D1523666

Source Books on Education
(Vol. 42)

EDUCATING YOUNG
ADOLESCENTS

GARLAND REFERENCE LIBRARY
OF SOCIAL SCIENCE
(VOL. 866)

EDUCATING YOUNG ADOLESCENTS

Life in the Middle

Edited by
Michael J. Wavering

GARLAND PUBLISHING, INC.
New York & London / 1995

Library of Congress Cataloging-in-Publication Data

Educating young adolescents : life in the middle / edited by Michael
J. Wavering.
     p. cm. — (Garland reference library of social science ; vol.
866. Source books on education ; vol. 42)
   Includes bibliographical references and index.
   ISBN 0-8153-1021-8 (alk. paper)
   1. Middle schools—United States. 2. Education, Secondary—
United States. 3. Adolescence—United States. 4. Middle school
teachers—Training of—United States. I. Wavering, Michael James.
II. Series: Garland reference library of social science ; v. 866.
III. Series: Garland reference library of social science. Source
books on education ; vol. 42.
LB1623.5.E38   1995
373.2'36—dc20   94-31028
                                                               CIP

Printed on acid-free, 250-year-life paper
Manufactured in the United States of America

I dedicate this book to my parents, Joseph and Dolores, who gave me life and direction and who with their lives have provided me with an example of how to be a good person. And to Karen, without whom life would hold little meaning.

Contents

Acknowledgments

I must admit that when I was asked to edit a book about the education of young adolescents, I was pleased yet apprehensive. I was serving as department head at the time, and I wasn't sure that I would have the time necessary to accomplish the task satisfactorily. Once I had decided to tackle the project, my apprehensions started to disappear as I contacted colleagues to test their interest in writing chapters for this book. I have been fortunate in my career to have worked with outstanding educators whose experiences have been exceptional.

Once these individuals had signed on, I still had a number of chapters that needed some attention. At that point, I contacted Tom Dickinson, who at the time was editor of the *Middle School Journal* and a former colleague at the Model Laboratory School at Eastern Kentucky University. Tom, as always, was very helpful and suggested a number of individuals with expertise in the areas of young adolescent education. The individuals he suggested had outstanding experiences with young adolescents and were very ready to contribute a chapter in their areas of expertise. I thank Tom for his invaluable assistance and for the opportunity to get to know these fine authors through their writing and numerous telephone conversations. All the authors have made this project a joy and a high point in my career.

I also acknowledge the hard work of the secretarial staff in the Department of Curriculum and Instruction at the University of Arkansas, especially Mary Phebus, Laura Pierce, and Barbara Fuller who handled the correspondence and necessary copying tasks during the course of this project. These ladies were always helpful and reentered chapters into word processing programs when our technical staff was unable to get diskettes translated. I thank them for their assistance on this task which was in addition to their normal secretarial duties.

The work of the production services staff of the College of Education of the University of Arkansas was outstanding. This is the first major project I have attempted using a computer as the basis for composing and sharing information between the editor and the chapter authors. I thank Bart Cohen, whose computer expertise allowed me to take diskettes from authors using at least five different word processing programs and translate them into something my computer could read, and, additionally, Bart, Gary Day, and Bobby Craig for preparing camera-ready copy for the graphics in the text.

Also, Jack Helfeldt, my department head, deserves special thanks for finding the money to purchase updated computers for the faculty of the department. My new Macintosh surely saved a tremendous amount of time. Further, I wish to thank Dean Rod McDavis of the College of Education at the time, who encouraged me to pursue this project. His friendship and encouragement are appreciated greatly.

Elizabeth McKee, who specializes in resources for education at the University of Arkansas library, provided excellent assistance in answering my many reference citation questions. Over the years Elizabeth has been efficient, very professional, and extremely pleasant to work with.

Thanks to my wife Karen Wavering, not because she is my wife (even though that is of utmost importance to me), but because she did the cleanup work on this book. Karen made sure all the words were spelled correctly, the computer translations did not garble the formatting, checked and corrected references, and caught any grammar problems that remained in the chapters after numerous readings by the authors and me. Her diligence in this task in no small measure has made this book possible. Our friend Lynn Cleaveland reviewed several chapters as the deadline approached. Karen and I both thank her.

Finally, I thank the staff of Garland Publishing, especially Marie Ellen Lacarda. She not only encouraged me to submit the original idea, but she also served as one of Garland's editors for this book, and to Adrienne Makowski, who put this book into its final form.

I hope I have not missed anyone who made a contribution to the realization of this book. It has been a pleasure for me to be associated with the authors of each chapter, and the pleasure has been increased by the assistance I have received from those mentioned above. Projects such as this are never the work of a single individual, although I take responsibility for any errors in this book.

Michael J. Wavering
University of Arkansas

Introduction

Michael J. Wavering

> Young adolescents face significant turning points. For
> many youth 10 to 15 years old, early adolescence offers
> opportunities to choose a path toward a productive and
> fulfilling life. For many others, it represents their last best
> chance to avoid a diminished future. (Carnegie Council on
> Adolescent Development, 1989, p. 8)

Just a few years ago, with these words, the Carnegie Council set
the stage for a continuing discussion of education for young
adolescents. Just as the National Commission on Excellence in
Education (1983) declared the nation's education system placed
us "at risk," the Carnegie Council (1989) pinpointed a focus for
educational efforts for emerging adolescents.

While the Carnegie Council (1989) defined the young
adolescent age group as 10 to 15 years old, other authorities may
define this same grouping using other ages. For example,
Stevenson (1992) defined the young adolescent age group as age
10 to 14. The ages cited are not as important as it is to recognize
and respect the emotional, social, intellectual, and physical
developmental changes and needs occurring during this vitally
important period in young adolescent lives.

With the focus on children in the age group 10 to 15 years
old becoming sharper, a book about educating these young
adolescents should be helpful to all who are involved in the
education of this volatile group. *Educating Young Adolescents: Life
in the Middle* is meant to serve as a reference, a starting point, for
those parents, educators, and policymakers, whose primary

concern is schools that serve the needs of young adolescents and, in turn, the society which they inhabit.

This book is divided into five sections. The first section lays the philosophical and historical basis for the education of young adolescents. In the following chapter, Michael James describes the need for clearly understanding the philosophical bases and biases of education for this age group. Philosophy should help provide guidance and justification for the policies and methodologies used with students at the middle.

Judy Brough describes the historical development of education for young adolescents and the birth of the middle school movement from the demise of the junior high school. This chapter serves to place middle level reform solidly in the school reform movement of the late twentieth century.

The second section outlines the characteristics of 10- to 15-year-olds. It can be said easily that change is the major characteristic of this age group. Change that is sometimes quite startling, not only to the adults involved in the life of the individual, but also to the individual. In the first chapter in this section, Dionne Walker and Cathy Lirgg describe the physical development of this age group. The most obvious changes taking place in the young adolescent are physical.

Rebecca Bowers discusses the social and emotional development of early adolescents. Next to physical development, social-emotional development is the most visible set of changes that these youth experience. Some educators refer to youth in this age group with a variety of disparaging comments. These comments usually refer to the emotional and social ups and downs, the herding behavior, and other characteristic behaviors.

The last chapter in this section addresses the cognitive development of young adolescents. The editor of *Educating Young Adolescents: Life in the Middle* writes about the changes that take place in the cognitive and moral development of young adolescents. As with the other developmental areas discussed, cognitive development occurs at varying rates and different times during the interval of young adolescent development. The changes are confusing and disturbing, yet marvelous, to these youth as they begin to develop into young adulthood.

The third section explores the nature and preparation of teachers who work with young adolescents. Rebecca Farris Mills writes of the concerns of those who prepare teachers for middle level education. In this chapter, she describes how colleges and universities are meeting the needs of schools for specially trained middle level educators.

In the next chapter, Mary Ann Davies describes the ideal middle-level teacher. She answers the question, "What kind of person is needed to undertake the task of teaching the middle level student?" Because very few individuals pursue a teaching career with the middle level as their first choice, this is a question of utmost importance.

The fourth section outlines administrative concerns in middle level schools. A supportive administrative structure is acknowledged by most educators as a necessity for an effective school for young adolescents. Beverly Reed and Charles Russell describe leadership in the middle level school in a broad stroke with leadership coming from and being encouraged in all of the participants in the process.

In the next chapter, DeWayne Mason describes the evolving structure of the middle level school. He envisions the directions this school structure will take as the restructuring movement progresses.

In the final section, the issues of curriculum in middle level schools are addressed. Jeanneine Jones starts this section with a discussion of what is a core curriculum for young adolescents. In the next chapter, Jim Gill writes about the need for clarity and direction in the exploratory curriculum. These two initial chapters outline the issues and concerns of the content matter at the middle level.

Annette Digby, Samuel Totten, and Dennis Snider discuss the affective domain for young adolescent education. Advisor-advisee programs supply counseling support with teachers and administrators becoming responsible for the affective needs of small groups of youth.

Mary Ann Davies explores teaching strategies that are appropriate for teaching young adolescents in the next chapter. In the ensuing chapter, Bruce Smith takes an expanded view of classroom management, in which he explores the development of the classroom as a caring community. In the final chapter of this section, Cathy Lirgg places physical education and athletics in the perspectives of the needs of young adolescents and the middle school philosophy.

Although written separately, these chapters express a unity of purpose and viewpoint. I asked each of the authors to approach his or her task from a constructivist viewpoint and to present a synthesis of research and/or best practice in the education of middle level youth. I believe they have succeeded in this venture.

REFERENCES

Carnegie Council on Adolescent Development. (1989). *Turning points: Preparing American youth for the 21st century*. Washington, DC: Author.

National Commission on Excellence in Education. (1983). *A nation at risk: The imperative for educational reform*. Washington, DC: Government Printing Office.

Stevenson, C. (1992). *Teaching ten to fourteen year olds*. New York: Longman.

Educating Young Adolescents

CHAPTER 1

Philosophy: A Guide to Middle School Program Development

Michael James

Introduction

Power (1990) suggests that regardless of the focus of a debate, we always argue from a "platform of conviction," and, when action is taken, these decisions are supported by "good and convincing justification" (p. 3). Why then have those of us involved at all levels of middle grades education—students to college professors—been so reluctant to look at the philosophical bases of our convictions and further back up our decisions with historical and/or contemporary justifications? Many such inquiries would result in eclectic positions or options but, according to Shane (1981), it is all right if we analyze the origins of these values, opinions, and convictions and construct a meaningful synthesis that is our public and private platform for the elements of our reforms, be those at national levels or within our classrooms.

This chapter will review several distant and proximal positions advertised and/or advocated by national, local, and on-site organizations and educational leaders. Whenever productive, these positions will be tied back to modern philosophies of education or contemporary theories of schooling. The major distinguishing questions to guide the reader's inquiries are:

1. What should we be doing in middle grades education and why? (Appropriately classified as philosophical issues.)
2. How should we do what we think is right— developmentally, morally and ethically? (Appropriately classified as psychological and philosophical issues.)

It should be noted that this is not an unbiased nor dispassionate assessment. The author of this chapter has had 25 years of teaching, researching, and reflectively promoting the best of middle grades education. In combination, the training, experiences, inquiry, and justification have led to the following definition of a *viable middle school*.

> A model middle school is a set of educational plans designed for early and young adolescents after carefully analyzing the characteristics, needs, and concerns of this age group which specify organizational, administrative, curricular, and instructional opportunities for learners in the school.

These plans emerge after rigorous inquiry into the what, why, and how of appropriate middle grades education and structuring. Everything from the master schedule to the empowerment of staff, from the involvement of students in decision-making to the support of and by auxiliary units, or from the "sign-posts" of valued practices to the number of "up" slips issued ("Your son improved in math today") needs to be reviewed. Each element singularly and collectively speaks loudly of our philosophical and psychological foundations.

From a constructivist orientation, this chapter will be developed by raising three guiding questions: (1) What do we know?, (2) What do we want to know?, (3) How will our knowledge be manifested usefully?

A Framework for Inquiry

Again, Power (1990) suggests that we can use several philosophical lenses through which to view and review our purposes, in this case as middle level educators and advocates.

- As an inspirational enterprise educational philosophy means to put on exhibit as a model some organization of teaching and learning that is judged ideal. (p. 5)

- Every educational philosopher . . . is prepared to be critical and analytical in separating principle and policy into their component parts and holding them up for scrutiny of their meaning. (p. 7)

- Educational philosophers who see prescription as the principal purpose of their discipline . . . [act] intelligently [to] use their talent to discover the nature of . . . design and try to conduct their lives in ways consistent with it. (p. 9)

- An educational philosophy whose purpose is investigation and inquiry refuses to accept or practice leadership. It finds its proper role, instead, in a prudent exercise of the art of delay. . . . Organize . . . devise pedagogical techniques . . . [and later] evaluate for justification and for needed commentaries on practice. (p. 14)

Therefore, as you join the journey toward better philosophical and psychological understandings of middle grades education, become an analytical, investigative inquirer as you seek inspiration and become prescriptive as a middle grades educator and advocate.

What Do We Know?

We can turn, as middle grades educators, to many powerful, published sources of direction for inspirational and prescriptive focuses. Recent publications, described below, are excellent examples.

Turning Points

Turning Points: Preparing American Youth for the 21st Century (1989), by the Carnegie Council on Adolescent

Development, Carnegie Corporation of New York, provides a noneducational perspective of what is and what should be for students, staffs, and organizations concerned with people 10 to 14 years old. The significance of *Turning Points* lies in its basic recommendations that society working collaboratively should:

1. Improve the educational experience of all middle grades students by creating small "communities of learners" within large schools (compared to the elementary feeder-schools), teaching an academic program with high expectations to master critical thinking and decision-making skills and participating in service learning activities, eliminating tracking and utilizing cooperative learning strategies, and increasing teachers' autonomy through empowerment.

2. These improved educational experiences should produce 15-year-olds who are reflective intellectually; healthy, caring, and ethical in behavior; good citizens; and well on their way to a lifetime of meaningful work by networking schools with families and community to increase access to such services as health and counseling facilities and to reengage the family, however defined, in the governance and support for the learning processes at home and school.

A Portrait of Young Adolescents in the 1990s

A Portrait of Young Adolescents in the 1990s: Implications for Promoting Healthy Growth and Development (1991) was written by Peter C. Scales for the Center for Early Adolescence, a highly respected research-based educational organization concerned with early adolescents. In this work Scales makes a passionate plea to consider the macro-portrait of youth—today and in the future—rather than any micro-imperfection. Although the personal and social demographic information presented in this report is less than optimistic, the overall approach to improving the education, health, and well-being of youth is very positive. For once, a report attacks the *big* issues that not only undergird the problems of the 1990s but also herald the resolutions so that all youth benefit. As in the previous source, the "turning points" are pointed toward the positive resolution of many societal problems, e.g., poverty and health care, that affect a growing population of 10- to 14-year-olds.

This We Believe

This We Believe is a 1982 landmark publication of the National Middle School Association, *the* preeminent organizational voice for all of middle grades education and educators. This book, revised in 1992, clearly sets forth guiding beliefs and conditions of schools serving youth at the middle level of education and provides 10 conditions or characteristics, called *essential elements*, of a "true" middle school.

1. Educators knowledgeable about and committed to young adolescents.
2. A balanced curriculum based on the needs of young adolescents.
3. A range of organizational arrangements.
4. Varied instructional strategies.
5. A full exploratory program.
6. Comprehensive advising and counseling.
7. Continuous progress for students.
8. Evaluation procedures compatible with the nature of young adolescent needs.
9. Cooperative planning.
10. Positive school climate. (NMSA, 1992, p. 27)

In addition, NMSA sets forth the association's seven beliefs about middle level students.

- [The] middle school is an educational response to the needs and characteristics of youngsters during the transition from childhood to adolescence and, as such, deals with the full range of intellectual and developmental needs.

- [Y]oung people going through the rapid growth and extensive maturation that occurs in early adolescence need an educational program that is distinctively different from either the elementary or the secondary model.

- [E]xisting programs for this age group have all too often lacked focus on young adolescent characteristics and needs.

- [E]ducators, school board members, parents, and citizens generally need to become more cognizant of this age group and what an effective educational program for this group requires.

- [N]o other age level is of more enduring importance because the determinants of one's behavior as an adult, self-concept, learning interests and skills, and values largely are formed in this period of life.

- [T]he developmental diversity of this age group makes it especially difficult to organize an educational program that adequately meets the needs of all.

- [T]he academic needs of middle school students are affected greatly by their physical, social, and emotional needs which also must be addressed directly in the school program. (NMSA, 1992, p. 26)

The Exemplary Middle School

George and Alexander, in their 1993 *The Exemplary Middle School*, identify 10 characteristics of exemplary middle schools.

1. The primary focus of the middle school should be on the learners in these schools, usually about ages 10–14 and having the many unique needs and interests of early adolescents.
2. Middle school planning should recognize as fully as possible historical factors in the development of this school and level, and its rationale and desired characteristics.
3. The middle school curriculum should include provision for its three basic domains or areas: personal development, continued learning skills, and basic knowledge areas.
4. [C]urrent information from theory, practice, and research as to instructional methodology should be utilized fully in every middle school and classroom.

5. The middle school should provide an adequate guidance program, with special attention to types and plans for teacher-based guidance.
6. An interdisciplinary team organization is characteristic of an effective middle school.
7. Exemplary middle schools can and should utilize appropriate means of grouping students.
8. Flexible scheduling and various types of space utilization should be planned for each middle school for its maximum effectiveness.
9. Exemplary middle schools depend upon effective planning and implementation. Furthermore, middle schools, new and established, should be evaluated on the extent to which they attain goals related to needs of the students who are their clients.
10. [S]ooner or later every middle school takes on the characteristics of its leadership. (p. 52)

Philosophy Statements

Sometimes you have to look far and wide to find it, but chances are that every middle school or school district with more than two middle schools will have a statement of "middle school philosophy." These statements may be the product of a staff development activity to inform the parents and community of impending changes; of a preaccreditation visit inquiry to ready documentation for the visit; or, as is the case cited below, a district-wide, implementation committee's report to a local school board detailing major focal changes in middle grades education. Examine the following statements of philosophy and note the values that emerge just through the language chosen.

> The students being educated today will be living in a rapidly changing society where the ability to access information and use it to formulate viable solutions will determine their measure of success in life. A successful, innovative, and dynamic program of learning must be developed to meet the needs of these students.
> Middle level education is a program separate from either elementary or high school education. The program

serves a group of students in transition, students who are undergoing dramatic changes in their intellectual, physical, social, and emotional development. A middle school program, therefore, provides a bridge between the nurturing and support of the elementary classroom and the independence and self-discipline required at the high school level. A successful middle school program has four major purposes:

1. An emphasis upon academic excellence—mastery of academic basics is a goal for all learners.
2. An emphasis on personal growth and social and emotional development for all learners.
3. An introduction to all disciplines of study for all learners.
4. The development of critical thinking, decision-making, and problem-solving abilities for all learners.

A successful middle school program will provide the learners with the opportunity to achieve their maximum potential, both academically and personally. (Wichita Public Schools, 1988, p. 2)

Every major educational philosophy has its definitions of "what is real." This is called the *metaphysics of a belief system.* Perennialists believe that life has meaning in the context of the collective wisdom of Western culture. Essentialists believe that what is relevant is what helps an individual live well and benefits humanity. Progressivists believe that meaning is in the context of the individual who is a problem solver. And, existentialists believe that reality is always in terms of our relationship to existence with no meaning outside ourselves.

What is real in the above-cited example of a district's philosophy statement is an obvious eclectic mixture of metaphysical interpretations. This is not uncommon when statements developed by committees are accepted. Consider the backgrounds and belief systems of the committee members!

A Walk on the "Wild Side"— Or, In Search of Value Sign-Posts

Walk around, in, or through any middle grades school and you instantly sense what that school, staff, and student population—with parental and community support—value. Reflect on these examples:

1. An official-looking, rectangular sign posted 50 yards beyond the school property proclaiming "GUN-FREE and DRUG-FREE ZONE—By City Ordinance."
   •Value=protectionism.
2. A school announcement board listing upcoming events: "Girls' volleyball tourney—Thursday, 4:30 P.M.—GO PANTHERS!"
   "Boys' basketball vs. Midway MS—Thursday, 6:00 P.M. EAT 'EM ALIVE, PANTHERS!
   •Values=elitism, sexism, athleticism.
3. Clean, litter-free, fenced school grounds with security guards near external entrances.
   •Values=law and order, form before function.
4. An honor roll plaque prominently displayed near the entrance to the school office.
   •Values=scholasticism, academic elitism, favoritism.
5. A display case in the entry area of the school featuring students' products from a recent science fair.
   •Values=academic favoritism, extended success opportunities, competition.
6. Laughter and excitement within classrooms while students are working on a project.
   •Values="fun" (a characteristic kids enjoy), active learning, and/or engagement in knowledge production.
7. Bells announcing the beginning and ending of periods plus intercom announcements and administrative interruptions.
   •Values=conformity, structures imposed by others, power and control.
8. Administrators with cellular phones or walkie-talkies attached to their belts as they roam the halls.

• Values=authority availability, overload of responsibilities, increased crisis prevention and intervention.

9. A team of teachers during their planning period discussing student progress and planning the upcoming interdisciplinary unit on "conflict and conflict resolution."
   • Values=collegiality, responsiveness, care and concern.

10. A student "greeter" in the office who volunteers to show you how exciting her school is.
    • Values=student empowerment, relevant responsibility-taking, school as life.

11. A parent meeting in progress where teachers, administrators, and parents are working together to support positive youth development.
    • Values=proactive support, networking, positive involvement.

12 Cheerleading practice during school time.
    • Values=elitism, social-emotional pressuring, seg-regation.

13. Published and posted school rules starting with, "DO NOT . . . "
    • Values=authoritarianism, lack of trust, negativism.

This baker's dozen of "value signs" in and around our middle schools can be categorized by philosophical orientation. By reviewing the axiology (the values, ethics, etc.) of four educational philosophies, each value sign is a visible and viable example or personification of a belief system.

Philosophical Orientation: Axiology

Perennialism	Essentialism	Progressivism	Existentialism
Changeless. Determined by culture.	Determined by the natural order of things. Values exist in the best of culture.	Determined by each individual in interaction with his or her culture.	Determined by the individual. Stresses values clarification.
Value Signs:			
3, 4, 8, 13	1, 2, 7, 12	5, 9, 11	6, 10

Based on this review, where would the reader place the following value signs?

- An advisement class that is fostering prosocial skill development by designing and implementing a service learning project outside the school environment.
- A peer mentoring and/or governance plan used for orientation into the new middle school experience, maintenance and indoctrination as a middle school member, and promotion out to the high school.
- Classroom discussions of relevant topics fostering amplification and verification but encouraging opinions that are supported by evidence.
- A cooperative learning strategy—Jigsaw II—employed during an interdisciplinary unit thematically incorporating academic and exploratory related disciplines on "Why am I like this?"
- Meaningless homework assignments.
- School assemblies honoring recovering drug addicts, criminals, and/or eating disordered students.
- Repeat-testing practices allowing students to learn from their mistakes and improve their knowledge base.
- All students assigned the same number of math problems for homework regardless of readiness levels.
- A prescriptive dress code—males wearing dark colored trousers and plaid shirts, and the females in patterned skirts and white blouses.
- An individualized math class with pretest, practice, and posttest options that can only be awarded a "D" grade because it focuses on basic consumer math.

Listening to Teachers Talk

In this author's more than 20 years as a teacher educator with a primary responsibility for providing middle grades training opportunities, he has encountered hundreds of teachers—either in preservice or in-service status—with differing philosophical bases. That one's "belief system" is seldom labeled, defended, or open to scrutiny is not surprising, considering the myriad of demands made on teachers by schedules, pupils, parents, team members, and themselves. When, during a faculty meeting, team planning time, or while driving to work, does someone ask if your ideas are progressivist, perennialistic, existential, or essentialist? Yet, in conversations, in papers and projects, and embedded in the team's newly developed interdisciplinary unit, the belief systems speak loudly, proudly, and powerfully. Perhaps the beauty and the frustration of eclecticism among middle school educators are the textural complexities of the educational experiences they craft for early adolescent learners. When all ideas are weighed and each piece is sewn into place, the learners benefit from the planners' convictions.

Listen to four very unique and committed middle grades educators as they talk about themselves as teachers, the pupils they teach, what they teach, and how they do it. Each voice is a composite of voices this author has heard over time, portrayed as an exaggeration of one or more philosophical viewpoints. Maybe the reader knows someone like Walter, Maria, Rick, or Sue. Perhaps the reader would like to work on a team with one or more of them. No voice is entirely right. Certainly no voice is wrong if the goal is to construct opportunities for learners to connect their world of knowledge to the larger picture of a changing and interdependent world.

Walter, a Perennialist

Walter is secondary certified in comprehensive social studies, has his Ph.D. in history, is a veteran of the junior high school days, currently teaches eighth grade social studies in a large middle school, and is a staunch advocate of Hirsch's *Cultural Literacy* (1987) initiatives. He sees himself as a conduit for passing on to future generations the accumulated wisdom of the past. Thereby, in team meetings he advocates the use of universal and recurring themes only for unit development.

Walter says:

No need to reinvent the wheel. We have plenty of classic materials that reflect and cultivate the rationality of great

people and their works and ideas. Our job as teachers is to
teach kids how and what others thought. I think and show
my thoughts while I teach. Kids should model their
thinking and rational powers after me and the masters
who are our culture's best.

Believing this, Walter uses mostly lecture/recitation class
periods with frequent paper and pencil tests to assess
understandings. He seldom deviates from his detailed lecture
notes and does not encourage much student-to-student
interaction. Walter is respected for his intellect and strong set of
no-nonsense values. Yet, he is feared by some students and peers
because he is seen as being too tough, opinionated, and set in his
ways. He is an outspoken critic of either a concerns-driven or
skills-based curriculum for the middle school. What was the best
of the past is good enough for now!

Maria, an Essentialist

Maria is in her second year of teaching in a school-within-
a-school middle school as an elementary certified/middle level
endorsed teacher. She formerly had a brief, but challenging,
career in the aircraft construction industry. Maria is very task
oriented and sees schools as places where pupils come to learn
what they need to know. Basic but essential skills, coupled with
disciplined knowledge, form the core of Maria's curriculum. Yet,
lately, she has worked excitedly with her other four team
members to implement and augment the Bank Street's *Voyage of
the Mimi II*—a multidisciplinary, technologically varied
simulation. Maria departs from the hard-line stance of some
essentialists when it comes to how students learn best.

I believe we have to create a very exciting and hands-on
way to engage middle school learners. Sure, I know a lot
about mathematics and the sciences, but if I can't find a
relevant way to turn kids on to these subjects, then I am
failing them and my disciplines. *The Voyage of the Mimi II*
is an excellent example of how we can use media and
technologies to bring kids into contact with relevant
content and essential skills. I supplement each segment of
the unit with ideas and materials I have gained through

aerospace workshops I attended and the Junior Astronauts Program I sponsor at school.

Maria's classroom reflects her dual philosophical perspectives. At any given time you might find live animals caged but cared for by students, a wealth of resource materials— some in classroom sets and others at interest centers, small groups carrying out projects or appropriate experiments, and the teacher serving more as a facilitator than an expert. Notwithstanding, when the team plans a new integrated unit for their sixth graders, Maria wants assurances that the appropriate science and mathematics standards/outcomes will be met during the run of the unit, or she will need some extra time between units to specifically teach to them.

"I don't mind trying new ways to integrate curriculum," Maria says. "But, someone is going to have to tell me exactly what they want me to do because I'm not very creative in these endeavors. Then I will do it!"

Sue, a Progressivist

Sue's involvements in middle grades education are varied and impressive. Having taught in the upper grades in an elementary school in Texas and being a certified elementary media specialist, Sue applied for a middle school language arts position when a large, urban school district moved from 7–9 junior high schools to a paradigm-driven 6–8 middle school organization. Prior to her second year on the team, she was chosen as team leader. Under a very dynamic administrator, Sue pushed her team members into expanding their role as curriculum developers. For three years after that, Sue was a district-level middle school teaching specialist with major responsibilities for helping teams in all 15 of the middle schools master teaming processes, implement viable advisory programs, and develop concerns-driven interdisciplinary units of instruction. This year, being also administrator certified, Sue is an assistant principal of a medium-sized middle school. She is in charge of developing staff and supporting change within and between the teams.

Because of her experiences, Sue is a very patient and knowledgeable facilitator of change within middle schools. By using democratic procedures and group processes that encourage consensus-making, she helps students, teachers, and staff do what they need and want to do. The real, everyday problems of being a team member, engaging an at-risk student, or scheduling exploratory teachers for planning time with core academic teachers are all centered on the needs and concerns of the participants and form the sum and substance of Sue's middle school "curriculum."

> When I am asked, "How do we do such-and-such," like relate advisory classes to the focus of an interdisciplinary unit, I usually say, "Well, what are the givens? Who do you want to solve this problem? What are the obstacles to overcome?" Then I help them focus on the problem and encourage creative problem solutions, leaving them alone to come up with their best solutions. Of course, I always am available to them as a resource, but basically I trust them and will support their actions *if it is best for the students.*

Rick, an Existentialist

Rick is an enigma of sorts. While he is certified in secondary English and a language arts teacher on a seventh grade team, Rick also is the coordinator of gifted students' education, Grades 6–8. A recognized, frequently published poet, Rick is young and serious minded yet free to make his own meanings of "truth."

Despite the institutional strictures in Rick's very traditional junior-high-school-like middle school, he attempts to create a learning environment for students' self-definitions through an emphasis in the humanities and arts. Responsibility-taking and making personal choices are his challenges to his students.

At times he finds himself very alone with his thoughts and personal freedoms. But reflectively, he expresses his ideas in very scholarly and unique ways, including restoring an 1890s home in his spare time. Rick allows his students the same introspective "think time" and encourages them to develop "personal statement products."

> I want my kids—all kids for that matter—to exercise their reflective abilities in order to stand back and witness their own unfolding. There is so much beauty inside each of us; we must help these kids go beyond the mundane pablum of traditional curriculum and establish their own agendas for excellence. My job is to be a supportive provocateur for freedom, seeking abilities while stressing a person's responsibilities for the choices made.

Summation of Teacher Talk

Each of these composite middle school educators espouses a fairly clear philosophical perspective or perspectives. Walter's love of the classics makes him primarily a perennialist. Yet, even with an earned doctorate, he chose to be on an interdisciplinary team and teach middle school youngsters.

Maria leans more toward the essentialist ideas of task orientation, a teacher as an expert, and an emphasis on basic skill development. But, she welcomes change and wants to learn how to better engage her students in meaningful learning experiences.

Sue most clearly acts on neoprogressivist beliefs. She sees one of life's main purposes as solving real problems that are of interest to the participants. "Curriculum has to be integrated," according to her words and actions, "because life is integrated."

Rick, while surrounded by many traditional trappings of schooling, is a free-spirited, artistic problem generator and solver whose values and beliefs coincide with the tenets of existential philosophy. "Let freedoms ring," he says, "because we have to respect our own freedoms in order to understand and appreciate anyone else's freedoms and expressions."

Listening to Student Talk

Perhaps the most under-used and under-appreciated sources in the decision-making process for learning opportunities are the middle grades students being taught. Somehow, adults think they know what these kids need to know and how to deliver it. This is a power position that adults can justify when dealing with early adolescent learning if they metaphorically think of them as "brain dead," "walking hormones," or worse yet, "the range of the strange."

These are such inaccurate metaphors. They only support a defensive adult position when they are unable to get in touch with what 10- to 14-year-olds really think about substantive issues. The key to understanding this age group's concerns resides in the educator's ability to actively listen to what is said, analyze, and classify their responses, and act on the information in a constructive manner.

James and Kuhns (1993) reported how sixth and seventh grade students were canvassed for their ideas about immediate interests and concerns—both personal and social. When asked what kind of classes they "don't like," students responded: "dull," "boring," and "routine." However, when asked what kind of classes they "do like," the same students (n = 300+) responded enthusiastically: "hands-on," "exciting," and, of course, "fun." Fun may be interpreted by some teachers as nonlearning, but the middle school learner defines those experiences as ones "in which they are engaged in more hands-on activities and projects . . . " (p. 26).

This type of evidence should remind middle school teachers that the learners have valuable insights on *what* they want to learn and *how* they prefer to be engaged in their own learning. This form of student empowerment encourages a constructivist view of learning: "Let me inquire into something that has meaning for me or is of immediate concern. Then, give me the space to learn my way."

What Do We Want to Know?

At least three major professional associations, the National Middle School Association (NMSA), the National Council of Teachers of Mathematics (NCTM), and the American Association for the Advancement of Science (AAAS), are advocating major changes toward constructivist teaching and learning. What they are positing is an active, sustained reformation in the way we think about the two critical processes associated with schooling. Both NCTM and AAAS, representing major disciplines, now see their future mission as one of exploring options and opening up the world of knowledge to learners connectively.

National Middle School Association

The NMSA Task Force on Curriculum, in a draft statement made available to interested participants, identifies many constructivist belief statements.

> We strongly support learning experiences which
> help young adolescents make sense of themselves and the world about them . . .
> are highly integrated, so that students see the connectedness of life . . .
> open doors to new ideas, evoking curiosity, exploration, and at times, awe and wonder . . .
> actively engage students in problem-solving and a variety of experiential learning opportunities.

National Council of Teachers of Mathematics

NCTM's (1989) call for reforms includes 13 standards for Grades 5–8 that include (1) mathematics as communication, (2) mathematics as connections, and (3) mathematics as problem-solving.

Among the summary of change notions built into the NCTM's guidelines are "increased attention" to

- Actively involving students individually and in groups in exploring, conjecturing, analyzing, and applying mathematics in both a mathematical and a real-world context,
- Asessing learning as an integral part of instruction.

Within the three cited "standards," NCTM proposes opportunities for students to

> [R]eflect on and clarify their own thinking . . . use the skills of reading, listening, and viewing to interpret and evaluate mathematical ideas . . . discuss mathematical ideas and make conjectures and convincing arguments. . . . (p. 78)

In addition, NCTM cites ways to use mathematics to develop problem-solving skills and suggests teachers "formulate problems from situations within and outside mathematics" (p. 75), and, when investigating mathematical connections, teachers should "apply mathematical thinking and modeling to solve problems that arise in other disciplines, such as art, music, psychology, science, and business" (p. 84).

American Association for the Advancement of Science

AAAS's *1993 Benchmarks for Science Literacy—Project 2061* (the year Haley's Comet is supposed to reappear near Earth) identifies what all students should know or be able to do in science, mathematics, and technology by the end of Grades 2, 5, 8, and 12. By the end of the eighth grade, students should know "[s]cientific knowledge is subject to modification as new information challenges prevailing theories. . . . Some scientific knowledge is very old and yet is still applicable today" (p. 7).

As far as scientific inquiry is concerned, AAAS suggests that eighth grade students need to know that

> Although there is no fixed set of steps that scientists follow, scientific investigations usually involve the collection of relevant evidence, the use of logical reasoning, and the application of imagination in devising hypotheses and explanations to make sense of the

collected evidence. . . . What people expect to observe often affects what they actually do observe. (p. 12)

Overlapping Constructivists' Practices with Progressivist Philosophy

Brooks and Brooks, in *In Search of Understanding* (1993), list 12 descriptors that highlight practices constructivist teachers can use to help learners "search for their own understandings rather than follow other peoples' logic" (p. 118). These are

1. Constructivist teachers encourage and accept student autonomy and initiative.
2. Constructivist teachers use raw data and primary sources, along with manipulative, interactive, and physical materials.
3. When framing tasks, constructivist teachers use cognitive terminology such as "classify," "analyze," "predict," and "create."
4. Constructivist teachers allow student responses to drive lessons, shift instructional strategies, and alter content.
5. Constructivist teachers inquire about students' understandings of concepts before sharing their own understandings of those concepts.
6. Constructivist teachers encourage students to engage in dialogue, both with the teacher and with one another.
7. Constructivist teachers encourage student inquiry by asking thoughtful, open-ended questions and encouraging students to ask questions of each other.
8. Constructivist teachers seek elaboration of students' initial responses.
9. Constructivist teachers engage students in experiences that might engender contradictions to their initial hypotheses and then encourage discussion.
10. Constructivist teachers allow wait time after posing questions.
11. Constructivist teachers provide time for students to construct relationships and create metaphors.

12. Constructivist teachers nurture students' natural curiosity through frequent use of the learning cycle model (unstructured opportunity to interact with selected materials or discovery, concept introduction, and concept application).

Couple this with its logical philosophical underpinnings of neoprogressivism and you have the perfect platform for major reform in today's middle schools. Power (1990) cites some neoprogressivist thought values:

> Education is primarily a social enterprise.
> Cultural transmission is essential . . . in a pluriform society.
> The school's curriculum must not be dominated by either a majority or a preferred culture.
> [A]ctivity methods are endorsed.
> The cultural values students bring to school have worth. Personal dignity and social responsibility are enhanced when respect is accorded all cultural backgrounds.
> Teachers must exhibit genuine respect . . . for all cultures. (excerpted from p. 187)

Conclusion

Tomorrow's middle schools can look and feel and be quite different if the values that drive them are examined, analyzed, extended, and realized—especially when kids come first! Noddings (1984) says that to care as a teacher is to be ethically bound to understand one's students. This has to be the key to inspired middle schools of the future. Ten-to fourteen-year-old learners cannot be ignored, overlooked, or taken for granted. They are our future, and we owe them the very best educational learning opportunities.

We will have to better understand constructivist learning and teaching and provide meaningful instructional variety and authentic assessments. The classroom will need to be a true microcosm of our democracy—full of high expectations and love—where "community" can be developed and felt. Teams of teachers will have to really work together for the common good and be empowered to do what they know is best for the students. Support systems will need to be initiated both in the school and outside, with community taking on more and more responsibility for promoting positive youth development. Parents will have to be more involved in the growth and development of their children.

All this takes understanding and patience, which the schools can help nurture. Administration and school board members will need to know that the middle school years are probably the most important turning point for youth. If the turn is to be toward positive interdependency and a productive life, then they hold the power to make policies consistent with what we know to be right for and about kids.

REFERENCES

American Association for the Advancement of Science. (1993). *Benchmarks for science literacy: Project 2061*. New York: Oxford University Press.

Brooks, J. G. and Brooks, M. G. (1993). *In search of understanding: The case for constructivist classrooms*. Alexandria, VA: Association for Supervision and Curriculum Development.

Carnegie Council on Adolescent Development. (1989). *Turning points: Preparing American youth for the 21st century*. Washington, DC: Author.

George, P. and Alexander, W. (1993). *The exemplary middle school* (2nd Ed.). Fort Worth, TX: Harcourt Brace Jovanovich.

Hirsch, E.D. (1987). *Cultural literacy: What every American needs to know*. Boston, MA: Houghton Mifflin Company.

James, M. and Kuhns, B. (1993). Who should write the middle school curriculum? *Transescence: The Journal on Emerging Adolescent Education 21* (1): 25–29.

National Council of Teachers of Mathematics. (1989). *Curriculum and evaluation standards for school mathematics*. Reston, VA: Author.

National Middle School Association. (1992). *This we believe*. Columbus, OH: Author.

Noddings, N. (1984). *Caring: A feminine approach to ethic and moral education*. Berkeley, CA: University of California Press.

Power, E. J. (1990). *Philosophy of education: Studies in philosophies, schooling, and educational policies*. Prospect Heights, IL: Waveland Press, Inc.

Scales, P. C. (1991). *A portrait of young adolescents in the 1990s: Implications for promoting healthy growth and development*. Carrboro, NC: The Center for Early Adolescence.

Shane, H. G. (1981). "Complexities of curriculum planning for tomorrow's world." In G. Hass, *Curriculum planning: A new approach* (4th Ed.) (pp. 34–41). Needham Heights, MA: Allyn & Bacon.

Stevenson, C. (1992). *Teaching ten to fourteen year olds*. New York: Longman.

Wichita Public Schools. (1988). *Middle level implementation committee report*. Wichita, KS: Author.

CHAPTER 2

Middle Level Education: An Historical Perspective

Judith A. Brough

Like most trends in society in general and education in particular, the evolution of the junior high and middle school cannot be traced to one particular event, person, or cause. Rather, it was a movement fed through various tributaries, some not even related to young adolescents in our schools.

The idea of separate schooling for young adolescents can be found as far back as the Greeks and Romans. Quintilian (A.D. 35–95), for example, advocated schooling on three levels, with one geared toward the child aged 7 to 14 (Ornstein and Levine, 1993). But most historians credit events and people around the turn of the twentieth century with the creation of a school organization designed expressly for students in and around the seventh and eighth grades.

Reorganization of the Secondary Schools

During the latter half of the nineteenth century, the dominant educational organization was eight years of elementary schooling and four years of secondary schooling. This eight-four organization prevailed across the United States except in the South, where most schools practiced a seven-year elementary plan, and New England, which had a nine-year elementary program (Gruhn and Douglass, 1956).

But then a series of events and conversations took place that called this plan into question. Most of the educational recommendations and debates arose from the annual conferences of the National Education Association (NEA). Perusal of the association's *Journals of Proceedings* during the decades surrounding the turn of the century give the educational historian a complete perspective of thought at that time.

The onset of the school reorganization debates has been credited to Charles W. Eliot, then president of Harvard University, in 1888. Eliot was not interested necessarily in the education of young adolescents, secondary education in general, or even secondary school reorganization. Rather, he, like many college presidents of the time, was concerned about the increasing age of boys at their time of admission to college. Eliot railed before a gathered body of the Department of Superintendence in February, 1888, that the average age of boys entering college had risen to an alarming 18 years and 10 months. By the time they graduated and received formal job preparation for a professional career, a young man entered the job market at the age of 27. Rather than suggest a change in the college curriculum, Eliot chose to criticize the prevailing eight-four plan. He recommended that the secondary program be "shortened and enriched" (Eliot, 1898, p. 151) in order for young men to be better prepared for college in a shorter amount of time.

Eliot's criticisms were echoed by college leaders across the country. For the next two decades, numerous reports were commissioned by the National Education Association to address this nagging problem. The Committee of Ten (1884), comprised mainly of college presidents and headed by Eliot, and the Committee of Fifteen (1885), comprised mostly of school administrators, studied their own problems and suggested for their own purposes a realignment of the grades from an eight-four organization to a six-six plan. The Committee on College Entrance Requirements (1899) and the Standing Committee on Six-Year Courses of High School (1907) each supported the six-year secondary education plan. The Committee on Economy of Time (1913), which studied the problem of "waste" in education, and the Commission on the Reorganization of Secondary

Education (1918) suggested that the secondary program be separated into junior and senior divisions.

It is interesting to note the rationale the committees used to support their recommendations. For example, the Committee on College Entrance Requirements reported that, "The most necessary and far-reaching reforms in secondary education must begin in the seventh and eighth grades of our schools" (NEA, 1899, p. 659). The report included the following reasons for favoring a six-year high school program that started with the seventh grade:

1. [Grades 7 and 8 needed to be] enriched by eliminating non-essentials and adding new subjects formerly taught only in the high school.
2. [The] lack of qualified teachers and competent supervision [in the teaching of Latin, German, mathematics, and science].
3. The seventh grade, rather than ninth, is the natural turning-point in the pupil's life, as the age of adolescence demands new methods and wiser direction.
4. The transition from the elementary to the secondary period may be made natural and easy by changing gradually from the one-teacher regimen to the system of special teachers, thus avoiding the violent shock now commonly felt on entering the high school.
5. Under the system proposed, an inefficient teacher in the seventh or eighth grade would do less harm in blasting bright intellects and in turning able students away from higher study.
6. [The number of students leaving school at the end of sixth grade was significantly fewer than those leaving at the close of seventh and eighth grades.] By the proposed change, the students in seventh and eighth grades would gradually gain the inspiration of the high school life, and the desire to go farther in the languages and sciences which they have already begun under favorable conditions. The result would doubtless be a more closely articulated system, with a larger percentage of high-school graduates.

7. [Placing the seventh and eighth graders with the upper grades in the same building was perceived to result in] better scholarship.

8. The gradual change to this system would probably lead to the establishment of a larger number of less expensive high schools, thus placing the "people's college" nearer their homes without additional expense to the taxpayer, but with a saving in money and strength to students attending the high school. (NEA, 1899, pp. 659–660)

The significance of the Commission on the Reorganization of the Secondary Education (which published its Cardinal Principles of Secondary Education in 1918) is that it called for the liberation of secondary education from the dominance of college admission requirements. Bossing and Cramer (1965) referred to the report as education's "Magna Carta" (p. 21). The report, which sought to clarify the functions of the junior and senior divisions, recommended:

In the junior period emphasis should be placed upon the attempt to help the pupil to explore his own aptitudes and to make at least provisional choice of the kinds of work to which he will devote himself. In the senior period emphasis should be given to training in the fields thus chosen. . . . In the junior high school there should be the gradual introduction of departmental instruction, some choice of subjects under guidance, promotion by subjects, pre-vocational courses, and a social organization that calls forth initiative and develops the sense of personal responsibility for the welfare of the group. (Bossing and Cramer, 1965, p. 22)

It should be noted that the first junior high schools actually were implemented before the national commissions recommended the separation between junior and senior high school divisions. Three-year junior high schools were established first in 1909 in Columbus, Ohio, and in Berkeley, California, in 1910. However, Richmond, Indiana, actually began an intermediate school program for young adolescents as early as 1896, but it was not widely publicized (Toepfer, (1962). The NEA reports did not call for a junior high division until 1913.

Therefore, other phenomena were causing school directors to rethink their school grade configuration.

Cultural Factors

As Van Til, Vars, and Lounsbury (1961, p. 19) put it, "The cultural context is always a prime determiner of educational practice." Changes in our society were rampant as the twentieth century dawned. Technology boomed as the industrial era began with steam and electrical power. Our country moved from a rural agricultural setting to an emphasis on factories and urbanization. "In 1880 half of all the American workers were employed in agriculture; by 1920 only one in four held an agricultural job" (Van Til et al., 1961, pp. 19–20). Immigrants poured into the country. This industrialization, urbanization, and immigration created new societal problems.

> Crowded ghettos, inadequate urban services, and a population primarily rural in origin contributed to unsanitary living conditions and the spread of disease. Added to these real conditions was a belief held by many Americans that a sense of community was being lost with the growth of urban America and that this loss would cause the urban population to suffer alienation, a breakdown in traditional forms of social control, and, as a consequence, increased crime and poverty. A fear also arose that the new immigrants would destroy traditional American values and create a strong following for radical economic and political ideas.
>
> The school was considered a logical institution to prevent these problems by providing social services, teaching new behaviors, and creating a community center. Nurses, health facilities, and showers were added to schools in order to control the spread of disease, and special instructional programs were introduced to educate children about sanitary conditions. Americanization programs were offered as a means of assimilating children of immigrants in American life and preventing the spread of radical ideologies. Playgrounds were attached to schools to provide after-school activities for children that,

it was hoped, would reduce juvenile delinquency. To curb a sense of alienation caused by urban living, auditoriums and special facilities for adults were provided by schools to serve as centers for community activities. (Spring, 1986, p. 159)

Thus, the role of schools as social agencies took on greater significance. This was true especially of schools that housed sixth, seventh, and eighth graders where the increase in dropout rate was staggering. Van Til, Vars, and Lounsbury reported that during the years 1907–1911 only slightly more than a third of the students in public schools continued schooling to Grade 9, and only about 1 in 10 first graders continued through completion of high school (pp. 13–14).

The high dropout rate was blamed on the difficulty of transition from elementary to secondary school, the difficulty of students to adjust to the high school, an irrelevant and unrealistic curriculum, and retention in grade, then known as *retardation* (Salmeri, 1985). Schools of the time were formal, traditional, and harsh. All students were taught the same curriculum of perceived essentials, which had little or no relevance to students' lives. Teachers made no attempt to connect classwork, which was repetitious and tedious, to everyday practical applications. There was no special consideration for individual needs of students, particularly the less academically able and poor readers. Students then entered the ninth grade and faced the high school curriculum and its pedagogy, which was even more formal and presented by many teachers of the specialized subjects. No attempt at transition or articulation was undertaken. Frequently, students who faced failure quit school and entered the job market unprepared (Van Til et al., 1961).

With the advancing technology and industrialization, more skilled and, therefore, better educated workers were needed. It was hoped that the new junior high school structure would invigorate the curriculum and the students it supposedly served.

Psychological Factors

As educators were devising ways to entice youngsters to stay in school, psychologists, most significantly G. Stanley Hall, were busy studying adolescence and individual differences. In Hall's 1905 classic work, *Adolescence*, he described children around the age of puberty as social persons. Thus, institutions that served them needed to address adolescents' sexual-social drives in positive social ways (Spring, 1986). Hall (1905) described the young adolescent:

> The pupil is in the age of spontaneous variation which at no period of life is so great. He does not want a standardized, overpeptonized mental diet. It palls on his appetite. He suffers from mental ennui and dyspepsia, and this is why so many and an increasing number refuse some of the best prepared courses. (p. 509)

In other words, schools needed to meet the developmental needs of the students they served, and young adolescents were unique individuals with unique needs.

Prior to the study of individual differences, students were thought to be basically alike. A person's school failure could be attributed to laziness or lack of motivation. But studies in the early twentieth century showed that individual differences could be found not only from person to person, but also *within* an individual. This variation was apparent especially among young adolescents who exemplified a wide range of physical development, emotional maturity, social skills, interests, and abilities. Seventh, eighth, and ninth graders, unique in their wide range of development levels, needed an educational program better suited to their needs. The concept of the junior high school housing these youngsters together seemed logical. "[T]he development of the new science of individual differences in the early twentieth century provided another justification for the organization of the junior high school" (Van Til et al., 1961, p. 18).

The Rise of the Junior High School

In support of the six-three-three school organization, Briggs (1920) listed the following criticisms of the eight-four organization:

1. The eight-four organization is not justified by (a) psychology, (b) comparative education, (c) historical development, or (d) results.
2. Isolated and small grammar schools are uneconomical in that (a) the plant, if equipped with special rooms (shops laboratories, auditorium, gymnasium, and library), is not fully used; (b) special teachers and supervisors in going from building to building lose much time; (c) upper classes are frequently not filled; and (d) they do not permit differentiated curricula, departmental teaching, and promotion by subject.
3. The costly building and equipment of the high school are unnecessary for the adequate training of ninth grade pupils.
4. The work of the elementary school does not prepare for life activities.
5. The work of the elementary school does not satisfactorily prepare for higher schools.
6. The progress of pupils in the grammar grades is not marked as in other periods in school life.
7. In early adolescence pupils do not get the needed influence of teachers of both sexes.
8. Elementary or childish methods of teaching are too long continued and too suddenly changed.
9. The eight-four organization makes inadequate provision for the varying needs of pupils due to individual differences.
10. The eight-four organization causes an unnecessary and unjustifiable elimination because (a) the break between lower and upper schools is too sharp; and (b) it comes at the wrong time.
11. There is inadequate provision for personal guidance or direction—social, educational, and vocational—either in the elementary or in the high school. (excerpted from pp. 4–19)

Briggs (1920) also criticized the motives of those who first reorganized the educational organization. He charged school superintendents with reorganizing their schools without adequate facilities, teachers, curricula, materials, or thought of articulation. In some instances Briggs accused schools of making the change because of overcrowding in the high school, use of an outgrown high school, or student population distribution. Van Til, Vars, and Lounsbury (1961) also acknowledged that a school building shortage may have had a significant impact on the expansion of junior high schools. Not only were there too few buildings (perhaps due to the lack of new construction during World War I), but also many existing buildings were in need of renovation and repair. But, as Briggs stated, even if the junior high schools were established for less-than-honorable rea-sons, often the reorganization led to a "desirable advance in educational matters so as to justify themselves" (Briggs, 1920, p. 33).

As the junior high school division of secondary education took hold in the United States, the schools' functions had to be defined. The functions incorporated many of the variables that caused the reorganization of the secondary school. Koos (1927) listed the "peculiar functions" for the junior high school:

- Realizing a democratic school system through retention of pupils, economy of time, recognition of individual differences, exploration and guidance, and beginnings of vocational education.
- Recognizing the nature of the child at adolescence.
- Providing the conditions for better teaching.
- Securing better scholarship.
- Improving the disciplinary situation and socializing opportunities.
- Effecting financial economy.
- Relieving the building situation.
- Continuing the influence of the home.
- Hastening reform in grades above and below.
- Normalizing the size of classes.
- Relieving teachers. (adapted from p. 17)

During the 1930s, educational programs designed to meet the needs and nature of early adolescence gained wider acceptance. Bossing and Cramer said the "few voices" raised on behalf of early adolescents at the turn of the century had been turned into a "chorus" by 1940 (1965, p. 37). "That the junior high school idea became firmly established during this period is reflected in the rapid growth of separate three-year schools— from 387 in 1922 to 2,372 in 1938—and of junior-senior high schools—from 1,088 in 1922 to 6,203 in 1938" (Bossing and Cramer, 1965, p. 38).

Recognition of the uniqueness of the students provoked thought about uniqueness of the school program. This led to the next major shift in emphasis in the junior high movement, which was described as a move from a focus on grade organization "toward educational function" (Bossing and Cramer, 1965, p. 38). And, the functions had changed. What had been considered advantages of the new junior division during the first several decades of the twentieth century became irrelevant by the 1940s and 1950s, even though another similar increase in student enrollments besieged the schools. What was becoming clear, however, was the need to build the school program around the students. Gruhn and Douglass (1956) defined the junior high school as:

> *[A]n educational program which is designed particularly to meet the needs, the interests, and the abilities of the boys and girls during early adolescence.* A school building, grade organization, and certain administrative features are important to the junior high school only to the extent that they have a bearing on that educational program. (p. 4, italics in original)

By synthesizing the best thinking of the time, Gruhn and Douglass (1956) recommended the following functions of the junior high school of the 1950s:

1. Integration—To provide learning experiences in which pupils may use [previously learned knowledge], skills, attitudes, [and] interests in such a way that they will become coordinated and integrated into effective and wholesome pupil behavior. To provide . . . a broad, general, and common education . . . which will lead to wholesome, well-integrated behavior, attitudes, interests, ideals, and understandings.

2. Exploration—To lead pupils to discover and explore their specialized interests, aptitudes, and abilities as a basis for decisions regarding educational opportunities ... as a basis for present and future vocational decisions. ... To [help] pupils ... develop a continually widening range of cultural, social, civic, avocational, and recreational interests.

3. Guidance—To assist pupils to make intelligent decisions regarding present [and future educational and vocational activities and opportunities]. To assist pupils to make satisfactory mental, emotional, and social adjustments in their growth toward wholesome, well-adjusted personalities. To stimulate and prepare pupils to participate as effectively as possible in learning activities, so that they may reach the maximum development of their personal powers and qualities.

4. Differentiation—To provide differentiated educational facilities and opportunities suited to the varying backgrounds, interests, aptitudes, abilities, personalities, and needs of pupils, in order that each pupil may realize most economically and completely the ultimate aims of education.

5. Socialization—To provide increasingly for learning experiences designed to prepare pupils for effective and satisfying participation in the present complex social order. To provide increasingly for learning experiences designed to prepare pupils to adjust themselves and contribute to future developments and changes in that social order.

6. Articulation—To provide a gradual transition from preadolescent education to an educational program suited to the needs and interests of adolescents. (excerpted from pp. 31–32)

Mounting Dissatisfaction with the Junior High School

But in 1956, even as Gruhn and Douglass published the second edition of their book, *The Modern Junior High School*, criticisms of the junior high were mounting. Again, several unrelated events led to thoughts of school reorganization. One major influence was the Soviet launch of Sputnik in 1957, which caused a public outcry of dissatisfaction with our nation's schools. It spawned educational innovation and restructuring, especially in mathematics and science. Attention and funds were awarded to curriculum development, pedagogy, and process. The time was ripe for change.

Much of the literature in the 1960s was written about education for young adolescents and drew attention to a growing dissatisfaction with the junior high. The criticisms were leveled not so much at the grade organization as they were at the programs so prevalent in our schools for students in their middle grade years. Repeated surveys and numerous articles bemoaned the apparent fact that the junior high had turned into a miniature senior high, aping the latter's curriculum, pedagogy, and schedule. The junior high school, it seemed, was not fulfilling its functions as proposed by Koos, Briggs, and Gruhn, and Douglass; it was not meeting the unique needs of its students. Kindred, Wolotkiewicz, Mickelson, Coplein, and Dyson (1976) explained that the function of the junior high as a transitional bridge between the elementary and senior high schools had been lost. The school, instead, had taken on a preparatory function and operated much like the senior high with its emphasis on content rather than exploration, departmentalization rather than integration, and an adherence to a rigid schedule.

In 1960 James Conant, a distinguished educator and diplomat, introduced his *Recommendations for Education in the Junior High School Years*. Conant, too, stated that grade organization was less important than the school program, but he warned about inherent problems of the junior high.

> The school board and the professional staff must always keep in mind the danger that the three-year junior high school may become a replica of the senior high school with its attendant social pressures. *Interscholastic athletics and marching bands are to be condemned in junior high schools: there is no sound educational reason for them and too often they serve merely as public entertainment* [italics in original]. Community desires to glorify the role of the "senior" in the junior high school must also be watched carefully.

Graduation ceremonies with diplomas and cap and gown
have no place at the junior high level. (p. 42)

Conant (1960) continued by pointing out the difficulties
but importance of academic articulation between the junior and
senior high schools, especially considering the unique program
of the ninth grade. He considered placement of the ninth grade
in the senior high school as an articulation as well as a social
advantage, but he was not complimentary of a two-year junior
high because of the rapid turnover. Conant noted that a few
systems were incorporating Grade 6 with the seventh and eighth
grades but that educators disagreed strongly about the
effectiveness of such a plan.

Moss (1969) also acknowledged the problem of ninth
grade placement. Most college requirements included a four-
year preparatory program based on Carnegie Units. The
curriculum of the ninth grade was connected more to the senior
high school than to the junior high where it was housed.
Therefore, the junior high could not maintain a "coherent and
unique three-year sequence" (p. 13). Thus, ideas began to brew
that involved the moving of the ninth grade to the high school,
allowing for a more cohesive junior high program.

Changes in Society

As with the rise of the junior high, its decreasing popularity can
be linked partly to societal factors. Our society of the 1960s and
1970s was again changing rapidly. Industrialization was
adapting to an emphasis on more advanced technology. Sputnik
had caused a national frenzy. Generalized knowledge was
becoming less important than specialized knowledge and skills.
Innovation became valued.

The Civil Rights Movement had begun. Civil rights
protests of the 1950s and 1960s rocked tradition, and schools
were challenged to meet desegregation mandates. In *Brown* v.
The Board of Education of Topeka, Kansas (1954), the Supreme Court
struck down the separate-but-equal doctrine that had kept our
schools segregated. By 1971 plans for school desegregation had

to be designed. Many school districts responded with plans for reorganization.

A population shift was occurring. Secondary schools, which had seen a population explosion, suddenly were faced with declining enrollments. Teachers were laid off; schools were closing. At the same time, a baby "boomlet" was appearing. More students were entering our elementary schools (George, Stevenson, Thomason, and Beane, 1992). The concepts of early childhood education and kindergarten were gaining in popularity and educational acceptance. But with the introduction of these programs for young children, school rooms were commandeered. "Their growth, stimulated by federal social and educational legislation and grants to aid them, made popular in many districts the notion to move the kindergarten in, and the sixth grade out" (Alexander, 1984, pp. 19–20). School reorganizations became commonplace once again.

Young Adolescent Development

The unique needs and characteristics of young adolescents had been touted as contributory reasons for implementing a junior high school. Years later, the same rationale was used as evidence for building a middle school program. In the 1960s, however, it was noted that young adolescents were maturing physically earlier than their counterparts at the turn of the century. Tanner reported in 1962 that the age at menarche was decreasing about four months per decade (Eichhorn, 1966). Therefore, biologically, the eighth grader of the 1960s came to resemble the ninth grader of the turn of the century.

Information available on young adolescent growth and development, including attention span, interests, and learning needs, pointed to an awareness that these youngsters were unique and diverse individuals. Middle school advocates, while acknowledging myriad reasons for developing separate programs for young adolescents, referred to the developmental needs argument as the most compelling.

It was in response to young adolescent characteristics and needs that new middle schools were established in 1961 in

Saginaw Township Community School District, Michigan, and in 1963 in Armory, Mississippi. The Armory superintendent of schools was quoted as stating that, "[An] eighth grade student has more in common with sixth grade friends than with high school juniors and seniors who are already smoking, dating, and using cosmetics" (Abramson, 1963, pp. 86–87).

Perhaps the most widely known case of new middle schools was in Upper St. Clair, Pennsylvania, and championed by Donald H. Eichhorn. He had studied young adolescents in his doctoral program at the University of Pittsburgh and had developed a middle level program based on his own conception of a sociopsychological model. Eichhorn, in concert with Dr. Allan Drash from Children's Hospital in Pittsburgh, had undertaken the nation's first complete health study of young adolescents. The results of the Boyce Medical Study were the bases for the programs implemented at Fort Couch and Boyce Middle Schools. The following were among the reasons given for the transition to a six three-three organization in Upper St. Clair in 1959:

1. From the physical and psychological point of view it is a more natural grouping. There appears to be less of a differential in maturity between the sixth and eighth grade than between the seventh and the ninth grade.
2. The social patterns are more nearly the same in grades 6, 7, and 8 than in the conventional pattern of grades 7, 8, and 9. The social maturity of the ninth grade student more nearly parallels that of the older students. At the present time the ninth grade sets the pattern which is too advanced for the younger students. A better social program could be carried on without the ninth grade student.
3. The transition from the self-contained classroom to a departmentalized program may be more gradual. . . . (Eichhorn, 1966, pp. 2–3).

The Middle School Movement

The following years saw a rapid growth of middle schools (Grades 6, 7, 8 or 5, 6, 7, 8) and a decline of the junior high (see table 1).

During the 1960s and 1970s, educational associations added middle school components to try to fill the gap in professional development in middle level education. The Association for Supervision and Curriculum Development (ASCD), for example, developed its Working Group on the Middle School and the Early Adolescent Learner. The members of this group developed multimedia programs that were used extensively by schools moving to the middle school concept. Donald Eichhorn, Conrad Toepfer, and John Lounsbury, among others, presented papers, workshops, and "Action Labs" for middle level educators across the nation. Many educators began advocating the move of the ninth grade to the high school. Eichhorn, in particular, fought for this move on the basis of what he had learned about young adolescent development (personal conversations with Conrad Toepfer, July, 1992, and Donald Eichhorn, June, 1993).

In the Midwest, two middle school conferences were held in 1967, one at Miami University in Ohio and one at the University of Toledo. At the conclusion of a similar middle school conference in 1970, the Midwest Middle School Association was formed:

> (a) [T]o promote the development and growth of the middle school as a distinct and necessary entity in the structure of American education; (b) [T]o disseminate information about the middle school movement in the states serviced by the Association; and (c) [T]o promote forums for the sharing of ideas and innovations among middle school professionals" (Pickett, 1984, pp. 157–158).

Over the next few years, the association expanded from its original 22 members, and in 1973 the organization voted to become the National Middle School Association (NMSA) (Pickett, 1984). The first National Middle School Conference was

Table 1
Number of Middle Level Schools with Various Grade Organizations,
1970–71 and 1986–87

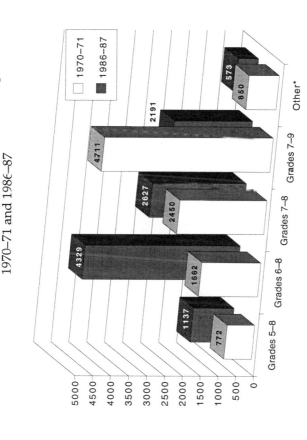

*5th or higher, with the highest grade 7th to 9th
(Alexander and McEwin, 1989) p. 3. Used by permission of National Middle School Association.

held in Columbus, Ohio, in 1974. Today this association registers 165,000 institutional members (a number that includes all the staffs of schools that are registered as institutional members) and 19,000 voting members (personal conversation with Sue Swaim, Executive Director of NMSA, February 22, 1994).

In 1975 ASCD published its position statement, *The Middle School We Need*, which again emphasized the necessity of developing school programs around the needs and characteristics of young adolescents. But the authors acknowledged the gap between theory and practice. Few middle schools, like their predecessors the junior high schools, were implementing in actual practice those components advocated for optimum educational experiences for students aged 10 to 14.

John Swaim, president of the National Middle School Association in 1980, appointed a committee to develop a position paper for the association. The committee was comprised of William Alexander, Alfred Arth, Charles Cherry, Donald Eichhorn, Conrad Toepfer, and Gordon Vars. Later, John Lounsbury was appointed as editor. The NMSA position paper, *This We Believe*, was published in 1982 and became *the* definitive statement of the middle school concept. Based on characteristics of young adolescents, the rationale of the middle school was explained and the 10 essential elements listed:

1. Educators knowledgeable about and committed to young adolescents.
2. A balanced curriculum based on the needs of young adolescents.
3. A range of organizational arrangements.
4. Varied instructional strategies.
5. A full exploratory program.
6. Comprehensive advising and counseling.
7. Continuous progress for students.
8. Evaluation procedures compatible with the nature of young adolescent needs.
9. Cooperative planning.
10. Positive school climate. (NMSA, 1992, p. 27)

Some middle level schools began tinkering with their programs, adding advisory programs and team teaching, but overall structure and curriculum remained static. Other schools began a revisioning of the all-school program. In 1985 the National Association of Secondary School Principals published *An Agenda for Excellence in Middle Level Education,* a statement written by the association's Middle Level Council. The authors, who had assisted in the restructuring of many of the "lighthouse" middle schools, explained 12 key areas of consideration for middle level schools: core values, culture and climate, student development, curriculum, learning and instruction, school organization, technology, teachers, transition, principals, connections, and client centeredness. The authors strove to help middle level schools change their overall educational presentation—to build school programs specifically for young adolescents.

Throughout the 1970s and 1980s these documents, associations, and scholars molded the development of middle level schools. Unfortunately, middle level education still lacked its own identity. Both the junior high and the middle school seemed destined to remain in the shadow of the more dominant high school system. In 1984 Lounsbury noted that although approximately 12,000 middle level schools existed in the United States, "They are grossly underrepresented in state certification, college teacher education programs, and in professional recognition and leadership. At the same time, public awareness and understanding of middle level education is drastically lacking" (Lounsbury, 1984, pp. 2–3). Information from research studies (e.g., Boyer-Brough, 1983; McEwin, 1991) supported Lounsbury's statement after data confirmed the existence of few middle level teacher preparation programs or components.

The Shadow Studies (e.g., Lounsbury and Clark, 1990; Lounsbury and Johnston, 1988) carried out by the National Association of Secondary School Principals (NASSP), clearly showed that although schools were attempting to break from the dominance of the senior high, many of the traditional techniques and structures remained. Although preferred program elements had been widely publicized by at least three national education organizations (ASCD, NMSA, and NASSP), schools were slow to implement the recommendations. Several states, California and Maryland, for example, chose to develop their own responses to middle level education by publishing their concepts of middle level educational curricula and components.

The document that has had the most recent impact not only on nascent middle level programs but also on the middle level restructuring and revitalization movement, was the Carnegie Council on Adolescent Development's *Turning Points*, published in 1989. This important report was the result of the work of the Carnegie Corporation's Task Force on Education of Young Adolescents. The report included the following charges to middle grade schools:

- Create small communities for learning. . . . The key elements . . . are schools-within-schools or houses [where] students and teachers [are] grouped as teams.
- Teach a core academic program [leading to student literacy, critical thinking, a healthy lifestyle, ethical behavior, and responsible citizenship]. Youth service to promote values for citizenship is an essential part of the core academic program.
- Ensure success for all students through elimination of tracking . . . and promotion of cooperative learning, flexibility in arranging instructional time, and adequate resources for teachers.
- Empower teachers and administrators to make decisions about the experiences of middle grade students.
- Staff middle grade schools with teachers who are expert at teaching young adolescents.
- Improve academic performance through fostering health and fitness for the young adolescents.
- Reengage families in the education of young adolescents.
- Connect schools with communities. (excerpted from Carnegie, 1989, p. 9)

The Carnegie Council then offered grants to 27 states which submitted competitive plans for improvement of middle level education. By doing so, the task force's recommendations were put into practice. The combination of the publication of *Turning Points* and the follow-up funding put middle level education in the spotlight. States where middle level education was not even recognized began studying the educational programs presented to young adolescents. Interest in NMSA's 10 essential elements and NASSP's *Agenda for Excellence* (1985) was renewed.

The Middle Level School
of the Present and Future

In 1988 Epstein and Mac Iver surveyed principals of schools, regardless of school configuration, which housed Grade 7. While about two-thirds of the principals reported homeroom or advisory periods (without indicating the actual practices in these periods), few other recognized middle school elements were so widely used. Drill and practice and passive rather than active student involvement still dominated. Fifty-eight percent of the students did not receive instruction from interdisciplinary teams of teachers (Epstein and Mac Iver, 1990). The researchers concluded that, "The data show clearly that in present practice there are not commonly agreed upon 'best' or 'essential' practices for middle grades education in this country" (p. 8).

Cuban (1992) remarked:

> After a quarter of a century of experience with middle schools, there is much evidence that what has most changed in the new middle schools has been the policy talk, the formal names of schools, and the vocabulary of educators. In addition to the shifts in talk and adoption of policies, there have been incremental changes in organization, curriculum, and instruction. These add-ons have occurred in great frequency in many middle schools, as reported in surveys of teachers, principals, and superintendents. But the vast majority of schools housing early adolescents, especially in cities, resemble the junior highs they were supposed to reform. (p. 246)

Today, increasing numbers of middle level educators and scholars are focusing on the educational program for young adolescents rather than on the grade levels housed in their schools. It is an accepted fact that too many variables other than the needs of students affect the grade configuration of the schools. The descriptor *middle level* is being used with some frequency to indicate reference to young adolescent education, rather than specific designation of middle school, junior high, or intermediate school education.

The emphasis, instead, has turned to appropriate curriculum, pedagogy, process, and teacher preparation. Middle level conferences list sessions on such topics as "Advisor-Advisee Programs," "Integrated Curriculum," "Transition to a Middle Level Concept," and "Teaming." The National Council for Accreditation of Teacher Education (NCATE) recently approved undergraduate and graduate level teacher preparation curriculum guidelines prepared by NMSA's Professional Preparation and Certification Committee (NMSA, 1991).

Our nation's schools struggle again with varying perspectives on the social functions of education. For example, educators and their communities now grapple with the appropriate degree and intensity of emphasis on multiculturalism and diversity, the teaching of values, and conflict resolution. We debate benefits of various curriculum approaches, such as departmentalization, subject matter integration, and interdisciplinary and multidisciplinary models. We fight over outcomes-based education and authentic versus traditional assessment.

By rereading the rationale for the birth and subsequent decline of the junior high model, one can notice a similarity to the life cycle of the middle school model. For over 60 years our nation has articulated a need to define and implement an educational program appropriate for children between the ages of 10 and 14. For these 60 years, other issues—some related, some not—have clouded our objective; many and diverse priorities and points of view affect the educational programs we deliver.

It seems apparent that the future of middle level education depends quite directly on its ability to break from the dominance of the high school and form its own identity and clarity of goals. But it is through the study of and attention to the needs and characteristics of the clients, young adolescents themselves, that we will ultimately succeed in building a truly responsive and responsible middle level program.

REFERENCES

Abramson, P. (1963). Why one district is building a middle school. *School Management 7*: 86–88.

Alexander, W. (1969). *The emergent middle school* (2nd ed.). New York: Holt, Rinehart, & Winston.

Alexander, W. (1984). The middle school emerges and flourishes. In J. Lounsbury (Ed.), *Perspectives: Middle school education, 1964–1984* (pp. 14–29). Columbus, OH: National Middle School Association.

Alexander, W., and McEwin, C. K. (1989). *Schools in the middle: Status and progress*. Columbus, OH: National Middle School Association.

Association for Supervision and Curriculum Development. (1975). *The middle school we need*. Washington, D.C.: Author.

Bossing, N., and Cramer, R. (1965). *The junior high school*. Boston: Houghton Mifflin Co.

Boyer Brough, J. A. (1983). A study of middle level teacher education components. Unpublished doctoral dissertation, State University of New York at Buffalo.

Briggs, T. (1920). *The junior high school*. Cambridge: The Riverside Press.

Carnegie Council on Adolescent Development. (1989). *Turning points: Preparing American youth for the 21st century*. Washington, DC: Author.

Conant, J. B. (1959). *The American high school today: A first report to citizens*. New York: McGraw-Hill.

Conant, J. B. (1960). *Recommendations for education in the junior high school years*. Princeton, NJ: Educational Testing Service.

Cuban, L. (1992). What happens to reforms that last? The case of the junior high school. *American Educational Research Journal 29*: 227–251.

Eichhorn, D. H. (1966). *The middle school*. New York: The Center for Applied Research in Education.

Eliot, C. W. (1898). *Educational reform: Essays and addresses*. New York: The Century Co.

Epstein, J., and Mac Iver, D. (1990). Implementation and effects of middle grades practices. *CREMS Report*. Baltimore: Center for Research on Elementary and Middle Schools, Johns Hopkins University.

George, P. S., Stevenson, C., Thomason, J., and Beane, J. (1992). *The middle school—and beyond.* Alexandria, VA: Association for Supervision and Curriculum Development.

Gruhn, W., and Douglass, H. (1956). *The modern junior high school* (2nd ed.). New York: Ronald Press.

Hall, G. S. (1905). *Adolescence: Its psychology and its relations to physiology, anthropology, sociology, sex, crime, religion and education* (Vol. II). New York: D. Appleton & Co.

Kindred, L., Wolotkiewicz, R., Mickelson, J., Coplein, L., and Dyson, E. (1976). *The middle school curriculum: A practitioner's handbook.* Needham Heights, MA: Allyn & Bacon.

Koos, L. (1927). *The junior high school.* New York: Ginn & Co.

Lounsbury, J. H. (1984). Prologue. In J. Lounsbury (Ed.), *Perspectives: Middle school education 1964–1984* (pp. 1–4). Columbus, OH: National Middle School Association.

Lounsbury, J. H., and Johnston, J. H. (1988). *Life in the three sixth grades.* Reston, VA: National Association of Secondary School Principals.

Lounsbury, J. H., and Clark, D. C. (1990). *Inside grade eight: From apathy to excitement.* Reston, VA: National Association of Secondary School Principals.

McEwin, C. K (1991). *Middle level teacher certification practices in 1990: A national perspective.* Boone, NC: Appalachian State University.

Moss, T. (1969). *Middle school.* New York: Houghton Mifflin.

National Association of Secondary School Principals Middle Level Council. (1985). *Agenda for excellence in middle level education.* Reston, VA: Author.

National Education Association. (1899). Report of the committee on college entrance requirements. *Journal of proceedings and addresses of the thirty-eighth annual meeting* (pp. 632–817). Los Angeles: Author.

National Middle School Association. (1982, 1992). *This we believe.* Columbus, OH: Author.

National Middle School Association. (1991). *Professional certification and preparation for the middle level.* Columbus, OH: Author.

Ornstein, A., and Levine, D. (1993). *Foundations of education* (5th ed.). Boston: Houghton Mifflin.

Pickett, W. (1984). The development of the national middle school association. In J. Lounsbury (Ed.), *Perspectives: Middle school education 1964–1984* (pp. 157–168). Columbus, OH: National Middle School Association.

Salmeri, E. (1985). A comparison and analysis of the junior high program antecedents of the middle school from 1910 to 1982 in relation to the ten essential elements. Unpublished doctoral dissertation, University of Wyoming, Laramie.

Spring, J. (1986). *The American school 1642–1985*. New York: Longman.

Toepfer, C. F. (1962). Evolving curricular patterns in junior high school: An historical study. Unpublished doctoral dissertation, State University of New York at Buffalo.

Van Til, W., Vars. G., and Lounsbury, J. (1961). *Modern education for the junior high school years*. New York: Bobbs-Merrill.

CHAPTER 3

Growth and Development during the Middle School Years

Dionne M. Walker and Cathy D. Lirgg

Throughout the chapters of this book, it readily becomes apparent that the middle school years encompass a time of great change. Psychological, social, physical, cognitive, and personality changes are inevitable for young adolescents. Division of these developmental areas is quite simple and somewhat necessary for the purpose of this chapter. However, it is nearly impossible to separate the facets of adolescent development in reality. In fact, the changes that take place within every young adolescent are so strongly related that a shift in one aspect of development is almost certain to bring about variations in others.

Because physical changes often are the most obvious and least understood, they tend to be the center around which other areas of development revolve. Even the advent of the middle school concept was partially in response to the earlier maturation trend of today's students (Berzonsky, 1981; Hannan, 1974; Lawrence, 1980), a trend that has occurred primarily in a physical sense. As students mature earlier physically, their cognitive, social, and psychological needs change as well. Elementary schools are often no longer the ideal place for young adolescents between the ages of 10 and 14, many of whom may be well into puberty and quite physically and socially mature.

The main purpose of this chapter is to explore the physical and sexual growth and development that occurs during the middle school years. Important physiological changes that underlie the more apparent physical ones will be described briefly as well. An examination of the various methods used in determining maturity levels (*developmental age*) also will be included. Finally, the factors that affect growth and maturation rates will be noted and the way in which these variable growth rates most often affect males and females will be explained.

Physical Growth during the Middle School Years

One of the many physical changes associated with puberty is the adolescent *growth spurt*. This term is used usually to refer to the accelerated rate of increase in height and weight that occurs during early adolescence. The adolescent growth spurt occurs at some point in all children, although it varies greatly in intensity and duration from one child to another. Differences also can be seen when comparing the onset of the growth spurt in boys and girls. In boys the growth spurt usually takes place from ages 12.5–15, while in girls it occurs most often between the ages of 10.5–13 (Tanner, 1978).

The growth spurt, which includes increases in both height and weight as well as other physical changes, is responsible for the ultimate difference in size between adult men and women. Prior to this spurt, boys and girls are very similar in size and other biological characteristics. In boys, a height increase of about 20 cm (7.9"), a weight increase of about 20 kg (44 lbs.), and a peak velocity of height growth near 10 cm/year (4"/year) occur during this period. For girls, the spurt is smaller in scope with an average growth of 8 cm/year (3.1"/year) during puberty (Tanner, 1962). For both genders, peak weight velocity (PWV) occurs after peak height velocity (PHV). Growth curves for both height and body weight are shown in figure 1.

Mean Stature and Body Weight from 9–16 Years
of Age in American Children

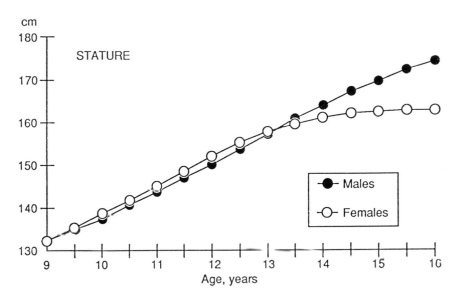

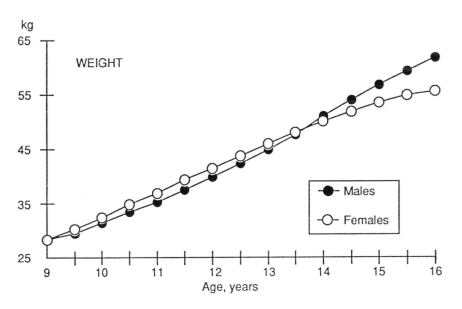

Although overall increases in weight and height are the most obvious changes that occur during the adolescent growth spurt, growth spurts that occur in other dimensions should not be overlooked. In fact, practically all skeletal and muscular dimensions take part in the adolescent spurt (Tanner, 1978). Some of the physiological changes, such as the increase in the size and weight of the heart which nearly doubles at puberty (Coleman, 1980), are not outwardly observable. However, many of the changes that take place in other physical dimensions (e.g., anthropometric, muscular, and body composition changes) easily are seen.

Anthropometric Changes

According to Tanner (1978), there is a fairly regular order in which the dimensions of the adolescent accelerate. Leg length will, in most children, reach its peak first, followed directly by increases in the body breadths (hips and shoulders), and, approximately a year later, by trunk length. In fact, most of the spurt in height is due to trunk growth rather than growth of the legs. This explains the coordination problems seen in many young middle schoolers who, at times, may be fittingly described as "all legs." This natural procession of growth needs to be carefully considered by teachers, coaches, and parents as the child begins to participate in certain sports and recreational activities (see Lirgg, this volume). As stated earlier, because peak height velocity occurs before peak weight velocity, students, at certain points in their development, may not be as strong as they appear (Payne and Issacs, 1991). For this reason, collision and contact sports should be supervised and proper equipment should be worn.

Muscular Changes

Approximately three to six months after peak height velocity, the muscles begin the peak of their spurt (Malina, 1990; Tanner, 1962). With this comes a sharp increase in the strength of the muscles, especially in boys. This is the point at which differences in strength, particularly arm strength, begin to occur between genders. In boys, the spurt in arm muscle growth is approximately twice the magnitude of that for girls. In contrast to the arm, peak gain in the calf muscle during the growth spurt is only slightly greater in boys than girls (Tanner, Hughes, and Whitehouse, 1981). In fact, boys and girls will have nearly identical strength in the legs (Jones, Wells, Peters, and Johnson, 1993).

Changes in Body Composition

In addition to muscular development and growth in height and weight, a change in the composition of the body occurs during this time. According to Malina (1990), fat free mass (FFM) follows a growth pattern comparable to that of height and weight. Boys tend to have, on average, a larger FFM than girls at all ages, and, while both boys and girls experience a gain in FFM, the increase in boys is about twice that of girls This accounts for the gender difference in FFM which is apparent during adulthood.

Regarding fat mass (FM), girls increase at a greater rate than boys from childhood to adolescence, and, in boys, FM appears to reach a plateau near the time of the growth spurt (Malina, 1990). In comparing the two genders, at all ages girls have a greater percentage of body fat than boys. It is this increase in body fat that often precipitates the weight consciousness and continual dieting that is practiced by many women, young and old alike. A further explanation regarding the implication of this constant dieting and weight consciousness during the adolescent years can be found later in the chapter.

Physiological Changes

During the adolescent growth spurt, a considerable number of physiological changes occur. It is at this time that gender differences, especially those related to physical performance, first begin to surface. As stated earlier in this chapter, before the occurrence of the adolescent growth spurt, boys and girls are very similar in most physiological measurements. In this section, a brief explanation of the physiological changes that occur during adolescence is given.

Heart rate. Throughout the entire period of growth, heart rate is decreasing continually in both males and females. In fact, until approximately age 11, both genders are very similar in heart rate. It is at this point that females' heart rates begin to decrease less than males'; this ultimately leads to a significant difference between genders at around age 12 (Tanner, 1962). There are two possible reasons for this gender difference, a difference that remains throughout adulthood: (a) the greater size of the male heart, and (b) the difference in body temperature, which also occurs at this time.

Body temperature. The changes in body temperature that occur during adolescence are similar to those for heart rate. Body temperature also decreases with age in both sexes, and, again, a gender difference becomes apparent at approximately age 12. As with heart rate, girls reach their adult values for body temperature earlier than boys, while boys continue decreasing, causing them to have a lower basal body temperature at least into young adulthood.

Blood pressure. Throughout childhood systolic blood pressure rises at a steady pace. However, during adolescence it increases more rapidly and quickly approaches adult levels (Gabbard, 1992). Girls experience this rise in systolic blood pressure earlier than boys; however, when boys do experience an increase, it is greater than that for girls (Tanner, 1962). This difference, which is believed to be caused by either the greater stroke volume or increased blood volume of the male, occurs around age 12 and continues into adulthood. Diastolic blood pressure does not change nearly as much as systolic pressure does. Furthermore, there is virtually no gender difference in diastolic blood pressure.

Blood volume. The gender difference in blood volume, mentioned above, is attributed largely to the greater increase in hemoglobin experienced by males during puberty. Hemoglobin, which determines the oxygen carrying capacity of the blood, is believed to be related to the percentage of lean body mass (muscle) a person possesses. This accounts for the greater levels of hemoglobin found in most males after puberty (Gabbard, 1992; Tanner, 1962). Because females do not experience an equivalent rise in the number of red blood cells, and thus hemoglobin, physiological function in adults will differ between the sexes.

Respiratory function. Throughout childhood and adolescence, respiratory rate steadily decreases for both males and females. Changes also occur in respiratory volume, vital capacity, and maximum breathing capacity at this time with increases in all areas for both genders. Boys, however, increase more significantly than girls, accounting for the differences observed between adult males and females (Keogh and Sugden, 1985; Tanner, 1962). These differences between the genders is believed to be due primarily to the greater growth of the lungs and overall body size that occurs in boys during puberty.

Response to exercise. The physiological changes stated above are not the only ones that take place during adolescence. They are, however, largely responsible for the adult gender differences in response to physical exertion. Males, with their larger hearts, higher hemoglobin content, increased respiratory function, and greater lean body mass, are, on average, ultimately more physiologically efficient than their female counterparts. These differences are most easily observed by evaluation of maximal oxygen consumption (VO_2 max), which increases in males until about age 18, while females cease to improve beyond the age of 14 (Gabbard, 1992). However, it is possible for both males and females to improve their aerobic capacity with proper training.

Sexual Maturation during the Middle School Years

Closely linked to the physical changes described above is sexual maturation, which also takes place for most students during the middle school years. Although the timing of these events is completely individual, they follow a pattern that again resembles that of the height and weight growth spurt. In other words, while each individual child will experience the onset and stages of sexual maturation at different chronological ages, the order in which these changes occur will vary little between children. As with every other aspect of development, the events of sexual maturation occur approximately 18–24 months later for boys than girls.

Sexual Maturation in Males

For boys, the first sign of puberty is usually an increase in the size and rate of growth of the testes (which produce sperm and testosterone) and the scrotum. Following this, growth of pubic hair begins but proceeds slowly until the general growth spurt occurs (Tanner, 1978). About a year later, an acceleration in height and growth of the penis begins with the penis growing in both length and width and the head becoming larger. Prostatic activity (i.e., the ejaculation of semen and sperm) is a key pubertal event and most often begins upon completion of penis growth. Although the first ejaculation often occurs through masturbation, spontaneous emission of seminal fluid usually will begin to take place during sleep about a year after penis growth commences (Berzonsky, 1981).

In many ways the first ejaculation may be analogous to the female menarche (the first menstrual period) (Muth & Averman, 1992). This occurrence marks the point of transition from childhood to adolescence in the minds of many, and the young boy may now begin to feel like a "man." Studies have shown, however, that this is often a time of shame and fear for the young male if he has not been properly informed concerning the events he will experience. In fact, in studies comparing young girls and boys, it has been determined that females usually are much better informed about and prepared for menarche than males are for their first ejaculation (Zani, 1991).

Approximately two years after the appearance of pubic hair, the male will begin to see axillary and facial hair appearing. It is most common for facial hair to first increase in length and pigmentation at the corners of the upper lip with final growth of facial hair occurring along the sides and border of the chin (Tanner, 1978). Shortly after the spurt in height, the larynx enlarges and the voice begins to deepen. This deepening in the voice occurs as the development of the penis approaches completion.

A final development that may occur in some boys during puberty is slight breast enlargement. For the majority of boys this is temporary and disappears quickly. However, slight breast enlargement is a development for which many boys are unprepared and a source of much unnecessary alarm. Again, proper education and correct information can make these changes much less stressful for the young adolescent.

Sexual Maturation in Females

In girls, the beginning of breast development and the growth of pubic hair are the first signs of puberty. However, these two series of events show "considerable independence" (Tanner, 1978, p. 32). In some girls, breast development may be almost complete while pubic hair growth has not begun. It also is common for girls in the early stages of breast development to have pubic hair that has reached adult stages.

Because of the above-stated discrepancies, menarche most commonly is used as the landmark of sexual development in females. Menarche almost always occurs after the peak of the height spurt has elapsed. In the average female, this puts menarche at approximately 13 years of age, although the normal range for the first menstrual period is ages 10–16 (Tanner, 1990).

Much research has been conducted to determine what factors may affect age at menarche. Muth and Alverman (1992) introduced findings that showed menarche to be highly correlated with weight. In this research it was determined that menarche occurs around 106 pounds, regardless of age. Although most people could find exceptions to this rule, this relationship is supported by the fact that menstruation begins early in obese females and amenorrhea (abnormal suppression or absence of menstruation) commonly occurs in females whose weight drops below this critical point.

The occurrence of menarche denotes the final maturation stage of vaginal and uterine growth. This, however, does not necessarily mark the attainment of full reproductive function.

Tanner (1978) discusses a possible period of infertility of a year or 18 months following the initial menstrual period in many cases. At the same time, it is important to note that it is possible for a female to have full reproductive capabilities at the onset of menstruation.

Sexuality and the Middle School Student

With the average age of menarche at approximately 13 years, and the average age for the growth of the penis at $12^1/2$ years, the ability for females to conceive and for males to father children is quite possible during the middle school years. Along with this development comes responsibility—responsibility that many of these young adolescents have not been prepared to address.

Young adolescents need to know the facts concerning their sexual development. Educators, counselors, and parents are in the best possible position to provide information and assurance during this time of uncertainty for the adolescent. If an adolescent who is cautiously but diligently searching for answers does not receive them in time, he or she will be forced to learn through experimentation or, possibly, through the often inaccurate portrayals found in magazines, movies, and television.

Because the decisions these adolescents make concerning sexual activity impact their future in so many ways, these choices should be of great concern to parents and middle school educators. One needs only to open the daily newspaper to find that the percentages of middle-school-aged youths who have experienced sexual intercourse at least once, or the number of girls at this age who are pregnant, are on the rise (Dornbusch, 1989). In fact, according to the National Research Council, approximately 17 percent of boys and 5 percent of girls, had sexual intercourse by age 15 in 1983. By 1988 the numbers had risen to 33 percent and 27 percent for boys and girls, respectively (Scales, 1991). This shocking realization, coupled with the ever present threat of STDs and HIV infection, may explain why more than 85 percent of adults now favor sexuality education in American schools (Budlong and Franken, 1992).

Until this point, an effort has been made to describe the physical and sexual changes that occur during adolescence, with limited reference to the chronological ages at which they present themselves. As has been stated several times, both physical and sexual maturation follow a course that is individualized for each child. Because of this, it is almost impossible to give "normal" ages for the onset of certain developments. It was possible, however, to report age ranges that encompassed the point at which the average male and female experience certain events at puberty.

The next section will examine various methods for determining maturity. Through the use of these methods it is possible to assign a *developmental* rather than *chronological* age to a growing child. In order to better understand and fully appreciate subsequent sections of this chapter, it is important for the reader to examine the table referred to in the following text and the explanation that accompanies it.

Determining Stages of Maturity

Because individuals vary so greatly in the age at which they reach certain stages of development, the statement that a child is 14 years of age often is much too vague to be of value. In fact, for certain clinical and research purposes, chronological age may be of almost no value at all. It is for this reason that a developmental rather than chronological age may be assigned to a growing child. For the purpose of assigning a developmental age to a growing child, there are four systems currently being used (Tanner, 1962). They are (1) sexual age, (2) dental age, (3) morphological age, and (4) skeletal age.

Sexual Age

The basis for assessing the sexual maturation of a child is the development of the secondary sex characteristics. A relatively simple scheme has been proposed by Tanner (1962) and can be found in many publications that cover the development of adolescents. In this model, breast development in girls, genital development in boys, and stage of pubic hair growth in both sexes provide the basis for assessment. For both males and females the ratings are on a scale from 1–5. Stage 1 indicates an absence of development of the particular characteristic, while stage 2 indicates the beginning of development. Stages 3 and 4 are considered the intermediate stages of development, and stage 5 is indicative of mature status.

In reporting these stages of development, it is a common practice to state the characteristic first, followed by the stage of development. In doing this, stage 2 of breast development would be reported as B2, for example, and stage 4 of pubic hair development as PH4. Table 1 summarizes the sequence of pubertal events for boys and girls in North America and Europe.

Table 1

Sequence of Pubertal Events in North American
and European Girls and Boys

Girls		Boys	
Event	Range of Reported Ages	Event	Range of Reported Ages
B2	10.6–11.4	G2	11.0–12.4
PH2	10.4–12.1	PH2	12.2–13.4
PH3	11.9–13.1	PH3	13.1–13.9
PHV	11.5–12.1	G4	13.4–14.7
PH4	12.5–13.5	PHV	13.8–14.1
B4	12.2–13.8	PH4	13.9–15.1
M	12.8–13.5	G5	14.6–17.3
PH5	13.9–15.2	G5	14.6–17.3
B5	13.7–15.6	PH5	14.9–16.1

Note: Pubertal events are as follows: B2–BS, G2–G5, PH2–PH5 refer to breast, genital, and pubic hair stages 2 through 5 respectively; PHV refers to peak height velocity; M refers to menarche. Range of reported ages refers to mean or median ages (years) for each pubertal event.

Dental Age

The age at which certain teeth begin to erupt also provides information concerning the approximate level of maturation. The deciduous dentition (temporary teeth) erupt between the ages of 6 months to 2 years. Permanent teeth generally appear from about 6–13 years of age.

Although the eruption of teeth is quite a predictable event in most cases, this method of assigning developmental age is of little use beyond age 13. However, Gabbard (1992) discusses research that mentions dental calcification seen in X-rays as a possible indicator of dental age.

Morphological Age

The term *morphology* refers to the form or structure of an individual (Gabbard, 1992). In determining morphological age, estimations usually are made by determining a child's height and comparing that measure to a height percentile chart. By doing this, it is possible to indicate where an individual ranks for his or her age and gender.

Although this method frequently is used in determining a person's maturity, a measure of height alone is often a poor indicator. Because individuals vary so greatly in mature height, being assessed as above or below average at a specific time may signify either a rapid, slow, or average rate of growth for a child who ultimately may be above or below average in height as an adult.

Skeletal Age

Skeletal age is perhaps the most widely used and effective means of estimating maturity. In this method assessment is made by comparing the X-ray of a given child with a predetermined set of standards. Skeletal maturity, also referred to as *bone age*, usually is measured by taking an X-ray of the left wrist and hand. The continual enlargement and shape changes that occur in the 29 separate ossification centers of the wrist and hand can be easily detected on X-ray. With the use of this method, it also is possible to determine the maturity of the bone by observing its denseness or visibility on the X-ray.

The four preceding methods of assigning developmental age, along with the use of chronological age, make it quite simple to determine and explain a child's stage of development. What is it, though, that makes young adolescents vary so greatly in their rates of development? And why do some young adolescents never seem to "catch up" to their peers in development and size? Although the majority of the influence concerning maturation is internal, some external forces may play a role as well.

Factors Affecting Rate of Growth

Various factors are known to affect the adolescent growth spurt and rate of development in children. Some of these factors are strictly genetic in nature, some are considered environmental, and still others may be an interaction of the two. Following is a brief explanation of the most common factors believed to affect growth rate and age at puberty.

Heredity

Genetics is "probably the single most important source of variation in physical growth" (Brunk, 1975, p. 50). The rate of a person's development, the point at which the growth spurt and the onset of puberty occur, and the ultimate size and height of an individual are greatly influenced by heredity. One of the greatest sources of evidence for this is the inheritance of age at menarche.

Studies have been conducted that compare the difference, in months, of age at menarche between identical twins, nonidentical twins, siblings, and unrelated women (Tanner, 1962). As expected, the difference is much less for identical twins than for nonidentical twins or sisters. However, the difference for sisters is still considerably lower than that for unrelated women.

Another piece of "evidence" that points toward heredity as an important factor affecting growth is the way in which "children come to resemble their parents in height, weight, and other measurements more as they grow older" (Tanner, 1962, p. 117). This family resemblance between parents and children, as well as siblings, seems at times to be just common sense. Tanner (1990), however, stresses that still more longitudinal growth studies are needed before conclusions can be drawn regarding the strength of the relationship between genetics and growth rates.

Nutrition

The effects of malnutrition on growth and puberty have been well documented. Using victims of war as subjects, it has been possible to determine the effects of malnutrition on childhood growth and the adolescent growth spurt (Tanner, 1978).

In general, it can be said that malnutrition during childhood delays growth, and malnutrition in the years preceding adolescence delays the onset of the adolescent growth spurt (Forbes, 1968). It has also been found that the areas of the body growing the fastest at the time poor nutrition occurs will show the greatest loss of development.

Although the effects of poor nutrition and even starvation can influence greatly the maturation process, the body is very forgiving. In both animals and humans, the body is quite adept at recuperating, provided the adverse conditions have not been present for a substantial period of time. Severe malnutrition that has occurred during a large part of the growth period, however, may cause some permanent stunting.

Illness

When reporting the effects of illness on rate of growth, it is important to distinguish between major illnesses, such as kidney disease, and minor ones, such as measles and pneumonia. Longitudinal studies throughout the growth period, which have carefully recorded all illnesses, show that minor illnesses do not play a role in hampering growth. Major illnesses that lead to prolonged hospitalization, however, may cause a considerable slowing of the growth process. Tanner (1978) explains that the most probable cause for this delay in development hinges upon the changes in endocrine balance that occur with certain disorders.

Delays in growth due to illness are similar to those caused by malnutrition in that a "catch-up" period occurs in both cases upon removal of the negative stimuli (Mosier, 1989). In fact, ultimate body size and development seem to be virtually unaffected unless the illness is chronic.

SES and Family Size

Although the effects of socioeconomic status (SES) and family size on rate of growth are not substantial, they do exist. This is one area, however, in which confounding variables abound. Because SES, family size, and overall home conditions are so often interrelated, it is difficult to distinguish between these and other factors in regard to maturation rate. It can generally be said that children who come from lower-class families and those who have several siblings tend to lag behind in rate of growth (Tanner, 1962). Menarche, body size, and even permanent tooth eruption tend to differ between social classes and with the size of the family.

The reason for the differences between social classes vary. Nutrition is one contributing factor along with several other good health habits, such as proper amounts of sleep, exercise, and grooming. The effects caused by family size are most likely similar. With a greater number of children to care for and more mouths to feed, certain nutritional and health-related benefits are apt to be overlooked. Although these factors may play a significant role in affecting rate of growth in some countries, in the United States the effect has not been substantial.

Exercise

Although a survey of the literature concerning the influence of physical exercise on growth reveals few absolute conclusions, it is generally understood that a certain minimal amount of physical activity is necessary for normal human growth to occur. Parents and teachers alike can attest to the fact that most young adolescents naturally are drawn to and enjoy physical activity. This innate desire to play and be physically active is seen in most young animals, making it apparent that it is probably a necessary condition for growth (Bailey, Malina & Rasmussen, 1978).

As stated earlier, few concrete conclusions regarding the effects of physical activity on growth can be found in the literature. This, along with the many variables that surround physical activity, such as the type of activity and the extent to which it is pursued, makes it difficult to comment with certainty on the effect it ultimately will have on growth. Following is a brief summary of the possible effects of exercise on muscular and bone development, body composition, and physiological function.

Muscle and bone development. In regard to muscle and bone development, resistance activities have been found to increase strength, width, and density of the skeletal structure as well as size, strength, and endurance of the muscular system (Arnheim, 1985). Although these desired results may be obtained through activities such as weight lifting, most authors caution against the use of heavy resistance training or strength specialization in growing adolescents (Arnheim, 1985). The use of low weight and high repetitions or the use of isokinetic methods are much safer and will produce similar results.

Body composition. Body composition is another area that is positively affected by physical activity. Although more effort is generally directed toward the correction of fatness rather than its prevention, studies have shown that physical training early in life reduces the rate of fat cell accumulation, which is an ongoing process until early adolescence (Bailey et al., 1978). Physical training, in general, produces an increase in lean body mass and, thus, a decrease in body fat. It is somewhat difficult, however, to separate the effects of exercise from the effects of natural growth in young adolescents.

Physiological function. The effects of exercise on physiological function is another area of interest to many, especially as its usefulness in disease prevention becomes more apparent. Bailey et al. (1978) discussed several studies that have examined the effects of childhood physical activity on development and functional capacity during adulthood. Most studies have concluded that physical training, provided it is not too strenuous, does not elicit harmful effects in children. It does, however, tend to affect the long-term health and physiological function of the individual in a positive manner.

Although it is not within the scope of this chapter to discuss the role of physical education and athletics within the middle school, the positive effects of exercise mentioned above make it impossible to overlook the importance of daily, quality physical education in our school systems. Not all young adolescents will have the opportunity to benefit from participation in athletics or even intramural sports and, with the advent of video games and cable television, few are motivated to be physically active at home. A quality physical education program with a qualified physical education teacher is paramount if today's middle school students are to become healthy adults.

Secular Trend

Another factor known to affect rate of growth has influenced entire generations in many sections of the world. This phenomenon is known as the *secular trend*. The term secular trend "has been used to describe the biological fact that over the last hundred years the rate of physical growth of children and adolescents has accelerated, leading to faster and thus earlier maturation" (Coleman, 1980, p. 19). Although there have been many studies conducted to collect data on the secular trend, several questions still remain. For example, "What exactly is it that has caused this trend toward earlier development?" "What are the effects of the secular trend, both socially and in regard to physical performance?" And, "To what extent will the secular trend continue?"

The secular trend is believed to be predominantly due to advances in environmental conditions, especially nutrition and health care (Berzonsky, 1981; Coleman, 1980; Malina, 1979; Tanner, 1962). Another explanation includes genetic influences caused primarily by outbreeding or the "marrying of individuals from outside an intact community" (Berzonsky, 1981, p. 143). Malina (1979) has compiled a list of "causative or associated" factors believed to contribute to the secular trend. Among those factors are

> [D]ietary changes, especially increased fat and sugar consumption; changing patterns of infant nutrition; improved health conditions as reflected in reduced infant and childhood mortality and increased life expectancy; urbanization and industrialization; reduction in child labor; reduction in family size, natural selection; and outbreeding. (p. 213)

Implications of the secular trend may, at first glance, seem minimal. What difference does it really make if the children of today are taller, heavier, and reaching puberty earlier than children of the same age several generations ago? Malina (1979) also has compiled a list in regard to this question which states that secular trends in size and maturation can lead to

> [L]engthened reproductive span; increase in teenage births; overnutrition and increased physical inactivity; the need for updated growth reference data both as growth charts and for use in design and manufacture of children's clothing, furniture, and public facilities; and educational and social implications, for example, sex education and parent-child interactions. (p. 213)

Because strength and motor performance are related partially to body size and stage of maturity, the secular trend also has implications for physical performance. The absolute magnitude of these implications are somewhat difficult to measure, however. Malina (1979) discusses the impact of possible differences in methods of measurement, socioeconomic status, and racial/ethnic composition of subjects used to determine the extent of the trend in regard to physical performance. For example, the results of a study conducted on boys in Saginaw, Michigan, in 1899 and again in 1963–1964 show increases in strength for the latter group. Although both groups of students attended the same school, the composition of the Saginaw population may not have remained the same during that 65-year period. Thus, it is difficult to determine exactly how much of the increase was due to the secular trend and how much was due to other confounding variables.

Two of the areas in which data on increases in strength and motor performance are collected most easily are the fitness tests that are conducted in the majority of our nation's physical education classes and in the Olympics, in which records are continually being broken. Again, there are differences, other than size and weight, that must be considered. Differences in the curriculum of physical education classes of today compared with those of 50 years ago, as well as the population's heightened interest in physical fitness, have played a significant role in influencing the motor performance of today's children (Malina, 1979).

In regard to the Olympics, today's world-class athletes have shown considerable secular improvement in many events over the past 80 years or so (Malina, 1979). Some data also suggest that the body size of athletes has shown a greater secular trend than that of the general population. However, it is quite possible that the continual improvement and record-breaking performances seen in the last 80 years are due to more than just the secular trend in body size. Today's athlete often gets an earlier start at specializing in a particular sport or event, the training levels and selection of top athletes is more stringent, and coaching techniques have improved as well. Although the increase in the size of the athlete may play a role in the secular improvement of world-class athletes, it is most likely a combination of the above-stated factors that has caused the trend. But what are the limits to this trend? And how much longer will it continue?

Although there are those who have images of children someday reaching puberty by the age of five years and an average adult height of eight feet, researchers such as Tanner

(1962), Malina (1979), Coleman (1980), and Damon (1974), just to name a few, have suggested a slowing, or even stopping of the secular trend in some countries. The suggestion that the secular trend is nearing its end is based on experimental results as well as the belief that physical development can be accelerated only within certain biological limits for any given population (Coleman, 1980).

Most authors agree that while the trend toward earlier development and greater body size is slowing, it is not occurring in an abrupt fashion. Instead, where the age of menarche has been reducing approximately four months per decade during the twentieth century, it may slow to a reduction of only one month per decade in the next century. Secular trends for size and physical performance will most likely occur in the same manner. Thus, while the distance that a world-class athlete is able to throw the discus will continue to increase, the amount by which the record is broken each year will gradually decrease. The extent to which the secular trend does continue to occur is most likely largely dependent upon the degree to which environmental conditions continue to improve.

Research regarding the effects of certain inherited and environmental factors on rate of growth is somewhat inconclusive; however, a basic understanding of the concepts presented in the section above is still important. Just as important for parents, teachers, and others who deal with middle school youths is an understanding of how those who mature earlier or later than average are affected by their atypical rate of development. Following is an explanation of the impact of early and late maturation rates on young adolescents and how the effects are different for boys and girls.

Early versus Late Maturation

The evaluation of one's physical appearance has important and lasting effects (Wood and Hillman, 1992). Young adolescents who are perceived as physically attractive tend to have more positive relationships with peers and adults and are often believed to have higher academic ability than young adolescents who are perceived as physically unattractive (Lerner and Lerner, 1977).

The way a child is perceived by others is not the only factor affected by maturation rate. Children's beliefs concerning their own popularity and academic potential often are affected as well. In other words, a child's self-concept ultimately may be determined by something over which that child has absolutely no control. For this reason alone, it is important for middle school students to be educated about their developing bodies and the various rates of development they will observe among their peers.

Boys

For boys it clearly is advantageous to be an "early bloomer." The characteristics of male puberty, such as increased height and muscle mass, are considered a positive development, and most boys look forward to this time of change. If a boy matures earlier than the average, he will have decisive advantages over his later-maturing peers, both physically and socially (Hillman, 1991; Stafford, 1982; Tanner, 1962). These boys often are looked up to, respected by their classmates, and considered by teachers to be more socially mature (Berzonsky, 1981). Early-maturing boys also are more likely to succeed in sports at a younger age and are thus given more opportunities to participate in sporting activities than late-maturing boys (Martens, 1978).

Boys who mature later than the average are completely on the other end of the spectrum. Instead of being respected and well liked, these boys tend to be viewed as socially immature and less capable. Due in part to expectancy effects, these boys tend to engage in more deviant behaviors, especially in the school setting. Boys who lag behind in development also tend to have a lower self-image than boys who mature ahead of their peers (Duncan, Ritter, Dornbusch, Gross, and Carlsmith, 1985).

Girls

The effects of early and late maturation for girls basically are the opposite of those found in boys. For girls early maturation tends to be a disadvantage, while late maturation is somewhat more socially acceptable. The reason for this difference between girls and boys is really quite easily explained. While the bodily changes that occur in boys (e.g., broadening of the shoulders, increased strength, and muscle mass) are considered positive, the changes that occur in girls (e.g., increase in adipose tissue and widening of the hips) are not. Even young girls realize that in today's society "thin is in."

Girls who mature early generally are heavier for their height and age than girls who mature late. This often leads to weight consciousness which, more than any other factor, tends to cause body image dissatisfaction. The early maturing girl may not feel good about herself, and, because she sometimes does not "fit the mold" of the physically attractive middle schooler, relationships with peers and adults tend to suffer. Along with this, earlier-maturing girls have been found to engage in more deviant behaviors and have more school-related difficulties than girls who mature later (Duncan et al., 1985). Of course, this is not to say that all girls who mature earlier than average respond in this manner.

Because the early-maturing female is experiencing changes she perceives as negative, she often finds herself feeling as though she has lost control over her own body. Anorexia nervosa, which often starts as an attempt to gain back some of this control, occurs in young girls at this critical time. In fact, the greatest number of those who suffer from anorexia nervosa are females 12 to 18 years old (Romeo, 1984).

Anorexia nervosa is a mental illness that manifests itself in individuals extremely overweight or exceptionally thin. Just because a child seems to be a model student or because she is considered already physically attractive by her peers does not mean she is not susceptible. All parents and teachers should be aware of the warning signs surrounding anorexia nervosa, as should middle school students themselves. Students who have a clear understanding of anorexia nervosa may be more conscious of their own dietary habits and may be more apt to notice the signs of anorexia nervosa among their friends (Romeo, 1984).

Conclusion

An illness such as anorexia nervosa is just one example of the problems that often surface when young adolescents become confused and overwhelmed by the changes they are quickly undergoing. At no other time in life, other than the two years following birth, does the human body and mind change as much as it does during the middle school years. This great change, coupled with uncertainty, often leads to fear and feelings of helplessness. For this reason, young adolescents need to be surrounded by parents, teachers, counselors, and others who truly understand the importance of educating young adolescents regarding their physical, sexual, and emotional development.

Where the middle school student receives this education (e.g., at home or in the school) has become an area of much controversy. Many believe it is not the place of the public school to educate young adolescents regarding their impending development, while others argue that schools may be the only place some students can ever hope to get the information they so desperately need. Whether or not our schools are a primary source of information in this area, one thing is certain: Our middle schools must become a place where young girls and boys can begin to feel good about their developing bodies and not be ashamed or fearful of the exceptionalities that make them special.

REFERENCES

Arnheim, D. D. (1985). *Modern principles of athletic training*. St. Louis: Times Mirror/Mosby College Publishing.

Bailey, D., Malina, R., and Rasmussen, R. (1978). The influence of exercise, physical activity, and athletic performance on the dynamics of human growth. In Falkner and J. M. Tanner (Eds.), *Human growth: Volume 2—Postnatal growth* (pp. 475–505). New York: Plenum.

Berzonsky, M. (1981). *Adolescent development.* New York: Macmillan.

Brunk, J. (1975). *Child & adolescent development.* New York: John Wiley & Sons.

Budlong, C., and Franken, M. (1992). Sexuality education in the middle school curriculum. *Middle School Journal* 23(3): 29–33.

Coleman, J. (1980). *The nature of adolescence.* New York: Methuen.

Damon, A. (1974). Larger body size and earlier menarche: The end may be in sight. *Social Biology* 21: 8–11.

Dornbusch, S. (1989). The sociology of adolescence. *Annual Review of Sociology* 15: 233–259.

Duncan, P., Ritter, P., Dornbusch, S., Gross, R., and Carlsmith, M. (1985). The effects of pubertal timing on body image, school behavior, and deviance. *Journal of Youth and Adolescence* 14: 227–235.

Forbes, G. (1968). Physical aspects of early adolescents. In T. Curtis (Ed.), *The Middle School* (pp. 25–42). New York: F.S.A.

Gabbard, C. (1992). *Lifelong motor development.* Dubuque, IA: Wm. C. Brown.

Hannan, T. P. (1974). Middle school: The need to establish a unique identity. *Middle School Journal* 5(1): 9–10.

Hillman, S. (1991). What developmental psychology has to say about early adolescence. *Middle School Journal,* 23(1): 3–8.

Jones, J. J., Wells, L. J., Peters, R. E., and Johnson, D. J. (1993). *Guide to effective coaching.* Dubuque, IA: Brown & Benchmark.

Keogh, J., and Sugden, D. (1985). *Movement skill development.* New York: Macmillan.

Lawrence, G. (1980). Do programs reflect what research says about physical development? *Middle School Journal* 11(2): 12–14.

Lerner, R. M., and Lerner, J. V. (1977). Effects of age, sex, and physical attractiveness on child-peer relations, academic performance, and elementary school adjustment. *Developmental Psychology* 13: 585–590.

Malina, R. (1979). Secular changes in growth, maturation, and physical performance. In R. S. Hutton (Ed.), *Exercise and Sport Sciences Reviews* (pp. 203–255). Hillsdale, NJ: Franklin Institute Press.

Malina, R. (1990). Physical growth and performance during the transitional years (9–16). In R. Montemayor and G. Adams (Eds.), *From childhood to adolescence* (pp. 41–62). Newbury Park, CA: Sage Publications.

Martens, R. (1978). *Joy and sadness in children's sports*. Champaign, IL: Human Kinetics Publishing.

Mosier, H. D. (1989). Catch-up growth and target size in experimental animals. In J. M. Tanner and M. A. Preece (Eds.), *The physiology of human growth* (pp. 29–46). New York: Cambridge University Press.

Muth, D. K., and Alvermann, D. E. (1992). *Teaching and learning in the middle grades*. Needham Heights, MA: Allyn & Bacon.

Payne, V. G., and Isaacs, L. D. (1991). *Human motor development: A lifespan approach*. Mountain View, CA: Mayfield.

Romeo, F. (1984). Anorexia nervosa in the middle school. *Middle School Journal* 15(4): 16–18.

Scales, P. C. (1991). *A portrait of young adolescents in the 1990's*. Carrboro, NC: University of North Carolina at Chapel Hill.

Stafford, E. (1982). The unique middle school student: An unknown ingredient. *The Physical Educator* 39: 38–42.

Tanner, J. M. (1962). *Growth at adolescence*. London: Blackwell Scientific Publications.

Tanner, J. M. (1978). *Education and physical growth*. New York: International Universities Press.

Tanner, J. M. (1990). *Foetus into man*. Cambridge, MA: Harvard University Press.

Tanner, J. M., Hughes, P., and Whitehouse, R. H. (1981). Radiographically determined widths of bone, muscle and fat in the upper arm and calf from 3–18 years. *Annals of Human Biology 8*: 495–517.

Wood, P., and Hillman, S. (1992). Developmental issues of very young adolescents. *Middle School Journal* 23(4): 14–19.

Zani, B. (1991). Male and female patterns in the discovery of sexuality during adolescence. *Journal of Adolescence* 14: 163–178.

CHAPTER 4

Early Adolescent Social and Emotional Development: A Constructivist Perspective

*Rebecca S. Bowers**

When Donald Eichhorn (1966) coined the term *transescence* to describe the passage from childhood to adolescence, he was emphasizing the distinctively transitional characteristic of this stage of development. The word *transition* is rooted in a Latin term for "going across"—moving from one position to another. Early adolescence is a "going-across" in which enormous changes are occurring—physically, cognitively, emotionally, and socially. Contextual changes also are occurring, most notably the transition from elementary school to middle school or junior high, an experience that may be stressful for some students (Crockett, Petersen, Graber, Schulenberg, and Ebata, 1989; Fenzel, 1989). An increasing number of scientists believe that these biological, psychological, and social changes are "interdependent and dynamically interactive" (Lerner and Lerner, 1989, p. 175).

Thus, early adolescence—the going-across period between childhood and adolescence—must be viewed as much more than a prefabricated bridge spanning the chasm between two familiar landscapes. From a constructivist perspective, the characteristics of this stage result from dynamic interactions on many fronts. The individual young adolescent is looking at and relating to others in new ways (social development) and becoming aware of his or her feelings at a much deeper level than before (emotional development). It is a time of trying to make sense of things for oneself instead of passively accepting a prestructured worldview handed down from others.

"Development, then, is not governed by internal maturation or external teachings," wrote Crain (1980) in summarizing the constructivist emphasis in Piaget's developmental theory. "It is an active construction process, in which children, through their own activities, build increasingly differentiated and comprehensive cognitive structures" (p. 77). But the process is not automatic. As Wadsworth (1978) reiterated Piaget's position, "Each and every child *constructs* the world from his or her *actions* on it. The child must act on the environment for development to occur. These actions are the raw materials for assimilation and accommodation, and generate the development of mental structures or schemata" (p. 21, italics in original).

Piaget's (1973) constructivist emphasis does not by any means stand alone in the world of ideas. Constructivism is an epistemology that has emerged from studies in anthropology, sociology, philosophy, cognitive science, linguistics, science and science history, and mathematics. In summarizing the theoretical approach of Vygotsky, John-Steiner and Souberman (1978) emphasized his interest in "the psychological implications of the fact that humans are active, vigorous participants in their own existence" (p. 123). Constructivists, because of their belief that students create their own reality, knowledge, beliefs, attitudes, and meaning, reject the traditional cultural transmission view in which students are seen as empty vessels into which knowledge is poured. Nor are students to be regarded as clean slates upon which predigested wisdom is written, nor lumps of clay to be shaped into some predetermined mold. Rather, constructivists maintain that students make meaning of the world around them by "constructing stories that fit this world" (Roth, 1992, p. 308). In other words, individuals weave the events, experiences, and observations of their lives into personalized narratives that make sense and provide meaning. Roth (1992) noted that researchers have found that "this weaving of stories is a function of the context in which it happens and that knowing and doing are inseparably tied together" (p. 308).

Thus, the social environment—or culture—provides a framework in which the person composes or constructs his or her life. "The developing child and the cultural environment of the child are intrinsically related," wrote Valsiner (1987) in his summary of Vygotsky's learning theory. "The cultural environment is organized by active members of the culture who belong to the generations older than the child. That environment itself guides the child toward the personal (but socially assisted) invention of culture" (p. 64). The reality of this cultural framework mandates the consideration of numerous factors that are salient in understanding adolescent social and emotional development, especially gender, multicultural, and other diversity factors.

An Overall Picture

"Who am I?" "How do I feel about myself?" "What do others think of me?" "Where do I fit?" These are all important issues for the early adolescent because the transitional time between childhood and adolescence is a time of finding oneself in relation to the rest of the world. The early adolescent is moving toward a sociocentric view of the self—increasingly seeing himself or herself as a part of society as it is organized around roles, rules, requirements, responsibilities, and relationships. At the same time, the egocentricism characteristic of the middle level years means that young adolescents tend to perceive that they are constantly on "center stage" (Elkind, 1967). People around them may be viewed as either an admiring or a fault-finding audience that is as intrigued by what the young adolescent is wearing, saying, or doing as he himself or she herself is.

The tension between egocentricism and sociocentrism is only one of the tensions faced by young adolescents. George and Lawrence (1982) have cataloged numerous competing forces operating in the social and emotional development of early adolescents. For example, the young adolescent wants to conform to peer group standards but at the same time wants to be recognized as unique. He or she may feel a need to seek peer group acceptance, support, and companionship (experiencing the outer world), but at the same time may be introspective and engrossed in experiencing the inner world of "a new emotionality—strong subjective moods, feelings, and sensations" (p. 79). Reaching out to peers as a primary reference group may also compete with "a reluctance to break the long-standing, supporting family relationship" (p. 77). Similarly, the desire to think for oneself and form one's own belief and value system competes with lifelong beliefs handed down from parents.

George and Lawrence also speak of the inner struggle between the early adolescent's desire to explore romantic attractions and the fear of rejection and inadequacy. The anticipation of entering the adult world, along with the "desire to exercise the new powers of body and mind," competes with "the comfort of childhood habits and the protective cushion that adults provide for children" (p. 79). Tension also may be felt as the young adolescent grapples with an emerging awareness of flaws and faults in many adults, resulting in disappointment and disenchantment at the same time she or he is yearning for heroes and role models. A conflict between idealism and realism produces additional tension at this stage. Strain may occur also when a young adolescent's degree of physical maturation does not correspond to his or her chronological age, social maturity, or cognitive development.

However, the competing claims with which early adolescents struggle do not mean that this period is one of unceasing turbulence in which 10- to 14-year-old adolescents are helplessly tossed about on a sea of raging hormones. Changes are taking place, to be sure. The physical changes that are part of sexual development do affect emotions. But the young adolescent is not a passive object at the mercy of inside or outside forces acting upon her or him, but rather is an active and conscious participant in the person she or he is in the process of becoming. According to constructivism, young adolescence is not only a time of *finding* oneself in relation to the rest of the world but is a time of *producing* oneself as a unique individual with a distinct part to play in that world. To do this, the early adolescent engages in two main actions: *interpretation* of events, experiences, and information, on the one hand, and *making choices* based upon those interpretations, on the other. Both actions are involved in social-emotional development. And to understand how these two actions are involved, we need to examine the development of the self.

The Self in Social-Emotional Development

Secord and Backman (1974) listed three aspects of a person's attitude toward himself or herself—the cognitive, the affective, and the behavioral. "The *cognitive* component represents the content of the self, illustrated by such thoughts as, 'I am intelligent, honest, sincere, ambitious, tall, strong, overweight, etc.,'" they wrote (p. 524, italics added). How one feels about oneself comprises the *affective* component, and how one acts toward oneself comprises the third, or *behavioral*, component. (In explaining this third component, these authors cited self-deprecation and self-indulgence as examples of ways persons may behave toward themselves.)

In a similar vein, Beane, Lipka, and Ludewig (1980) pointed out three dimensions of self-perception: *self-concept* ("the description we hold of ourselves based on the roles we play and personal attributes we believe we possess"), *self-esteem* ("the level of satisfaction we attach to that description or parts of it"), and *values* ("what is important to us") (p. 84). (See also Beane and Lipka, 1984).

By drawing upon and expanding these observations by both sets of authors and adding another component, *self-efficacy* (Bandura, 1982), we might conceptualize the self-development of early adolescents as consisting of the following elements.

Self-Perception

Figure 1

Cognitive Dimension	Affective Dimension	Behavioral Dimension
Self-concept (The way I see myself)	**Two parts:** *Self-esteem* (How I feel about myself) and *Self-efficacy* (What I believe I am capable of achieving)	*Value-based choices and conduct* (How I choose to act on the basis of what I believe and how I feel about myself and about other people)

The Cognitive Dimension of Self-Perception: Self-Concept

The social theorist George Herbert Mead (1934) emphasized that the self develops through interaction with other people. It is a *social* self, constructed as a young child, that mimics the words and actions of others and later engages in make-believe play in which the child imagines being in another person's place, thus learning to take "the role of the other" in interaction with himself or herself. Eventually, through engaging in games and other organized activities, the child begins to grasp a concept that Mead called the *generalized other* (a mental image of all that comprises society and societal expectations). In these various ways, the person constructs her or his own unique sense of self.

Crain (1980) has summarized Erik Erikson's (1959) theory of *ego identity*, pointing out that both identification with esteemed others and the accomplishment of tasks and skills (for example, learning to stand, walk, read, write, and so on) contribute to its formation. A person thus comes to see him or herself as someone who has distinctive attributes and abilities—

someone who is able to do things. This process of identity formation continues throughout life.

However, "the process of identity reaches its crisis at adolescence," wrote Crain (1980).

> It is at this time that so many inner changes are taking place, and so much in terms of future commitment is at stake. At this time, one's earlier identity seems inadequate for all the choices and decisions one must make. (p. 156)

The adolescent "in-group" arises from such concerns over personal identity in the midst of so many changes. In-groups or cliques (often characterized by distinctive clothing and hairstyles) were viewed by Erikson as providing a sense of collective identity for those young adolescents who are privileged to belong to these groups. But others who are looked upon as "different" may not only be excluded from the group but may be treated cruelly.

Sometimes, however, the young adolescent who is regarded as different may be perceived as having something valuable to offer the group. For example, the athletically or musically gifted student who might otherwise be frozen out because of his socioeconomic status may be welcomed into the in-group because of his or her unique talents. I observed one situation in which a student from a school for the deaf was mainstreamed because her parents wanted her to learn to speak and lip-read through interaction with middle school classmates in a local public school. Many of the students at that school were known for their cliquishness, unwillingness to welcome newcomers as part of the group, and intolerance toward those from other socioeconomic and racial groups or who were in any way considered different. Teachers were uncertain about how these students would receive someone with a physical disability. Instead of treating the new student as an outsider, however, the students were fascinated by her signing abilities and thought of her as an asset to the group. In fact, their interest in having her teach them sign language took precedence over their helping her to learn to vocalize and lip-read.

Body image also is an important part of the young adolescent's developing self-concept (Erikson, 1968). Adams, Day, Dyk, Frede, and Rogers (1992) have summarized numerous clinical and empirical studies indicating that the rapid, multiple changes occurring during early adolescence affect the way early adolescents think about themselves as well as how others perceive them and act toward them. For example, these authors pointed out that while early breast growth may, on the one hand, contribute to a more positive body image, there may be a negative side as well—specifically, the familial teasing about their growing breasts that early developing girls often face, resulting in intense embarrassment, self-consciousness, and anger. "In this case, discordance exists between chronological age of the girl and her rate of breast development," they explained (p. 360). They also cited research showing that, because of American society's emphasis on an ideal of extreme thinness, early maturing girls (who tend to be naturally heavier than their peers) are less satisfied with their body image. As Hancock (1989) demonstrates, the changes in body image may be especially stressful for the athletically inclined girl approaching puberty.

> An exuberant athlete at nine, many a girl is a careful young lady at eleven as female appendages begin to intrude on pure physical prowess: unwieldy breasts, broadening hips, softening contours, clutter the taut streamlined body of her androgynous youth. No matter how proud she may be of "becoming a woman," these physical changes hamper a girl's freedom and weaken the confidence she earlier placed in her physical skills. . . . The skills that assured her place among peers now jeopardize a girl's popularity; a sinewy body, impressive height, and forceful strength belong to the males. . . . [A boy's] freedoms are dramatically expanded while hers are curtailed. (pp. 19–20)

Because of society's more expansive view of what boys' pubertal changes signify, young males have been found to have more positive attitudes toward their bodies than young females. Koff, Rierdan, and Stubbs (1990) pointed out the cultural objectification of the female body as a "physically attractive interpersonal stimulus," whereas the male body is viewed primarily "as a means of effectively operating in the external environment" (p. 57). These researchers noted that "as the majority of girls reach puberty . . . they begin to move away from the lean, lithe, prepubertal body currently in favor." This disjuncture between the cultural ideal that is presently in vogue and the reality of physical maturation accounts for the less satisfactory body image held by many young females as compared to that held by their male counterparts. On the other hand, the fulfillment of the male cultural ideal—"the valued attributes of masculine physique, tallness and muscularity, which are closely associated with instrumental effectiveness" (p. 58)—can be anticipated as a natural outcome of a boy's experience of puberty. Thus, young adolescent males in general tend to report increasing satisfaction with their developing bodies.

The importance of body image to the construction of the early adolescent's self-concept is one reason gender issues cannot be ignored. Similarly, issues of *ethnic group membership* should not be overlooked. Thus, Maldonado (1975) spoke of ethnic self-identity as "central to the development of the personal identity of minority group members" (p. 621). Interested in understanding how ethnic identity develops among minority group adolescents, Phinney (1989) utilized Marcia's (1966, 1980) operationalization of Erikson's theory of ego identity development.

Marcia had suggested a paradigm of four ego-identity statuses to describe the particular point at which an adolescent may be located in his or her personal journey in self-discovery: *achieved identity* status (a sense of knowing who one is through having undergone a crisis that led to a personal exploration of various choices followed by a firm commitment to one's chosen beliefs and life goals), *identity foreclosure* status (a commitment to the values handed down from others, particularly one's parents, having experienced no need to question, explore, and come to one's own conclusions), *moratorium* status (a time of *exploring* during which concerns about making firm commitments are suspended—a time of being in a sense "on hold"), and *identity diffusion* status (a nonfocused identity in which commitments to a particular way of thinking about themselves and the world around them have not been made and there is little concern about exploration or lack of goals). Marcia's four statuses do not necessarily indicate a developmental progression, "although an achieved identity is seen as the most sophisticated identity status" (Phinney, 1989, p. 35).

Applying this ego-identity paradigm to ethnic identity development, Phinney conducted in-depth interviews with 91 Asian-American, African-American, Hispanic, and white tenth grade students and reported that the study provided "empirical evidence for three stages of ethnic identity development among American-born minority adolescents" (p. 45), with similar numbers of subjects in each category across groups. (Three rather than four stages were discussed because the overlap between the diffuse and foreclosure categories in this study logically suggested a combined category.)

Regardless of their ethnic background, these adolescents indicated "a similar need to deal with the fact of their membership in an ethnic minority group in a predominantly White society" (p. 45). The white students in the study were found to have no concept of their own ethnicity and considered themselves simply American, leading Phinney to conclude that there was implied "an ethnocentric view that is out of touch with the increasingly pluralistic nature of society" (p. 45). Slightly over half of the minority tenth graders had given little concern to the issue of ethnic identity or else passively had accepted the views of others (whether negative, positive, or indifferent) without searching out the topic for themselves. The other nearly one-half of the subjects gave clear evidence of an ethnic identity search and were nearly evenly divided between those who were in an exploration or moratorium stage and those who had already achieved a "confident sense of self as a minority group member," after having actively explored the meaning of their ethnicity as a component of their self-identity (p. 46). Since, in an earlier study, Phinney and Tarver (1988) had found that only one-third of black eighth graders had engaged in an ethnic identity search, the possibility was raised that interest in searching out the meaning of one's ethnic identity may increase with age. In both studies, there was more evidence of ethnic identity exploration and commitment among black females than among black males.

Phinney (1989) found more negative attitudes about their ethnicity among Asian-American adolescents than among the other groups and suggested that this finding may reflect the lack of a social movement emphasizing ethnic pride similar to those available to blacks and Mexican-Americans. The Asian-American students, for example, had trouble naming Asian-Americans noted for their achievements. "Generally, their attitudes tended more toward assimilation than toward ethnic pride and pluralism," explained Phinney (p. 47).

The concerns of minority adolescents in Phinney's sample as they constructed their ethnic identity varied according to group membership. Asian-Americans were concerned about academic achievement pressures and the quotas that make their entrance into good colleges more difficult, and they worried about being mistaken for recent immigrants. Hispanic adolescents spoke about the prejudice they encountered and told of conflicts between their own cultural values and those of the white majority culture. Many African-American females expressed concerns over the white culture's beauty standards for skin color and hairstyles. African-American males worried about being judged according to negative stereotypes of black adolescent males, and they were concerned about encountering job discrimination.

Phinney also cited Ogbu's (1987, p. 166) observation of the "oppositional identity" chosen by some black youth who want their self-definition to contrast with white culture even though it may mean acting in ways disapproved of by that culture, and the dilemma faced by students who feel pressure to choose between what is defined as "acting black" or "acting white."

The Affective Dimension of Self-Perception, Part 1: Self-Esteem

Although a person's *self-concept* might be expected to include a description of himself or herself as a member of a particular ethnic group or the occupant of a particular role, social status, or possessor of some specific attribute, it is the person's *self-esteem* that must be examined if we wish to understand how he or she feels about this self-description. Beane and Lipka (1980, 1984) have warned that imprecision in the use of the two terms can be confusing and pointed out the difficulties in comparing research studies when the terms are used interchangeably. According to these authors, "self-esteem . . . refers to the evaluation one makes of the self-concept description and, more specifically, to the degree to which one is satisfied or dissatisfied with it, in whole or in part" (Beane and Lipka, 1984, p. 6).

When the American Association of University Women (AAUW) commissioned a nationwide poll of 3,000 male and female students from Grades 4 through 10, the findings on self-esteem stood out noticeably. Both boys and girls were found to have a decrease in self-esteem as they approached and entered adolescence, but "the loss is most dramatic and has the most long-lasting effect for girls" (AAUW, 1991, p. 3). The poll was undertaken to provide better understanding of these middle grade years through assessing the interaction among self-esteem, career aspirations, and educational experiences (with particular attention to interest and skills in math and science).

Pointing out that more boys than girls enter adolescence and leave adolescence with high self-esteem, the researchers wrote:

> Girls, aged eight and nine, are confident, assertive, and feel authoritative about themselves. They emerge from adolescence with a poor self-image, constrained views of their future and their place in society, and much less confidence about themselves and their abilities. (p. 4)

Whereas 60 percent of the elementary school girls in the survey reported being "happy the way I am" (one of five measures utilized in calculating a Self-Esteem Index), only 29 percent of high school young women reported such positive feelings about themselves. Among boys in the survey, 67 percent of those in elementary school reported being happy with themselves, and 46 percent of high school young men also reported being happy with themselves.

When asked what they liked most about themselves, boys were more likely than girls to cite their talents, whereas girls were more likely to name some physical characteristic. "Physical appearance is most important for girls in middle school, the time of greatest decline in self-esteem" (p. 7), the researchers emphasized, pointing out that the confidence boys had in their talents (including athletic talents, an area in which their confidence was found to be four times as high as that of girls) "cushioned" any uneasiness that boys may have felt about their changing physical appearance.

Girls, on the other hand, were found to have internalized society's message that "their worth is dependent on their appearance" (p. 7). Their displeasure with the changes taking place in their bodies and their perceived inability to meet societal beauty standards contributes to their decreased self-esteem. Many young adolescent girls attempt to increase their self-esteem through desperate attempts at conformity to societal thinness standards, thus becoming vulnerable to eating disorders, such as anorexia nervosa and bulimia.

The AAUW survey also showed that boys had greater career dreams and expectations of success than was true of girls. Girls had less confidence in their abilities, and their declining self-esteem during the middle grade years inhibited their endeavors and lowered their career aspirations. Girls were more likely than boys to consider themselves "not smart enough" or "not good enough" for careers they might desire but believed were beyond their reach.

Because boys were found to "feel good about a lot of things" and to have a higher degree of confidence in their ability to do things than was true of girls, boys tended to exhibit different behaviors in school. They were found to be more willing to speak up in the classroom and to argue with their teachers when they disagreed with them. Self-esteem in boys was fostered by the societal assumption that males can do things and the expectation that they will achieve. In contrast, the research showed that girls encounter people, including their teachers, who believe they cannot accomplish what they believe they can accomplish, which plays a major role in girls' lower self-esteem.

A review of research on adolescence prompted Stern (1991) to go so far as to call adolescence "a time of great psychological danger for girls" (p. 114), a point also made by

Schultz (1991). Schultz called attention to various studies that
have shown that "girls react much more negatively than boys to
the psychological and physiological aspects of puberty and are
therefore at risk for eating disorders, substance abuse,
depression, suicide attempts, dropping out of school, and early
childbearing" (p. 1).

When the Minnesota Adolescent Health Survey of over
36,000 students in Grades 7 through 12 was conducted during
the 1986–1987 school year, it was found that 30 percent of junior
high girls (Grades 7 through 9) reported a negative body image,
as did 40 percent of females in the senior high years. The
comparable figures for boys were 12 percent and 15 percent,
respectively. The researchers reported that "among Minnesota
youth, at every grade level after the seventh, twice as many
females as males reported having attempted suicide at least
once" (Harris, Blum, and Resnick, 1991, p. 123). By the time they
were seniors, 9 percent of boys and 18 percent of girls reported
having attempted suicide.

When the researchers looked at overall emotional stress
among this population of young people, they again found
significant differences by gender. The questions used to measure
level of stress included questions about nervousness, sadness
and anxiety, hopelessness, the degree of being in control,
dissatisfaction with life, and so on. Over 25 percent of junior high
school girls and 14 percent of junior high boys indicated high
levels of stress. Among senior high students, over one-third of
girls (36 percent) and one-fifth of boys (20 percent) were found
to manifest high stress levels.

Gender differences were found not only in levels of stress
but also in how stress was handled. Male students were more
likely than female students to express distress through *acting
out*—engaging in aggression, vandalism, and other antisocial
behaviors; taking excessive risks (such as combining drinking
and driving, refusing to use seat belts, taking risks with
motorcycles and recreational vehicles, and the like); and through
substance abuse. Female students were more likely than males to
"muffle" their psychological distress, turning it inward where
self-destructive behaviors were less easily observed by others.
"Suicidal tendencies, disordered patterns of eating and

emotional stress do not often call attention to themselves until the damage is severe" (Harris et al., 1991, p. 132).

The overwhelming evidence that the transition to adolescence is more problematic for girls than for boys led Stern (1991) to assert that a "disavowal of self" occurs for many young women at this stage. Even though a "solid sense of self" may have been demonstrated during the years prior to adolescence, the transition to adolescence is a time in which many girls begin "to renounce and devalue their perceptions, beliefs, thoughts, and feelings" (p. 105). Because this phenomenon has been observed both in girls who are functioning well in school and in those who have exhibited symptoms of psychological distress, such as those just discussed, Stern and numerous other scholars perceive the problem to be rooted in conflicting societal and personal demands. Gilligan (1992), for example, offers the following explanation:

> Girls are encouraged to give up their own experiences and tune into the way other people want them to see things. They replace their detailed knowledge of the social world with an idealized, stereotyped notion of relationships and of the type of girl people admire. This nice or perfect girl isn't angry or selfish, and she certainly doesn't disagree in public. (p. 20)

As girls attempt to reconstruct their image of themselves to meet societal requirements for young womanhood (out of fear that they will displease others and disrupt relationships if they do not comply), their self-esteem drops. They tend to become less sure of themselves and less confident of their abilities.

In the AAUW study, black girls were found to have considerably higher self-esteem than white girls during the elementary, middle school, and high school years. Black young women did not undergo the dramatic drop in self-esteem that was experienced by white young women and to an even greater degree by Hispanic young women. In response to the "happy the way I am" item in the survey, 65 percent of black female elementary school students answered that the statement was always true for them, as did 59 percent of middle school respondents and 58 percent of high school respondents, in this racial and gender category. There was thus a drop in self-esteem of only 7 percentage points among black young women, as compared to a 33-point drop among white and a 30-point drop among Hispanic young women.

Although personal self-esteem was found to be high among black young women, academic self-esteem was not. For many black girls, the support they draw from their families and communities, along with the value black culture places on assertiveness and strength in women, tends to reinforce positive self-esteem. At the same time, their confidence may be undermined through their school experience. Among data summarized in an extensive review of the literature for another AAUW report (1992) was the finding that "African-American girls have fewer interactions with teachers than do white girls, despite evidence that they attempt to initiate interactions more frequently" (p. 2). It also was found that when black girls do as well as white boys, teachers tend to assume that the girls have worked hard but that the white boys have not worked up to their full potential. Research has shown also that teachers are more likely to praise black girls for behavior than for their academic performance (Schultz, 1991, p. 10).

Contrary to the popular conception that a young adolescent's self-esteem is most affected by peer relationships, research has shown that the family and school have a greater impact than peers on self-esteem and aspirations (AAUW, 1991). In one study, students attending middle schools that used interdisciplinary teaming were found to have higher self-esteem than did students in schools not using interdisciplinary teaming (Stefanich, Wills, and Buss, 1991). Families have been found to be of prime importance in predicting a young person's emotional well-being and ability to cope with stress (Harris et al., 1991).

Although academic self-esteem has been found to be of prime importance in the self-esteem of girls, only 49 percent of elementary school girls surveyed for the AAUW (1991) study reported feeling proud of their academic performance. By high school, only 12 percent voiced such feelings of pride in their schoolwork. The percentage of boys feeling such pride also dropped between elementary and high school (from 53 percent to 16 percent), but the research showed that academic pride was of much less importance in boys' self-esteem. The researchers found that "for young men, the sense of confidence in their ability to do things correlates more strongly with general self-esteem than with other aspects of academic confidence" (AAUW, 1991, p. 10). These findings bring us to the second part of the affective dimension of self-perception—self-efficacy.

The Affective Dimension of Self-Perception, Part 2: Self-Efficacy

Bandura (1982) used the term *self-efficacy* in reference to people's perceived ability "to produce and regulate events in their lives" (p. 122). A personal sense of competence or mastery—a belief that one is capable of carrying out a necessary course of action to achieve a desired outcome—affects the choices people make, the amount of effort they are willing to expend, and the length of time they are willing to persist when confronted with difficulties. "When beset with difficulties people who entertain serious doubts about their capabilities slacken their efforts or give up altogether, whereas those who have a strong sense of efficacy exert greater effort to master the challenges," wrote Bandura (1982, p. 123). Bandura pointed out that in some circumstances people give up trying, not because of doubt about their own capabilities but rather because of a negative environment that is unresponsive to their efforts and fails to recognize and reward their accomplishments.

Conceptualizing self-esteem and self-efficacy as two separate aspects of the affective dimension of self-perception is useful in understanding, for instance, why raising self-esteem does not necessarily guarantee a young adolescent's academic success. The AAUW (1991) study showed the self-esteem of black girls to be higher than that of any other group. But at the same time, black young women drop out of school in large numbers. Brown (1991), drawing upon the research of Fine and Zane (1991), called attention to the fact that "more often than not, it may be the most responsible and psychologically astute female students who choose to drop out of inner-city public high schools—a choice on their part to actively resist conditions insensitive to the complexities of their lives and which render them psychically at risk" (p. 68). Robinson and Ward (1991) likewise have taken into account the student's construction of reality by emphasizing that the act of dropping out of a nonsupportive environment may be "the calculated move of an adolescent who has made a decision for herself that is psychologically empowering" (p. 96). While warning of the shortsightedness and detrimental consequences of such a move, these scholars pointed out that "in this light, school failure can be seen as a survival strategy adopted by teens who, feeling bored, devalued and unrecognized, attempt to resist a school system they experience as both disrespectful of, and irrelevant to, their lives" (p. 96).

According to the self-worth theory of achievement motivation set forth by Covington (1984), students will try to protect their sense of self-worth by avoiding situations in which failure is likely. Toward this end, they may employ strategies such as procrastination, excuses, and refusing to try—thereby accentuating a value-clash with teachers who embrace the prevailing work ethic.

"Early adolescence is a particularly important time in the development of self-perceptions of ability," wrote Kramer (1991), "because it is a time when students' understanding of the meaning of ability changes" (p. 358). Among younger children, effort and ability are not viewed as two distinct entities at odds with one another. For them, self-worth is enhanced by effort, and effort says nothing about the possession or lack of ability. As Covington (1984) has pointed out, "They believe they can improve their performance (and by implication, their ability) through diligence. Thus, young children do not necessarily view poor performance as threatening or indicative of their future promise" (p. 14). However, numerous studies have indicated that in early adolescence students begin believing that the greater the effort required the lower is the person's ability. "As the amount of effort needed to attain a given achievement increases, the less able the individual is perceived to be" (Covington, 1984, p. 15).

A "why try?" attitude may thus develop in some cases. The AAUW study (1991) showed that, between elementary and middle school and continuing into high school, both boys and girls indicated a drop in their enjoyment of and their ability to do well in math and science—the two subjects that were found to be most associated with self-esteem and career aspirations. The decline was much greater among girls than boys, and the reactions to the decline differed by gender. Boys who expressed lower levels of enjoyment and a perceived lack of ability in these subjects tended to attribute the problem to the subject matter, claiming the subjects were not useful or important to them. Girls who disliked math and science tended to be self-blamers, believing that the problem lay in themselves as manifested in their poor math grades and failure to find science interesting.

Covington (1984) emphasized that "because ability is seen as a critical component of success, and inability a prime cause of failure, self-perceptions of ability become a significant part of one's self-definition" (p. 8). Thus, as students begin viewing ability "as the dominant causal factor in achievement" (p. 16), as is true of young adolescents, they become anxious about the humiliation of being judged incompetent. If they must put forth a great deal of effort to accomplish what someone else has accomplished with less effort, they perceive themselves to have less ability than the other person. If they put forth great effort and fail nevertheless, they may be perceived as totally lacking ability. In order to protect their sense of self-worth, therefore, they may elect not to try. Failure due to little or no effort will not necessarily call their ability into question "since low effort alone is a sufficient explanation for failure and therefore should minimize shame" (p. 11).

Calsyn and Kenny (1977) found that self-esteem is more likely to be raised by academic achievement (the "skill development model of education") than that academic achievement will follow efforts to raise self-esteem (the "self-enhancement" model) (p. 136). The Jaime Escalante Math Program in East Los Angeles was built on this principle. Escalante (Escalante and Dirmann, 1990) has eschewed

> [T]he prevailing opinion that requiring academic excellence from poverty-level students presents a grave risk to those students' "fragile" self-esteem. . . . When students of any race, ethnicity, or economic status are

expected to work hard, they usually rise to the occasion, devote themselves to the task, and do the work. (p. 416)

Escalante has watched self-efficacy increase as he convinces his students (the majority of whom are female) that, if they contract with him to learn math, "they can do anything" (p. 416). Having examined the two parts of the affective dimension of self-perception, *self-esteem* (how I feel about myself) and *self-efficacy* (what I believe I am capable of achieving), we now move to the behavioral dimension.

The Behavioral Dimension of Self-Perception

Constructivism provides a lens for viewing the behavior of young adolescents within their own reality. They are meaning-makers as they interpret experiences, the events around them, and the information to which they have access. What they do and say, the choices they make about themselves and other people, the actions they do or do not take, spring from the meanings they thus construct. The values on which they base their actions also must be viewed in light of their perceptions about what is important and what is not.

Tierno (1991) has pointed out that the growing importance of peer relationships and peer influence during early adolescence can be attributed to more than the social and sexual drives that are awakening at puberty. Also emerging at this stage are abstract cognitive abilities that include a developing ability to, in Tierno's words, "think about thoughts"—an ability he views as lying behind the self-consciousness displayed by middle school students. Being able to think about thoughts "includes the ability to think about the thoughts of others, including what they might be thinking about the adolescent" (p. 572). Self-doubts and worries about possible negative evaluations by others may cause early adolescents to act in ways designed to gain peer approval, even though such behaviors are at odds with adult norms and may seem to teachers to be "silly, obnoxious, or even antisocial" (p. 572).

O'Connor and Nikolic (1990) linked adolescent self-consciousness and egocentrism to the identity development process. As adolescents are constructing an image of who they are, they may "assume that others will survey them closely for signs of individuality, since budding individuality is expected at this time of life" (p. 150). Further, these researchers wrote, "the self-concerns and social demands of the identity development process may lead adolescents to confuse their own concerns with the concerns of others" (p. 150).

The three principles of the well-known "looking-glass self" construct of Cooley (1902) are applicable to the process of identity development that young adolescents are experiencing as they perceive themselves reflected in the eyes of others. They imagine, first, how others view them. Second, they imagine what judgments others probably are making about them based upon this view. And third, they react to this imagined judgment, perhaps with pride or embarrassment.

In her research on gifted middle school girls, Kramer (1991) found that the girls in her study believed giftedness implied to others that one always knew the answers. Because they knew that frequently they found themselves in situations where they did not know the correct answers, they perceived teachers and peers to look down upon them. "These situations inhibited girls' performance and contributed to their beliefs that they were not smart, but only had potential," Kramer wrote (p. 358). "This distinction offered girls a safe explanation for not always knowing the expected answer, while, at the same time, it created the acceptable role of someone-who-tries in place of the socially unacceptable role of someone-who-knows, 'the brain'." Kramer found that the girls did not want to risk speaking up and debating various viewpoints, as the gifted boys in their group did. Rather, the girls wanted above all to please their teachers and parents, be well liked by peers, and "fit in." Social acceptance was considered an achievement in itself.

Roberts and Peterson (1992) emphasized the importance of considering the individual within her or his peer group in order to ascertain the way academic achievement affects that person's feelings of social acceptance. "Peer influences may either encourage or discourage academic success depending on the dominant value within the peer group," they wrote (p. 198). Their study focused on the effects of academic achievement upon social self-image among middle school students oriented toward academics, athletics, or popularity.

As Beane and Lipka (1984) pointed out, teachers are sometimes perplexed by the behavior of students who have demonstrated an ability to achieve academically but who do not consider such achievements a source of self-esteem and, therefore, refuse to strive for academic success. Such students may place greater value on acceptance by a peer group that looks down upon school success. Beane and Lipka warned that a teacher, unaware of the student's value-base, might unwittingly complicate the situation further by attempting to elevate the student's self-esteem "by praising the student's work in front of peers who devalue school success" (p. 6).

Data from one program, in which minority college students were utilized to mentor urban at-risk middle school students, indicated that, although middle school students in the program did better academically than those in a control group, the students with the highest grade point averages had the lowest self-esteem. "It suggests," wrote researchers Simon, Reed, and Clark (1990), "that being 'book smart' is something that many students avoid because it may not fit in with their perception of being popular" (p. 19). Emphasizing that high-achieving students might meet with ridicule from their peers rather than praise for their accomplishments, these authors suggested that groups of close friends be kept together in special mentoring programs.

Peer relationships have been shown to have great importance in the lives of middle school students (Benenson, 1990). Research by Raffaelli and Duckett (1989) indicated that young adolescents discuss age-related concerns with their peers while at the same time continuing to talk about everyday issues with their families. "Talk with friends did not appear to replace talk with family members but rather represented a new facet of the social world, supplementing existing family relationships," wrote these authors (p. 567). East (1989) found that young adolescents who sustain close relationships outside their families "are more apt to enhance their well-being than if they relied predominantly on family support" (p. 389).

There is some evidence of a gender difference in social networks in the middle grades. Although both sexes were found to have the same number of best friends in a study by Benenson (1990), she found middle grade boys to have larger social networks than girls and to be concerned with attributes related to status in the peer group. Girls tended to emphasize attributes considered essential in relating to a few friends.

The findings of East (1989) indicate that early adolescents who are lonely or who have feelings of low self-worth tend to think of personal relationships as being risky and costly. "Their negative social orientation may operate as a kind of self-regulation strategy," explained East, "one that acts to reduce the likelihood of embarrassment or rejection and concomitant feelings of failure" (p. 391). Anticipating hurt, they try to protect themselves by simply avoiding close relationships. Early adolescents who were found to be depressed thought of social relationships as providing fewer benefits than did their nondepressed counterparts. "Thus," wrote East, "it could be argued that perceptions of low social benefit lead the depressed to avoid social situations, which thereby exacerbates their depression" (p. 391).

The linkage between questions of personal identity and relationships, both with others and the world at large, cannot be overlooked in considering the social and emotional development of early adolescents. Gilligan (1988) has emphasized that the work of Kohlberg and Erikson, as well as her own work, shows that "adolescents are passionately interested in moral questions" (p. xvi). However, by not including girls in studies of moral development, researchers until recently presented an incomplete picture. Kohlberg (1976), for example, developed his six stages of moral reasoning from a 12-year study of 75 boys.

Gilligan (1982, 1988) and her colleagues, however, have found that a different picture emerges—a different voice is heard—when girls and women are included in research on moral reasoning. People tend to construct a moral perspective in one of two ways: either by focusing on a *justice* perspective that is concerned with inequality, unfairness, and individual rights, or by focusing on a *care* perspective that views moral questions in terms of disconnection and abandonment, the importance of relationship with others, and being responsive to one another's concerns. Gilligan (1982) emphasized that the "different voice" of the care perspective "is not characterized by gender but theme" (p. 2), and said that finding it to be more characteristic of the moral reasoning of girls and women than of boys and men was nothing more than an empirical observation.

Eleven-to-fifteen-year-olds of both sexes have been shown to employ either of the themes in wrestling with moral questions, although individuals tend to favor one moral orientation over the other, with males more likely to emphasize a justice/rights perspective and females more likely to emphasize a care/response perspective (Johnston, 1988). In a study of adolescents from an urban area characterized by high rates of violence, Ward (1988) found that both male and female students used both moral orientations in trying to understand and explain the tragic acts of violence that were part of their everyday lives, tending to use justice reasoning more often when describing neighborhood violence and a care perspective when describing family violence. However, she also found that not all student responses fit one category or the other; some responses indicated a combination of the two ways of thinking.

Conclusion

As young adolescents observe and interpret events around them, they are constructing a view of themselves and the universe in which they live, a view that encompasses the multiple aspects of their own social and emotional development and guides them as they make choices and prepare to take their place in tomorrow's world. However, this production of the young adolescent self does not occur in isolation, and perceptive educators will recognize opportunities to play an important role in the process. By demonstrating an understanding of the concerns of young adolescents, by being sensitive to their anxieties, by recognizing their yearning for acknowledgment and respect as individuals along with their desire to be accepted as part of a group, educators can contribute significantly to the development of their students.

The constructivist approach provides a way to examine early adolescent social and emotional development by emphasizing the following salient features on the cognitive, affective, and behavioral levels:

- Cognitive—Self-concept: The young adolescent is forming a personal identity, developing a peer-group identity, experiencing changing body-image perceptions, and searching for ethnic and/or racial group identity.
- Affective—Self-esteem: At the same time, the early adolescent is becoming aware of emerging feelings of self-satisfaction or dissatisfaction based upon how he or she thinks about him or herself and emerging feelings of self-satisfaction or dissatisfaction in relation to how he or she thinks others perceive him or her.
- Affective—Self-efficacy: The young adolescent also is characterized by an emerging belief that he or she can (or cannot) create and/or regulate events in his or her life, by decision-making with regard to the effort and time he or she is willing to devote to tasks and events, by evaluation of responsiveness to his or her efforts, and by increasing or decreasing belief in his or her ability and competence.
- Behavioral—Self-perception: On the behavioral level, the young adolescent is acting in ways to gain peer group approval, basing academic performance on external influences (peer group, parents, and teacher ex-pectations), developing personal relationships, and building a personal moral and value structure as a basis for thinking about the world around her or him and for decision-making and action.

In view of all that is happening in the young adolescent's life, it might be useful for educators to consider some insights from James Beane (1990.) Beane has suggested an interdisciplinary-based curriculum and instructional approach that takes into account the unique developmental needs and personal concerns of early adolescents. According to Beane, an appropriate middle school interdisciplinary curriculum would include such life skills as reflective thinking about the meanings and consequences of ideas and behaviors, describing and evaluating personal interests and ambitions, and identifying and defining personal beliefs and principles. In addition, Beane suggests that an interdisciplinary curricular design supportive of adolescent development should include themes such as understanding and making transitions in the context of a changing world, independence and interdependence, diversity, and consumerism and commercialism.

Further support for early adolescent social and emotional developmental needs is provided by interdisciplinary teacher teaming in which teachers have opportunities to know students and to work together to provide educational activities to address their interests, aspirations, and developmental needs. Cooperative learning, implemented by a skillful teacher, can be the vehicle for young adolescents to develop interpersonal social skills and communication skills, enhance academic mastery, and acquire confidence in their abilities and talents. The middle school environment thus can support and encourage young adolescents as they continue in their characteristic venture, interpreting and making meaning of the events around them and constructing a view of themselves as they live in the present and prepare for their futures.

NOTE

*The author wishes to thank Letha Dawson Scanzoni for her research and editorial assistance in the preparation of this chapter.

REFERENCES

Adams, G. R., Day, T., Dyk, P. H., Frede, E., and Rogers, D. R. B. (1992). On the dialectics of pubescence and psychological development. *Journal of Early Adolescence 12*: 348–365.

American Association of University Women Foundation. (1991). *Shortchanging girls, shortchanging America* (Executive Summary). Washington, DC: Author.

American Association of University Women Foundation. (1992). *The AAUW report: How schools shortchange girls* (Executive Summary). Washington, DC: Author.

Bandura, A. (1982). Self-efficacy mechanism in human agency. *American Psychologist 37* (2): 122–147.

Beane, J. A. (1990) *A middle school curriculum: From rhetoric to reality.* Columbus, OH: National Middle School Association.

Beane, J. A., and Lipka, R. P. (1980). Self-concept and self-esteem: A construct differentiation. *Child Study Journal 10*: 1–6.

Beane, J. A., and Lipka, R. P. (1984). *Self-concept, self-esteem, and the curriculum.* Needham Heights, MA: Allyn and Bacon.

Beane, J. A., Lipka, R. P., and Ludewig, J. W. (1980). Synthesis of research on self-concept. *Educational Leadership 38*(1): 84–89.

Benenson, J. F. (1990). Gender differences in social networks. *Journal of Early Adolescence 10*: 472–495.

Brown, L. M. (1991). A problem of vision: The development of voice and relational knowledge in girls ages seven to sixteen. *Women Studies Quarterly 19*(1): 52–71.

Calsyn, R. J., and Kenny, D. A. (1977). Self-concept of ability and perceived evaluation of others: Cause or effect of academic achievement? *Journal of Educational Psychology 69*(2): 136–145.

Cooley, C. H. (1902). *Human nature and the social order.* New York: Charles Scribner's Sons.

Covington, M. V. (1984). The self-worth theory of achievement motivation: Findings and implications. *The Elementary School Journal 85* : 5–19.

Crain, W. C. (1980). *Theories of development: Concepts and applications.* Englewood Cliffs, NJ: Prentice-Hall.

Crockett, L. J., Petersen, A. C., Graber, J. A., Schulenberg, J. E., and Ebata, A. (1989). School transitions and adjustment during early adolescence. *Journal of Early Adolescence 9*: 181–210.

East, P. L. (1989). Early adolescents' perceived interpersonal risks and benefits: Relations to social support and psychological functioning. *Journal of Early Adolescence 9*: 374–395.

Eichhorn, D. H. (1966). *The middle school*. New York: The Center for Research in Education.

Elkind, D. (1967). Egocentrism in adolescents. *Childhood Development 38*: 1025–1034.

Erikson, E. H. (1959). Identity and the life cycle. *Psychological Issues 1*: 1–173.

Erikson, E. H. (1968). *Identity: Youth and Crisis*. New York: Norton.

Escalante, J., and Dirmann, J. (1990). The Jaime Escalante math program. *The Journal of Negro Education 59*: 407–423.

Fenzel, L. M. (1989). Role strains and the transition to middle school: longitudinal trends and sex differences. *Journal of Early Adolescence 9*: 211–226.

Fine, M., and Zane, N. (1991). Bein' wrapped too tight: When low-income women drop out of high school. *Women's Studies Quarterly 19*(1): 77–99.

George, P., and Lawrence, G. (1982). *Handbook for middle school teaching*. Glenview, IL: Scott, Foresman.

Gilligan, C. (1982). *In a different voice: Psychological theory and women's development*. Cambridge, MA: Harvard University Press.

Gilligan, C. (1988). Prologue: Adolescent development reconsidered. In C. Gilligan, J. V. Ward, and J. M. Taylor (Eds.), *Mapping the moral domain* (pp. vii–xxxix). Cambridge, MA: Harvard University Press.

Gilligan, C. (1992). Girls at 11: An interview with Carol Gilligan. In A. Steinberg (Ed.), *The Best of the Harvard Education Letter* (pp. 19–21). Cambridge, MA: Harvard University Graduate School of Education.

Hancock, E. (1989). *The girl within*. New York: Fawcett Columbine.

Harris, L., Blum, R. W., and Resnick, M. (1991). Teen females in Minnesota: A portrait of quiet disturbance. In C. Gilligan, A. G. Rogers, and D. L. Tolman (Eds.), *Women, Girls, and Psychotherapy: Reframing Resistance* (pp. 119–135). Binghamton, NY: Harrington Park Press.

John-Steiner, V., and Souberman, E. (1978). Afterward. In L. S. Vygotsky, *Mind in Society* (pp. 121–133). Cambridge, MA: Harvard University Press.

Johnston, D. K. (1988). Adolescent solutions to dilemmas in fables: Two moral orientations—two problem solving strategies. In C. Gilligan, J. V. Ward, and J. M. Taylor (Eds.), *Mapping the moral domain* (pp. 49–69). Cambridge, MA: Harvard University Press.

Koff, E., Rierdan, J., and Stubbs, M. L. (1990). Gender, body image, and self-concept in early adolescence. *Journal of Early Adolescence 10*: 56–67.

Kohlberg, L. (1976). Moral stage and moralization. In T. Lickona (Ed.), *Moral development and behavior* (pp. 31–53). New York: Holt.

Kramer, L. R. (1991). The social construction of ability perceptions: An ethnographic study of gifted adolescent girls. *Journal of Early Adolescence 11*: 340–362.

Lerner, J. V., and Lerner, R. M. (1989). Introduction: Longitudinal analyses of biological, psychological, and social interactions across the transitions of early adolescence. *Journal of Early Adolescence 9*. 175 180.

Malonado, D., Jr. (1975). Ethnic self-identity and self-understanding. *Social Casework 56*: 618–622.

Marcia, J. (1966). Development and validation of ego-identity status. *Journal of Personality and Social Psychology 3*: 551–558.

Marcia, J. (1980). Identity in adolescence. In J. Adelson (Ed.), *Handbook of adolescent psychology* (pp. 159–187). New York: Wiley.

Mead, G. H. (1934). *Mind, self, and society*. Chicago: University of Chicago Press.

O'Connor, B. P., and Nikolic, J. (1990). Identity development and formal operations as sources of adolescent egocentrism. *Journal of Youth and Adolescence 19*: 149–158.

Ogbu, J. (1987). Opportunity structure, cultural boundaries, and literacy. In J. Langer (Ed.), *Language, literacy, and culture: Issues of society and schooling* (pp. 149–177). Norwood, NJ: Ablex.

Phinney, J. (1989). Stages of ethnic identity development in minority group adolescents. *Journal of Early Adolescence 9*: 34–49.

Phinney, J., and Tarver, S. (1988). Ethnic identity search and commitment in black and white eighth graders. *Journal of Early Adolescence 8*: 265–277.

Piaget, J. (1973). *To understand is to invent*. New York: Viking.

Raffaelli, M., and Duckett, E. (1989). "We were just talking . . .":
Conversations in early adolescence. *Journal of Youth and
Adolescence 18*: 567–582.

Roberts, L. R., and Petersen, A. C. (1992). The relationship between
academic achievement and social self-image during early
adolescence. *Journal of Early Adolescence 12*: 197–219.

Robinson, T., and Ward, J. V. (1991). "A belief in self far greater than
anyone's disbelief": Cultivating resistance among African-
American female adolescents. In C. Gilligan, A. G. Rogers, and D.
L. Tolman (Eds.), *Women, girls, and psychotherapy* (pp. 87–103).
Binghamton, NY: Harrington Park Press.

Roth, W. M. (1992). Bridging the gap between school and real life:
Toward and integration of science, mathematics, and technology
in the context of authentic practice. *School Science and Mathematics
92*: 307–317.

Schultz, D. L. (July 1991). *Risk, resiliency, and resistance: Current research
on adolescent girls.* Ms. Foundation for Women National Girls
Initiative Report. New York: National Council for Research on
Women.

Secord, P. F., and Backman, C. W. (1974). *Social Psychology* (2nd ed.).
New York: McGraw-Hill.

Simon, D. J., Reed, D. F., and Clark, M. (1990). The effect of cross-age
mentoring on the achievement and self-esteem of at-risk students
in middle school. *Research in Middle Level Education 14*(1): 11–22.

Stefanich, G. P., Wills, F. A., and Buss, R. R. (1991). The use of
interdisciplinary teaming and its influence on student self-
concept in middle schools. *Journal of Early Adolescence 11*: 404–419.

Stern, L. (1991). Disavowing the self in female adolescence. In C.
Gilligan, A. F. Rogers, and D. L. Tolman (Eds.), *Women, girls, and
psychotherapy: Reframing Resistance* (pp. 105–117). Binghamton,
NY: Harrington Park Press.

Tierno, M. J. (1991). Responding to the socially motivated behaviors of
early adolescents: Recommendations for classroom management.
Adolescence 26: 569–577.

Valsiner, J. (1987). *Culture and the development of children's action.*
Chichester, U. K.: John Wiley and Sons.

Wadsworth, B. J. (1978). *Piaget for the classroom teacher.* New York:
Longman.

Ward, J. V. (1988). Urban adolescents' conceptions of violence. In C. Gilligan, J. V. Ward, and J. M. Taylor (Eds.), *Mapping the moral domain* (pp. 175–200). Cambridge, MA: Harvard University Press.

CHAPTER 5

Cognitive Development of Young Adolescents

*Michael J. Wavering**

> The direction of development is channeled by the specific as well as the universal givens of the human physical and social endowment. That is, all humans share a great deal of universal activity because of the biological and cultural heritage that we have in common as a species (e.g., two legs, communication through language, helpless infancy, organization in groups, and capacity to invent tools), and at the same time, each of us varies because of differences in our physical and interpersonal circumstances (e.g., acuity, strength, family constellation, means of making a living, familiarity with specific languages). To understand development, it is essential to understand both the underlying cultural and biological similarities across individuals and groups, and the essential differences between them. (Rogoff, 1990, p. 11)

Barbara Rogoff neatly outlines the task of this chapter, that is, to discuss the similarities and differences in development, specifically that of the young adolescent. This will be done within the cultural and biological framework and within the areas of cognitive and moral development.

From the beginning of the middle school movement in the 1960s, founding fathers such as Donald Eichhorn (1966) and Conrad Toepfer (1982) have recognized the importance of understanding cognitive development. In *The Middle School*, Eichhorn underscored the importance of teachers understanding

111

cognitive development in order to develop curricula appropriate to the needs of development. In one chapter, Eichhorn outlined cognitive development according to the paradigm developed by Jean Piaget (Inhelder and Piaget, 1958, 1969; Piaget, 1987a, 1987b; Piaget and Garcia, 1991). Subsequently, Piaget's model became the required frame of reference for middle level educators and the starting point for speculative brain growth claims (Brazee, 1983; Epstein and Toepfer, 1978; Strahan, 1985). Since then much has changed in the studies of cognitive development, and much has remained the same. What follows is (1) a discussion of relevant Piagetian theory of cognitive development; (2) a short discussion of the theory of Lev Vygotsky; (3) Howard Gardner's theory of multiple intelligences; (4) moral development according to Lawrence Kohlberg, Carol Gilligan, and Nel Noddings; and (5) recommendations concerning the relevance for educating young adolescents.

The general framework for the discussion of cognitive development is that of the philosophy of constructivism. Constructivism posits that the development of intelligence or meaning is an active construction of the individual acting in the matrix of the culture in which he resides. Rogoff (1990) stated it this way:

> I assume that thinking is functional, active, and grounded in goal-directed action. Problem solving involves interpersonal and practical goals, addressed deliberately (not necessarily consciously or rationally). It is purposeful, involving flexible improvisation toward goals as diverse as planning a meal, writing an essay, convincing or entertaining others, exploring the properties of an idea or unfamiliar terrain or objects, or remembering or inferring the location of one's keys. (pp. 8–9)

Piaget's Theory of Cognitive Development

> Development is a process of ongoing qualitative change, of transformations proceeding in a progressive, orderly manner. Development proceeds with various systems, biological and psychological. These systemic changes are

interdependent. There is a synergistic quality to the transformation, so that while the child does not change in one system, the system changes. (Sigel, 1990, p. 78)

The task at hand is to explain how this constructive development takes place in the young adolescent. Piaget's (Inhelder and Piaget, 1958, 1969) theory is a developmental theory that describes general development from birth to adulthood and proposes that all humans develop cognitively through a series of stages, with each stage being necessary to the development of subsequent stages.

The first of these stages is the sensorimotor, which lasts from birth to about 2 years of age; next is the preoperational stage from 2 to approximately 7 years of age; following this is the concrete operational stage from 7 to around 12 years of age; finally, the formal operational stage ranges from 12 years of age and up. The ages listed are approximations, and not everyone in those age ranges will be able to demonstrate thinking processes associated with a given stage. At each stage, there are characteristic types of cognitive processes that are typical for an individual who is able to use them. One of the criticisms of Piagetian theory is that it describes logico-mathematical reasoning and excludes other forms of reasoning, such as artistic expression, creativity, and musical talents, among others (e.g., see Gardner, 1983).

Overview of Piaget's Theory

Piaget's theory also describes the factors that are necessary for development to occur: physical maturation, physical experience, social transmission, and equilibration. Each of these factors is necessary but not sufficient by itself for cognitive development.

Physical maturation must occur for development. Throughout the life of the individual the brain and the nervous system develop and grow. Such growth, of course, takes place even before the birth of the child. This growth is important because without it normal development does not occur. At no other time, with the exception of the development of the fetus up to about three years of age, do so many physical changes take place in the human being than during the onset of puberty (Roche, 1992).

Physical experience also is necessary for cognitive development. According to Piagetian theory, the individual develops mental reasoning structures (referred to as schema) by mentally internalizing physical action. The actions internalized are experiences with the environment. Initially, with the young child, the internalization is that of an action scheme. For older children and young adolescents, the action schemes are replaced by operative structures (mental schema that are used to reason about information from the environment), which are described below.

Social transmission is another necessary factor for cognitive development. Commonly, we might think of schooling as a form of social transmission (and it is), but there are many other forms of social transmission, including parental attention, interaction with playmates, and, certainly, the effects of modern technologies. Social transmission in Piaget's theory is necessary but not sufficient to cognitive development. Consequently, the effects of schooling on cognitive development (one of this chapter's concerns) are of primary importance. Cognitive development is worked out in a matrix of interaction with others. This interaction with others is the source of disequilibrium; data from the environment are seen by the individual as sources of mental conflict. Piaget does not develop the effects of social transmission adequately. Therefore, other theories, such as Vygotsky's, need to be consulted (see Rogoff, 1990; Tharp and Gallimore, 1988).

Equilibration is a final factor necessary for cognitive development. Equilibration is the mechanism for cognitive development, the motor that pushes development forward. The human being in terms of cognition is self-regulating. That is, the individual is in a state of equilibrium with his environment. When information is taken in from the environment, the information sometimes creates a state of disequilibrium. The state of disequilibrium is resolved by an equilibration, a movement of the mind to a new state of equilibrium. This is done by the process of adaptation described below. "To summarize, cognitive advance occurs as a function of appropriate neurological development, a proper social environment, experience with things, and internal cognitive reorganization" (Ginsburg and Opper, 1988, p. 206).

Relevance for the Development of Young Adolescents

Since most young adolescents function at the concrete and formal operational stages, I will focus on these two stages. A very few students, those with cognitive impairment, may still be functioning at the preoperational stage of development. (See Campione, Brown, and Ferrara, 1982; Feuerstein, 1979; Kramer, Piersel, and Glover, 1988; and Taylor, 1988, for methods to assist these students.)

For Piaget the development of intelligence occurs through the active adaptation of the individual to his social and physical environment. Adaptation takes place in two forms: assimilation and accommodation. *Assimilation* refers to the individual's attempt to make novel environmental happenings fit with the cognitive constructions that already exist. On the other hand, *accommodation* is the restructuring of cognitive constructions to fit with environmental happenings that cannot be assimilated otherwise. This adaptation takes place initially during the months immediately after birth, through direct action on objects and persons in the environment, for example, the grasping schemes of infant children to bring objects close to them for detailed inspection. These direct-action schemes gradually become internalized in the brain of the child, where there is mental manipulation of the objects and ideas encountered in the environment. External action becomes mental action. At the concrete and formal operational stages, mental action is the mode of intelligent behavior, although at the concrete stage manipulation of objects initially is required for the development of operational thought. Operations are "actions which are not only *internalized* but are also *integrated* with other actions to form general *reversible* systems" (Inhelder and Piaget, 1958, p. 6, italics in original).

Concrete operational reasoning. Concrete operational reasoning is the stage at which most 10-year-olds find themselves. This stage of reasoning is characterized by direct action on objects from which concepts, categories, spatial relations, etc., become mental constructions (a schema of relationships) that are used to reason logically about events in the life of the individual. The actions are internalized mentally to form structures that are integrated with other reasoning structures and are reversible, meaning that actions can mentally be reversed, by negation or by reciprocity. For example, doing the reverse mental action, the negation of 4+5=9 is 9–5=4. Or, returning to a starting point in a chain of thought by a mental route different than negation, a reciprocal of 4+5=9 is 9–2–3=4.

Concrete operations are described by structures that include conservations, classification, ordering, time, number, measurement, and spatial reasoning (topological, projective, and Euclidean). The reasoning structures are not composed of lists of content but are structures that process content. For example, addition, subtraction, multiplication, and division are examples of processes encompassed in reasoning structures, but math facts are not. An individual will be able to solve a problem for which he has not acquired certain math facts, if he has developed the appropriate mental structures. This is the difference between rote learning and meaningful learning. The structures of concrete operational reasoning are described in great detail by Phillips (1981).

Formal operational reasoning. Even though the concrete operational reasoning structures are capable of processing diverse forms of experience, they are limited. Concrete structures are limited to initial direct experience with the environment, to interpolation and limited extrapolation, and possibility is limited to experience. These limitations are resolved at the stage of formal operational thought. Formal operational thought is referred to as *thinking about thinking.*

After the young adolescent has developed the structures of concrete operational reasoning and assuming adequate physical maturation, physical experience, social transmission, and equilibration, she or he begins to develop formal operational reasoning ability. This happens approximately at 12 years of age. There is a great deal of variance when this occurs, and studies have demonstrated that this development may not happen for many adolescents and young adults (Kelsey, 1980; Wavering,

Kelsey, and Perry, 1987). Ginsburg and Opper (1988) offered the
following opinion:

> [S]ome adolescents and adults fail to show evidence of the
> ability to use formal operations on some tasks. This may
> be due to a lack of environmental stimulation which
> results in a slowing down or stoppage of development. Or
> it may be due to the use of limited testing procedures
> which are biased in favor of adolescents from particular
> backgrounds. Perhaps all adolescents can use formal
> operations in situations of interest to them. (p. 205)

As with concrete operational thinking, Piaget characterizes
formal operational thought by structures that process content
from the environment and from within the individual. The
structures Piaget proposes at the formal operational level are the
combinatorial structure, proportions, coordination of two
systems of reference and the relativity of motion or acceleration,
mechanical equilibrium, probability, correlation, multiplicative
compensations, and the forms of conservation that go beyond
direct empirical verification (Inhelder and Piaget, 1958). These
structures are used with a form of propositional logic and a
group of four operations that allow the individual to mentally
manipulate statements about content, such as mathematics or
science. This propositional logic is not the formal logic of the
philosophers, but a mental logic of which the individual may not
be directly aware. The areas studied by Piaget at the formal
operational level are chiefly mathematics and science reasoning.
Even though he claimed that these structures were essential to
other areas of thought, it has not been well established that this
is the case.

Van Hoose and Strahan (1988) nicely summed up the
change in young adolescents during this crucial period of
intellectual development:

> It is during this time that students first develop powers of
> abstract reasoning. They begin to think of the world
> around them and themselves in new ways. For the first
> time, young adolescents can "think about thinking"—
> which often confuses them. This "reflexive thinking"
> allows them to form sophisticated self-concepts that are
> shaped by interactions between their experiences and new

powers of reasoning. Understanding the development of abstract reasoning and reflexive thinking is especially important for successful teaching at the middle level. (p. 13)

Development According to Vygotsky

As mentioned above, Piaget's theory does not adequately describe the social aspects of cognitive development. The sociohistorical theory of development of Lev Vygotsky offers interesting insights and is worth inspection by those concerned with the education of young adolescents.

> Vygotsky argued that a child's development cannot be understood by a study of the individual; one must also examine the external social world in which that individual life has developed. In schools, we can understand the child's developing mind by studying the social interactions of teaching and learning. (Tharp and Gallimore, 1988, p. 19)

And from Rogoff (1990):

> Societal practices that support children's development are tied to the values and skills considered important. . . . For middle-class American children, the skills of schooling may relate closely to the skills required for participation in many aspects of adult life, and many of the practices of middle-class American families and educators may be well adapted to support development of formal operational, scientific reasoning, literate communication, mathematical facility, and other skills that may be useful for children's eventual participation in the economic and political institutions of their society. In other communities (in the United States and elsewhere), other goals and practices take prominence. (p. 12)

These statements support the conclusion that middle level educators need to be aware of the culture of the child, their own, and that of the school in order to understand and be more closely attuned to the intellectual development of young adolescents. Any or all of these cultures may be in harmony or in conflict, resulting in desired or undesired educational outcomes. Tharp and Gallimore (1988) further stated:

> [T]he cognitive and social development of the child (to the extent that the biological substrate is present) proceeds as an unfolding of potential through the reciprocal influences of child and social environment. Through guided reinvention, higher mental   functions that are part of the social and cultural heritage of the child will move from the social plane to the psychological plane, from the intermental to the intramental, from the socially regulated to the self-regulated. The child, through the regulating actions and speech of others, is brought to engage in independent action and speech. In the resulting interaction, the child performs through assistance and cooperative activity, at developmental levels quite beyond the individual level of achievement. In the beginning of the transformation to the intramental plane, the child need not understand the activity as the adult understands it, need not be aware of its reasons or its articulation with other activities. For skills and functions to develop into internalized, self-regulated capacity, all that is needed is performance, through assisting interaction. Through this process, the child acquires the "plane of consciousness" of the natal society and is socialized, acculturated, made human. (pp. 29–30)

In this view of development, the individual learns when more capable others, who have developed cognition at a higher level or socially valued skills, assist the individual to perform a task that the individual could not perform without assistance. Assistance is provided in continually decreasing increments as the individual becomes able to perform various aspects of the activity, until all assistance is withdrawn when the individual is able to perform the activity on her or his own. Vygotsky (Tharp and Gallimore, 1988) referred to this area of development as the *zone of proximal development (ZPD)*. In the ZPD, capable others provide a scaffold that supports performance and gradually is removed as the individual demonstrates more capable performance.

Assisted performance defines what a child can do with
help, with the support of the environment, of others, and
of the self. For Vygotsky, the contrast between assisted
performance and unassisted performance identified the
fundamental nexus of development and learning that he
called the zone of proximal development (ZPD). (Tharp
and Gallimore, 1988, p. 30)

Gardner's Multiple Intelligences

In the early 1980s, Howard Gardner (1983) unveiled his theory of
multiple intelligences. Gardner's work is included in this chapter
because it derives from the work of Piaget and Vygotsky
(Gardner, 1983, 1991). His theory of multiple intelligences
represents an attempt to synthesize the findings of the scholars
of cognition to develop a "point of view that . . . may prove of
genuine utility to those policy makers and practitioners charged
with 'the development of other individuals'" (Gardner, 1983, p.
10).

In his book *Frames of Mind: The Theory of Multiple
Intelligences*, Gardner (1983) devoted an extended section to the
debunking of intelligence as a single factor that governs all
realms of cognition. He took to task the psychometric school of
psychology and the misuse of single numbers, such as IQ, to
characterize someone as intelligent. (For a good exposé of
intelligence testing, refer to *The Mismeasure of Man* by Stephen J.
Gould, 1981.) Instead, Gardner proposed that there are at least
seven intelligences: language, logico-mathematical analysis,
spatial representation, musical thinking, the use of the body to
solve problems or to make things, an understanding of other
individuals, and an understanding of ourselves (Gardner, 1991).
Gardner (1983) chose these as intelligences because they met his
criteria for an intelligence.

To my mind, a human intellectual competence must entail
a set of skills of problem solving—enabling the individual
to resolve genuine problems or difficulties that he or she
encounters and, when appropriate, to create an effective
product—and must also entail the potential for *finding or*

creating problems —thereby laying the groundwork for the acquisition of new knowledge. These prerequisites represent my effort to focus on those intellectual strengths that prove of some importance within a cultural context. At the same time, I recognize that the ideal of what is valued will differ markedly, sometimes even radically, across human cultures, within the creation of new products or posing of new questions being of relatively little importance in some settings. (pp. 60–61, italics in original)

Gardner's Intelligences

Language intelligence appears to be an intelligence that virtually everyone develops to some extent. Most humans develop a facility with language to an extent that enables them to survive in their cultural setting. On the other hand, only a few individuals in a society develop linguistic skills to the level that they are recognized as experts or accomplished. Great writers, poets, and orators have demonstrated the highest levels of accomplishment in linguistic intelligence.

Logico-mathematical analysis is an intelligence that we prize and recognize in our society. We often say, "It doesn't take a rocket scientist to understand it," recognizing that great intelligence of a scientific-mathematical nature is not needed. This phrase, conversely, sets aside logico-mathematical analysis as an intelligence that is held in esteem; and its accomplished forms are not attained by all. What is not recognized is that everyone possesses at least some level of understanding in this area of intelligence.

Spatial representation. We all possess to some extent the intelligence of spatial representation. The ability to recognize shapes, transform them, recognize different perspectives, and create objects are examples of the use of spatial representation.

Musical thinking is an intelligence concerned with sound and, especially, how harmonious sounds can be created and performed with various instruments. Again, as humans we all possess this intelligence to some extent, even though it may be very limited.

Body use. The use of the body to create and solve problems or to make things sounds like a strange intelligence, but movement can be a very refined and sophisticated form of intelligence. This ability takes many forms, ranging from purposeful movement to get from one side of a crowded room to the other, to the lithe movements of a graceful dance, or to the dodging of players for the purpose of slamming a basketball into a goal. Certainly, aspects of this form of intelligence are regarded highly in our society.

Understanding others is a form of intelligence that is important to the survival of the human race. The level of conflict in many schools is an indication that this intelligence needs to be a visible component of the curriculum.

Understanding of ourselves is the final intelligence outlined by Gardner. The ancient philosophers counseled us to "know thyself." This intelligence may be the most elusive of the intelligences, but it is certainly important in schools, as evidenced through the statements of many schools about enhancing self-concept. (These concerns are more fully developed in other chapters in this book).

These intelligences appear to have levels of development, ranging from a novice or naive level, with a very limited range of application, to an expert or mastery level, with a wide range of demonstration. Dreyfus and Dreyfus (1986) have described a sequence of development from novice to expert that bears reading in light of Gardner's (1983) theory of multiple intelligences. Individuals will show varying ranges of development on each of these intelligences. They may be accomplished on some but relatively unaccomplished on others.

The theory of multiple intelligences deserves careful scrutiny by educators of young adolescents. If nothing else, it suggests that our schools too narrowly define intelligence and definitely do not evaluate students appropriately to determine if learning is merely rote or truly meaningful. Gardner (1993) and his colleagues have made some attempts to use the theory of multiple intelligences to improve schooling for young adolescents. One of these attempts is described in chapter 8 of Gardner's (1993, pp. 119–133) book *Multiple Intelligences: The Theory in Practice.*

Moral Development according to Kohlberg and Gilligan

Intellectual development and moral development go hand-in-hand. Moral development represents the intersection of the intellectual and social development (B. Smith personal communication, January 1994). In the 1920s, Piaget (1976) first tackled the problem of the development of moral reasoning. After outlining a general development scheme in this area, he relinquished research to others. In the 1960s, Lawrence Kohlberg (1981) took up the research and published his influential levels of moral development. Kohlberg posited six stages of moral development: avoiding punishment, seeking reward, social approval, law and order, social contract, and universal ethics. These stages represent a developmental sequence that is roughly characteristic of an age group and is alterable on the basis of maturation, experience with others, and through disequilibrating experiences.

At stage one, an individual makes moral decisions to avoid punishment. At stage two, a child makes moral decisions on the basis of being rewarded for the behavior. Children make moral decisions to receive social approval at stage three. That is, will they be seen as good or bad for doing something? At stage four, individuals make moral decisions by the rules, the law and order orientation. Rules are not to be broken under any circumstances because if exceptions were made, no one would follow rules. A stage five individual makes moral judgments on the basis of a social contract, "Do unto others as you would have them do unto you." At stage six, individuals make moral decisions based on a universal ethic of compassion for humans. At the fifth and sixth stages, individuals would violate laws if they were seen as unjust and violated stated principles. Young adolescents exhibit moral reasoning behaviors that mainly are associated with stages three through five, with some young adolescents at the other stages of development. Kohlberg (1981) has proposed that students be challenged to understand moral choices they would make through the posing of moral dilemmas.

Kohlberg's theory is not without its dissenters. In the original research a disproportionate number of males demonstrated moral reasoning at stages five and six. Carol Gilligan (1982) proposed the explanation that more females exhibited what is being referred to as an ethic of caring (Noddings, 1993), which was not accounted for in Kohlberg's theory. Although moral development is not an area of instruction in most schools, the choices and behaviors of students in our middle level schools are of great concern to educators. Consequently, educators need to be aware of moral development and how it can be ethically incorporated into the education of young adolescents.

Recommendations for Middle Level Educators

> Contrary to much conventional belief, cognitive development during early adolescence is not on hold. Belief in such claims has had substantial and damaging effects on middle grade education, by limiting innovation in curriculum development that might require new and more advanced ways of thinking. A thorough review of recent studies on adolescent cognitive development found "no persuasive evidence" that young adolescents cannot engage in critical and higher order thinking. (Carnegie Council on Adolescent Development, 1989, p. 42)

This quotation from *Turning Points: Preparing American Youth for the 21st Century* sets the stage for the conclusion to this chapter. In the past, it has been fashionable to write off early adolescents as "brain dead." Some have even suggested, more than half-seriously, that the 10- to 15-year-olds should be locked up until the dramatic changes accompanying the onset of puberty have run their course. The theorists and the researchers inspired by the developmental theories reviewed here amply demonstrate that young adolescents are indeed in the throes of dramatic cognitive changes. They need in their schooling adults who understand thoroughly the changes that are affecting them—adults who are capable of designing and delivering educational experiences, respecting these changes and not ignoring them as something that will pass with time.

What do all these theorists on development have to say to the adults who teach at the middle level? First, we should respect the young humans who inhabit our classrooms. They are undergoing the most dramatic changes since the first few years of life. New intellectual capabilities are developing at the same time that a new body and new emotions are challenging this human.

Second, this being is not stupid or incapable of thinking, even though at one minute he or she may be incapable of solving a problem similar to the one he or she solved easily just yesterday. This human is an intelligent being who is trying to construct the world he or she inhabits on the basis of what he or she already understands. Consequently, making mistakes and the struggle to understand are necessary parts of development.

Third, the research and theory of Piaget, Vygotsky, Gardner, and Kohlberg suggest that we must make an effort to uncover what our students understand. A correct answer is not an indication that a young adolescent has mastered a given content. School-wise students have developed the ability to get the right answer (rote learning) without understanding (meaningful learning) the underlying principles. Since this correct answer is not tied to a long-term memory structure, the information is forgotten by most students within a short time after the testing situation. Another aspect of this point is that student understanding of a given piece of content is not that of the more mature or expert thinkers in the field. Novice conceptions are sometimes referred to as *naive conceptions*. Some of the best-developed research on naive conceptions has been done in science education (Connor, 1990). Educators need to be willing to ask students to justify their responses or demonstrate how they determined their answer and, at appropriate times, model the skills required.

Fourth, just knowing Piaget's stages or anyone else's stages is not enough. For example, it is often said that early adolescents are in the transitional stage from concrete to formal operations. Having said that, what do we really know and how does that help us work with these students? Educators, as well as young adolescents, must not be satisfied with rote learning. Theory has a bad name among educational practitioners, but as no less an authority than John Dewey (Hass, 1983, p. 296) said, "Theory is in the end, as has been well said, the most practical of all things. . . . " As educators, we do act from a theoretical base, even if it is only implicit and strictly idiosyncratic. Why not make it explicit and improve its efficacy by modifying the theoretical base with experience, both practical and the experience of others who might have done some research, too?

Fifth, cognitive development does not take place in a vacuum. Both Piaget's (Inhelder and Piaget, 1958) and Vygotsky's (Tharp and Gallimore, 1988) theories recognize the role of social transmission. In terms of those theories, development is an interactive process. The individual develops by interaction with fellow students and teachers and by confronting her or his own thoughts. The major role of the teacher becomes one of constructing activities that upset the comfortable equilibrium of the student so that she or he will attempt to reconcile what she or he is learning with what she or he understands. Doing this is less threatening in the presence of supportive peers and educators. "Piaget emphasized cooperation as the ideal form of social interaction promoting development because he believed that the social relations involved in cooperation are the same as the logical relations that children construct in regard to the physical world" (Rogoff, 1990, p. 140). This certainly points up the necessity of developing a learning community in the school. Doing this would necessitate teaching to the intelligence of understanding others, as described by Gardner (1991).

Sixth, Vygotsky's (Tharp and Gallimore, 1988) theory further emphasizes the role of the teacher as assisting the development of the student. To do this, the teacher must be a capable individual, able to do what he or she expects from the student or able to match the student with someone who can. In this role, teachers must be lifelong learners and can assist their students to become lifelong learners. The teacher, as a lifelong learner, must acquire new knowledge and skills about subject matter and how to teach that subject matter more effectively.

Grossman, Wilson, and Shulman (1989) call this *pedagogical content knowledge*.

Seventh, Gardner's (1983) theory of multiple intelligences calls for middle level educators to be aware that intelligence is not that which is narrowly defined by intelligence tests or the latest form of the state minimum performance test. There are at least seven areas of intelligence, all of which are important to our society. No one will excel at all of them. "Indeed, as currently constituted, our educational system is heavily biased toward linguistic modes of instruction and assessment and, to a somewhat lesser degree, toward logical-quantitative modes as well" (Gardner, 1991, p. 12). This is a call not only for a broader curriculum but also for authentic assessment, assessment that asks students to demonstrate their knowledge and abilities in ways appropriate to that type of intelligence.

Eighth, Kohlberg's (1981) moral development theory, with modifications to include the insights of Gilligan (1982) and Noddings (1993), points up the need to be concerned with the consequences of ignoring the ecology of the school in which moral development is occurring. Is the school community the type of community in which caring, moral adolescents have an opportunity to develop? Ignoring these concerns runs the risk of perpetuating the lack of concern that denies so many of our citizens the choices to make their lives more humane.

> Students learn in ways that are identifiably distinctive. The broad spectrum of students—and perhaps the society as a whole—would be better served if all disciplines could be presented in a number of ways and learning could be assessed through a variety of means. (Gardner, 1991, p. 12)

NOTE

*I would like to thank Annette Digby and Bruce Smith who provided me with invaluable and numerous comments that served to improve this chapter.

REFERENCES

Brazee, E. (1983). Brain periodization—Challenge. *Middle School Journal* 15(1): 8–9.

Campione, J., Brown, A., and Ferrara, R. (1982). Mental retardation and intelligence. In R. Sternberg (Ed.), *Handbook of human intelligence* (pp. 392–400). Cambridge, England: Cambridge University Press.

Carnegie Council on Adolescent Development. (1989). *Turning points: Preparing American youth for the 21st century.* Washington, DC: Author.

Connor, J. (1990). Naive conceptions and the school science curriculum. In M. Rowe (Ed.), *What research says to the science teacher* (Vol. 6): *The process of knowing* (pp. 5–18). Washington, DC: National Science Teachers Association.

Dreyfus, H., and Dreyfus, S. (1986). *Mind over machine: The power of human intuition and expertise in the era of the computer.* New York: Macmillan.

Eichhorn, D. (1966). *The middle school.* Columbus, OH: National Middle School Association.

Epstein, H., and Toepfer, C. F., Jr. (1978). A neuroscience basis for reorganizing middle grade education. *Educational Leadership 35*: 656–660.

Feuerstein, R. (1979). *The dynamic assessment of retarded performers: The learning potential assessment device, theory, instruments, and techniques.* Baltimore: University Park Press.

Gardner, H. (1983). *Frames of mind: The theory of multiple intelligences.* New York: Basic Books.

Gardner, H. (1991). *The unschooled mind: How children think and how schools should teach.* New York: Basic Books.

Gardner, H. (1993). *Multiple intelligences: The theory in practice.* New York: Basic Books.

Gilligan, C. (1982). *In a different voice.* Cambridge, MA: Harvard University Press.

Ginsburg, H., and Opper, S. (1988). *Piaget's theory of intellectual development* (3d. ed.). Englewood Cliffs, NJ: Prentice Hall.

Gould, S. (1981). *The mismeasure of man.* New York: W. W. Norton.

Grossman, P., Wilson, S., and Shulman, L. (1989). Teachers of substance: Subject matter knowledge for teaching. In M. Reynolds (Ed.),

Knowledge for the beginning teacher (pp. 23–36). New York: Pergamon Press.

Hass, G. (1983). *Curriculum planning: A new approach* (4th ed.). Needham Heights, MA: Allyn and Bacon.

Inhelder, B., and Piaget, J. (1958). *The growth of logical thinking: From childhood to adolescence*. New York: Basic Books.

Inhelder, B., and Piaget, J. (1969). *The early growth of logic in the child*. New York: W. W. Norton.

Kelsey, L. (1980). The performance of college astronomy students on two of Piaget's projective infralogical grouping tasks and their relationship to problems dealing with phases of the moon. Unpublished doctoral dissertation. University of Iowa, Iowa City.

Kohlberg, L. (1981). *The philosophy of moral development*. San Francisco: Harper and Row.

Kramer, J., Piersel, W., and Glover, J. (1988). Cognitive and social development of mildly retarded children. In M. Wang, M. Reynolds, and H. Walberg (Eds.), *Handbook of special education: Research and practice: Vol. 2. Mildly handicapped conditions* (pp. 43–58). Oxford, England: Pergamon Press.

Noddings, N. (1993). Caring: A feminist perspective. In K. Strike and P. Ternasky (Eds.), *Ethics for professional education: Perspectives for preparation and practice* (pp. 43–53). New York: Teachers College Press.

Phillips, D. (1981). *The structures of thinking: Elaboration, evaluation and applications of Piaget's model of intellectual development*. Iowa City, IA: Science Education Center.

Piaget, J. (1976). *Judgment and reasoning in the child*. Totowa, NJ: Littlefield, Adams, and Co.

Piaget, J. (1987a). *Possibility and necessity: The role of possibility in cognitive development* (Vol. 1). Minneapolis: University of Minnesota Press.

Piaget, J. (1987b). *Possibility and necessity: The role of necessity in cognitive development* (Vol. 2). Minneapolis: University of Minnesota Press.

Piaget, J., and Garcia, R. (1991). *Toward a logic of meanings*. Hillsdale, NJ: Lawrence Erlbaum Associates.

Roche, A. (1992). *Growth, maturation, and body composition: The Fels longitudinal study 1929–1991*. New York: Cambridge University Press.

Rogoff, B. (1990). *Apprenticeship in thinking: Cognitive development in social context*. New York: Oxford University Press.

Sigel, I. (1990). What teachers need to know about human development. In D. Dill (Ed.), *What teachers need to know* . . . (pp. 76–93). San Francisco: Jossey-Bass.

Strahan, D. (1985). Brain growth—Readiness the issue. *Middle School Journal 16*(2): 11–13.

Taylor, R. (1988). Psychological intervention with mildly retarded children: Prevention and remediation of cognitive skills. In M. Wang, M. Reynolds, and H. Walberg (Eds.), *Handbook of special education: Research and practice: Vol. 2. Mildly handicapped conditions* (pp. 59–75). Oxford, England: Pergamon Press.

Tharp, R., and Gallimore, R. (1988). *Rousing minds to life.* New York: Cambridge University Press.

Toepfer, C. F., Jr. (1982). Curriculum design and neuropsychological development. *Journal of Review and Development in Education 15*(3): 1–11.

Van Hoose, J., and Strahan, D. (1988). *Young adolescent development and school practices: Promoting harmony.* Columbus, OH: National Middle School Association.

Wavering, M., Kelsey, L., and Perry, B. (1987). Order of attainment of the mental structures for five of Piaget's logical, infralogical, and formal tasks. *Journal of Genetic Psychology 148*: 279–288.

CHAPTER 6

Preparing Teachers for Middle Level Schools: Meeting the Needs of Adolescents

Rebecca Farris Mills

Wendy, Bobbie, Cindy, and April began the school year as an interdisciplinary team of sixth grade teachers in a Grades 6–8 middle school. Wendy, the team leader, was a third-year teacher who recently had finished a teacher preparation program in secondary education with a major teaching field in social studies. Her teaching license certified her to teach in Grades 7–12; she had student taught with seventh graders at a junior high school in the local school district. Bobbie, a veteran of 11 years of elementary school teaching, had an area of concentration in reading in her elementary teacher education program and was the team's reading teacher. Her elementary license allowed her to teach Grades 1–8.

Cindy, who like Wendy had student taught in the middle grades, was a secondary education major licensed to teach English in Grades 7–12. This was her first year of teaching. Another first-year teacher, April, was a mathematics major who had student taught in a self-contained sixth grade at a K–8 school; her license was elementary.

All four of these women had chosen to teach in middle grades and were committed to the teaming concept. None had any course work specifically focused on middle level education or early adolescence. However, the group would have a daily team planning period to prepare meaningful learning experiences for the 120 students with whom they would work. Despite their differing backgrounds in teacher education and teaching experience, when the school year began, they were expected to work together effectively and efficiently.

This interdisciplinary team of teachers was expected, without explicit training or certification, to build a team culture among themselves and with their students; to plan interdisciplinary units for instruction; to make good use of team planning time; to learn to cooperate and to compromise in instructional planning; to hold shared parent and student conferences; to coordinate management policies, classroom routines, and homework schedules; to lead an advisory program; and to consider the concerns and feelings of the electives, "nonteam" teachers. All of these are among the common expectations for middle school teachers.

The team described above is not atypical. Often middle level teams of teachers include elementary and secondary education majors who are expected to work together with little prior experience and virtually no modeling of effective teaming. Not surprisingly, Scales (1992) found that the "typical middle-grades teacher is prepared at the undergraduate level in an elementary or secondary program that does not focus centrally on the young adolescent as a middle-grades program should" (p. 16). Yet *Turning Points*, a report of the Carnegie Council on Adolescent Development (1989), calls for teachers who have been specially educated to teach young adolescents.

This chapter will address preparing to teach at the middle level; it will begin with a description of current issues of concern in teacher education generally and middle level teacher education specifically. A discussion of the responsibilities of middle school teachers and issues surrounding middle level certification and licensure will be followed by recommendations for teacher education programs that have been made by professional organizations and middle school teachers. The chapter will conclude with a further look at our team of teachers and a discussion about better preparing teachers to meet the challenges of middle school teaching.

Current Issues in Teacher Education

Decisions about middle level teacher preparation cannot be made without a strong understanding of teacher education concerns generally. Currently, teacher educators are calling for the professionalization of teaching and for teacher preparation programs that provide opportunities for teachers to become *reflective* practitioners capable of making sound decisions (e.g., Russell, Munby, Spafford, and Johnston, 1988; Schön, 1983, 1987). The literature is replete with encouragement for teacher candidates to examine their fundamental beliefs about teaching, learners, learning, and subject matter (e.g., Connelly and Clandinin, 1985; Elbaz, 1983). Shulman (1986) wrote that teachers have both content knowledge and general pedagogical knowledge. Moreover, he contended that content knowledge consists of subject matter content knowledge, pedagogical content knowledge, and curricular knowledge; and he encouraged teacher educators to better understand the knowledge base that exists for teaching.

Shulman's work has implications not only for teacher education but for teacher assessment as well. *Alternative assessment*, in the form of portfolios, is being called for in both public school and teacher education classrooms by such writers as Glazer and Brown (1993) and Mitchell (1992).

Case teaching is finding a home in teacher education classes, in which preservice teacher candidates are being asked to examine real-life teaching dilemmas, pose possible solutions, and examine implications of their proposed solutions (e.g., Doyle, 1990; Silverman, Welty, and Lyon, 1991; Sykes and Bird, 1992). Courses in multicultural education and social foundations are receiving greater emphasis because of the recognition that new teachers enter schools where students' needs virtually overwhelm their ability to learn.

Writers such as Fullan (1991) have called for teacher education to prepare individuals to become *change agents*. New teachers often need a special strength not only to survive but to flourish in a system that often resists or impedes change. In addition to these general concerns, the literature also focuses on specific concerns in preparing teachers for middle level classrooms.

Challenging Issues in Middle Level Teacher Education

Decisions about middle level teacher preparation are situated in the context described above. However, preparing prospective teachers to work with young adolescents requires that other issues also be addressed. A number of challenges await those individuals who plan to teach in middle level schools and the teacher educators who work to prepare them. Nevertheless, a number of current trends make it a welcoming climate for those who are entering the profession as middle school teachers. Middle level teaching is receiving emphasis in the work of a number of professional organizations, and professionals are encouraged to recognize that teaching young adolescents fundamentally is different from teaching either elementary or high school students.

Professional organizations such as the National Middle School Association (NMSA), the National Board of Professional Teaching Standards (NBPTS), and the National Association of Secondary School Principals (NASSP) recognize that teaching at the middle level is a profession that demands fundamentally different tasks and strengths than those expected of classroom teachers at other levels. In addition, according to NMSA's Curriculum Guidelines (1991), which were approved by the National Council for the Accreditation of Teacher Education (NCATE):

> [NCATE] recognizes that roles and responsibilities of middle level educators are unique and that they demand and deserve specifically designed preparation programs. These programs should provide educators with the special knowledge, skills, concepts, and attitudes that will help them achieve high levels of success in working with early adolescents. (p. 31)

The changing needs of today's early adolescents are recognized by our society and the education profession. Books, such as *Fateful Choices* (Hechinger, 1992), focus attention on the nature of today's adolescents and the dilemmas they face. An emphasis on the human relations element of teaching has found its way into teacher education generally and middle level teacher education specifically. Writers, such as Eitzen (1992) and Schoor (1988), encourage middle level teachers to see themselves as part of a wider resource for social services to meet the needs of their students. Middle level teachers, like teachers at other levels, face increasingly complex cultural diversity and gender equity issues. As a profession, we are working to achieve consensus in identifying the experiences students should have in schools during early adolescence. *Turning Points* (Carnegie, 1989), Wiles and Bondi (1993), and Stevenson (1992) make clear distinctions between teaching at the middle level and any other level of schooling and examine effective characteristics of middle grade schools.

A focus on youth often is reflected in the media today. Activists such as Marion Wright Edelman, entertainers like Bill Cosby, and theorists like Jonathan Kozol remind us through their work that today's young people deserve and demand our attention and our services. We constantly are reminded that today's young adolescent is tomorrow's community leader. Daily, the media bombard the public with statistics about teenage pregnancy, suicide, and poverty. Today's young adolescents increasingly face consequences from alcohol and drug abuse, HIV infection, and violent crimes. Despite such grim reminders of the difficulties of adolescence, the public's awareness of and concern about these issues increase the likelihood they will be addressed through educational and social agencies and action. Candidates for middle level teaching need not only recognize the difficulties but must also respond sensitively and effectively to their students who face them daily. Middle level teachers should be educated carefully in order to prepare them for their role in programs such as advisor-advisee. It is through such planning and preparation that student's concerns more likely will be addressed.

New views of teacher assessment are apparent in the literature. In fact, in one early project the NBPTS (1989) drafted criteria for middle grades English and language arts teachers that might be used in national board certification. The work, an attempt to describe what constitutes highly accomplished practice, was done in collaboration with the NMSA, middle level English teachers, university English professors, and others. It is still in the draft stages. Another set of criteria recently drafted addresses the general characteristics to be assessed of all middle level teachers.

Yet another skill required of middle level teachers is the ability to work with other teachers to integrate subject matter. The ability to prepare interdisciplinary thematic units is not inherent in a novice teacher. It requires a conceptual knowledge of one's subject matter, a willingness to learn about other subject matter, and a holistic view of the teaching and learning processes. Teacher education courses that address this topic also might model effective interdisciplinary teaching so that candidates have a realistic sense of what it looks like and how it is done. It is safe to assume that the majority of current teacher candidates have not been taught in this manner; to expect them to teach as they have not been taught puts additional responsibility on both the teacher candidate and teacher educator.

Teacher Characteristics for Middle Level Teaching

The time seems right for school districts to embrace fully the middle school concept. Its focus on the young adolescent student and on developmentally appropriate instruction addresses the concerns that have been raised about middle level education and young adolescents. There seems to be general agreement that the traditional junior high school does not adequately meet the needs of the majority of middle level students. The middle school concept seems to be a reasonable, workable way to address the myriad needs of today's youth. In order for the middle school concept to be implemented more widely, both preservice and in-service teacher education will need to change. Teacher educators must provide both course and field experiences that prepare teachers who can meet the recent calls for individuals who have been specially trained to work at the middle level.

The NBPTS policy statement explains what teachers generally should know and be able to do. Of course, the board's work has implications for middle level teachers specifically. The NBPTS (1989) calls for teachers who:

- Are committed to students and their learning.
- Know their subjects and how to teach it to students.
- Can manage and monitor students' learning.
- Think systematically about their practice.
- Learn from their experiences.
- Work as members of learning communities. (excerpted from pp. 13–15)

In its *Inventory of the Professional Functions of Middle School Teachers* (1989), the Educational Testing Service grouped middle school teaching tasks into the following categories: planning and preparing for instruction, managing the classroom, implementing instruction, evaluating student learning and instructional effectiveness, conducting administrative and other professional responsibilities. Teacher educators must recognize and respond to the variety of sources that provide a sense of the characteristics teachers will need in order to meet the myriad challenges of middle school teaching.

Turning Points (Carnegie, 1989) has become a widely accepted document for outlining the goals and expectations for middle schools. Meeting its recommendations will require teachers who can create communities for learning, teach a core of common knowledge, improve student health and fitness, ensure success for all students, reengage families in their children's education, and connect schools with communities. The council also recognized the need to empower middle level teachers and asserted that middle level schools need teachers who are "specially educated to teach young adolescents" (p. 58). The *Turning Points* authors' "expert teachers" of young adolescents understand adolescent development, are sensitive to cultural differences, learn to work as a team, educate one another about their subject matters, understand principles of guidance for use in an advisory role, and work with families of all sorts. Each of these recommendations has implications for teacher certification and teacher education.

Teacher Certification or Licensure for Middle Level Teaching

Individuals have been calling for special preparation of middle school teachers for more than 50 years; however, teacher education program plans and teacher certification/licensure decisions virtually are inextricable. George and McEwin (1978), writing in the *Journal of Teacher Education*, claimed that certification and teacher education "simply cannot be separated. Students will not prepare for careers for which there is no license to practice, and practicing teachers need greater inducements than altruism" (p. 16). A call for special certification and preparation for middle level educators has been issued by the NMSA in publications such as *Professional Certification and Preparation for the Middle Level* (NMSA, 1991), *Preparing to Teach in Middle Level Schools* (Alexander and McEwin, 1988), and *On Site: Preparing Middle Level Teachers through Field Experiences* (Butler, Davies, and Dickinson, 1991).

The progress toward a separate certification, license, or endorsement has been steady. In 1969, Pumerantz found 2 states that issued middle grades certificates; that number had increased to 15 in 1978 (Gillan). Most recently, McEwin (1990) reported that 28 states had special certification requirements for middle grades teachers.

Turning Points (Carnegie, 1989) suggested that preservice candidates who wish to teach at the middle level develop a solid core of knowledge in one or more subject areas during their bachelor degree programs and be given, as early as their freshman year, opportunities to interact with young adolescents. The Carnegie Council further suggested that teacher preparation, upon completion of the bachelor degree program, include paid internships in middle grades schools, where interns would teach half time and work with mentor teachers. Only after completing graduate courses on understanding young adolescents, the art of teaching, and the learning process, and after undergoing on-the-job assessment, could individuals become fully licensed teachers of middle level students. The Carnegie Council called for a supplemental endorsement above an elementary or secondary license or certificate in order to recognize a middle level teacher's special talents and training, to encourage schools of education to offer special courses, and to legitimize the status of middle grades teachers.

Teacher Education for Middle Level Teaching

Although a Metropolitan Life survey (Harris, 1991) reported that 16 percent of that year's 1,002 new preservice teacher graduates expected to teach junior high or middle school in 1990–91, numerous studies have confirmed the serious lack of special preparation programs for middle level teachers (Alexander and McEwin, 1989; Gatewood and Mills, 1973; Valentine, Clark, Nickerson, and Keefe, 1981). A 1987 American Association for Colleges of Teacher Education study (McEwin and Alexander, 1987) showed that 34 percent of responding institutions had a special middle grades program at one or more degree levels. The NMSA's (1992) *Directory of Middle Level Teacher Preparation Programs* included 241 institutions that reported they had available specialized middle level teacher preparation programs.

As mentioned earlier, among attempts to identify the specific body of knowledge necessary to become an effective middle level teacher, some general consensus exists. Scales (1992) mentioned that core knowledge in middle level teacher preparation should include a knowledge of how adolescents develop, how teachers promote the physical, social, and emotional growth of young adolescents, and how teachers design curriculum and instruction that responds appropriately to young adolescent developmental needs.

Alexander and McEwin's (1988) list of recommended requirements for preservice middle school teachers included, in addition to those Scales cited, a broad academic background, special methods and reading courses, and early and continuous field experiences in good middle schools. George and McEwin (1978) listed the following items as a consensus about the characteristics of effective middle school teacher education programs.

- Emphasize knowledge about young adolescents.
- Understand the middle school concept.
- Improve field experiences.
- Provide more about developmentally responsive teaching and assessment techniques.
- Increase depth of coverage of classroom management strategies.
- Provide more comprehensive coverage of academic content areas.
- Increase understanding of early adolescent development. (pp. 13–16)

In a more recent attempt not only "to identify areas of consensus and contention [about] . . . the preparation of middle-grades teachers" but also "to suggest ways of improving their education" (p. 1), Scales (1992) randomly selected middle grades teachers in eight states (Arkansas, California, Florida, Georgia, Indiana, New York, North Carolina, and Washington) where middle level issues were considered to be a relatively high priority. The middle grades teachers in Scales' study most frequently made the following recommendations to improve teacher preparation for middle grades teachers:

- Improve field experiences.
- Provide more about developmentally responsible teaching and assessment techniques.
- Increase depth of coverage of classroom management strategies.
- Provide more comprehensive coverage of academic content areas.
- Increase understanding of early adolescent development. (p. 68)

Scales' study (1992), which included feedback not only from classroom teachers but also from deans of teacher education programs and chief state school officers, led to seven primary recommendations for improving middle grades teacher preparation.

1. Clarify definitions and strengthen standards.
2. Foster leadership among middle-grades professionals.
3. Improve teacher education curriculum and field experiences by focusing on young adolescents . . . and creating a professional development schools approach.
4. Target public relations to potential future teachers.
5. Advocate for the whole young adolescent.
6. Incorporate tools for systemic school change into the teacher education program.
7. Conduct further research that helps improve middle grades teacher preparation programs. (p. 106)

Developing the teaching force for middle schools, which many studies and organizations call for, will require that we provide teachers with incentives to teach at the middle level and encourage their commitment to teach young adolescents. Despite the consensus on what middle level teachers should know and do, the image of middle grades teaching sometimes suffers, and pervasive stereotypes of middle level teaching exist. The NMSA's own call for proposals at its national conference admonishes prospective presenters to avoid negative language when describing young adolescents in presentation titles and content. Generally, the literature reports that many teachers see the middle level as a "stopping-off point" on their way to high school teaching, and middle grades teachers not only lack confidence in their ability to teach young adolescents but also feel overwhelmed by the middle school environment (Carnegie, 1989). Given all this, how can teacher education support and prepare prospective teachers for middle level teaching?

Recommendations for teacher education, all of which can be addressed through course offerings, field experiences, and school-based research, fall in five basic areas. Teacher education programs designed to prepare middle level teachers need to provide opportunities for candidates to learn about the nature of the young adolescent, middle level teaching, middle level curriculum, developmentally appropriate pedagogy, and authentic assessment of learning.

Understandably, basic courses in educational psychology devote but a portion of their time to adolescent development. Prospective teachers need to take courses that focus on that topic and need to participate in field experiences that demonstrate clearly the nature of the young adolescent learner. It seems logical that the best way to prepare teachers to deal with the unique nature of the young adolescent is to give them experience doing so. Therefore, prospective middle level teachers need to spend considerable time observing and interacting with middle grade students.

If middle level teachers are to be capable of successfully implementing the middle school concept, they must fully understand the nature of middle level teaching and its requirements. Studies indicate that interdisciplinary teaming is one way to address the issue of low morale among middle school teachers because it reduces the typical isolation and alienation of secondary teachers (Arhar, Johnston, and Markle, 1988; Mills, Powell, and Pollak, 1992). Works like those of Erb and Doda (1989) and Johnston, Markle, and Arhar (1988) provide much needed information about the skills teachers need to successfully work in middle schools as members of interdisciplinary teams. Research must continue to focus on the challenges and rewards of middle level teaching.

Middle level teachers are called upon to meet a number of demands, such as serving in an advisor–advisee program, involving parents and communities in adolescents' education, implementing service projects with students, and responding to the unique needs of the young adolescent. Teacher education courses can better prepare individuals for the multiple roles middle level teachers are expected to assume, and field experiences can provide opportunities to practice and gain comfort in those roles.

The National Middle School Association's Curriculum Committee currently is circulating a position paper on what the middle level curriculum should and should not include. The position paper, not unlike other works, calls for an integrated, thematic approach to subject matter. This requires a conceptual understanding of subject matter and a working knowledge of curriculum development. Teacher education programs must require candidates to demonstrate mastery of the subject matter(s) for which they are certified and must provide their middle level candidates with opportunities to plan interdisciplinary units and to implement them in real classrooms. This process, a time-consuming one, greatly increases the likelihood that the prospective teachers will, indeed, teach in an integrated manner when left to their own devices. Middle level teachers are more likely to plan curricular experiences that focus on the learner when they themselves have been involved, as students, in curriculum planning. Therefore, teacher educators could and should demonstrate the process of encouraging and allowing students ownership in their learning.

Developmentally appropriate pedagogy includes, but certainly is not limited to, opportunities for students to learn by doing, to practice problem solving, to explore various media for learning, and to set their goals for learning. Student-centered classrooms provide a variety of ways and a number of opportunities for students to explore matters in which they are interested and follow ideas by which they are compelled. Young adolescents need freedom of movement, interaction with peers, opportunities for success, and support in failure. Professors who teach methodology courses in teacher education should not only mention but also demonstrate a variety of strategies for encouraging student understanding. Teacher candidates should have a chance to work with the latest technologies. For example, those who have learned by using an effective computer simulation will be more likely to encourage their students to learn in a similar manner. If teacher candidates were required to interview young adolescents about their interests, about their learning styles, and about their school experiences, they might better be prepared to deliver instruction appropriately for their students.

Authentic assessment, a frequent term in today's literature, represents another range of techniques that must be demonstrated by teacher educators. If middle level schools are going to ensure all students' successes, there certainly must be a change in the way we assess and evaluate students' learning. Teacher education programs might consider having their candidates assemble portfolios after setting goals for themselves. Certainly teacher education students' ability to identify and pose solutions for classroom problems can be demonstrated through case-teaching discussions much better than by objective test items.

Teacher education programs must address each of these areas in order to adequately prepare their candidates for the middle level schools called for in *Turning Points* (Carnegie, 1989). Courses in teacher education must be research based, and candidates must be taught the process of action research and encouraged to explore their own teaching. Requiring an action research approach to teacher education would demonstrate a value for the practical knowledge many teachers possess and provide a structure for systematic inquiry into the process of teaching that could be used by prospective teachers. It also would encourage prospective teachers to recognize their role as decision makers and to formulate effective decision-making procedures. Teacher educators also must continue to focus their research on the challenges and rewards of middle level teaching. Such research informs teacher education curriculum development.

It will be no small task to develop teachers who not only recognize the need for 10- to 15-year-olds who are intellectually reflective, healthy, caring, and ethical persons en route to a lifetime of meaningful work and good citizenship (Carnegie, 1989), but who also know how to shape educational experiences that encourage the development of such young adults. Teacher educators, state and district school officials, community leaders, and students' parents who embrace the recommendations of the Carnegie Council, certainly, will need to continue to scrutinize and refine the experiences that lead an individual to certification, licensure, or endorsement for middle level teaching. With such efforts in teacher education, it seems likely that more middle level students will be taught by teachers who themselves are intellectually reflective, caring, ethical, healthy citizens, who see themselves engaged in meaningful work.

Wendy, Bobbie, Cindy, and April Revisited

To conclude, we will return to our interdisciplinary team of teachers at the end of their first school year as a team. It is for teachers like these that teacher education must focus specifically on issues unique to middle level teaching. If teacher education course work and research focus on the middle level, candidates might have greater knowledge and relevant experience from which to draw. Then their efforts as middle level teachers on interdisciplinary teams likely would be effective and efficient.

The middle school in which our teachers taught, in its first year of full-school teaming, grappled with such issues as incorporating electives' teachers, providing adequate planning time, and maintaining flexible scheduling. Some teachers resisted the changes, and the local teachers' union representatives visited the school frequently. Despite all of this, Wendy, Bobbie, Cindy, and April were successful individually and collectively. They learned to depend on one another's support both in and out of school. They extended their team planning sessions through lunch, into their personal preparation time, and often after school. They were determined to make teaming work, and they did.

In their first year, the team worked together daily and created three interdisciplinary units: a unit about the presidential election, another around United States social studies, and a third for the science fair. In addition to the interdisciplinary units, students benefited from the consistency and reinforcement that resulted from teachers sharing routines and plans. The team of teachers and students planned service activities which included a Veteran's Day celebration honoring the school's custodian and holiday decorations for local hospital patients. They also took field trips, celebrated team successes, and participated in intramural activities. Teachers felt empowered to make decisions about their classrooms and their teaching, and learning experiences focused on issues and activities that were relevant to and appropriate for young adolescents. All was not perfect, but the commitment to making the team work allowed a successful outcome. Teachers and students worked together in a meaningful learning journey.

REFERENCES

Alexander, W. M., and McEwin, C. K. (1988). *Preparing to teach in middle level schools*. Columbus, OH: National Middle School Association.

Alexander, W. M., and McEwin, C. K. (1989). *Schools in the middle: Status and progress*. Columbus, OH: National Middle School Association.

Arhar, J. M., Johnston, J. H., and Markle, G. C. (1988). The effects of teaming and other collaborative arrangements. *Middle School Journal* 19(4): 122–125.

Butler, D. A., Davies, M. A., and Dickinson, T. S. (1991). *On site: Preparing middle level teachers through field experiences*. Columbus, OH: National Middle School Association.

Carnegie Council on Adolescent Development. (1989). *Turning points: Preparing American youth for the 21st century*. Washington, DC: Author.

Connelly, F. M., and Clandinin, D. J. (1985). Personal practical knowledge and the modes of knowing: Relevance for teaching and learning. In E. Eisner (Ed.), *Learning and teaching the ways of knowing*. Eighty-fourth Yearbook of the National Society for the Study of Education, Part 2. (pp. 174–178). Chicago: University of Chicago Press.

Doyle, W. (1990). Case methods in the education of teachers. *Teacher Education Quarterly* 17(1): 7–15.

Educational Testing Service. (1989). *Inventory of the professional functions of middle school teachers*. Princeton, NJ: Author.

Eitzen, D. S. (1992). Problem students: The sociocultural roots. *Phi Delta Kappan* 73: 585–590.

Elbaz, F. (1983). *Teacher thinking: A study of practical knowledge*. London: Croom Helm.

Erb, T. O., and Doda, N. M. (1989). *Team organization: Promise— practices and possibilities*. Washington DC: National Education Association.

Fullan, M. G. (1991). *The new meaning of educational change* (2nd ed.). New York: Teachers College Press.

Gatewood, T. E., and Mills, R. C. (1973). *Preparing teachers for the middle school, junior high: A survey and a model*. Mt. Pleasant: Central Michigan University.

George, P. S., and McEwin, C. K. (1978). Middle school teacher education: A progress report. *Journal of Teacher Education* 29(5): 13–16.

Gillan, R. E. (1978). *Teacher preparation and certification for the middle school grades.* ERIC Document Reproduction Service No. ED 178 463.

Glazer, S. M., and Brown, C. S. (1993). *Portfolios and beyond: Collaborative assessment in reading and writing.* Norwood, MA: Christopher-Gordon.

Harris, L. and Associates. (1991) *The Metropolitan Life survey of the American teacher, 1991.* New York: Author.

Hechinger, F. M. (1992). *Fateful choices: Healthy youth for the 21st century.* New York: Carnegie Corporation.

Johnston, J. H., Markle, G. C., and Arhar, J. M. (1988). Cooperation, collaboration, and professional development of teachers. *Middle School Journal* 29(3): 28–32.

McEwin, C. K. (1990). *Middle level certification practices: Report of a national study.* Boone, NC: Appalachian State University.

McEwin, C. K., and Alexander, W. M. (1987). *Report of middle level teacher education programs: A second survey (1986 87).* Boone, NC: Appalachian State University.

Mills, R. A., Powell, R. R., and Pollak, J. P. (1992). The influence of middle level interdisciplinary teaming on teacher isolation: A case study. *Research in Middle Level Education* 15(2): 9–25.

Mitchell, R. (1992). *Testing for learning: How new approaches to evaluation can improve American schools.* New York: The Free Press.

National Board for Professional Teaching Standards. (1989). *Toward high and rigorous standards for the teaching profession: Initial policies and perspectives of the National Board for Professional Teaching Standards.* Detroit: Author.

National Middle School Association. (1991). *NMSA Curriculum Guidelines.* Columbus, OH: Author.

National Middle School Association. (1991). *Professional certification and preparation for the middle level: A position paper of National Middle School Association.* Columbus, OH: Author.

National Middle School Association. (1992). *Directory of middle level teacher preparation programs.* Columbus, OH: Author.

Pumerantz, P. (1969). Few states certify teachers for growing middle schools. *Phi Delta Kappan* 5(2): 102.

Russell, T., Munby, H., Spafford, C., and Johnston, P. (1988). Learning the professional knowledge of teaching: Metaphors, puzzles, and the theory-practice relationship. In P. Grimmett and G. Erickson (Eds.), *Reflection in teacher education* (pp. 67–90). New York: Teachers College Press.

Scales, P. C. (1992). *Windows of opportunity: improving middle grades teacher preparation*. Carrboro, N. C.: The Center for Early Adolescence.

Schön, D. A. (1983). *The reflective practitioner: How professionals think in action*. New York: Basic Books.

Schön, D. A. (1987). *Educating the reflective practitioner: Toward a new design for teaching and learning in the professions*. San Francisco: Jossey-Bass.

Schorr, L. B. (1988). *Within our reach: Breaking the cycle of disadvantage.* New York: Doubleday.

Shulman, L. S. (1986). Those who understand: Knowledge growth in teaching. *Educational Researcher XXX*: 4–14.

Silverman, R., Welty, W. H., and Lyon, S. (1991). *Case studies for teacher problem solving*. New York: McGraw-Hill.

Stevenson, C. (1992). *Teaching ten to fourteen year olds*. New York: Longman.

Sykes, G., and Bird, T. (1992). *Teacher education and the case idea*. East Lansing: Michigan State University, National Center for Research on Teacher Learning.

Valentine, J., Clark, D., Nickerson, N., and Keefe, J. (1981). *The middle level principalship: A survey of middle level principals and programs* (Vol. 1). Reston, VA: National Association of Secondary School Principals.

Wiles, J., and Bondi, J. (1993). *The essential middle school* (2nd ed.). New York: Macmillan.

CHAPTER 7

The Ideal Middle Level Teacher

Mary Ann Davies

> Middle level youngsters require special kinds of attention and teaching. Therefore, it is important that only the very best teachers—those who understand the subjects they teach and the development of early adolescents— be permitted to work with these dynamic youngsters. (National Association of Secondary School Principal's Council on Middle Level Education [NASSP], 1985, p. 13)

It takes a special kind of person to effectively teach 10- to 14-year-olds. Not all teachers find a match between the characteristics of these young people and their own needs. This chapter presents a portrait of the ideal middle level teacher.

Effective middle level teachers *choose* to teach this age (George, Stevenson, Thomason, and Beane, 1992; Lipsitz, 1984; Thomason and Grebing, 1990). Rather than ending up in the middle grades by default, they opt to be there because they enjoy these youngsters. They understand their students and thrive on the energy and enthusiasm generated from being among these "between-agers." A match exists between the teacher's disposition and the very nature of young adolescents. One often hears these teachers comment, "It helps to be just as squirrely as the kids."

The Carnegie Council on Adolescent Development reinforces these desirable teacher qualities in its document *Turning Points: Preparing American Youth for the 21st century*. It calls for middle level educators who "understand and want to teach young adolescents and find the middle grade school a rewarding place to work" (1989, p. 58). A national survey of 540 middle level teachers found that the two most frequently cited reasons for teaching were a "strong desire to work with young people" and a belief "that it is an important service" (Henson, Buttery, and Chissom, 1985, p. 15). Effective middle level teachers choose this age and believe they can make a difference. As a result, they do make a difference.

Research provides further insight on the ideal middle level teacher. A summary of the research-based characteristics of effective middle level teachers is found in table 1.

> The image of the competent middle school teacher that emerges from this research is thus a self-confident "personable" professional who demonstrates awareness of both student needs and varied learning strategies. While this image is not unlike that which emerges from "arm chair" listings of competencies, this image has the added validity of empirical research. (Johnston and Markle, 1986, p. 18)

Effective teachers are more than the sum total of these listed competencies. There exists a complex interaction between personal and professional characteristics. As shown in figure 1, a tree analogy helps illustrate the interaction between these behaviors. The personal qualities are like the roots of the tree. An extensive root system enables the tree to grow tall, strong, and branch out. Likewise, a teacher's "self-rootedness" and positive esteem support professional growth, enabling one to stand tall and firmly for young adolescents, to take risks in the classroom, and to model personal growth for students. May we follow Socrates words of wisdom, "Know thyself." Before teachers can believe in the worthiness of their students, they must first believe in themselves. This is the taproot of life. Self-knowledge feeds the root system and, thus, strengthens the entire tree.

Table 1
Summary of the Characteristics of
Effective Middle Level Teachers

Personal Qualities *Effective teachers*	Professional Characteristics *Effective teachers*
• Have positive self-concepts (1, 2, 5)	• Understand young adolescent developmental characteristics (1, 2, 3, 4)
• Display optimism (1,4, 5)	• Adapt curriculum and instruction to developmental needs (1, 2, 3, 4)
• Show enthusiasm (1, 4, 5)	• Address individual learning needs (1, 2, 3, 4, 5)
• Exhibit a good sense of humor (5)	• Use varied activities and materials (1, 2, 3, 4, 5)
• Demonstrate flexibility (1, 2, 5)	• Ask varied questions and promote thinking (1, 3, 4, 5)
• Act spontaneously (1, 5)	• Promote successful experiences (1, 2, 3, 4, 5)
• Demonstrate caring (1, 2, 4, 5)	• Teach communication skills (2, 4)
• Respect and accept others (1, 2, 4, 5)	• Evaluate fairly (2, 4, 5)
• Are good listeners and communicators (1, 2, 4, 5)	• Encourage self-responsibility (2, 3, 4, 5)
• Cooperate with others (2, 3, 4)	• Maintain classroom control (2, 3, 4, 5)
	• Monitor learning (1, 4, 5)
	• Structure instruction (1, 4, 5)
	• Easy to understand (4, 5)
	• Know subject matter (1, 2, 4, 5)
	• Self-evaluate for professional growth (2, 3, 4)

Research studies supporting identified characteristics (numbers in parentheses, above):
  1. Johnston and Markle, 1986
  2. National Middle School Association, 1981
  3. Walter and Fanslow, 1980
  4. National Association of Secondary School Principals, 1985
  5. Buckner and Bickel, 1991

Figure 1
Ideal Middle Level Teacher: An Analogy

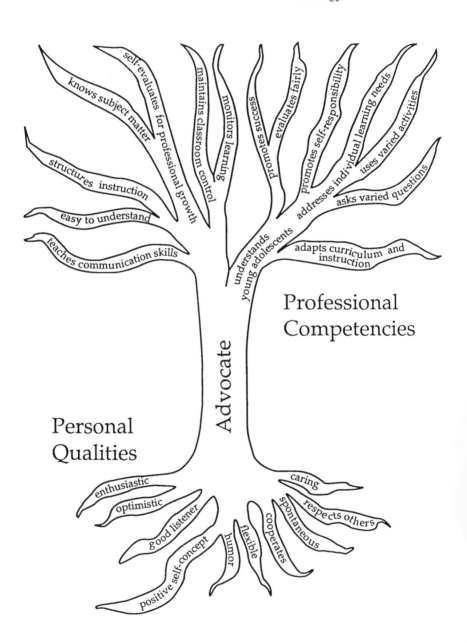

Personal Qualities: Who You Are
Is What You Teach

"Quality education in the middle grades requires quality teachers" (National Middle School Association [NMSA], 1981, p. 17). The developmental needs of young adolescents require teachers personally prepare to meet those needs. Periods of rapid change are stressful and *change* is a key descriptor of middle level students. The physical, emotional, social, and intellectual changes of young people inherently are stressful, requiring teachers capable of creating positive, supportive environments. Such support helps reduce the impact of developmental changes. In addition, these youngsters are seeking answers to the developmental question, "Who am I?" In attempting to answer this question, they look to adults for guidance. Thus, who you are as a teacher helps shape and support these young people.

Middle level students express greater concern over their teachers' personal qualities than their professional skills. Buckner and Bickel (1991) surveyed approximately 400 students in Grades 5–8 regarding the qualities of excellent middle school teachers. Almost two-thirds of the students felt that it was very important that their teachers "are willing to listen, are respectful toward students, accept students, are easy to talk with, demonstrate warmth and kindness, and are friendly" (p. 27). In another study, academically successful young adolescents typically described their preferred teachers as "nice." When students perceive their teachers as having positive affective qualities, they tend to experience greater academic success and satisfaction (Beane and Lipka, 1986).

Role Models: Walk What You Talk

John Lounsbury (1991) underscores the need for positive teacher role models.

> Paraphrasing a few lines from that familiar "Children Learn What They Live," by Dorothy Nolte, we can say if young adolescents are taught with ridicule, they learn to be shy, but if they are taught with tolerance, they learn to

be patient. If they are taught with criticism, they learn to condemn, but if they are taught with approval, they learn to like themselves. Character is like measles. It can only be caught by close contact with someone who has it." (p. 86)

Successful middle level teachers are aware that they serve as role models for young adolescents all the time, in and out of the classroom (George et al., 1992; Merenbloom 1988). Teaching character as much as content, these teachers monitor themselves and the messages they are conveying to these young people. They realize that the early adolescents' search for identity is very much colored by the character of the significant adults in their lives.

Sense of self. Positive modeling starts with the teacher's sense of self. Excellent middle level teachers display positive self-concepts (Buckner and Bickel, 1991; Johnston and Markle, 1986; NMSA, 1981). They "are secure, open, self-confident, and fully comfortable with kids and themselves" (Lounsbury, 1991, p. 41). They view life optimistically and live it enthusiastically. This positive view of self and life energizes them, making them "high on life." When faced with problems, they seek solutions. When faced with pain, they remember joy. When faced with the ups and downs of life, they live it fully and honestly, never avoiding that which challenges them to grow. An individual with high self-esteem is not afraid to say, "I don't know" or, "I could improve upon that." Modeling a positive self-concept assists young people in developing a positive sense of self.

Students relate best to teachers who display high self-esteem. Rozanne Sparks and Donald Rye (1990) found that eighth graders were satisfied most in classes taught by teachers who scored the highest on a self-concept scale and "who were enthusiastic, bold, group-oriented, relaxed, and extroverted" (p. 32). They concluded:

> [M]odeling is one of the most effective ways students learn so it could be assumed that the teacher who feels good about himself or herself and who expresses warmth, genuineness, and a congruency in communicating with students will be the most influential. (p. 33)

Significant adults with high self-esteem are positive influences in the lives of those shaping their own characters.

Sense of humor. A positive sense of self enables one to more readily laugh at himself or herself along with the foibles of the world. The ideal teacher looks for the comedy embedded within the apparent tragedy. When things seem to fall apart in the classroom, he or she resorts to "humor not holler." Nancy Doda, Paul George, and Ken McEwin (1987) postulate humor as one of the 10 "current truths" about effective middle schools: "Effective middle level teachers have a sense of humor" (p. 5). The teacher uses humor to redirect behavior and encourage and assist the young person in not "awfulizing" about the normal daily events of the student's life.

Playful—enjoys life. Along with a sense of humor, the effective teacher models taking time to play and enjoy life. Like the youngsters they teach, they look for opportunities to combine work and play. While teaching at Eastern Kentucky University's Model Laboratory School, my colleagues found many such opportunities. Teachers regularly dressed up as "punks," their favorite movie stars, etc., to surprise their students. After confiscating a forbidden water gun, a teacher opened fire on the offending student. Another colleague unexpectedly brought his entire class into my room during a lesson. Such playfulness guides students in maintaining balance in their own lives and encourages them to not lose sight of their childhood.

Flexible. Successful middle level teachers model flexibility (Buckner and Bickel, 1991; Johnston and Markle, 1986; NMSA, 1981). The demands of teaching young adolescents require flexibility in the classroom. If a lesson is not going well or if an incident occurs that captures students' emotions, ideal middle level teachers are prepared to shift gears and do that which best meets their students' immediate needs or interests. When the space shuttle Challenger exploded, the preplanned social studies lesson on the judicial branch was replaced quickly with an open forum for expression of emotional reactions. The adolescents' development of a healthy, emotional self requires opportunities to honestly express emotions.

Flexible teachers are open-minded, risk-takers, and act spontaneously. This means being willing to try something unusual, be creative, and look for the teachable moment. One teacher aptly describes his risk-taking, "I said things they didn't expect me to say, did things they didn't expect me to do, and asked them to do things they never expected to do in school" (Dyer, 1980, p. 3). Yes, it helps to be in tune with the kids!

Caring: Operate from the Heart

Effective middle level schools create environments of "pervasive caring" (George and Oldaker, 1985; Johnston and Markle, 1986). Joan Lipsitz's (1984) study of four exemplary middle schools concluded that "[S]uccessful schools insist on the common humanity of their inhabitants. They insist on the schools as community—and the students assent. . . . Most striking is the level of caring in the schools" (p. 181). These teachers are committed to young adolescents. They work hard to build a climate of mutual respect, trust, open communication, and acceptance of differences (George et al., 1992). A study of the "very best teams" in the "very best schools" reinforces the importance of caring teachers. It found that "[T]he most consistent characterization of teachers on the exemplary teams referred to the respect, understanding, and commitment teachers manifest in their relationships with their students" (George and Stevenson, 1989, p. 11).

Teachers demonstrate caring in many ways. For example, they create secure, positive classroom environments that nurture students' success and growth. They look for opportunities to interact with students outside of class at extracurricular activities, during lunch, before and after school, on field trips— anyway imaginable (Van Hoose and Strahan, 1988). These positive interactions carry over into the school day, building respect, trust, and special bonds. These teachers take advantage of what John Lounsbury termed *wayside* teaching (Lounsbury, 1991, p. 30), the teacher/student relationship that emerges from modeling and noninstructional interactions.

Caring teachers like young adolescents, understand their students, and enjoy talking to them. The words of an eighth grader capture these traits.

> My homeroom teacher is my favorite teacher. She is always nice in the morning when you come in. On Mondays she always asks about our weekends and tells us what she and her husband did. She knows a lot about plants and has spider plants all over the classroom. One time she brought in an orange cactus. A boy accidentally knocked it off the cabinet and all the dirt went everywhere. He was really scared that he was going to get in trouble cause she likes plants and all but she just laughed and said it was her fault for putting it in someone's way. Then the boy laughed too and they cleaned it up. The next day she brought the cactus back in new dirt and got the boy to find a safe place for it. At the end of the year she gives her plants away. (Van Hoose and Strahan, 1988, p. 34)

Effective teachers create symbols of caring. A sampling of these symbols are public display of students' work; awards and reinforcements; parties; special events, such as breakfasts or pot luck dinners; recognition of students through bulletin boards, newsletters, or some public forum; field trips, clubs; team names, logos, exchange programs; community service projects; warm and inviting classrooms; peer teaching/tutoring; and tee shirts— anything to build a sense of community. These teachers look for ways to demonstrate caring.

The ideal middle level teacher also communicates caring by remembering what it was like to be a 10- to 14-year-old. These memories evoke empathy, and empathic teachers relate more effectively to young people. Teachers operating from the heart touch more hearts.

The poetic words of one early adolescent underscore the need for such understanding.

> There's a time for us in life
> that no one understands.
> We grow and change in
> many ways and later find
> out why.
> We face new problems
> every day and sometimes
> it's just so unbearable
> We have to break down
> and cry.

During these times there
are good and bad
And we hope our parents
will just understand,
For what is happening to us
cannot be controlled,
No matter what we are told.
So bear with us,
grow with us,
learn to love us through it. (Ricken, 1987, pp. 2–3)

Teachers who compassionately identify with their students foster this same quality in them (Healy, 1987). Early adolescence provides a developmental opportunity for nurturing empathy. It is a critical period of neural development in the prefrontal cortex (Healy, 1987), the area of the brain responsible for a wide variety of adaptive behaviors, including putting oneself in another's shoes (Caine and Caine, 1991; Restak, 1984). Not using these newly established connections can result in atrophy (Golton, 1983). Our world cannot afford dispassionate future generations. Development of the prefrontal cortex provides hope for addressing the increasingly complex problems of the world with compassion and empathy. Excellent middle level teachers nurture this hope.

"Effective middle school teachers work to weasel their way into the hearts of the young adolescents they teach" (Doda, George, and McEwin, 1987, p. 5). They reach out and touch their students. They accept them as they are—in all their moods. They encourage them to seek their dreams and reach for the sky— becoming the best person they can.

Cooperative: Together We Make a Difference

Effective middle level teachers collaborate with colleagues, administrators, and parents to better meet the needs of the students they teach (Zorfass and Remz, 1992). The team structure facilitates this process. In *Turning Points* (1989), the Carnegie Council recommends that middle level teachers "learn to work as members of a team" (p. 59).

Paul George and Chris Stevenson's (1989) study of the "very best teams" provides insight regarding the characteristics of effective team members. Principals described these teachers as "personally mature," willing to work with others, supportive of colleagues, accepting of differences, good listeners and communicators, willing to compromise, hard workers, and individuals whose "egos were under control, who understood and respected the complexity of their work, who weren't competing with their teammates and other colleagues" (p. 12).

These same skills aid them in effectively collaborating with parents. Together, they work towards the mutual goal of helping the young person grow. These teachers regularly communicate with parents via positive phone calls, newsletters, progress reports, parent/teacher conferences, and home visits. In addition, they seek ways to bring parents and the community into the educational process, e.g., guest speakers, mentors, chaperones, aides, family homework assignments, and parenting workshops.

Ideal teachers cooperate with others. By modeling cooperation, they assist young adolescents in both valuing cooperation and in developing collaborative skills. These skills, in turn, promote their social development.

Professional Characteristics

A number of teaching competencies are associated with effective middle level teaching. Although early adolescents place greater importance on the personal qualities of teachers, they are quick to recognize perceived deficiencies in professional character- istics. Successful teachers display the following competencies.

Understand Young Adolescent Development

The emergence of the middle school movement stems from a perceived need to create more developmentally responsive schools for young adolescents. Students in this age group experience developmental growth in all aspects of their being:

physical, intellectual, social, and emotional. No other period of human development, except that immediately after birth, is characterized by such dramatic changes. These developmental characteristics make early adolescents unique. Effective middle level teachers understand this uniqueness (Johnston and Markle, 1986; NASSP, 1985; NMSA, 1981; Walter and Fanslow, 1980).

Successful teachers recognize that all middle level students are *at risk* as a result of developmental and societal changes (Butte, 1993; Ruff, 1993; Wylie, 1992). They use teaching strategies that challenge and promote success with all students rather than selectively labeling students (Taylor and Reeves, 1993; Xenos-Whiston and Leroux, 1992).

Adapt Curriculum and Instruction to Developmental Needs

Effective middle level teachers not only understand the developmental characteristics of early adolescents but also adapt their instruction to better meet these needs. They address physical needs by incorporating opportunities for movement into instruction and deemphasizing competitiveness in physical education and sports. These teachers use cooperative learning, games, and other strategies to enable youngsters to move frequently and, thus, reduce some of the discomfort associated with rapid physical growth. They also help these between-agers understand and accept their rapidly changing bodies.

The ideal teacher understands that middle schoolers largely are concrete thinkers who are beginning to develop the ability to manipulate abstractions.

> Successful teachers "build" concepts. They often begin with opportunities for students to think about what they already know about the topic and activities that build motivation and set induction. For example, one teacher observed began a lesson on "balancing equations" with a discussion of balance. When one student suggested that "you have to balance on a balance beam," the teacher asked him to come to the front of the class and demonstrate walking on a thin line. She then asked students to describe what they saw. Several students

suggested that when he leaned one way, he had to put his arm the other way. They defined *balance* as "evening things out." She then used a balance scale and weights to demonstrate a different type of balance. Students then defined *balance* as "keeping both sides even." At this point, the teacher demonstrated how to balance several equations. Students then generated a mathematical definition. In this lesson, they did not start reading and answering questions until they had generated the critical concept they needed for success. (Van Hoose and Strahan, 1988, p. 42)

Lessons facilitate understanding by bringing "students as close to the real thing as possible" (Doda et al., 1987, p. 5). They include hands-on activities, multisensory experiences, relevant examples, pictures, videos/movies, simulations, and field trips.

Effective teachers are sensitive to the social and emotional needs of students. They nurture a positive self-concept and provide opportunities for young people to develop a sense of identity. These professionals look for ways to assist early adolescents in exploring the questions that are most important to them.

Will you teach me how to sail,
through space upon a comet's tail?
Will you teach me how to fly,
to sail the skies on wings untried?
Will you teach me how to soar,
to see things never seen before?
But most importantly of all,
Will you teach me how to fall?
Will you teach me how to cry?
to release feelings deep inside?
Will you teach me how to laugh,
and travel off the beaten path?
Will you teach me how to dream,
to face the future sight-unseen?
Will you teach me how to be,
the only thing I can be,
me. (Ricken, 1987, p.28)

Address individual learning needs. An understanding of the developmental diversity of this age group drives successful teachers to adapt instruction to meet these varied needs (DeLeon, 1992; Vatterott and Yard, 1993). They vary questions, offer choices in assignments, create learning centers, use contracts and learning activity packages, and stay sensitive to each student's needs. When asked, middle level students said that excellent teachers "are aware some students need extra help and take more time for those who need it when explaining things" (Buckner and Bickel, 1991, p. 28).

Use varied activities and materials. Effective schools' research stresses the importance of using a variety of teaching strategies (Johnston and Markle, 1986). Varied instructional approaches motivate students and address differences in learning styles, thus setting them up for success. Changing activities three to four times in a class period acknowledges students' developmentally short attention spans.

Ask varied questions/promote thinking. Teachers address different learning needs and levels of cognitive development by varying the questions asked. They ask questions that move students from the recollection of facts to higher levels of thinking. Their questions foster independent learning and lifelong learning skills. These teachers recognize the need to assist young adolescents in coping with a rapidly changing world by teaching them how to learn. "Because we cannot teach them all they need to know, we must teach them how to learn and how to adjust their lives to the changes that will surround them" (NASSP, 1985, p.1). This means teaching problem-solving, self-monitoring skills, and a broad repertoire of learning strategies.

Promote successful experiences. Excellent teachers assure that all students have an equal chance of achieving success. This requires addressing their varied needs. By providing "achievable challenges" (George et al., 1992), students do better and, in turn, feel better about themselves. Students are recognized publicly for many different achievements, and evaluations focus on students' progress and what they can do. These teachers believe in their students and know that success breeds success.

Teach communication skills. Part of assuring successful experiences means providing students with the requisite skills. This includes teaching them how to speak, listen, read, and write effectively. All teachers share the responsibility of assisting students in mastering these skills (NASSP, 1985; NMSA, 1981).

Promote self-responsibility. Effective schools provide opportunities for developing student responsibility (Johnston and Markle, 1986). Teachers in these schools nurture self-discipline, offer choices, teach self-evaluation and goal-setting skills, make themselves dispensable, teach decision-making, and seek student input in curricular decisions. They know developing responsibility requires practice, so they offer students many practice opportunities.

Maintain classroom control. Successful teachers know that young adolescents "value order, consistency, and fair play" (George et al., 1992, p. 21). They meet their students' need for a safe environment by establishing clear rules and procedures and by consistently enforcing them. This consistency creates a climate wherein students know what to expect and, thus, feel more secure. These teachers model trust and fairness by providing for student input in rule-making and emphasizing choices and consequences in students' actions. The clear boundaries of their classrooms aid students in developing self-discipline—an important developmental goal.

Monitor learning. Effective schools' research supports the importance of monitoring learning in order to enhance achievement (Johnston and Markle, 1986). Excellent middle level instructors teach on their feet. This enables them to better keep students at task, assess the need for modifying instruction, and actively involve students.

Structure instruction. Lessons with a clear purpose, direction, and organized structure facilitate learning. Think of examples of teachers from your own experiences who made learning easier or more difficult. Have you ever attended a class where the instructor rambled on and on? Where you were unsure what was important and how to prepare for tests? If you answered "yes," then your experiences help you understand how a poorly organized lesson interferes with learning.

In addition to organization, effective teachers structure their lessons to move from concrete to more abstract examples. By building concepts upon the foundation of students' prior knowledge, they enhance meaningfulness and understanding

(Buckner and Bickel, 1991; Johnston and Markle, 1986; Van Hoose and Strahan, 1988; Woolfolk, 1993).

Easy to understand. Young adolescents value teachers who are clear, relate learning to their lives, and adapt instruction to their varied learning needs. This requires a thorough understanding of how early adolescents think. It means being aware of their interests and feelings. What do your students like to do in their free time? What movies or videos do they watch? What things are most important to them at this point in their lives? Recall your own early adolescent years and *think* like your students. Now you are easier to understand (Buckner and Bickel, 1991; Lipsitz, 1984; NASSP, 1985)!

Know subject matter. At a time in their lives when their cognitive development begins enabling them to think abstractly, young adolescents expect their teachers to be knowledgeable about their subjects. Driven by curiosity and a need to better understand the world around them, they turn to teachers for answers. Teachers whose responses avoid oversimplification and highlight the interconnectedness of the world are respected for their knowledge (Buckner and Bickel, 1991; Johnston and Markle, 1986; NASSP, 1985; NMSA, 1981).

Self-Evaluate for Professional Growth

Teaching, like learning, requires continuous self-assessment in order to sustain its dynamic nature. Successful teachers use reflection to better meet the needs of their students. The following steps serve to guide teacher reflection:

> First, teachers should be encouraged to trust their own judgments about what kind of instructional treatments students require at any given time. Lock-step approaches to teaching should be avoided. Second, teachers should be skilled in reading student feedback and adjusting their feedback, quickly, on the basis of that feedback. Further, they must be encouraged to evaluate each approach they use and reflect thoughtfully on their performance each day. Finally, teachers must have the opportunity to discuss their teaching with other professionals in a nonevaluative setting. This means that groups of teachers

should meet for the expressed purpose of talking about their teaching in their context with their students. (Johnston and Markle, 1986, p. 7)

The ideal teacher sees continued personal and professional growth as the key to successful teaching. Reflection acts as the fuel that fires such growth.

ACT: Advocates Can Together

Excellent middle level teachers take proactive roles in assuring that early adolescent developmental needs are met. These teachers believe they *do* make a difference in the lives of young people. Their inner strengths and professional skills enable them to stand tall and effect change. They act as advocates for between-agers.

Comments of middle level educators in a graduate program at Western Michigan University underscore the characteristics of middle school advocates.

- "An effective middle grades advocate must truly believe in the middle school philosophy."
- "Commitment to 'what is best for kids' is required."
- "The advocate must practice what is preached."
- "Be able to work effectively with staff and students. Be able to take risks in order to experiment with new techniques."
- "Values parent and community support and involvement. This furthers the understanding of the importance of middle level education."
- "You must be willing and able to urge, cajole, lobby, and push the school system to improve its program so that it fully meets the needs of those it seeks to serve. One must speak forcefully, knowledgeably, and articulately."
- "A middle school advocate is compassionate, which ties in with being knowledgeable about adolescents."
- "It takes a great deal of knowledge and enthusiasm to be an effective middle grades advocate."
- "I absolutely LOVE what I'm doing!"

Advocates look for ways to support appropriate education for young adolescents. Their actions range from seeking to better meet the needs of students in their classes to promoting major schoolwide reforms. Advocates believe they *can* make a difference. As a result, they *do* make a difference.

Summary

Ideal middle level teachers combine personal qualities and professional characteristics that assist young adolescents in their development. Their students place a high value on the kind of people they are. Effective teachers model a positive self-concept, optimism, enthusiasm, flexibility, spontaneity, cooperation, communication skills, and sense of humor. They operate from the heart, letting young people know that they care for and respect them. These teachers model qualities that match with young adolescents' developmental needs.

In addition, successful middle level educators display professional characteristics that enable them to adapt instruction to the developmental characteristics of this age group. They recognize the diversity of their students by teaching with variety. Effective teachers create safe and orderly classroom environments that facilitate the development of self-responsibility. Furthermore, they promote student success by teaching in a clear and organized manner, monitoring learning, and being knowledgeable in their subject matters. These teachers challenge students and assist them in meeting their expectations by fostering skill development. Excellent teachers promote student growth through fair evaluative feedback and model self-evaluation skills.

Ideal middle level teachers blend personal and professional growth to nurture the development of the young people in their care. Teachers who feel they have no more to learn, have nothing more to offer.

REFERENCES

Beane, J., and Lipka, R. (1986). *Self-concept, self-esteem, and the curriculum.* New York: Teachers College Press.

Butte, H. (1993). Developing curriculum to reduce emotional stress in middle schoolers. *Middle School Journal* 24(4): 41–46.

Buckner, J. H., and Bickel, F. (1991). If you want to know about effective teaching, why not ask your middle school kids? *Middle School Journal,* 22(3): 26–29.

Caine, R. N., and Caine, G. (1991). *Making connections: Teaching and the human brain.* Alexandria, VA: Association for Supervision and Curriculum Development.

Carnegie Council on Adolescent Development. (1989). *Turning points: Preparing American youth for the 21st century.* Washington, DC: Author.

DeLeon, J. (1992). Let the students' voices be heard! *Middle School Journal* 23(5): 27–30.

Doda, N., George, P., and McEwin, K. (1987). The current truths about effective schools. *Middle School Journal* 18(3): 3–5.

Dyer, D. (1980). You gotta be crazy to teach. *Middle School Journal* 11(2): 3–5, 24.

George, P., and Oldaker, L. L. (1985). *Evidence for the middle school.* Columbus, OH: National Middle School Association.

George, P. S., and Stevenson, C. (1989). The "very best teams" in "the very best schools" as described by middle school principals. *TEAM* 3(5): 6–14.

George, P. S., Stevenson, C., Thomason, J., and Beane, J. (1992). *The middle school and beyond.* Alexandria, VA: Association for Supervision and Curriculum Development.

Golton, M. A. (1983). *Your brain at work: A new view of personality and behavior.* New York: Frank Publications.

Healy, J. M. (1987). *Your child's growing mind.* New York: Doubleday.

Henson, K. T., Buttery, T. J., and Chissom, B. (1985). The middle school teacher as a member of the community. *Middle School Journal* 16(4): 13–15.

Johnston, J. H., and Markle, G. C. (1986). *What research says to the middle level practitioner.* Columbus, OH: National Middle School Association.

Lipsitz, J. (1984). *Successful schools for young adolescents*. New Brunswick: Transition Books.

Lounsbury, J. H. (1991). *As I see it*. Columbus, OH: National Middle School Association.

Merenbloom, E. Y. (1988). *Developing effective middle schools through faculty participation*. Columbus, OH: National Middle School Association.

National Association of Secondary School Principal's Council on Middle Level Education. (1985). *An agenda for excellence at the middle level*. Reston, VA: National Association of Secondary School Principals.

National Middle School Association Position Paper Committee. (1981). Preparing teachers for the middle grades. *Middle School Journal* 12(4): 17–19.

Restak, R. (1984). *The brain*. New York: Bantam Books.

Ricken, R. (1987). *Love me when I'm most unlovable*. Reston, VA: National Association of Secondary School Principals.

Ruff, T. P. (1993). Middle school students at risk: What do we do with the most vulnerable children in American education? *Middle School Journal* 24(5): 10–12.

Sparks, R., and Rye, D. R. (1990). Teacher self-esteem and personality: The major ingredient in teacher-student relationships. *Middle School Journal* 22(1): 32–33.

Taylor, R., and Reeves, V. (1993). More is better: Raising expectations for students at risk. *Middle School Journal* 24(5): 13–18.

Thomason, J. T., and Grebing, W. (1990). *We who laugh last*. Columbus, OH: National Middle School Association.

Van Hoose, J. V., and Strahan, D. (1988). *Young adolescent development and school practices: Promoting harmony*. Columbus, OH: National Middle School Association.

Vatterott, C., and Yard, G. J. (1993). Accommodating individual differences through instructional adaptations. *Middle School Journal* 24(5): 23–28.

Walter, J. M., and Fanslow, A. M. (1980). Professional competencies for middle school teachers. *Middle School Journal* 11(3): 23–24, 29.

Woolfolk, A. (1993). *Educational psychology*. Needham Heights, MA: Allyn and Bacon.

Wylie, V. L. (1992). The risk in being average. *Middle School Journal* 23(4): 33–35.

Xenos-Whiston, M., and Leroux, J. A. (1992). Gifted education: Isn't this good for all children? *Middle School Journal* 23(4): 36–39.

Zorfass, J., and Remz, A. R. (1992). Successful technology integration: The role of communication and collaboration. *Middle School Journal* 23(5): 39–43.

CHAPTER 8

Leadership in the Middle Level School

Beverly Reed and Charles Russell

Middle school leadership requires both general leadership skills and behaviors—those practiced by effective leaders everywhere, in both school and nonschool settings—and those specifically appropriate to the middle school. As a result, this chapter is organized into three distinct sections.

Section one draws on some of the "popular" business literature to identify characteristics of effective leaders in business and to generalize those characteristics to the school setting. Although the authors do not subscribe to the idea that schools should be operated "like a business," they do believe that school leaders can learn much from the business community.

The second section identifies leadership skills and behaviors specifically applicable to the middle school. The authors have attempted to go beyond general school issues and focus on those suited to the unique needs of middle level leaders. Finally, section three relates "tips" offered by outstanding practicing middle school administrators and other practitioners.

The authors intend that the organization and content of this chapter will make a clear link between theory and practice and will demonstrate that middle level leadership can—and should—be exhibited by a wide range of people, including central office staff, building administrators, teachers, parents, students, and community members. Indeed, all of these groups should see it as their responsibility to *share* leadership in the middle level school.

The reader will find little in this chapter addressing the traditional role of the administrator (planning, organizing, supervising, etc.). The first reason for this is the belief that leadership is not an *administrative* function but, as indicated in the preceding paragraph, rather a function to be shared by many in the effective middle school. Second, this traditional view of administration/leadership is, in fact, embedded in the three sections of this chapter; it is simply not offered as a recipe-type approach to leadership.

The Business Connection

In Search of Excellence

The first business connection is the classic *In Search of Excellence: Lessons from America's Best-Run Companies* (Peters and Waterman, 1982), which identified eight characteristics of effective companies. Peters and Waterman pointed out that excellence in a particular company is not necessarily marked by the presence of *all eight* but rather by a *preponderance* of the characteristics.

A bias for action. Companies displaying this characteristic are marked by informal, simple communication; organizational flexibility, which allows and encourages people to try a lot of ideas; management by wandering around (MBWA, more informal communication); and work teams comprised of volunteers who set their own goals. Organizations with a bias for action do not spend a lot of time trying to overcome employees' resistance. They focus, instead, on finding out what people are ready to do and then let the organization's action be influenced by this readiness. Problems are converted to manageable "chunks" then attacked vigorously.

A school must first answer the question of whether it *wants* to have a bias for action. (Bureaucracies are known for maintaining the status quo, not for encouraging and supporting change.) If a school does want to encourage such behavior, it should look at how it communicates, organizes, tackles problems, and encourages its faculty and staff.

Communication should be simple and informal. Write short memos instead of longer, policy-type statements full of jargon; communicate orally as you pass in the hall or talk in the faculty lounge; allow faculty meetings to become forums for real discussion and problem-solving; and do not worry too much about "chain of command" issues, but, rather, promote the regular exchange of information.

Organization should be flexible and should support attempts at improvement, even when they fail. Encourage work teams that form voluntarily and spontaneously, set their own goals, and may exist for a limited time.

Break large problems into manageable chunks and encourage teams or individuals to attack each chunk with a variety of ideas, approaches, and resources. Schools often are paralyzed into inactivity because of the magnitude of their problems.

Focus on people's strengths and willingness to try to improve. Avoid focusing on their weaknesses and resistance to change.

Close to the customer. Companies displaying this characteristic are marked by an obsession with quality and service. They are intolerant of any failure to serve the customer and view their customers as their first priority.

Schools that follow this precept will make decisions based on what is best for students (*then* on what works for teachers). They will insist on high quality in *all* services provided to both students (teaching, curriculum, facilities, psychological environment, etc.) and employees (salaries, materials, job security, supervision, etc.). Finally, schools should refuse to accept failure as the final effort by employees and by students.

Autonomy and entrepreneurship. Companies exhibiting this characteristic encourage innovation and creativity, promote informal—but intense—communication, support champions of new ideas, and are tolerant of failure when it represents an effort to improve.

While this characteristic may seem unrelated to school leadership, it is not. Schools have the opportunity to

- Encourage and protect innovators, even when a particular attempt fails, as long as the innovation is an effort to improve the school's performance or that of individuals in the school.
- Promote follow-through on new ideas.
- Reward efforts to improve on the assumption that many attempts will lead to some improvement.
- Communicate informally, but intensely, keeping everyone informed of new ideas.

Failure to encourage innovators and innovation may lead to a stagnant school that survives on reputation and history rather than on creativity and improvement.

Productivity through people. The successful companies see that their success is a result of the people who work for them. As a result, they treat employees with respect and dignity, as partners in the enterprise—as *adults*. At the same time, expectations and accountability are extremely high. People-oriented language and a sense of "family" are prevalent.

Schools can develop this same people orientation by viewing *all* employees as the school's greatest resource and treating them with dignity and respect, as *partners* in the school's mission. Schools can hold all employees to high standards of performance and accountability but must set reasonable goals so that the school can have many "winners" rather than a few "stars." They can encourage the practice of MBWA, promoting a loose chain of command in daily communication. Finally, schools can look for reasons to celebrate even small successes and provide positive reinforcement.

Hands-on, value-driven. The companies that display this characteristic have a clear idea of what their institution stands for. Their values are stated in qualitative, not quantitative terms. Efforts are made to inspire and create pride even in those employees at the very bottom of the organization. Leaders make a personal commitment to the values they wish to impart to others.

Schools choosing to make this commitment must first agree on the values that will drive the organization—not short-term goals, but those for which the school wants to be known in 10 or 20 years. Once this has been done, schools should

- Prominently display that which is valued (slogans, newsletters, banners, posters, letterheads, etc.) so that the values become known to all.
- Instill pride in and commitment to those values in all school employees, then in students, parents, and the community.
- Practice MBWA.
- Choose innovation over the status quo if the innovation advances the school's values.
- Choose informality over formality.
- Choose people over "control."
- Be sure those in leadership positions have a personal commitment to the school's values and that they exhibit those values in their everyday dealings with students, staff, and parents.

Stick to the knitting. Successful companies focus on those things they do well, those things identified in their values. They do not try to be "all things to all people."

Successful schools will behave similarly. They will be "value-driven" and will not attempt those things that are not derived from their values. If a middle school believes in homogeneous grouping, classes will be organized in that manner. If it believes that interscholastic athletics are incongruent with the values of a middle school, it will educate its public to that value and will refuse to accommodate those who believe differently.

Simple form, lean staff. Companies that exhibit this characteristic have an organizational structure that provides for stability, entrepreneurship, and innovation. While these characteristics might seem contradictory for both businesses and schools, they are not. A school's organizational structure must provide a stable environment to ensure that the school's mission and purpose are always kept in the forefront. At the same time, that structure should foster innovative ways to achieve the mission and purpose through its flexibility, informality, lack of attention to chain-of-command issues, trust in and attention to people, and bias for action.

Simultaneous loose-tight properties. Successful companies are marked by a loose structure that is informal, flexible, and people oriented. However, their culture and values provide discipline and control and assure that everyone has the "big picture" of where the organization is headed.

Schools should work toward clear goals and purposes; a culture focusing on these goals and purposes; informal, flexible structure; regular communication; peer pressure, to ensure compliance with the school's mission and its attention to excellence; quick feedback; concise paperwork; and a consistent focus on what is best for the student.

Many of these eight characteristics will be difficult for schools. Some of the eight are even antithetical to the typical school bureaucracy. Yet there is much in *In Search of Excellence* for schools to learn. Those schools that attempt to do so should keep in mind a warning from Peters and Waterman. While the eight characteristics appear to be "motherhood and apple pie" issues, the reason they are not such simplistic issues in the excellent companies is the *intensity* with which these companies execute them. Schools would be advised that they must pursue these characteristics vigorously, not just paying lip service and saying words that are not supported by commitment.

ZAPP! The Lightning of Empowerment

The second business reference is *ZAPP! The Lightning of Empowerment* (Byham and Cox, 1990). The authors of this little book encouraged leaders to make work *personally* important to people by sharing with them responsibility, authority, identity, energy, and power.

Byham and Cox identified a four-step process to accomplish this:

1. Maintain people's self-esteem.
2. Listen and respond with empathy.
3. Ask for help in solving problems; get ideas, information, and suggestions from others.
4. Offer help without taking responsibility.

Again, these are not always easy to practice in the school setting. But the value of ZAPPing people (students, staff, and parents) appears to be self-evident.

The 7 Habits of Highly Effective People

A third business reference is *The 7 Habits of Highly Effective People* (Covey, 1989). As the title suggests, Covey identified seven behaviors that characterize effective people.

Be proactive. Effective people are self-aware and accept responsibility for their own lives. They take the initiative, place their values above their feelings, and learn from their mistakes. They clearly see that behavior is a function of *decisions,* not conditions. All of these characteristics give them the opportunity to develop *personal vision.*

School leaders who see themselves as victims of circumstances, rather than as actors who have choices and who can initiate action, are unlikely to be effective. Personal vision, which allows school leaders to see that the future can be shaped by decisions, is necessary for effective leadership. This point should not be lost on those who select middle school leaders; they should look for proactiveness in prospective teachers and administrators.

Begin with the end in mind. Effective people can "see" the end they have in mind. They understand that all things are created twice—first mentally, then physically. They know that leadership is based on *imagination* and *conscience* and that leadership (doing the right things) takes precedence. Deeply held principles lead to a personal mission statement, which provides security, guidance, wisdom, and power. All of this allows the effective person to develop *personal leadership.*

All of the attention to mission statements and the like is intended to get leaders and others to "see" the ideal, to have the "end in mind." Someone has said, "If you don't know where you're going, you may end up somewhere else." This is a trap into which many schools, and school leaders, fall. Beginning with the end in mind will allow them to take the necessary steps to arrive at the desired destination; otherwise, they are operating randomly, without purpose or direction.

Put first things first. This habit allows one to fulfill the vision created through habits one and two. If leadership is doing the right things, this habit represents the *management* function— doing things right. This habit allows a person to organize and execute around priorities; to do things that need to be done, even when those things are tedious or unpleasant; and to focus on things that are important but not urgent. Based on independent will, this habit is the key to *personal management*.

School administrators are notorious for being crisis managers—for dealing with what is urgent but not necessarily important. Obviously, doing things right presumes that one has first determined what needs to be done. Too often in schools leaders lose sight of their priorities and drift through the day randomly, dealing with one event after another. Practicing putting first things first will overcome this tendency.

Think win/win. Effective people look for ways to resolve situations so that everyone wins. This habit grows out of an understanding that development of *character* leads to the development of *relationships*, which in turn leads to mutually acceptable *agreements*. This habit leads to *interpersonal leadership*.

Schools easily can become adversarial environments where administrators fight with teachers, teachers fight with students, school personnel fight with parents, etc. Someone must win and someone must lose in each of these relationships. Once the participants in these games understand that *character* should be the driving force in these relationships—that people should behave based on what is right instead of what will allow them to defeat their adversaries—they will work sincerely to reach agreements that are satisfactory to all.

Seek first to understand, then to be understood. Empathic listening should precede speaking because it provides understanding for you and affirmation and validation to the other party. Development of this habit creates *empathic communication*.

In schools it is easy for listening to become little more than waiting for one's next opportunity to speak. This obviously is not the way to create real understanding and to encourage the sincere exchange of ideas. Covey encourages leaders to diagnose before they prescribe and to avoid autobiographical responses, which tend to invalidate others' experiences. This habit has implications for administrators who are dealing with students, teachers, other staff members, parents, community members, and other administrators.

Synergize. This habit teaches that the whole is greater than the sum of its parts. Effective people value the mental, emotional, and psychological differences in people. Once they understand that all people (including themselves) see the world through their own set of experiences, they can begin to appreciate those experiences and realize that the truth is much more likely to lie somewhere within the total set of experiences than in a single person's experience. This realization leads to problem-solving through habits four and five and to *creative cooperation.*

School leaders, no different from other people, are influenced greatly by their own experiences and find it difficult to place as much confidence in other people's experiences. Once this habit is mastered, however, the synergy in communication, classrooms, and schools becomes obvious. Effective school leaders then begin to look for real alternative solutions to problems, not those that call for either/or solutions or compromise choices.

Sharpen the saw. This is Covey's label for maintaining personal physical, social/emotional, spiritual, and mental fitness. Every self-respecting school person pays homage to the value of in-service, even though genuine personal renewal often takes a back seat to the everyday demands of day-to-day work responsibilities. Covey's idea of keeping ourselves properly sharpened is that we must be just as committed to spending time on personal renewal as on job and family. By doing so, we actually begin to develop more productive relationships at home and at work.

These seven habits seem to be just as appropriate for developing effectiveness in school leaders as in business leaders. All seven are *learned* behaviors that can be mastered by anyone willing to invest the time and effort.

The Fifth Discipline

Our final reference from the business literature is *The Fifth Discipline: The Art and Practice of the Learning Organization* (Senge, 1990). Senge contended that we need to build *learning organizations*—those organizations that have a commitment to and a capacity for learning. Before he identified the five disciplines that allow and encourage the development of such organizations, he identified certain learning disabilities that may be present in an organization. Among these are the following:

- The "I am my position" syndrome, which leads to narrow, individual thinking and learning and failure to see one's role in the larger organization. For example, principals may see their role as "just" a principal, without really understanding how they fit into the school, school system, community, etc. They may fail to recognize that the decisions they make affect not only students and teachers in their own building, but also those in other buildings as well as custodians, parents, other administrators, etc.

- The "enemy is out there" syndrome, which attributes all problems to other internal or external agents, ignoring the impact of one's own decisions. In education it is easy to blame the superintendent, school board, state education office, parents, etc., without ever looking inwardly for causes of problems and solutions to those problems.

- A fixation on events, which causes a constant focus on the short term. Schools regularly look for simple cause-effect relationships to explain problems, without understanding that most problems are not "event"-related but are instead the result of slow, gradual processes.

- The myth of the management team leads organizations to believe that, because they can resolve simple issues, teams also can resolve complex issues. When confronted with really difficult problems, teams usually work toward compromise or advocacy rather than resolution. They begin to squelch disagreement, protect their turf, and avoid stating reservations and looking bad. All school people have had experiences with teams that produced compromise agreements that satisfied no one but offered everyone something, or those in which team members would not openly voice disagreement and reservations but later disavowed their part in the team's decision.

Senge contended that the five learning disciplines can overcome these and other organizational disabilities and can lead to healthy, growing, and productive organizations. The disciplines are outlined below.

Personal mastery. In Senge's view this is the spiritual foundation of the learning organization. It requires each individual to clarify and deepen personal vision, focus energies, develop patience, learn to see reality objectively—to become *proficient*. Compulsory training is not a solution to developing personal mastery, which must come from a sincere desire to improve.

Schools can foster personal mastery by creating a climate in which:

- Personal growth is valued.
- Proficiency is acknowledged and rewarded.
- It is safe for people to create visions.
- Inquiry and commitment to the truth are the norm.
- Challenging the status quo is expected.
- All leaders serve as models of personal mastery.
- All five learning disciplines are actively developed.

Mental models. Individuals must verbalize openly the assumptions and generalizations that describe how they perceive the world and that determine why they behave as they do. By exposing these "mental models" of their world and discussing them openly, individuals have the opportunity to discover limitations in their own models and develop new models incorporating their own thinking and that of others.

Schools, like other organizations, must encourage people to understand that there are many perceptions of truth and that exposing and discussing the various perceptions provides an opportunity for organizations to learn. All of us have been in situations in which progress could not be made because the participants all desperately held on to their own set of assumptions and generalizations. It is a human tendency to believe that our own view of the world is factual, but stubborn adherence to such beliefs clearly limits the growth of the individual and the organization.

Building shared vision. This refers to genuine commitment to and enrollment in some shared picture of the future, as opposed to compliance and lip service to some vision/mission statement imposed upon people. A truly shared vision provides the focus and energy for learning in the organization, encouraging each individual and group to learn whatever is necessary to achieve the vision.

Schools should create visions that clearly are understood and widely accepted by teachers, other staff, students, parents, and administrators. Once this is accomplished, the vision will drive actions and decisions within the school. This is not an easy task, since persons in the school must come to believe that they can shape their own future and can generate change instead of merely reacting to it. (Note how important the first two disciplines and the next two are in helping create this belief.)

Team learning. Senge defined this as dialogue that leads to thinking aloud together, to recognizing patterns of interactions that undermine learning. He distinguished between *discussion* (presenting and defending ideas in order to select the best one) and *dialogue* (listening carefully and suspending one's own views). Although we tend to be more skillful at the former than the latter, the fact is that we need to practice both.

Schools that want to develop skills in this discipline must help people understand the difference between discussion and dialogue and must provide opportunities for people to practice both, especially dialogue.

Systems thinking. This fifth discipline is the key discipline that integrates the other disciplines and allows people to see the *whole.* Without systems thinking, we see our organization and our world as sets of unrelated people and activities. With systems thinking, we begin to see how actions and events are interrelated, how our own actions create our problems and can also create solutions, how people can become active participants in shaping their reality, and how we can overcome the organizational learning disabilities mentioned earlier. Viewing the world as a set of interrelated systems causes people to see the importance of personal mastery, the value of mental models, the power of shared vision and team learning.

If schools are to become learning organizations, they must come to understand that decisions made in the third grade have implications for high school teachers and students. Decisions made in the school affect the community (in the long term if not the short), and actions taken by principals have an impact on the lives of teachers, students, parents, and others.

Senge pointed out that these could be called *leadership disciplines* instead of learning disciplines. Effective leaders spend lifetimes developing conceptual and communication skills, reflecting on personal values, aligning personal behavior with those values, learning to listen, learning to appreciate others and their ideas, and being committed to the truth. Without these characteristics, leaders have style without substance and cripple organizations by making people less able to think for themselves and to make wise choices.

Senge proposed that these learning disciplines will move us from the view of the leader as *hero*—setting direction, making key decisions, energizing the troops—to a view of the leader as the

- *Designer* of the organization as a learning organization, integrating all five disciplines and creating learning processes for people to develop mastery of the disciplines.
- *Steward* of the real vision and purpose of the organization—the keeper of the flame. Although the vision and purpose may be constantly evolving, the leader has the role of being responsible for the vision and purpose without being possessive of them.
- *Teacher* who fosters learning in all; who helps people see reality as an opportunity for creativity rather than as a source of limitation; and who helps people view reality as events, patterns of behavior, systemic structures, and purpose but leads them to focus on the last two.

These four books certainly do not exhaust the lessons school leaders can learn from the business community. They simply illustrate that the need for leadership, motivation, communication, and thoughtful behavior are common to all professions. School leaders would make a terrible mistake to ignore or feel compelled to reinvent what has been learned by the business community in recent years. These lessons are applicable to *all* school leaders. The next section of this chapter will deal with those leadership skills and behaviors of particular use in the middle school.

The Middle School Connection

Turning Points

Perhaps any discussion of middle school leadership should begin with *Turning Points: Preparing American Youth for the 21st Century* (Carnegie, 1989). This report of the Task Force on Education of Young Adolescents, sponsored by the Carnegie Corporation's Council on Adolescent Development, made eight recommendations for improving middle schools.

1. Create small communities for learning where sustained adult and peer relationships lead to intellectual and personal development for all middle grade students. Particular techniques for accomplishing this would include schools-within-schools, teams of students and teachers, and advisory groups.

2. Teach a core academic program, including youth service, which results in language, math, and scientific literacy; critical thinking; healthy living; ethical behavior; and responsible citizenship.

3. Ensure success for all students by eliminating achievement–based tracking, promoting cooperative learning and flexible time arrangements, and providing adequate resources for teachers.

4. Decentralize decision-making to the school and subschool level, especially for those decisions regarding the day-to-day experiences of middle grade students.

5. Select middle school teachers who have developed and demonstrated expertise through training and/or experience in working with middle grade students.

6. Improve academic performance by fostering the health and fitness of students. The report recommends a health coordinator for every school, ready access to health care and counseling services at school, and a health-promoting school environment.

7. Involve families in the education of young adolescents by giving them meaningful roles in school governance, communicating with them about school programs and student progress, and encouraging active participation in the learning process both at home and at school.

8. Connect schools with communities by identifying service opportunities in the community, establishing partnerships and collaborations, ensuring student access to health and social services, using community resources to supplement and enrich the instructional program, and discovering and developing opportunities for constructive after-school student activities.

Although *Turning Points* has been criticized for offering little in the way of substantive suggestions for achieving these recommendations, it is nevertheless recognized as *the* single document that best defines the proper *direction* for middle school improvement. *Turning Points* contends that implementation of the eight recommendations will result in the development of young adolescents who are intellectually reflective, en route to a lifetime of meaningful work, good citizens, caring and ethical individuals, and healthy persons.

So the easy answer to the question "What should the middle school leader do?" is that anyone—teacher, administrator, parent—desiring to be a middle school leader would take the actions necessary to see that the eight recommendations are implemented and would, of course, support others' efforts to implement these recommendations. Such action assumes that individuals and school communities are supportive of all eight recommendations. But even if all eight ideas are agreed to, the answer still is too easy. Nevertheless, the

Carnegie Council's recommendations do provide a handy and generally accepted framework against which the modern middle school may be measured.

Toepfer (1990) argued that *Turning Points* requires middle level leaders to address certain issues, including

- The physical, social, emotional, and intellectual diversity of middle level students (greater than that of either elementary or high school students) argues for instructional practices that *integrate* learning with students' lives.

- Lifelong learning must be emphasized, moving middle schools away from specific grade-based competencies toward students who value learning and the role of learning in their future lives.

- The increased power of self-concept for this age group argues for increased attention to this issue. Such attention should not only address the dropout problem but also "carry enthusiastic learners into high school who still believe they can succeed intellectually" (p. 19).

- Heterogeneous grouping and cooperative learning must be implemented more fully in middle schools, as suggested by a sound and increasingly large research base.

- Cognitive and intellectual growth for middle level students will come "through school experiences which facilitate [their] affective, emotional, and personal-social development" (p. 20).

It is easy to see how Toepfer's issues provide direction for those seeking to implement the recommendations found in *Turning Points*. He contended that addressing these issues will lead to programs that will allow middle school students "to learn as fast as they can, or as slow as they must" (p. 21).

Glasser's Views on Leadership

But what are some other ways we might focus on leadership in the middle school? Although William Glasser would not argue that his book *The Quality School* (1990), based on the ideas of W. Edwards Deming, applies only to middle schools, he does suggest that the ideas in that book and in his *Control Theory in the Classroom* (1986) are especially appropriate for the middle grades. This appropriateness is due to the increasing level of coercion in middle schools compared to elementary schools, the unique developmental characteristics of middle schoolers, and the heightened belief among students of this age that adults should be viewed as adversaries rather than as helpers and supporters.

Glasser (1990) advocated a move from "boss-management" to "lead-management" and identified four essential elements of the latter:

1. The leader engages workers in a discussion of the quality of the work to be done and the time needed to do it.
2. The leader, or someone else, models the work for the workers and continually asks for worker input regarding better ways to do the job.
3. The leader asks workers to become critics of their own work, evaluating it against agreed-upon standards of quality.
4. The leader facilitates the work by providing the best possible tools and materials, along with a noncoercive, cooperative workplace.

Such leadership can be exhibited by principals with teachers or by teachers with students. It especially is important for principals who want to lead-manage to learn the social and administrative skills necessary to mediate between the bosses above and the teachers in the school.

Lead-management will, in Glasser's view, move us toward schools in which almost all workers, teachers and students, are engaged actively in the pursuit of real quality and meaning in their work, in contrast to the typical school in which quality is measured by standardized test scores, behavioral compliance, and students' meeting "minimum" requirements. This approach appears particularly appropriate at the middle level, where many students are making conscious choices about the value of school and schooling. Glasser's quality school would appear to be comparable to what Sergiovanni (1991) described as the difference between *effective* schools, as measured solely by standardized tests, and *successful* schools, which are marked by high student achievement in basic skills and higher-level learning, responsible citizenship, active student involvement, agreement on values and beliefs, varied but high-quality instructional practices, high-quality human relationships, etc.

In an interview for the *Middle School Journal* (Chance and Bibens, 1990), Glasser discussed his view of the middle school and made suggestions for middle school leaders. Drawing on his books *Reality Therapy* (1965), *Schools without Failure* (1969), *Control Theory in the Classroom* (1986), and *The Quality School* (1990), Glasser made the following points relative to the middle school:

- Students should be encouraged to socialize with each other and to work in cooperative groups.
- They should be listened to when they express their needs to those in charge.
- Middle schools should diminish their focus on discipline, order, and coercion.
- Middle schools should design ways to allow students to express their emerging needs for power and sexual awareness.
- Middle schools should help students develop the notion of "quality."
- Middle schools need teachers who create an environment that is even less coercive than that of the elementary school.
- Middle schools need administrators who are "lead managers" rather than "boss managers."

Other Middle School Leadership Views

Further advice for the middle school leader came from Lipsitz (1984). In her summary of case studies of four successful middle schools, she reached some conclusions about principals and schools. The level of caring in all four schools was far beyond that typically found in schools. Students, staff, and parents were made to feel special. This enhanced staff morale retained parent support and gave students a sense of purpose that bound them to the school. School structures and practices encouraged adult communication and companionship, significantly decreasing adult isolation.

The four schools achieved unusual clarity about middle school purposes and middle school students. Each of the schools had clear academic and social missions that were pursued confidently in both word and practice.

Each of the schools had a principal with a driving vision, a person who gave meaning to decisions and practices, who emphasized *why* things were done as well as how, and who made decisions for reasons of principle. Significantly, the principals institutionalized their vision in both program and organizational structure.

The principals were not only visionary but also practical. They articulated and defined the schools' identities and purposes. They bound "philosophy to goals, goals to programs, and programs to practices" (Lipsitz, 1984, p. 175). In each school, the principal defined the special nature of the school and proclaimed that definition both internally and externally. Each school became special.

Principals were marked by drive, possessiveness, and, sometimes, defiance. They were critical to school success, but not indispensable.

The principals derived their authority from acknowledged competence. Although not authoritarian leaders, these principals often displayed an *undercurrent* of such behavior.

The principals saw instructional leadership as their major function. They sustained faculty commitment, set standards for performance, and established the norms and taboos for adult-child relationships. Each principal was committed—almost driven—to establish the best possible school environment for the age group.

Teachers set high expectations for themselves and believed that they could make a difference in their students' learning. They were highly autonomous and understood how and often why the whole school worked.

Many of these findings are confirmed by other researchers, although usually in a more general setting than the middle school. Nevertheless, some of these other general findings are worth mentioning to the middle school leader.

Bennis (1984) found that compelling vision was the critical characteristic of the leaders of the highly successful organizations he studied. Sergiovanni (1991) spoke of *leadership density*, the extent to which leadership roles are shared and exercised by many people in an organization. March (1984) found that the density of leadership was related directly to the success of schools. Sergiovanni (1991) suggested three ways people can be enabled to increase this density:

1. Empowering others by giving them the direction to function autonomously within the goals and purposes of the school.
2 Providing others with the support and training needed to function autonomously.
3. Removing bureaucratic obstacles that keep others from functioning autonomously.

Vaill (1984) found three critical attributes of the high-performing leaders he studied. They invested extraordinary amounts of time in the enterprise and had very strong feelings about their organizations' purposes. These leaders also focused on key issues and variables. Leadership is not an easy task and is not recommended for the fainthearted.

Susan Rosenholtz (1989) provided compelling evidence that principals must establish collegial environments to negate the teacher isolation common in schools. Principals were found to play a key role in creating cultures of collegiality, which in turn led to increased productivity, improved morale, and an enhanced sense of professionalism in teachers.

It is easy to allow a discussion of middle school leadership to degenerate into various lists, key criteria, and characteristics for success. In fact, there are no magic formulas for leadership in the middle school, or other schools for that matter. We can look at *The Junior High School We Need* (Grantes, Noyce, Patterson, and Robertson, 1961) or Ken Tye's more recent version (1985), and we find little difference. We have known for over 40 years that these early adolescents have special needs and require special schools. But our knowledge only infrequently has informed our practice.

We have reorganized grade groupings and assigned different labels without making any significant change in how we "hold school" for these special students. Elliot Merenbloom (Lounsbury, 1990) reminds us that middle school is "a curriculum and instructional issue, not an organizational issue" (p. 24). We know that many different types of leaders can be effective in the middle school (Smith and Andrews, 1989). Effectiveness does not require a particular style or personality. If there is magic for the middle school leader, it is most likely found in hard work, patience, commitment, understanding, and having a good heart attuned to the needs of middle school learners and those who teach them.

The Practitioner Connection

In this last section, we offer personal insights from a sampling of successful middle school principals and other practitioners about their unique brand of leadership. Is there a connection between popular business literature, specific middle level education skills, and the practitioner? To explore this connection, the authors sought advice from successful middle level principals and reviewed the data from an evaluation of a statewide leadership academy.

A survey asked principals of middle level schools, designated as Blue Ribbon Schools by the U. S. Department of Education's School Recognition Program, one question: "What is the most important leadership role a middle level principal can play for the benefit of the school?" Those principals offered the following advice:

> Managing human resources is absolutely the most important role a middle level principal has to perform in today's schools. Motivating staff to do their very best, to pursue staff development for their own personal and professional growth, and to constantly be positive in all situations is a must skill for any principal. The principal must remain active in discipline, set the tone, and gently demand responsible behavior of all students. (W. C. Lane personal communication, January 20, 1993)

> The number one role of a leader in a shared decision-making school is that of "listener." Let go of the power. Be open to what is shared. Don't just ask for input, use it. Become a participant yourself in the total process. Know what it is like on all levels of involvement by being there. The second most important role would be facilitator. (Helping others make things happen as smoothly as possible.) (L. Larson personal communication, January 6, 1993)

> I think that once all the organizational factors are in place (block scheduling, teams of academic teachers, common planning time, an advisor/advisee program, exploration, etc.), my role becomes that of a facilitator, cheerleader, and an instructional leader. I work to fine-tune the program, encourage innovation, both in classroom instruction and curriculum, and keep in constant touch with the teachers. I need to ensure that everything we do is to promote the well-being and education of our unique group of students. How all this is accomplished depends on the school and the individual principal. (W. W. Brewer personal communication, January 5, 1993)

> The most important function of a leader, in my opinion, is to empower others to develop themselves and contribute to the organization. I recognize talent, brains, and leadership, and try to release human potential. I get my staff involved in reading, talking, experimenting, writing, presenting, and proposing. I send them back to school, get them promoted, or promote them myself. They are interested and engaged. They do the same for their students.

I want each of my 90 teachers involved in exciting, challenging work. I get grants and programs, and encourage experimentation, to be sure this happens. I can't touch 1,350 students, but I can touch the teachers, and they'll take care of the students. (M. E. Levin personal communication, January 5, 1992)

After much consideration, I have decided that the one thing that seems to have had the greatest effect on my building is the effort that I have put into creating a positive climate for teaching and learning. When students and teachers are excited about school, attendance is higher, discipline is better, public support rises, and academic progress is more evident. When a positive attitude is prevalent, problems are dealt with at a lower level and challenges are faced from a problem-solving, rather than a finger-pointing perspective. We want students to arrive at school in a positive mental frame of mind because they left school the day before excited about what they had done. Our goal is to begin every day with students that are teachable and teachers that are prepared and excited about teaching. (K. B. Walker personal communication, January 11, 1993)

To benefit students a principal needs to know what is happening at the school, talk with the kids, have a sense of humor, care about the kids, and discipline with dignity and respect.

To benefit the staff a principal needs to be a leader— take risks, collaborate, listen, care—ask about families, and know the school—be aware of the issues teachers are facing.

To benefit the parents and community a principal needs to make school a friendly, warm, and inviting place—put out the welcome mat. Give them responsibilities and encourage them to be part of the decision-making. (J. K. Altersitz personal communication, January 19, 1993)

James McGregor Burns' Visionary Leader inspires teachers and students to model high ethical, moral values and treat us with respect and dignity. The principal must have and share "the vision." (J. Thornton personal communication, January, 1993)

I believe that a leader builds community; demonstrates moral courage; is centered in a belief system; has the strength of convictions; makes compassion an enduring value; has intuitive insights; values and models the intentions of the mission; understands that leadership is contextually grounded; believes in and is able to build collaborative relationships; builds a commitment to teamwork; brings people together to create and share a common information base; promotes collective commitment to a vision; is an interpreter and ambassador to the larger community; sees his or her role as one of stewardship. (D. M. Hillman personal communication, January 8, 1993)

In addition to polling principals of Blue Ribbon Schools, the authors reviewed an evaluation report of a statewide leadership academy. The academy, through a collaborative partnership, teaches leadership skills and knowledge from both business and education. This partnership includes universities, professional education associations, educational cooperatives, an educational television network, a state department of education, and two of the three most successful corporations in the world. It connects the worlds of business and education.

Frazier and Frazier (1993), in their evaluation report, interviewed more than 400 practitioners representing public schools, higher education, government, professional associations, and business to determine if the academy had targeted the appropriate leadership skills. Respondents cited the following skills as vital to successfully leading schools: action research, advocacy, accessing research, accessing best practice information, coaching, collaboration, communication, creative thinking, goal setting, modeling, networking, organizing, planning, policy development, problem-solving, team-learning, respect for diversity, risk-taking, shared decision-making, staff development, strategic planning, understanding change processes, and visioning.

In addition to focusing on skills needed to lead and manage change, the academy conducted strategic leadership institutes that piloted the following knowledge or content areas which seemingly promote successful leadership:

- Strategic planning processes.
- Stakeholder involvement strategies.
- Parent involvement programs.
- School-based management.
- Authentic assessment strategies.
- Interdisciplinary curriculum.
- Performance-based instruction.
- Responses to special interest groups.
- Design of curriculum frameworks.
- Definition of learner outcomes.
- Inclusionary practices.

The evaluation data indicate that these areas were deemed valuable to all school leaders. They appear to be consistent with the business literature, recommended practices for the middle school, and advice from middle school practitioners.

Conclusion

Who are the leaders of today's middle school? Who will be the leaders of the middle school of tomorrow? These leaders are not and will not be defined by position; they will be found among administrators, teachers, parents, and community members. They will not be defined by academic training alone, but rather by their willingness to be informed by the educational research, best practices in the private sector, their own intuition and experience, and the experiences of others. They will not be those who are easily categorized as "people" or "product" oriented or "process" versus "outcome" oriented (or on any similar dichotomous relationships). They will, instead, understand that balance is required in almost all of these relationships—that differences provide richness and texture in an organization, that a real learning organization invites and learns from such differences. Effective middle school leaders are not and will not be those who seek safety and sameness, but rather those who model and encourage risk-taking if the risk promises learning for the organization or for the individuals in the organization.

Middle school leaders of today and tomorrow must, of course, be passionate about advancing the social, emotional, and intellectual learning of students who are indeed "in the middle." The very uniqueness of these students defines the influence of the leaders needed in their schools—leaders who are struggling, developing, trying (and trying again) to find the right way.

If a summary is necessary, perhaps it is found in the adjacent figure. With apologies to Frazier and Frazier (1993), the effective middle school leader is, and will be, the one who can:

- Envision the middle school of the future—who can "see" what a middle school should be to serve its workers and its unique clients; who can create an informed vision that transcends personal experience, overcomes tradition and resistance, and gives direction and purpose to the entire organization.

- Manage the middle school work—who can plan, organize, schedule, and monitor the work necessary to achieve the vision, honoring process and product, effort and result, people and institution.

- Advance the middle school team—who can foster and model collaboration, who can communicate information and attitudes, who can capitalize on the expertise of others and develop expertise where it does not yet exist, and who can recognize the value of an organization that *learns* each day.

Figure 1

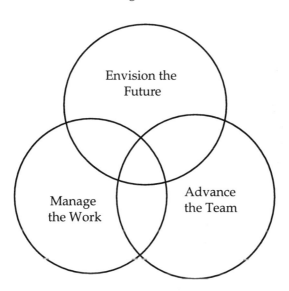

Middle schoolers will be well served when *all* the leaders in their schools demonstrate skills in these three areas.

REFERENCES

Bennis, W. (1984). Transformation power and leadership. In T. J. Sergiovanni and J. E. Corbally (Eds.), *Leadership and organizational culture* (pp. 64–71). Urbana: University of Illinois Press.

Byham, W. C., and Cox, Jr. (1990). *Zapp! The lightning of empowerment.* New York: Harmony Books.

Carnegie Council on Adolescent Development. (1989). *Turning points: Preparing American youth for the 21st century.* Washington, DC: Author.

Chance, E., and Bibens, R. (1990). Developing quality middle schools— An interview with Dr. William Glasser. *Middle School Journal*, 21(4): 1–4.

Covey, S. (1989). *The 7 habits of highly effective people*. New York: Simon and Schuster.

Frazier, G., and Frazier, R. (1993). *Evaluation report for the Arkansas academy for leadership training and school-based management*. Naples, FL: WEB Associates.

Glasser, W. (1965). *Reality Therapy*. New York: Harper and Row.

Glasser, W. (1969). *Schools without failure*. New York: Harper and Row.

Glasser, W. (1986). *Control theory in the classroom*. New York: Harper and Row.

Glasser, W. (1990). *The quality school*. New York: Harper and Row.

Grantes, J., Noyce, C., Patterson, F., and Robertson, J. (1961). *The junior high school we need*. Washington, DC: Association for Supervision and Curriculum Development.

Lipsitz, J. (1984). *Successful schools for young adolescents*. New Brunswick, NJ: Transaction Books.

Lounsbury, J. H. (Ed.). (1990). An interview with Elliot Y. Merenbloom. *Middle School Journal* 21(5): 22–25.

March, J. G. (1984). How we talk and how we act: Administrative theory and administrative life. In T. G. Sergiovanni and J. E. Corbally, (Eds.), *Leadership and Organizational Culture* (pp. 18–35). Urbana: University of Illinois Press.

Peters, T. J., and Waterman, R. H. (1982). *In search of excellence: Lessons from America's best-run companies.* New York: Harper and Row.

Rosenholtz, S. (1989). *Teacher's workplace: A social-organizational analysis.* New York: Longman.

Senge, P. (1990). *The fifth discipline: The art and practice of the learning organization*. New York: Doubleday Currency.

Sergiovanni, T. J. (1991). *The principalship: A reflective practice perspective*. Needham Heights: Allyn and Bacon.

Smith, W. F. and Andrews, R. L. (1989). *Instructional leadership: how principals make a difference*. Alexandria, VA: Association for Supervision and Curriculum Development.

Toepfer, C. F., Jr. (1990). Implementing turning points—Major issues to be faced. *Middle School Journal* 21(5): 18–21.

Tye, K. A. (1985). *The junior high: School in search of a mission*. New York: University Press of America.

Vaill, P. B. (1984). The purposing of high-performing systems. In T. J. Sergiovanni and J. E. Corbally (Eds.), *Leadership and Organizational Culture* (pp. 85–104). Urbana: University of Illinois Press.

CHAPTER 9

Organization of the Middle Level School: Evolution and a Vision for Restructuring

*DeWayne A. Mason**

> Organizational structure establishes continuity in adult-
> child relationships and opportunities for the lives of
> students and adults to cross in mutually meaningful ways
> (Joan Lipsitz, 1984, p. 181) *Successful Schools for Young
> Adolescents*

Organizational features can play an important role in facilitating a school's goals and objectives (Beane, 1990; Elmore, 1990; Lounsbury and Vars, 1978; Rowan, 1990). Indeed, research has shown that structural arrangements are linked closely to how organizations conduct their tasks (Simpson, 1985). Unfortunately, as the school restructuring literature points out so well, curriculum development, instruction, and quality student outcomes too often are circumscribed or totally obstructed by current organizational characteristics (e.g., see Elmore, 1990; Murphy, 1991). This chapter focuses on several organizational features that impact middle level program development, implementation, and student achievement broadly defined. It explores how the use of these organizational features has gradually changed as middle level philosophy has infiltrated schools, and it documents the current status of these features. Finally, the chapter provides a vision for restructuring three important features, a vision aimed at improving middle level education.

A broad range of features may be encompassed by the topic "organization of middle level schooling." A review of the literature, for example, reveals that organizational topics may be categorized into five areas: (1) organization of students (e.g., grade levels, daily time schedules, classroom ability grouping); (2) organization of teachers (e.g., subject specialists, interdisciplinary teams, differentiated staffing); (3) organization of curriculum (e.g., specialized vs. general, exploratory, activity programs); (4) organization of facilities (e.g., classrooms, team lecture or seminar rooms, small-group project areas); and (5) organization for administration and leadership (e.g., budgeting, staff development, restructuring). This chapter focuses specifically on organization of *students* and *teachers*. (Other organizational features are addressed in chapters 9, 11, 12, 13, 14, and 16 of this book.)

To review how students have been organized in middle level schools, I first discuss trends related to grade level organization, scheduling approaches, and classroom ability grouping. Second, to review how teachers are generally organized at the middle level, I discuss two approaches most often found in the literature: subject specialization or departmentalization and interdisciplinary teaming. Finally, I provide a vision for restructuring these organizational aspects to better support learning and teaching in middle level schools.

Evolution

Organization of Students

Grade level organization. Organizing schools with unique physical environments and programs geared to the developmental needs of young adolescents has been a slow process in the United States. When one-room schools gave way to graded schools during the later part of the nineteenth century, a dual system of grammar schools (Grades 1–8) and high schools (Grades 9–12) emerged as the major organizational pattern. Although the first middle level school was introduced in 1895 in

Richmond, Indiana, by 1920 only 3 percent of the students were enrolled in six-three-three or six-two-four grade arrangements featuring separate middle level schools, and 83 percent were still enrolled in a traditional eight-four arrangement (Howard and Stoumbis, 1970).

The early mission of the junior high school certainly was not clear cut. Frequently mentioned in the literature were goals related to reducing dropouts, broad-based preparation for employment, eliminating inefficiencies in graded schools, and introducing more subject specialists and advanced curricula, such as algebra and science. Other more progressive reformers, however, aimed at adapting middle level schools to the unique characteristics of young adolescents. Basing their ideas on studies in child psychology which showed teenagers as quite different than 8- and 9-year-olds, these educators sought a curriculum tied to students' interest in adult work and self-understanding, students' experiences, and instructional methods that addressed student diversity. Koos's (1920) early review of the junior high literature found that the movement was driven by retention of pupils, economy of time, recognition of individual differences, exploration for guidance, vocational education, recognition of the nature of the child, providing conditions for better teaching, securing better scholarship, and improving discipline and socialization opportunities. Whatever the vision, more and more districts chose to adopt some type of organizational pattern that included a junior high school.

The number of junior highs rose from 385 in 1920 to 1,850 in 1930 (Howard and Stoumbis, 1970), and Cuban (1992) reports that two- and three-year junior highs represented about 11 percent of the secondary schools by 1937–1938. By 1959, however, as enrollment in traditional eight-four arrangements declined to 18 percent and enrollment in six-six junior-senior high school arrangements increased to 32 percent, 50 percent of the students were enrolled in six-three-three or six-two-four arrangements featuring middle level schools (Howard and Stoumbis, 1970). As these numbers confirm and as Cuban (1992) asserts, "by 1970 the separate unit of the 2- and 3-year junior high school had become the dominant form of secondary school reorganization" (p. 238).

Beginning around 1960, however, dissatisfactions with traditional six-three-three or six-two-four junior high schools led to other grade level organizations and a new reform movement called *middle schools* (Alexander and McEwin, 1989). According to Cuban (1992), this movement was a reaction to junior high programs that had become narrowly focused on subject matters rather than students, extracurricular rather than intramural or activity programs, and curriculum depth rather than exploration.

Bolstered by the establishment of the National Middle School Association, middle level state organizations, and national journals, the middle school movement spread quickly. Alexander and McEwin (1989) report that Grades 5–8 and 6–8 middle schools grew by 125 percent from 1970–71 to 1986–87, while schools with Grades 7–8, 7–9, and other configurations declined by 33 percent. Of the 10,857 middle level schools in Alexander and McEwin's 1986–87 study, 5,466 (50.3 percent) showed a 5–8 or 6–8 grade configuration, while 5,391 (49.7 percent) reported 7–8, 7–9, or other organizational approaches. As Alexander and McEwin point out, these data clearly show "a large-scale movement toward the most common middle school grade organization (Grades 5–8 and, especially, 6–8) during the past 25 years" (p. 11). Therefore, by 1986–87, middle school grade configurations had replaced earlier junior high patterns as the predominant organizational approach for middle level education. Notably, a recent national survey conducted by the National Association of Secondary School Principals [NASSP] (Valentine, Clark, Irvin, Keefe, and Melton, 1993) has reported a continued growth in the number of middle level schools (to approximately 12,100) as well as in the percentage of schools with Grades 5–8 or 6–8 configurations (to approximately 62 percent).

A broader perspective may be drawn from a national survey of practices and trends completed by the Center for Research on Elementary and Middle Schools (CREMS) at Johns Hopkins University (e.g., see Epstein, 1990). These researchers found that U. S. schools enrolling seventh graders included 30 different grade spans. Middle schools (mainly Grades 6–8 schools but also 5–8, 5–7, and 6–7 schools) were organized in only about 25 percent of the schools sampled (serving 39 percent of the seventh graders), whereas K–8 and K–12 grade spans existed in about 43 percent of the schools (serving about 12 percent of the seventh graders). Junior high configurations (7–9), however, were found in only 8 percent of the schools (serving about 17 percent of the seventh graders).

A strong rationale has emerged supporting the displacement of ninth graders to the high school and inclusion of sixth (and often fifth) graders in middle level schools. Calhoun (1983), for example, reports that studies of maturity have found ninth graders to be more like tenth graders than eighth graders. Researchers also have found children maturing earlier and earlier during the past century, with many 10- to 14-year-olds beginning a difficult transition into puberty, new stages of intellectual development, and increased social and emotional awareness (e.g., see Curtis and Bidwell, 1977). Consequently, most middle school scholars argue that ninth graders belong with their similar peers at the high school, and that fifth and sixth graders should be included in middle level schools that focus on their unique characteristics and curriculum and instruction needs.

Schedule organization. Another major component of a school's organizational structure is the master schedule. The master schedule allocates and divides the time that students spend in school, and it accommodates or circumscribes a school's programmatic priorities. Alexander and George (1981) note that every schedule divides the school day into smaller units, and the major aspects of scheduling are unit size and control over adaptation of these units. Although various approaches to scheduling middle level schools have been identified in the literature (e.g., see Howard and Stoumbis, 1970), four approaches are most frequently used: self-contained schedules, block-of-time or interdisciplinary schedules, departmentalized schedules, and modular schedules.

Self-contained scheduling relies on the elementary school model of assigning students to a single teacher who then schedules and teaches all or most of his or her students' academic subjects, a practice that reduces student contact with other peers and teachers. This approach, which holds greater potential for developing personal, solicitous teacher-student relationships and adaptive teaching based on an enhanced understanding of students, contrasts starkly with the more impersonal departmentalized schedule commonly used in high schools. As middle level schools have developed alternative schedules aimed at bridging the gap between the small and personal elementary environment and the large and more impersonal high school setting, self-contained classes have declined steadily. Still, the advantages of self-contained classes frequently lead many middle level schools to use this approach for at-risk or special needs students.

Block-of-time or flexible schedules most frequently are used by interdisciplinary teams of teachers. These teachers, who are usually allocated 80–180 minutes of block time, typically agree on standard allocations for the various academic subjects and then regularly vary these schedules based on collaborative curriculum development and special day-to-day needs. According to Alexander and George (1981), block schedules provide a transition between the large block of time in the elementary school and the smaller periods at the high school, and they facilitate the basic organizational framework of the "exemplary" middle school—interdisciplinary team organization. Although the team approach does not provide a single teacher to accommodate students' needs, it certainly ensures a smaller haven for student-teacher and student-student relationships to develop than that of the loosely-coupled high school environment.

The major advantage of block scheduling is the flexibility it provides. Given blocks of time, teams of teachers may create unique and varied schedules that parallel their objectives and appropriately respond to fortuitous events that arise. For example, teachers may create schedules for large-group presentations to 150 students, extended laboratory or library inquiries, and small-group or individualized activities—all without upsetting the schedules of nonacademic classes and other teams in the school.

Departmentalized schedules, derived from the high school, typically divide the school day into six, seven, or eight standard periods of 40 to 55 minutes. Glatthorn and Spencer

(1986) argue that departmentalized schedules have persisted because they seem to work.

> It provides the teacher with enough time to teach a few concepts, check on student learning, and provide some directed practice. And it is not over-long for most secondary students; they can sit still for forty minutes without causing too much trouble or doing too much daydreaming. (p. 160)

Other scholars argue, however, that departmentalized schedules do not enable teachers to vary the time allocated to certain subjects; integrate curriculum; or adapt instruction for large-group, small-group, laboratory, or individualized formats (e.g., see Alexander and George, 1981).

Although exceptional schools may be able to develop integrated curriculum and adaptive instruction through departmentalization, these schedules typically constrain creative approaches that more fully meet the unique and varied needs of young adolescents. Alexander and George (1981) argue that effective middle level programs demand teacher autonomy and, therefore, master schedules that facilitate such. After reviewing the various scheduling options that schools have, these authors concluded that high school departmentalized schedules could never achieve the functions that middle school programs seek to attain (e.g., integration, differentiation, and guidance).

Modular scheduling, which arose in response to a need for more flexibility within secondary schools, uses shorter time increments (usually 15–25 minutes) as a way of organizing a school's schedule. With this approach, teachers can request the number of modules they need for a particular subject each day of the week and then, for example, meet for two "mods" on Monday, Wednesday, and Friday and three "mods" on Tuesday and Thursday. Similarly, programs may be organized around a brief 15–25 minute class (e.g., an advisory class) or a 75–100 minute laboratory, field, or library research experience.

Glatthorn and Spencer (1986) argue that modular schedules have two drawbacks that have limited their use in middle schools. First, modular master schedules are more difficult to develop than traditional departmentalized, block, or self-contained schedules. Secondly, once they're established, modular schedules can be as inflexible as departmentalized schedules. That is, it is difficult for teachers to know in advance whether they will need 25 or 75 minutes on any particular day; these needs can be altered by too many factors.

Special scheduling alternatives often are needed in middle level schools to facilitate such important programs as advisor-advisee, mini-courses, intramurals, independent study, and a full range of exploratory courses. Minimum-day schedules, an approach whereby classes meet for something less than their regular time allotment, often are used to permit these additional activities. Rotating schedules ("A and B days" or "odd or even days") also can be used to allow students to attend two different subjects concurrently (e.g., physical education and an exploratory course). Although other alternatives are available (e.g., floating and homebase periods), some scholars note that complex master schedules may be more appropriate for high schoolers than middle schoolers and that most special scheduling needs may be met best through flexible block approaches.

Alexander and McEwin (1989) provide indirect evidence of middle school scheduling trends by presenting data from 1968 and 1988 on "instructional organization" by subject matter and grade. Averages of the percentage of schools using various plans in Grades 5–8 basic subjects (language arts, mathematics, science, and social studies) showed that interdisciplinary organizational plans had increased from 6 percent to 30 percent over the 20-year period, with fifth and sixth grades accounting for the largest increases. Departmentalized plans, though predominant in both 1968 and 1988, showed a slight decline from 59 percent to 54 percent, with Grades 7 and 8 showing the largest decrease. Self-contained plans showed a slight decline from 22 percent to 16 percent, as Grade 5 decreased from 56 percent to 35 percent and Grade 6 decreased from 28 percent to 17 percent; Grades 7 and 8, however, each increased their use of self-containment from 1 percent to 5 percent. Notably, Alexander and McEwin (1989) found that middle schools used departmentalization an average of 17 percent less than junior high schools across the major subject areas.

Although a variety of scheduling approaches are currently used in middle level schools, no one arrangement is "best." middle level schools. Flexibility to use a variety of schedules is probably the key to effective schooling practices. The National Middle School Association's (NMSA) philosophical and programmatic statement about middle level education was explained by *This We Believe* (NMSA, 1992):

> Various organizational arrangements should be utilized within the middle school, since the students are so varied. . . . Organization should be a tool, not a master. Block scheduling, multi-age grouping, developmental age grouping, alternate schedules, and other ways of organizing for instruction belong in the middle school. A school-within-a-school arrangement may be needed, as may, on occasion, a self-contained or core situation. . . . In scheduling, the key question is, "Who needs what math?" rather than, "When will we teach math?" (pp. 16–17)

Assignment of students to classrooms. Student assignment policies and practices have significant effects on the type of curriculum and instruction that students receive, as well as on their achievement and prosocial development (e.g., see Gutiérrez and Slavin, 1992; Slavin, 1987; Slavin, 1990). This section details approaches used in organizing groups of students for classrooms, presents data on how schools presently organize classroom groups, and provides a discussion about research on these various approaches.

Glatthorn and Spencer (1986) write that student assignment centers around "the bases for grouping students and the size of instructional groups" (p. 157), and these authors identify six basic types of student assignment practices: tracking, ability grouping by subject, heterogeneous grouping, self-determined grouping, individual placement, and grouping by developmental level or learning style.

Tracking involves sorting students into two or more ability groups and assigning them to *all* classes on this basis. For example, low-ability students in a self-contained schedule would be assigned to a teacher with other low-ability peers for the whole day; and, in a departmentalized schedule, low-ability students would be assigned to classes each period with peers of similar ability. At the other end of the continuum, *heterogeneous grouping* takes place when schools assign students to classes randomly or systematically to ensure a range of student abilities and ethnic diversity.

Ability grouping by subject occurs when students are assigned to classes by their ability in particular subject areas. Thus, a student might be assigned to a high-ability mathematics class with other high achievers but take English in an average-ability class. Ability grouping by subject is typically less rigid than tracking; however, due to scheduling constraints in some schools, assignment to one or two subjects of a particular ability level often locks students into other classes of a similar nature. *Self-determined grouping* occurs when students, often in collaboration with parents, choose electives from among various levels of challenge or difficulty. Of course, this practice may occur in some or all academic areas.

Finally, students may be assigned to an *individualized* program or according to their *developmental level*. Individualized programs, which are used rarely in middle level schools, are typically based on a diagnosis of each student's present ability levels and a prescription of appropriate learning objectives. While such programs are advocated by many practitioners and scholars, research has shown that these approaches have not led to improved achievement at the elementary or secondary school levels (Bangert, Kulik, and Kulik, 1983; Gutiérrez and Slavin, 1992). Developmental placements are based on cognitive levels; learning styles; or social, physical, and academic maturity. These assignments often lead to multiage or nongraded groupings of students, an approach that leads to higher student achievement when accompanied by curricular and instructional changes (e.g., see Gutiérrez and Slavin, 1992).

Research is scant on the extent to which middle level schools use various student assignment approaches. Four surveys were found, however, that provide some evidence of trends related to grouping practices. Valentine, Clark, Nickerson, and Keefe (1981), in their NASSP survey of 1,413 middle level principals, found that ability grouping was used in 88 percent of the schools, and that standardized tests, staff judgments, and grades were used most frequently to place students differentially into classes. In response to a question about the scope of grouping policies in their schools, 59 percent reported grouping at all grade levels in certain subjects, while another 9 percent said they grouped at all grade levels in all subjects. Comparisons of these data with results from the NASSP 1966 *Report of the Junior High School Principalship* (Rock and Hemphill, 1966) found few differences.

Braddock's (1990) data on grouping from the CREMS survey parallel those of Valentine and his colleagues. Although between-class ability grouping varied by subject matter and grade level, Braddock reports that "roughly two-thirds or more of the nation's schools serving early adolescents report using at least some between-class ability grouping, and more than 20 percent assign students to all of their classes according to ability" (p. 446).

Epstein and Mac Iver (1988), in their analysis of the CREMS data, found that the number of students experiencing some homogeneous grouping increased from 70 percent of fifth graders to 85 percent of eighth graders and that the number of fully tracked students increased from 12 percent of fifth graders to 25 percent of sixth through eighth graders. Although Epstein and Mac Iver found that middle schools are less likely to have all classes grouped by ability than K–8 schools, they also reported that students in K–8, 7–12, and K–12 schools experience less between-class grouping than do students in schools dedicated only to middle grades.

The recent NASSP middle level survey by Valentine et al. (1993) did not investigate the full range of ability grouping practices, but these researchers found that 82 percent of the 570 responding principals reported using some degree of ability grouping, although 13 percent was within-class grouping by teachers. In response to this survey's question about describing the future of ability grouping in their schools, 36 percent of the principals who currently were using ability grouping were considering eliminating the practice, while only 1 percent of the principals said they were considering adding ability grouping to their schools.

As Becker (1987) notes, research about how alternative grouping approaches impact student outcomes has not been clear and consistent. While Slavin's (1987) review of research found that some ability-grouping approaches at the elementary school level provided achievement benefits when compared to self-contained classes (e.g., Joplin Plans, regrouping, and within-class ability grouping), he found that ability grouping at the middle grades and secondary school levels provided no achievement benefits (Slavin, 1990, 1993).

Organization of Teachers

How teachers are assigned to teach in middle level schools is a major organizational factor affecting quality of instruction and student-teacher relationships. Glatthorn and Spencer (1986) explain that four patterns of teacher assignment presently are used in middle grade schools, each of which typically reflects a school's schedule—in appearance if not in substance. At one end of the continuum is *self-contained assignment*, wherein a teacher is responsible for all areas of the curriculum and small number of students. At the other end is *departmentalized assignment*, where a teacher teaches one subject several times daily to several groups of students. In between these two extremes lies *departmentalized team assignment*, wherein a teacher works as a member of a subject specialty team that jointly plans and occasionally even team teaches large numbers of students in a variety of formats (large and small group). Finally, *interdisciplinary assignment* involves a team of teachers, each with competence in one of the academic disciplines, in collaborative planning aimed at guiding a common group of students through interdisciplinary or integrated units.

Independent of how schools assign teachers to particular organizational structures, teacher certification plays an important role in how middle level programs actually are oriented (McPartland, 1990). That is, despite certain administrative assignment patterns, teachers certified as subject specialists for departmentalized secondary schools tend to approach their instructional role from a "subject-matter" perspective, while teachers with multisubject credentials aimed at working in more self-contained elementary schools are more apt to exhibit a "student-centered" orientation. Since most scholars argue that middle level schools should serve as a balanced transition between the student-oriented approach typically found in elementary schools and the subject-oriented approach found in high schools (e.g., Alexander and George, 1981; Alexander, Williams, Compton, Hines, Prescott, and Kealy, 1968; NMSA, 1992), each orientation is important.

Subject or student specialists? Until middle level certification becomes standard practice across the U.S., a major organizational decision in staffing middle level schools will be choosing between teachers with single-subject or multisubject credentials. These different orientations can create subtle and not-so-subtle conflicts in how middle level programs are organized and in how curriculum and instruction are delivered.

Subject specialists, on the one hand, bring to their specific content areas greater expertise in curriculum development and instructional strategies. These teachers are more likely to have taken advanced coursework in their subject specialty, to have engaged in related in-service professional development, and to have joined specialized professional associations (e.g., the National Council for Teachers of Mathematics or National Teachers of English). Thus, it follows that they are more likely to stay abreast of research and other advancements in their subject specialties. Typically responsible for fewer preparations and capable of teaching the more demanding content or higher-level thinking skills that some theorists see as important for middle level curriculum, these teachers can spend more time developing activities that meet students' differential needs. Therefore, it seems reasonable to expect subject specialists to best meet those middle level goals associated with high-quality instruction and high-academic achievement.

Teachers with multisubject credentials, on the other hand, bring breadth of preparation to their teaching assignments. It is said that these teachers, more broadly trained and typically placed in more self-contained or semidepartmentalized settings with responsibility for smaller numbers of students, tend to become more attuned to the nonacademic needs of individual students and to more frequently integrate academic content and focus on noncognitive activities. Multisubject teachers, trained to teach at the elementary level, may be expected to emphasize development of the "whole child" and address goals more closely related to social, emotional, and physical development.

As the scheduling data provided above indicate, subject specialization clearly dominates middle level schools. McPartland (1990) reported that "middle-grade education in the U.S. is conducted primarily by teachers who are certified in specific subjects for secondary school instruction and who are assigned to highly departmentalized instructional roles" (p. 466). McPartland's data show, for example, that students at the fifth-grade level have an average of 2.5 teachers for their major academic subjects, but by seventh grade this average jumps to 4.6 teachers. Furthermore, McPartland found that 59 percent of the middle grade schools reported having 50–100 percent of their teachers certified at the secondary level, while only 20 percent reported having 50–100 percent of their teachers certified at the elementary level.

Middle level certification has increased from two states in 1968 to 28 states in 1987, with nine other states considering such a plan (Alexander and McEwin, 1988). Unfortunately, middle level certification at the state level has yet to be followed with appropriate teacher education programs. McEwin and Alexander (1982) found in their 1981 survey of all member institutions of the American Association of Colleges of Teacher Education that only 30 percent had special programs aimed at middle level education, and this percentage grew to only 33 percent five years later (McEwin and Alexander, 1987). These figures are disappointing, especially since a clear transitional role has emerged for middle level schools requiring balanced programming that meets the unique social, emotional, and physical needs of young adolescent students. Even more surprising is that the mainstay of teacher staffing in middle level philosophy—interdisciplinary team assignment—has not gained more popularity in schools.

Interdisciplinary teams. Scholars and practitioners from exemplary middle schools have argued that the most desirable approach for organizing teachers for middle level education is interdisciplinary teaming (Alexander and George, 1981; Arhar, 1992; Carnegie Council on Adolescent Development, 1989; George and Oldaker, 1985). Interdisciplinary teaming, rooted in the *core curriculum* movement of the 1920s and 1930s, is one of several approaches that Gruhn and Douglas (1947) identified almost 50 years ago for breaking down artificial barriers between subjects and better meeting the individual needs of students. Termed *cooperative planning* by these authors, this approach called for teachers from different subject areas to meet periodically either before school or during an extended lunch period to correlate learning activities for common groups of students. (See Gruhn and Douglas, 1947, for alternative self-contained or semidepartmentalized teaming approaches.) Recently, however, many schools have scheduled team planning periods for daily collaboration during the regular academic hours (e.g., see Valentine et al., 1993).

Interest in integrating subject matters arose as a reaction to the extreme departmentalization of early junior high schools—a feature that mirrored the high school—as well as to the abrupt change that students experienced in going from one teacher at the elementary level to seven or more teachers at the junior high level. Borrowing from Dewey (1902) and other progressive educators such as Johann Friedrich Herbart, these early advocates of integrated curriculum emphasized studying subject matter in settings that would lead to unified knowledge and applications in real-life situations, rather than mastery of fragmented bodies of subject matter. Theorists also emphasized the possibility of teachers remaining with groups of students for more than a single period for purposes of gaining knowledge of individual pupils, providing guidance opportunities, and developing conditions for better instruction (Gruhn and Douglass, 1947).

Numerous authors have discussed the benefits of interdisciplinary teaming (e.g., Alexander and George, 1981; Arhar, 1992; McCarthy, 1972; Pumerantz and Galano, 1972). Alexander and George (1981) assert that the advantages of interdisciplinary teaming fall into the areas of instruction, affect, and behavior. According to these authors, instruction is enhanced when team members collaboratively strive toward meeting the needs of individual students by combining their philosophical perspectives, creative talents, resources, and knowledge.

> Certainly teachers who develop trust in each other will
> learn new methods from one another, and this is
> particularly so in regard to the use of the team in the
> introduction and orientation of faculty new to the school
> or to the profession. (Alexander and George, p. 132)

Another advantage of interdisciplinary teaming is the
opportunity to collaboratively plan, evaluate, and engage in
problem-solving related to the instructional program and
student needs (social, developmental, behavioral, etc.).
Interdisciplinary teams rarely contain the territorial barriers that
departmentalized programs exhibit; thus, broad-based
curriculum planning and evaluation are more apt to occur and
lead to a range of ideas about program improvement. Alexander
and George (1981) note that interdisciplinary teams, having little
else in common, typically spend more time focused on planning
for what they do have in common—students. Certainly, any such
multiperspective discussion of an individual is more likely to
provide a balanced yet comprehensive view of that student.

> Deficiencies a student may have in one area can become
> known to the total group almost immediately. Students
> experiencing difficulties in more than one academic area
> can be identified, diagnosed and prescribed far much
> more accurately and efficiently when, in an
> interdisciplinary team setting, teachers in all the academic
> areas are present for discussions. (p. 133)

Interdisciplinary teaming also facilitates the smooth and
integrated functioning of other middle level programs such as
advisor-advisee, intramurals, and exploratory classes. For
example, as Alexander and George (1981) point out, a student is
better served when she or he has an advisor who teaches her or
him during the day and has other teachers who can regularly
communicate with the advisor about her or his progress and
other pertinent information. Furthermore, it is reasonable to
assume that teams of teachers working with exploratory teachers
to develop interdisciplinary activities are more prone to
encourage and find subject matter connections than individual
teachers working in isolation.

Interdisciplinary teams also may develop a "sense of
community," enhanced guidance opportunities with individuals,

a transition between the small elementary and large high school, improved communications with parents, and clearer expectations and improved standards for behavior. Arhar (1992) argues that social bonding and school membership are important mediators of school outcomes and that antisocial behavior results when students do not bond to teachers, peers, and their schooling experience. Citing the work of Hirschi (1969) and Wehlage, Rutter, Smith, Lesko, and Fernandez (1989), she argues that bonding and membership occur when students feel *attached*, when they are *committed* to and *involved* in group goals that reinforce their own immediate and long-term goals, and when they see the principles (*beliefs*) encouraged by the institution as valid.

Arhar (1992), Alexander and George (1981), and others (e.g., Carnegie, 1989) argue that interdisciplinary teams provide a vehicle for developing such common attachments, commitments, involvement, and beliefs. Social bonding and membership occur in interdisciplinary teams through breaking down an amorphous and largely anonymous school of 900 students, for example, into more personal teams of 150 students or less. Student interactions are focused on getting to know fewer teachers and students by reducing student movement throughout the building and by engaging in various small-group activities and programs (advisor-advisee, team assemblies, team meetings, team lectures or films, team field trips or community projects, etc.). Consequently, students develop more in-depth student and teacher relationships. As Alexander and George (1981) note, "the dimensions of the group that students must deal with are reduced dramatically. . . . " (p. 134), and this affords development of a smaller community atmosphere and an esprit de corps among students and teachers.

Given opportunities to use a flexible block schedule and an additional planning period, interdisciplinary teams may engage in a variety of guidance activities aimed at young adolescents. These activities may be as formal as large- or small-group advisor-advisee programs with a standard affective-oriented curriculum or as informal as occasional problem-solving discussions about students with various academic, social, or emotional problems. In one school in which the author worked, each team collaboratively identified students with special needs and then developed individually tailored plans for assisting them academically or behaviorally or both. The plans typically included one-on-one communication with students (usually a teacher to whom the student best related), short- and long-term goal setting, and reward schedules for successful goal achievement. Without flexible scheduling and a daily team-planning period, however, the comprehensiveness of these efforts would have been severely diminished.

Interdisciplinary teams also can improve communications with parents. Parent-team conferences can provide more informed and efficient communication, and problems may be addressed through consensual and cohesive strategies. These types of interactions show parents that students and not subject matter are receiving the highest priority, and increased parent cooperation and understanding are more likely to develop. Many schools are beginning to use a "student study team" approach in which parents, administrators, and teachers work collaboratively on academic improvement strategies, student behavior modifications, and social development and welfare.

Clearer expectations and improved standards for student behavior also are likely to accrue from interdisciplinary teams. In addition to the reduction of student movement around the building and the sense of pride and community that might contribute to enhanced behavior, teams of teachers tend to develop and communicate consensual rules for students on the team. Any such consensus and consistency of implementation would tend to improve student understanding of rules over time, and teachers who work collectively have a better chance of achieving a clear picture about the behavior patterns of individual students than when they work alone.

Finally, George (1975) and others (e.g., Arhar, 1992; Rosenholtz, 1989) argue that teachers who work collegially tend to have higher morale and job satisfaction and engage in more professional behavior aimed at leadership and self-development. Collaboration enables teachers to assist one another to improve and better use their pool of knowledge and resources, while isolated teachers fail to have links for solving problems related to curriculum, instruction, and student learning.

Roles and responsibilities of interdisciplinary teams differ, of course, depending on the approach used (e.g., see Alexander and George, 1981; Curtis and Bidwell, 1977; Van Til, Vars, and Lounsbury, 1961). Typically, team members assist with or make decisions about class scheduling and teacher assignments; student scheduling; student grouping for instruction; selection of curriculum and supplemental materials; development of units correlated among various subject areas; space allocation; budget expenditures; selection of new staff members; parent communication; special student placements; new student orientations; in-service staff development; and linkages with guidance counselors, administrators, and exploratory teachers. The major benefit of interdisciplinary teaming lies in the fact that block scheduling and common planning time enable teachers to communicate about each of these roles or responsibilities and make adaptive decisions according to their ever-changing curricular, instructional, and student needs.

Comparing 1968 to 1988, Alexander and McEwin (1989) found substantial increases in the percent of schools using interdisciplinary team organization for the major academic subjects. However, these authors reported that about two-thirds of the schools did not use this plan in Grades 5–8; and flexible scheduling, a key aspect in facilitating interdisciplinary team objectives, was not as common. Mac Iver's (1990) findings from the CREMS survey parallel those of Alexander and McEwin: only 32 percent of the public schools used interdisciplinary teaming in the seventh and eighth grades, and only 10 percent of the schools provided adequate time for team planning and activities. Epstein (1990) reported, however, that principals predicted an increase of 10 percent or more in teaming and common planning time for middle level teachers within three years. Such a prediction seems to have materialized, as Valentine and his colleagues (1993) found that 57 percent of the principals in the NASSP survey "indicated that their schools employed teams of teachers and students" (p. 69) and that 54 percent of these schools reported providing common planning time for team members plus individual planning time. While Valentine et al. (1993) concluded that the last decade has seen an increase in the use of interdisciplinary team organization, they also documented the need for progress in practical implementation, a challenge that must be addressed if middle level schools are to capitalize fully upon the potential of this key organizational feature.

A Vision for Restructuring

Some scholars argue that middle level schools have "yet to escape the shadow of the high school" or provide fundamental organizational, curriculum, and instructional reform (e.g., Cuban, 1992, p. 249). However, progress has been made philosophically and organizationally in many middle level schools (see Valentine et al., 1993). Alexander and McEwin (1989) report, "Our analysis of the characteristics of middle schools . . . comparing our 1968 and 1988 survey data revealed that considerable progress had been made in terms of the relative percents of schools exhibiting various characteristic features or earmarks" (p. 84).

> We believe the shadow studies make clear the reality that middle level education has been undergoing revision over the last three decades, and changes for the better can be noted. These changes are not as universal or widespread as one might hope, but they are evident. (Lounsbury and Clark, 1990, p. 133)

These authors add, however, that much improvement is still needed to serve fully the unique needs and characteristics of young adolescents, especially in the area of curriculum development and instructional practices. Lounsbury and Clark (1990) argue that middle level schools have developed recognition and activity programs, interdisciplinary teams, and unique classes or programs for special needs students; however, they assert that "the curriculum of content, the bread and butter of the school program, still is not reflective of what is known about the nature and needs of early adolescents" (p. 133). Mergendollar (1993a) adds that reformers too often have emphasized school-level structural changes that can be mandated rather than alternative goals and purposes, curriculum, and instructional models and strategies that enhance student motivation, engagement, and learning (also see Mergendollar, 1993b). Still, restructuring key organizational features can play a crucial role in facilitating a productive evolution of middle level goals, curriculum, and instruction.

This section presents a vision for reforming three organizational features that would increase the opportunities for bringing middle level practice more in line with what is known about quality education for young adolescents. First, I argue that interdisciplinary team approaches must replace the departmentalized structures that presently dominate most middle level schools. Second, to facilitate broad-based and meaning-centered curriculum, a variety of instructional models and strategies, and valid assessment of student learning, I argue that flexible block schedules must supplant standard-period schedules as the fundamental approach to organizing time in middle level schools. And third, I argue that the rigid tracking practices that currently are used in too many middle level subjects must be replaced by flexible grouping approaches, appropriate curriculum, and adaptive instructional practices.

Maintaining the Momentum toward Teaming

National reports and resolutions have highlighted interdisciplinary teaming as central in developing appropriate educational programming for middle grades education (e.g., Carnegie, 1989; NMSA, 1992). Although interdisciplinary teaming has increased significantly during the past few decades (Alexander and McEwin, 1989; Valentine et al., 1993), too many middle level schools have yet to adopt this valuable organizational structure, too many interdisciplinary teams exist within a departmentalized framework that stifles the benefits of teaming (Mac Iver, 1990), and appropriate implementation remains a major problem (Valentine et al., 1993). These problems are indeed unfortunate, especially since recent data from the CREMS survey indicate that "a well-organized interdisciplinary team approach can strengthen a school's overall program for students in the middle grades" (Mac Iver, 1990, p. 461).

Principals responding to the CREMS survey reported that use of interdisciplinary teams resulted in enhanced social support and understanding from other team members, more effective instruction because of increased integration and coordination across subjects and courses, faster recognition and solution of student problems, and increased student spirit, work habits, and attitudes (Mac Iver, 1990). These findings from practice correspond identically with the theoretical rationale for interdisciplinary teaming advanced by scholars (Alexander and George, 1981; Curtis and Bidwell, 1977; Van Til et al., 1962).

Based on these findings and the convincing theoretical benefits presented previously, future visions for developing exemplary middle level schooling must focus on interdisciplinary teaming as a key component. Once established, these teams must be empowered to develop real-world and application-oriented curriculum opportunities; alternative instructional models, strategies, and groupings; innovative guidance programs; and collegial relationships aimed at identifying student needs, improving instruction, and gaining support from parents. Since interdisciplinary teams, once established, often have their potential impact diluted by lack of implementation or structural support (e.g., see Valentine et al., 1993), it is important to recognize that this key component requires sufficient administrative support, appropriate staff development and time lines, adequate common planning time, and especially flexible block scheduling.

Developing Block Schedules for Flexibility

National reports and researchers also have asserted that teachers must become involved in making collaborative, responsive, and creative curriculum and instruction decisions that rely on their knowledge of individual groups of students and particular contexts (e.g., Carnegie, 1989; Lieberman, 1988; Rosenholtz, 1989). Unfortunately, teachers are empowered infrequently to make important decisions or afforded time for collegial problem-solving or creative curriculum development. Furthermore, beyond these issues of empowerment and time, teachers often find their creative solutions constrained by an antiquated structural nemesis—the standardized, depart-mentalized schedule. In the future, it is critical that boards of education, district administrators, principals, and staff members organize schedules that enable interdisciplinary teams to adapt their teaching strategies. This scheduling must include two components: (1) block schedules that enable a wide range of programmatic alternatives, and (2) common planning time for teachers.

It is important to understand how block scheduling facilitates the organization of transitional programs that meet the needs of early adolescents. Too often, standardized schedules translate into standardized programs with narrowed educational objectives and limited instructional methods that do not fit more expansive educational goals (e.g., concept development, active learning, independent learning, and cooperative learning) and nonstandardized groups of students needing a broad range of approaches (e.g., see Goodlad, 1984). Block schedules, however, facilitate the development of diverse programs and a broad range of objectives and methods, as well as the flexibility to drastically adapt such approaches when necessary. Block schedules, then, provide a flexible structure that enables educators to better serve diverse groups of students.

Educators knowledgeable about the diverse intellectual, social, emotional, and physical needs of young adolescents recognize the need to provide a balanced, relevant, and exploratory curriculum; various instruction and evaluation strategies; comprehensive advising and counseling; remediation and enrichment opportunities that assure continuous progress; and encouragement toward increased responsibility and independence while maintaining positive group affiliations and involvement (NMSA, 1992). Such a multidimensional program demands no less than a malleable, multidimensional schedule that permits educators to create multiple and ever-changing approaches to relating, guiding, creating, planning, instructing, learning, evaluating, remediating, and enriching.

Such activities, of course, require much collaboration and coordination between and among teachers and students. The extent to which and the quality with which each is conducted depend in large part on the time teachers have for joint planning and problem-solving. Departmentalized schedules afford practically no time for such activities. With block scheduling, however, the possibilities for collaboration and creative planning are practically limitless.

If teachers, for example, decide to develop an integrated curriculum around local government, and they are able to enlist the mayor and a council member to speak for 20 minutes about the government process and have a video illustrating the process of how a local problem can lead to a law, then they may reorganize their block schedule into a variety of formats to facilitate such. Furthermore, while two or three teachers supervise this presentation and video with their 150 or so students, two or three other teachers may engage in collaborative curriculum development aimed at supporting the unit, parental communication, guidance, or other activities. Such reorganization and collaboration never could have occurred within the confines of a departmentalized schedule.

An important ingredient in implementing block schedules is the provision of a common planning period for interdisciplinary team members, an allocation beyond their individual planning period. Although this allocation of both common and individual planning times has not been adopted rapidly by most school districts, most scholars and middle level leaders recognize the importance of this organizational feature, and recent research indicates an increase in its use (Valentine et al., 1993).

As a former principal of five middle level schools (four without the common planning period), I found that a second planning period for teachers in one school led to significantly more curriculum development and instructional innovation. This planning time also had important positive consequences for involvement in school leadership issues and decisions, student placement and counseling, parental communication, and extracurricular activities.

Reducing Tracking and Refining Ability Grouping

Research at the middle and secondary level generally demonstrates that few achievement benefits accrue through the use of tracking (George, 1988; Johnston and Markle, 1986; Oakes, 1985; Slavin, 1990, 1993). Given these empirical results and several plausible arguments against tracking (e.g., stigmatization and lowering of equity and democratic ideals), some scholars (e.g., Slavin, 1990) argue that proponents should bear the burden of proving the benefits of this practice. Unfortunately, this structural approach has been rigidly adopted by many middle level schools as the primary means to differentiate curriculum and instruction and, thus, to purportedly meet the needs of individual students.

Braddock (1990), for example, found that 20 percent of the schools serving middle level students assign *all* students to their classes by ability. Similarly, Lounsbury and Clark (1990) found widespread homogeneous grouping in their study of eighth grade classes. Echoing the comments of most middle level scholars about tracking and ability grouping, Lounsbury and Clark (1990) conclude that

> [T]he full implementation of the middle school concept will require a drastic reduction in the amount and degree of tracking and homogeneous grouping. Labels and accompanying assumptions about inherent ability can have serious and long-lasting effects at this key developmental stage." (p. 138)

Although Page (1991) writes that "tracking itself is not an omnipotent structure that renders lessons either inequitable or excellent" (p. 78) and that many factors combine to affect the meaning, processes, and effects of differential curriculum offerings, it appears that too many educators are unaware of the possible stereotypical and instructional trade-offs that may result when tracking is used. It also seems that too few educators are aware of alternative methods that might be used for adapting curriculum and instruction (e.g., personalized or integrated curriculum, cooperative learning, active teaching and learning, mastery learning, etc.). While it is important to acknowledge that the meaning and value of tracking depend on "how and with what knowledge teachers and students in particular contexts engage" (Page, 1991, p. 235), evidence from large-scale studies generally document that lower-track classes tend to have a slower learning pace, less variety, fewer opportunities for independence and enrichment, and less allocated time for instruction (e.g., see Oakes, 1985).

The foregoing is not to say that middle level schools should eliminate *all* differentiation or even tracking. My vision does advocate, however, that teachers and administrators in middle level schools engage in deliberative investigations and collaborations aimed at responding creatively to student differences and the implications that these differences hold for curriculum development. Such deliberations should focus beyond simple stereotypes of what students might need and what their standardized outcomes might be. These deliberations should focus on innovative school and classroom processes that involve students in a meaningful and challenging curriculum connected to their backgrounds and best aspirations.

To illustrate the types of deliberations and investigations that might be conducted to explore a decrease in rigid tracking and ability grouping, I offer two studies (one structural and one instructional) in which the author collaborated with teachers— one as a principal and one as a researcher. In the first, Mason, Schroeter, Combs, and Washington (1992) placed 34 average-achieving eighth graders (35th to 60th percentile) previously assigned to general track mathematics classes into high-track prealgebra classes with their higher-achieving peers. Results showed that these students achieved higher in concept development and equally well in computation and problem-solving than their similarly achieving cohorts from the two previous years. In addition to the fact that a good number of these "average achievers" outperformed many "high achievers," they went on to study substantially more advanced mathematics during high school and attain significantly higher grades in these classes than their cohort peers. Furthermore, we found that high-achieving students suffered no decrease in computation or problem-solving achievement, and they scored higher in concepts than their cohort peer groups from previous years.

In a study involving instructional adaptation, Mason and Good (1993) found that intermediate level students in classes featuring whole-class instruction and situational remediation and enrichment via small ad hoc groups outperformed students in classes featuring the teaching of two groups (high- and low-ability) in mathematics computation. Although this study was conducted in a context in which students had been regrouped, these authors argue that adaptive instruction, active learning, and situational remediation and enrichment can provide both academic and social benefits for students (e.g., more meaningful curriculum and instruction, increased individualization, less social labeling, and fewer low expectation effects).

In those cases in which tracks and ability groups must be formed, they might be used to enrich the curriculum and lives of students within these classrooms. As Page (1991) argues:

> Through discourse together, we may comprehend the spectacular diversity of American culture, critique the conditions that all too frequently constrain its manifestations in schools (for all students and teachers, but all too often particularly for those who are lower track or lower status), and act to value it as an affirmation of the distinctive humanity of each and all of us. (p. 252)

Conclusion

Organizational changes alone will not alter dramatically the educational experiences of middle grade students. Only new educational goals, enhanced curriculum, and improved instructional practices can strategically replace in-depth content coverage unrelated to students' experiences with students' real-world concerns and applications. As Lounsbury and Clark (1990) write:

> Developmental responsiveness carries with it major implications for school restructuring. It demands that middle level educators move beyond the "mere" form of middle level programs, such as interdisciplinary teaming and teacher advisories, and become increasingly concerned with the substance of these programs. (p. 134)

As Mergendollar (1993a) points out, "structural changes, by themselves, are too distal to significantly improve students' learning and attitudes" (p. 444). Instead, structural reforms can only facilitate more central changes in school goals, teaching, and learning outcomes.

This chapter has argued that flexible scheduling, interdisciplinary teaming, and adaptive grouping and instructional practices should replace departmentalized scheduling and rigid and uncritical grouping practices. Although it bears repeating that these structures alone cannot replace the day-in-and-day-out work of relating to students, developing a relevant curriculum, and using varied grouping and instructional strategies aimed at meeting the intellectual, social, emotional, and physical needs of young adolescents, they can play an important role in freeing teachers to communicate with parents and other school personnel and to creatively group, advise, instruct, and evaluate students.

NOTE

*I would like to thank Sandy Simpson for reviewing this chapter and making valuable suggestions. Any errors or shortcomings that remain are the author's alone.

REFERENCES

Alexander, W. M., and George, P. S. (1981). *The exemplary middle school.* New York: Holt, Rinehart and Winston.

Alexander, W. M., and McEwin, C. K. (1988). *Preparing to teach at the middle level.* Columbus, OH: National Middle School Association.

Alexander, W. M., and McEwin, C. K. (1989). *Schools in the middle: Status and progress.* Columbus, OH: National Middle School Association.

Alexander, W. M., Williams, E. I., Compton, M., Hines, V. A., Prescott, D., and Kealy, R. (1968). *The emergent middle school*. New York: Holt, Rinehart and Winston.

Arhar, J. M. (1992). Interdisciplinary teaming and the social bonding of middle level students. In J. L. Irvin (Ed.), *Transforming middle level education: Perspectives and possibilities* (pp. 139–161). Needham Heights, MA: Allyn and Bacon.

Bangert, R. L., Kulik, J. A., and Kulik, Chenn-Lin C. (1983). Individualized systems of instruction in secondary schools. *Review of Educational Research 53*: 143–158.

Beane, J. A. (1990). *A middle school curriculum: From rhetoric to reality*. Columbus, OH: National Middle School Association.

Becker, H. J. (1987, April). Addressing the needs of different groups of early adolescents: Effects of varying school and classroom organizational practices on students from different social backgrounds and ability groups. Paper presented at the meeting of the American Educational Research Association, Washington, DC.

Braddock, J. H. (1990). Tracking the middle grades: National patterns of grouping for instruction. *Phi Delta Kappan 71*: 445 –449.

Calhoun, F. D. (1983). *Organization of the middle grades: A summary of research*. Arlington, VA: Educational Research Services, Inc.

Carnegie Council on Adolescent Development. (1989). *Turning points: Preparing American youth for the 21st century*. Washington, DC: Author.

Cuban, L. (1992). What happens to reforms that last? The case of the junior high school. *American Educational Research Journal 29*: 227–251.

Curtis, T. E., and Bidwell, W. W. (1977). *Curriculum and instruction for emerging adolescents*. Reading, PA: Addison-Wesley.

Dewey, J. (1902). *The child and the curriculum/The school and society*. Chicago: University Press.

Elmore, R. F. (1990). *Restructuring schools: The next generation of educational reform*. San Francisco: Jossey-Bass.

Epstein, J. L., and Mac Iver, D. J. (1988). *Education in the middle grades: Overview of a national survey of practices and trends*. Baltimore, MD: Johns Hopkins University Center for Research on Elementary and Middle Schools.

Epstein, J. L. (1990). What matters in the middle grades—grade span or practices? *Phi Delta Kappan* 71: 438–444.

George, P. (1975, Spring). *Ten years of open space schools: A review of the research*. Gainesville, FL: The Florida Educational Research and Development Council), pp. 10–20.

George, P. (1988). Tracking and ability grouping. *Middle School Journal* 20(1): 21–28.

George, P., and Oldaker, L. (1985). *Evidence for the middle school*. Columbus, OH: National Middle School Association.

Glatthorn, A. A., and Spencer, N. K. (1986). *Middle school/junior high principal's handbook: A practical guide for developing better schools*. Englewood Cliffs, NJ: Prentice-Hall.

Goodlad, J. I. (1984). *A place called school: Prospects for the future*. New York: McGraw Hill.

Gruhn, W. T., and Douglass, H. R. (1947). *The modern junior high school*. New York: The Ronald Press.

Gutiérrez, R., and Slavin, R. E. (1992). Achievement effects of the nongraded elementary school: A best-evidence synthesis. *Review of Educational Research* 62(4): 333–376.

Hirschi, T. (1969). *Causes of delinquency*. Los Angeles: University of California Press.

Howard, A. W., and Stoumbis, G. C. (1970). *The junior high and middle school: Issues and practices*. Scranton, NJ: Intext.

Johnston, J. H., and Markle, G. C. (1986). *What research says to the middle level practitioner*. Columbus, OH: National Middle School Association.

Koos, L. (1920). The peculiar functions of the junior high school: Their relative importance. *School Review 28*: 673–681.

Lieberman, A. (Ed.). (1988). *Developing a professional culture in schools*. New York: Teachers College Press.

Lipsitz, J. (1984). *Successful schools for young adolescents*. New Brunswick, CT: Transaction.

Lounsbury, J. H., and Clark, D. C. (1990). *Inside grade eight: From apathy to excitement*. Reston, VA: National Association of Secondary School Principals.

Lounsbury, J. H. and Vars, G. F. (1978). *A curriculum for the middle school years*. New York: Harper and Row.

Mac Iver, D. J. (1990). Meeting the needs of young adolescents: Advisory groups, interdisciplinary teaching teams, and school transition programs. *Phi Delta Kappan 71*: 458–464.

Mason, D. A., and Good, T. L. (1993). Effects of two-group and whole-class teaching on regrouped elementary students' mathematics achievement. *American Educational Research Journal 30*: 328– 360.

Mason, D. A., Schroeter, D. D., Combs, R. K., and Washington, K. (1992). Assigning average-achieving eighth graders to advanced mathematics classes in an urban junior high. *Elementary School Journal 92*: 587–599.

McCarthy, R. J. (1972). *The ungraded middle school*. West Nyack, NJ: Parker.

McEwin, C. K., and Alexander, W. M. (1982). *The status of middle/junior high teacher education programs: A research report*. Boone, NC: Appalachian State University.

McEwin, C. K., and Alexander, W. M. (1987). *Research of middle level teacher education programs: A second survey (1986–1987)*. Boone, NC: Appalachian State University.

McPartland, J. M. (1990). Staffing decisions in the middle grades: Balancing quality instruction and teacher/student relations. *Phi Delta Kappan 71*: 465–469.

Mergendollar, J. R. (1993a). Introduction: The role of research in the reform of middle grades education. *The Elementary School Journal 93*: 443–446.

Mergendollar, J. R. (Ed.). (1993b). Middle grades research and reform [Special Issue]. *The Elementary School Journal 93*(5): 443–658.

Murphy, J. (1991). *Restructuring schools: Capturing and assessing the phenomena*. New York: Teachers College Press.

National Middle School Association. (1992). *This we believe*. Columbus, OH: Author.

National Middle School Association. (1992). *Resolutions*. Columbus, OH: Author.

Oakes, J. (1985). *Keeping track: How schools structure inequality*. New Haven, CT: Yale University Press.

Page, R. N. (1991). *Lower-track classrooms: A curricular and cultural perspective*. New York: Teachers College Press.

Pumerantz, P., and Galano, R. W. (1972). *Establishing interdisciplinary programs in the middle school*. West Nyack, NJ: Parker.

Rock, D. A., and Hemphill, J. K. (1966). *Report of the junior high school principalship.* Reston, VA: National Association of Secondary School Principals.

Rosenholtz, S. (1989). *Teachers workplace: A study of social organizations.* New York: Longman.

Rowan, B. (1990). Applying conceptions of teaching to organizational reform. In R. F. Elmore (Ed.), *Restructuring schools: The next generation of educational reform* (pp. 31–58). San Francisco: Jossey Bass.

Simpson, R. L. (1985). Social control of occupation and work. *Annual Review of Sociology 11*: 415–436.

Slavin, R. E. (1987). Ability grouping and student achievement in elementary schools: A best-evidence synthesis. *Review of Educational Research 57*: 293–336.

Slavin, R. E. (1990). Achievement effects of ability grouping in secondary schools: A best-evidence synthesis. *Review of Educational Research, 60*: 471–499.

Slavin, R. E. (1993). Ability grouping in the middle grades: Achievement effects and alternatives. In J. R. Mergendollar (Ed.)., Middle Grades Research and Reform [Special Issue]. *The Elementary School Journal 93*, 535–552.

Valentine, J., Clark, D. C., Irvin, J. L., Keefe, J. W., and Melton, G. (1993). *Leadership in middle level education: A national survey of middle level leaders and schools* (Vol. 1). Reston, VA: National Association of Secondary School Principals.

Valentine, J., Clark, D. C., Nickerson, N. C., and Keefe, J. W. (1981). *The middle level principalship: A survey of middle level principals and programs* (Vol. 1). Reston, VA: National Association of Secondary School Principals.

Van Til, W. T., Vars, G. F., and Lounsbury, J. H. (1961). *Modern education for the junior high school years.* New York: Bobbs- Merrill.

Wehlage, G. G., Rutter, R. A., Smith, G. A., Lesko, N., and Fernandez, R. R. (1989). *Reducing the risk: Schools as communities of support.* Philadelphia: Falmer Press.

CHAPTER 10

Reshaping Core Curriculum: Getting People Ready for the World

Jeanneine P. Jones

> Teachers ... help people learn and know how to live a full life. They also help you find your real self. On the other hand, teachers can also treat you like a passenger on a bus, not really caring for you. I think teachers are good, because they help the world keep on going. ... The most important thing teachers do is get people ready for the world. (An eighth grade student [Jones, 1990, p. 46])

Middle school advocates echo this challenge to "get people ready for the world." The Carnegie Council on Adolescent Development (1989) stressed that "successful participation in a technically based and interdependent world economy will require that we have a more skillful and adaptable workforce than ever before—at every level from the factory floor to top management" (p. 12). Stevenson and Carr (1993) characterized our task as one of preparing students who can "take responsibility for themselves, each other, and our planet" (p. 10). They encouraged teachers to be aware of learning when it is at its best: intriguing, challenging, and fulfilling, because, they assured us, "we are preparing our students for a world very different from that which we have known" (p. 10). Middle level experts collectively challenge us to change quickly the shape of things as they are and to look ahead with a clear focus to this task of getting our students ready to join the world as healthy, ethical, and successful adults (Arnold, 1991; Beane, 1992; Erb, 1991; George and Alexander, 1993; George, Stevenson,

Thomason, and Beane, 1992; Lounsbury, 1991a, 1991b; Stevenson, 1991; Stevenson and Carr, 1993; Toepfer, 1992).

This thought can be illustrated easily through an old cartoon strip wherein Pogo, the central character, declared that "we have met the enemy and he is us" (Lounsbury, 1991a, p. 33). Lounsbury pointed out that few samplings of common wisdom have been repeated as often as this addition to our culture's folklore. He found real meaning in this small phrase, adding that "while we may be the cause of most of our problems we are, at the same time, the real source of the solutions in almost all cases" (1991a, p. 33).

As middle level educators, we have come to recognize ourselves as crucial in this challenge of preparing adolescents for a healthy and successful life in a rapidly changing world. One key component in this challenge is a core curriculum that is more integrated, child centered, and literacy based than ever before.

Core curriculum has been called by any number of labels in the past, including block, general education, unified studies, common learning, basic education, and integrated program (George and Alexander, 1993; Wraga, 1992). Regardless of the label, educators historically have used it to reference either a set of learning objectives that are deemed vital to a child's basic education or a series of required courses (Wraga, 1992). Additionally, this aspect of schooling long has been segregated into traditional boundaries of language arts, social studies, mathematics, and science, where they often do little to address the personal interests and needs of young adolescents (Arnold, 1991; Beane, 1990, 1992; Lounsbury, 1991b; McDonough, 1991; Stevenson, 1991; Wraga, 1992). Rather, what is taught to middle school students frequently is shaped by many pressures, including standardized testing and curriculum mandates, departmentalization and other structures of tradition, and the expectations of both parents and the young adolescents who comprise the school's population (Beane, 1990). Not only do these classroom curriculums fail to address the personal interests and complexities of adolescence, but, as Beane noted, "The curriculum question has been an 'absent presence' in the middle school movement" (p. 1).

Stevenson (1991) reminded us that both teachers and parents have long harbored the belief that the primary task of the middle school is to prepare students for high school. Lounsbury (1991b) added, "The 3 R's are basic, but they do not constitute an education, any more than the silver, crystal, and china of a place setting comprise a fine dinner" (p. 5). He continued by noting that these schools exist to "guide, support, and educate youth during life's most critical phase, a significant and demanding task in and of itself. And if it does that successfully the high school will be negotiated successfully" (p. 6). Our young eighth grader would agree: a teacher's job is to get people ready for the world, not just the classroom beyond the current grade level.

This chapter will explore these thoughts by first surveying the realities that exist within many American middle schools. It will then focus on core curriculum practices as they should be if we are going to address and transcend these realities. The final section will synthesize suggestions for reshaping this curriculum and share an illustration of it.

The Realities of Middle School

Sketching the Picture

In 1989 the Carnegie Council on Adolescent Development issued a pivotal report titled *Turning Points: Preparing American Youth for the 21st Century*. This document awakened the public to a research base that focused national attention on the 10- to-15-year-old. It clearly described the current climate and setting as found in an abundance of America's middle level schools. It noted that many of them "function as mills that contain and process endless streams of students" (p. 37), often up to 2,000 in some areas. The Carnegie Council further asked that we consider what is expected of each of these developmentally diverse young adults:

> Every 50 minutes, perhaps 6 or 7 times each day, assemble with 30 or so of your peers, each time in a different group, sit silently in a chair in neat, frozen rows, and try to catch

> hold of knowledge as it whizzes by you in the words of an adult you met only at the beginning of this school year. The subject of one class has nothing to do with the subject of the next class. If a concept is confusing, don't ask for help, there isn't time to explain. If something interests you deeply, don't stop to think about it, there's too much to cover. If your feelings of awkwardness about your rapid growth make it difficult to concentrate, keep your concerns to yourself. And don't dare help or even talk to your fellow students in class; that may be considered cheating. (p. 37)

A recent study of eighth graders in this country also illustrated this gap between curriculum philosophy and implementation. The National Center for Education Statistics, U.S. Department of Education, conducted this investigation in three segments. The first phase described the experiences of American eighth graders in great detail (National Education Longitudinal Study of 1988 [NELS:88]). The second and third waves of the study followed in two-year intervals and described the same class of students as tenth graders and then as high school seniors.

The objective was simple yet serious.

> The longitudinal design of NELS:88 allows researchers to observe not only the critical transition of students from middle or junior high school to high school, but also to identify early student, school, and parental experiences that promote student learning. [The study was designed to] take into consideration the much larger environment in which the student functions and develops. The study assumes that a student's eighth grade experiences are critical to the student's further social, emotional, and academic development. (NELS:88, p. ix)

One of the major research questions that undergirds the study was identical to that asked repeatedly by camps of middle level educators: "Under what circumstances do our children flourish and succeed?"

The National Middle School Association (NMSA) discussed this study and its major research question in terms of America's middle level schools. It noted that the average middle school attends poorly to the adolescent needs and societal demands that have been previously described. Based on the results of the NELS:88 study, NMSA (1991) called for schools to become "communities of learning" if they are indeed to prove effective. It underscored the emphasis that must be placed on

> [A] climate that enhances intellectual dev-
> elopment . . . [has] high expectations of students,
> challenge(s) them with an integrated curriculum, offer(s)
> meaningful relationships with adults, and maintain(s) an
> environment where students feel safe. Such communities
> are places where students take schooling seriously, where
> they are motivated and ready to learn, and where they are
> engaged in their schoolwork. (NMSA, p. 8)

Unfortunately, the discussion continued, "[T]hese learning communities are not found in most of our schools. . . . The portrait painted by NELS:88 reveals the disparity between the schools we have and those we want for young adolescents" (NMSA, p. 8).

In outlining this belief, NMSA recognized three areas that it deemed vital to the successful schooling of developing young adolescents. It then counterpointed these areas with frightening pictures of reality, colored by the statistics offered from NELS:88. These three areas, with two examples each, include

> School Relationships. An important characteristic of
> effective schools is that students have stable, close, and
> mutually respectful relationships with teachers and other
> school personnel. But the data showed that by spring of
> the school year, one-third of eighth grade students said
> they had not talked with their teacher about coursework
> during the school year. Two-thirds of the schools had
> departmentalized instruction, where students move
> throughout the day from class to class, teacher to teacher.
>
> Students in Schools. The model of an effective school
> assumes that students take school seriously and arrive
> prepared to learn. But according to NELS:88, nearly one-
> half of the students said they were bored at least half of
> the time they spent in school. More than one-third of the
> students' parents had received a warning about their
> children's grades, and 22 percent had received a warning
> about the children's behavior.

School climate. To be effective, schools need to provide an environment that engages students. While many students are disengaged, other students see the disruptions caused by their disengaged classmates as significant problems. The NELS:88 data showed that about 40 percent of eighth graders reported class disruptions by other students often got in the way of their learning. While most eighth grade students felt safe in school, many students reported that physical conflicts, robbery or theft, vandalism of school property, alcohol, illegal drugs, and weapons were moderate to serious problems at their schools. (NMSA, p. 8)

Coloring in the Current Curriculum

Confronting these classrooms that are out of synchronization with adolescent needs is no small task, as Lipsitz (1984) noted: "Translating philosophy into curriculum is the most difficult feat for schools to accomplish. The translation to climate and organizational structure appears to be much easier for . . . schools than the translation of purpose into curriculum" (p. 188)

Beane (1990) agreed. Long a reflective advocate of middle level philosophy, he noted that this movement, barely 30 years old, has witnessed the mastery of many practices designed to meet the myriad of developmental diversities found within the emerging adolescent, such as interdisciplinary teaming, advisor-advisee sessions, flexible block scheduling, and exploratory programs. Yet most have failed to address the curriculum, which is the most crucial question of all.

The words *developmental responsiveness* have all but become a cliché in both basal textbooks and teacher-designed instruction. Arnold (1991) noted that schools may have well-conceived mission statements, but "practice amounts to little more than a few hands-on activities, an occasional field trip, a dash of Piagetian jargon, and business as usual" (p. 10). He pulled two illustrations from a society whose mixed messages often are ignored within the developmental considerations of the middle school curriculum.

The first illustration from Arnold (1991) featured adolescents who find it impossible to make societal contributions that will be recognized as useful or needed by the adults who surround them. Although opportunities may be out of the child's control due to age-related or financial limitations, the student still perceives the message as, "I am not valuable. I have little or nothing to offer to the adult world."

Arnold's (1991) second illustration stemmed from the American advertising industry, which goes to great lengths to portray youngsters who are physically, socially, and intellectually perfect in almost every way. To the developing adolescent, this message often causes a downward spiral in self-esteem. When middle school curricula neglect these messages, many opportunities for rich and meaningful teaching are lost.

Merenbloom (1988) long has insisted that a responsive curriculum must be designed around an interdisciplinary approach to learning that includes realistic messages such as those suggested by Arnold. However, Beane (1990) found that this generally is not achieved in today's middle schools. Teachers persist in identifying themselves by discipline orientation, and their teaching follows a fragmented suit. Likewise, the Middle Level Curriculum Project (McDonough, 1991) characterized the existing curriculum as one that features a segmented, segregated content and inactive students who exhibit poor social skills and insignificant levels of intellectual growth. The project's members added that

> [M]uch of the content contained in traditional subject areas is obsolete in an era of information and knowledge explosion. The very structure of these content areas is questionable in a world where multiplicity is valued and complexity is viewed as natural. (p. 34)

Toepfer (1992) cautioned that this tendency to maintain departmentalized instruction is the least desirable of all middle level organizational patterns, although strong teams can compensate for this in part. Teams must, however, first penetrate the segregated barriers that have long been characteristic of core curriculum practices. For example, interdisciplinary units of instruction are championed as a strategy that successfully promotes integrated, interactive curriculum. However, these units generally take on the restrictions of traditional discipline segregation and become multidisciplinary units as teams of teachers often stretch one theme to fit across individual requirements, as found in separate classrooms and separate textbooks, rather than blur the lines of demarcation (Beane, 1992; Stevenson and Carr, 1993).

Arnold (1991) summarized students' reactions to existing curriculum by noting that "too often young adolescents perceive that curriculum has nothing to do with them; there is nothing that excites their passions. It is viewed as something done to them, a series of hoops to jump through for extrinsic rewards" (p. 12). It would seem that we as teachers have made an effort to implement curriculum innovations. Yet, we have fallen short of taking that leap of faith that requires that we abandon the confines of our discipline expertise in favor of educating the whole child rather than finishing the whole text.

In short, middle level advocates proceed to champion an integrated approach to wholeness while they continue to witness a widening gap between philosophy and the realities of departmentalized curriculum implementation (Arnold, 1991; Beane, 1990; Capelluti and Brazee, 1992; Carnegie, 1989; George et al., 1992; Lipsitz, 1984; Lounsbury, 1991b; McDonough, 1991; Stevenson, 1991; Stevenson and Carr, 1993; Toepfer, 1992).

Lounsbury (1991b) found that "American education has continued to give homage to a curriculum that was established in the last century under vastly different circumstances and for a markedly different clientele" (p. 3). Tradition certainly has played a key role in this "business as usual" curriculum as found in contemporary schools. Capelluti and Brazee (1992) compiled and counterpointed five examples of common assumptions that are popular among today's educators.

1. There is a curriculum which is *the* standard against which all others should be measured. Curriculum in this case is seen as static, not ever-changing to meet the needs of students, community, and teachers.

2. Not all areas of the curriculum have equal importance or value. Core, academic, or basics are . . . generally considered more important than most other areas. And yet it is those other areas that often supply a learning spark which the core subjects do not.

3. Curriculum is a set of narrowly defined courses. In actuality, curriculum is all courses, learning, and activities which collectively make up the school day.
4. "The 'old style' curriculum was good enough for me, it should be good enough for my child." Stated simply, the curriculum of most middle level schools prepares students for life in the United States 40 years ago, not for today.
5. Curriculum is too important to leave to teachers. We need to allow teachers to use the knowledge and skills they have acquired to develop the most appropriate curriculum for their students. (pp. 11–12)

The Carnegie Council (1989) also underscored the dire need to teach life instead of isolated disciplines. It challenged adult society to participate fully and immediately in the healthy guidance of our emerging young adults, and it clearly stressed that middle level educators must make critical changes in curriculum and schooling if we are to successfully educate our children for life in 21st century America:

> Middle grade schools . . . are potentially society's most powerful force to recapture millions of youth adrift. Yet all too often they exacerbate the problems youth face.
>
> A volatile mismatch exists between the organization and curriculum of middle grade schools, and the intellectual, emotional, and interpersonal needs of young adolescents. . . . Today, as young adolescents move from elementary to middle or junior high schools, their involvement with learning diminishes and their rates of alienation, drug abuse, absenteeism, and dropping out begin to rise. . . .
>
> The ability of young adolescents to cope is often further jeopardized by a middle grade curriculum that assumes a need for an intellectual moratorium during early adolescence. . . . Furthermore, many middle grade schools pay little attention to the emotional, physical, and social development of their students. (p. 32)

Like the Carnegie Council and many others, Beane (1990) underscored this "volatile mismatch" between adolescent needs and school curriculum. He also took middle schools to task, noting that we have failed to give adequate attention to what is perhaps the most crucial question of all: "What should be the curriculum of the middle school?" This question has served to climax a discussion in progress, and it has further catapulted this curriculum conversation into a focused demand for immediate and drastic reform in our methods of schooling.

What Should Be the Curriculum . . . ?

> There is only one subject matter for education and that is Life in all its manifestations.
>
> Alfred North Whitehead (p. 10)

Beane (1990) crystallized a core curriculum question that now includes responses from the most respected scholars in today's educational arena. George and Alexander (1993) summarized a number of theses proposed by Beane, calling his work "a forceful case for this . . . concept" (p. 66) of a reorganized core curriculum. Their synthesis included the following:

1. The traditional curriculum is far from being developmentally appropriate for middle school students. It is, writes Beane, "alien to life" itself.
2. The success of the contemporary middle school movement is due, in part, to the refusal of middle school educators to challenge the deeply held subject matter loyalties of traditional secondary teachers and subject area coordinators.
3. Interdisciplinary team organization does not guarantee an interdisciplinary curriculum.
4. The advocates of a subject-centered curriculum have defeated every attempt at major modifications, and remain as politically powerful interest groups devoted to protecting their special interest at the expense of virtually any other component of the school program and experience.
5. A developmentally appropriate curriculum would be dramatically different. It would be permeated by the concepts of democracy, human dignity, peace, and justice.

6. A developmentally appropriate curriculum would be most effectively implemented through the design and teaching of interdisciplinary thematic units.

7. The middle school movement is uniquely positioned to take on the challenge of authentic curriculum change; the time for a new curriculum in the middle school is now. (p. 66)

Many others have strengthened this core curriculum conversation, and they too advocate for immediate restructuring away from traditionally segregated subject boundaries (Arnold, 1991; Erb, 1991; Lounsbury, 1991a, 1991b; McDonough, 1991; Merenbloom, 1988; Wraga, 1992). Wraga also recommended a rewording of the traditional definition of *core curriculum*, suggesting that "true core programs . . . apply knowledge and abilities to a consideration of personal social problems and issues free of any concern for the pretense of subject divisions" (p. 17).

Likewise, participants in the Middle Level Curriculum Project (McDonough, 1991) similarly defined successful approaches to learning. These participants summarized effective curriculum in terms that manifested the objectives of each individual member of the curriculum camp. This definition stated that an effective middle school curriculum was:

[T]hat which encompasses the dynamic interaction of all experiences during the young adolescent's school day. This includes the instructional strategies, organizational arrangements, integrated curricular content, and cultural environment experienced by the young adolescent. This curriculum is not imposed on the student by the institution. Instead, young adolescents and members of the school community (students, teachers, parents, and community members) create curriculum in the process of seeking answers to questions and concerns in their search for self and social meanings. (p. 29)

Organized in the spring of 1990, this group of teachers, administrators, state department personnel, and university professors pinpointed as its objective "a middle level curriculum . . . which can and will meet young adolescents and their teachers where they are at any moment in their development. It will extend their world to encompass what lies beyond the school walls" (McDonough, 1991, p. 29).

Arnold (1991) also discussed the curriculum that is integrated into and relevant to the early adolescent's personal agenda. He suggested three major characteristics that make this curriculum "rich in meaning." First, he noted that it is genuinely important and worth knowing. A positive illustration was taken from the struggling middle level reader who still managed to complete and comprehend *The Autobiography of Malcolm X*, simply because it was a work that was relevant and compelling.

Second, this curriculum deals with values. It encourages students to reflect upon issues and to question their own beliefs and attitudes. It in no way imposes the perspectives of others on the students; rather, it encourages each student to grow within the framework of her or his personal values system.

Finally, if curriculum is rich in meaning, it must relate to both the needs and interests of the growing adolescent. Arnold noted that developmental responsiveness is the string that ties together the curriculum, which is based upon important ideas and values. This characteristic must be interwoven skillfully throughout everything that is found in the middle school.

This stemmed, in part, from an earlier discussion in which Arnold (1985) stressed five characteristics of the responsive middle school curriculum, including (1) It must help students to understand themselves and their place in the world; (2) It must be developmentally appropriate; (3) Genuine knowledge (thinking, feeling, doing) must be emphasized over the memorization of isolated facts and unrelated skills; (4) It must promote real experiences; and (5) It must be taught by educators who are secure in their own knowledge, decision-making abilities, and instincts so that they might overcome the confines of traditional models and policies.

Further, Arnold (1985) offers baseline questions to guide initial curriculum development. Among these are

1. What are the really important issues/ideas/concepts principles involved in the topic?
2. What major values/ethical issues are involved?
3. How does this topic relate to students' lives here and now, and how can this relation be extended?

4. How can we develop activities that stimulate inquiry, promote firsthand knowledge, and encourage expression, taking into account questions 1–3? (p. 12)

Referencing Arnold's *Visions of Teaching and Learning: Eighty Exemplary Middle Level Projects* (1990) as an excellent example of just such a curriculum, Stevenson (1991) recommended that we each become "students of young adolescent development" (p. 15). Respected for his many years of conversations with and observations of young adolescents, Stevenson insisted that "development must be given context and balanced by continually expanding direct knowledge of our immediate students—the very ones we engage every day" (p. 15). He added that all educators must be curriculum theorists, as well, for we must remain informed, imaginative, and integrative if we are going to successfully teach our students to "take responsibility for themselves, each other, and our planet" (Stevenson and Carr, 1993, p. 10).

Stevenson (1991) described the results of this richly integrated curriculum by noting that it focused on "minds-on engagements" in which youngsters have "a personal intellectual investment in learning" (p. 14). He shared the following illustration as proof of this successful curriculum:

It is easy to recognize when young adolescents are engaged in authentic learning. They talk with each other a lot about what they are doing, and that talk is a young adolescent equivalent of the discourse shared by scientists in a laboratory. Young thinkers ache to flex their growing intellectual muscles. Their talk is problem centered, speculative, reflective, and often, though not always, analytical. It reflects high interest, genuine bewilderment, and commitment to resolution. And when learning is at its absolute best, we get glimpses of the manchild and womanchild manifesting newfound intellectual empowerment—an emerging, growing awareness of the intrigue of the world and an appreciation of their personal efficacy. Self-respect and dignity also derive from new enterprise. (p. 15)

Reshaping the Curriculum

Integrated and Child-Centered

It often is difficult to accomplish this goal of an integrated curriculum that is rich in meaning and, therefore, engages our students in "authentic learning." Surely, the first step is to establish a context in which the child is nurtured, stimulated, and challenged across the whole of the school setting. Both the Carnegie Council (1989) and NMSA (1991) share similar visions for this type of middle level education. Included in this description are the following principles, as suggested in the Carnegie Council's report, *Turning Points* (1989):

1. Large middle grade schools are divided into smaller communities for learning.
2. Middle grade schools transmit a core of common knowledge to all students.
3. Middle grade schools are organized to ensure success for all students.
4. Teachers and principals have the major responsibility and power to transform middle grade schools.
5. Teachers for the middle grades are specifically prepared to teach young adolescents.
6. Schools promote good health; the education and health of young adolescents are inextricably linked.
7. Families are allied with school staff through mutual respect, trust, and communication.
8. Schools and communities are partners in educating young adolescents. (p. 36)

When envisioning this campus and classroom setting, one turns a curious eye to Beane's (1990) question, "What ought to be the curriculum of the middle school?" In order to assist teachers in initiating a response, the Middle Level Curriculum Project (McDonough, 1991) identified a set of baseline questions, including

1. Who are young adolescents?
2. What questions do they have about themselves and their world?

3. What questions does the world pose for them?
4. In what kind of future world might they live?
5. How can adults help all students learn?
6. What activities should young adolescents engage in at school?
7. How do we design a curriculum that is good both for young adolescents as well as for the adults who share this world?
8. In the school experience, how do we utilize all ways of knowing and all areas of human experience? (pp. 29–30)

Calling these questions to task, the Middle Level Curriculum Project's participants set about making curriculum recommendations based on what is known about appropriate middle level education. Their suggested curriculum focuses on an adolescent's search for both self and social meaning, for this is essentially the most powerful concern of the emerging teenager. The sources for the development of this curriculum lie in the evolution of three types of questions

1. Inquiries which young adolescents generally have about themselves, including self-concept and self-esteem, the future, and personal experiences with developmental changes.
2. Questions that they often ask about their own world, including generalities or particulars concerning: family units, peer relationships, cultures and societies, as well as the global community.
3. Questions that frequently are not asked by early adolescents, yet which are important nonetheless, because they all live in a common world. For example, issues, problems, and concerns that are commonly confronted by all people because the world as a whole is interdependent: war and peace, human relations, school policies, environmental issues, prejudice, poverty, and others. (George et al., 1992, p. 93)

Perhaps these questions are best emphasized by Beane's (1990) suggestions for intersecting personal concerns, social issues, and whole-school core curriculum. He noted that in

crossing these, "We may find a promising way of
conceptualizing a general education that serves the dual purpose
of addressing the personal issues, needs, and problems of early
adolescents and the concerns of the larger world . . ." (p. 40).
Figure 1 presents Beane's (1990, p. 44) model, which explores the
intersection of 11 different adolescent and social concerns, and
then suggests topics for curriculum development based on these
common intersections.

Figure 1
Beane's Intersections Model for Curriculum Development

Early Adolescent Concerns	Curriculum Themes	Social Concerns
Understanding personal changes	TRANSITIONS	Living in a changing world
Developing a personal identity	IDENTITIES	Cultural diversity
Finding a place in the group	INTERDEPENDENCE	Global interdependence
Personal fitness	Wellness	Environmental protection
Social status	SOCIAL STRUCTURES	Class systems
Dealing with adults	INDEPENDENCE	Human rights
Peer conflict and gangs	CONFLICT RESOLUTION	Global conflict
Commercial pressures	COMMERCIALISM	Effects of media
Questioning authority	JUSTICE	Laws and social customs
Personal friendships	CARING	Social welfare
Living in the school	INSTITUTIONS	Social institutions

(Beane, 1990, p. 44), Used with permission of National Middle School
Association.

Beane (1990) continued an explanation by recommending
that specific skills also be applied to the intersections model for
curriculum development. Included in these must be the usual
school concerns. However, teachers also should add such things
as reflective thinking, critical ethics, problem-solving, valuing,

self-concept and self-esteem enhancement, social action skills, and searching for completeness and meaning. Because "middle schools do not exist in a vacuum," Beane further suggested that curriculum must display a respect for and involvement in "the enduring ideas upon which . . . society is based" (p. 43). Three of the most important of these ideas include democracy, human dignity, and diversity. Clearly stating that this curriculum should be *the* curriculum, Beane (1990) summarized by noting that "even though the idea of a needs- and problem-centered core is not new, I have departed from previous proposals by extending this view of the curriculum across the entire school" (p. 49).

This change to a truly integrated and relevant core curriculum—one that involves all teachers and all disciplines—can certainly prevent a curriculum that ignores the needs of students and social concerns from worsening and eventually will turn it around. For example, Glasser (1992) found that in the "quality school" one never forgets that

> [P]eople, not curriculum, are the desired outcomes of schooling. What we want to develop are students who have the skills to become active contributors to society, who are enthusiastic about what they have learned, and who are aware of how learning can be of use to them in the future. (p. 674)

The Carnegie Council (1989) also championed these outcomes of curriculum reform and discussed five characteristics that are associated with its vision of the healthy young adolescent. It described this child as one who is "an intellectually reflective person, a person en route to a lifetime of meaningful work, a good citizen, a caring and ethical individual, and a healthy person" (p. 15).

Perhaps these outcomes, and a plea to participate in their achievement, were best summarized by George et al. (1992).

> In the end, it is hard to believe that we would not support what these new curriculum visions offer to early adolescents. Here is the opportunity to help these students make closer connections with the world in which they live, to construct powerful meanings around their own concerns and those of the larger world, to integrate self

and social interests, to gain a sense of personal and social
efficacy, to experience learning as a whole and unified
activity, to bring knowledge and skill to life in meaningful
ways, and to have richer and fuller lives as early
adolescents. Isn't this what we should all want for early
adolescents and their middle schools? (p. 103)

Literacy-Based

In essence, one first must consider the entire spectrum of
the successful middle level curriculum and, then, mentally
connect it with students who build powerful meanings from
personal concerns, developmental issues, apprehensions, and
celebrations. When one considers the classroom in this light, one
quickly realizes that if schools are to be integrated successfully,
they also must be literacy based across the curriculum, for
increasingly sophisticated skills are required by all facets of our
global society.

The Commission on Reading's report, *Becoming a Nation of
Readers* (Anderson, Hiebert, Scott, and Wilkinson, 1985),
underscored the fact that "reading is a basic life skill. It is a
cornerstone for a child's success in school, and indeed,
throughout life. Without the ability to read well, opportunities
for personal fulfillment and job success inevitably will be lost"
(p. 1).

Glasser's (1992) vision of the successful student included
the "skills to become an active contributor to society" (p. 694).
This adolescent also is described as one "who could bring
knowledge and skill to life in meaningful ways . . . [thus having]
richer and fuller lives" (George et al., 1992, p. 103).

Many other educators emphasized reading instruction,
noting vocabulary, study skills, functional reading, and
comprehension as primary components in every school's
accounting (Anderson et al., 1985; Atwell, 1987; Kozol, 1985;
Merenbloom, 1988; NELS:88; Rudman, 1984). A number of these
educators found, however, that this facet of successful core
curriculum development also evidences wide gaps between
philosophy and implementation.

The Carnegie Council (1989) charged every middle school in this country to be aware that the current job market demands much higher levels of literacy than schools are producing. NELS:88 found that overall, 14 percent of eighth graders scored below a basic level of proficiency in reading, 52 percent scored competent at a basic level, and only 34 percent scored masterful at an advanced level. Kozol (1985) added dreary shades to this picture of reality by stating that

> [E]ven if the economic situation is improved, and opportunities for jobs expand, [these] will not be jobs that can be filled by people who can read at less than ninth grade level. "By the 1990s," according to Dorothy Shields, education director at the AFL-CIO, "anyone who doesn't have at least a twelfth grade reading, writing, and calculating level will be absolutely lost." (p. 58)

It is imperative that relevant reading instruction be stressed across the middle school curriculum, regardless of discipline. It has become increasingly harder for young adolescents to meet the demands that are levied by a contemporary and highly technological society. Again the Carnegie Council's account leaps to mind, for it reported that "a recent National Assessment of Educational Progress found that only 11 percent of 13-year-olds were 'adept' readers, that is, able to understand relatively complicated written information" (p. 27). This leaves behind an alarming 89 percent who scored somewhere below this "adept" level of literacy.

The Carnegie Council (1989) illustrated the future of the young adolescent as it continued Kozol's description.

> The economy will increasingly have little use for youth who are impaired by high-risk behaviors or who are intellectually unprepared for the challenges of a changing economy. Job growth is concentrated in occupations that require much more than basic literacy. . . . The domestic job market today reflects the intense international competition in which the United States finds itself. This nation needs a workforce capable of critical thinking and creative problem-solving. Yet we continue to educate youth for the smokestack economy of generations past.

As a nation, therefore, we face a paradox of our own making. We have created an economy that seeks literate, technically trained, and committed workers, while simultaneously we produce many young men and women who are semi-literate or functionally illiterate, unable to think critically and untrained in technical skills, hampered by high-risk lifestyles, and alienated from the social mainstream. (pp. 27–28)

An Illustration

Integrated, child-centered, literacy-based . . . rich in meaning, developmentally responsive, in search of both self and social meaning. . . . Putting these phrases and philosophies into tangible form often is difficult for those who are new to this call for curriculum reform. In the end, we do "support what these new curriculum visions offer to early adolescents" (George et al., 1992, p. 103). We are just not sure how to go about actually implementing them in a classroom.

The following sketch will serve as an illustration of the type of core curriculum we have been discussing. As such, it includes not only basic content and applied skills, but also group discussions and individual projects with student-defined parameters. It is integrated across disciplines and out into life; it is literacy based and developmentally responsive. It is, above all, rich in meaning, for it involves the writing of personal history in a way that is relevant and motivating. At Beane's suggestion, it directly touches the transitions of being, for it merges an understanding of personal changes with a concern for life in a changing world. It engulfs faculty, students, family, and community; its outcome is a strengthening of all that we have been and are and will ever be as a society.

Recording Culture: A Study of Bill and Vera Cleaver: Family, Self, and Community

The opening days of this six-week study introduce us to a family of four children who come to understand both themselves and their roles in a changing society. *Where the Lilies Bloom* (Cleaver and Cleaver, 1969) is the first of the two novels read aloud and discussed in class; its sequel, *Trial Valley* (Cleaver and Cleaver, 1977) follows.

Where the Lilies Bloom introduces us to the Luther children as it lures us into their mountain lives. We experience with them the death of their remaining parent, Roy Luther, and the overwhelming hardships that quickly follow. It is through the determination and leadership of the second child, Mary Call, that the other three children begin prospecting the plants on their mountain home, and the lucrative art of wildcrafting is born to them. Determined to keep social services at bay and, thus, their family together, they resort to almost anything in order to survive. Continued in *Trial Valley*, their tale is a poignant retelling of love and family, loneliness and maturation, poverty and life on the edge. Both books are acclaimed highly by all adolescents who share their reality.

When viewing these children from a realistic stance, survival is indeed the immediate problem for Mary Call, the leader. This desperate need leads to a great deal of both self-reliance and introspection on her part. This, in turn, provides a catalyst for personal change within her, which then ripples out and fosters change in the other children. A dependency on one another develops, with each coming to understand her or his own unique contributions to the family unit. They therefore learn that true survival involves much more than supplying tangible needs.

Through classroom discussions and introspective journal writing, the students, like the Luther children, come to realize an enhanced understanding of both self and society. Desperate to survive their introduction to adolescence while still maintaining their "coolness," these emerging young adults become more and more aware of self as they mature into a heightened sense of objectivity, commitment, and maturity. In doing so, they come to understand that they are a vital piece of a greater whole.

This enhanced understanding encompasses their own family heritage, for a discussion of the novels leads to a book of cultural journalism which the students themselves have written and published. Perhaps that is the best part of all; these students go from merely studying literature to writing the literature that they study—it is real and so very, very appropriate. The last day serves as a celebration of this class book, which is based on collections of oral history.

Gathered from family, self, and community, these writings underscore the belief that our roles in a changing world are to be celebrated and supported, rather than feared and isolated. When viewed collectively, all of the literature, both read and generated, wraps its arms around history, reading, writing, heritage, community, pride, success, family, and bonds that are worth working for.

The following summary serves as a very brief outline of this unit. Instructional details may be found in Jones (1991).

Before Reading the Novels

1. Introduce the Cleavers to the students and share brief excerpts from the two novels in the form of book talks.
2. Encourage the students to begin talking with older family or community members about childhood memories, the way life has changed in their area, school traditions, family customs, cultural differences, and any other items of interest. Explain that they will soon have an opportunity to interview these older folks, record their responses, and then publish them in a classroom collection of experiences. A discussion of local history is a natural focus, for older citizens will provide rich and colorful vignettes that are unmatched by any textbook.

Reading the Novels

3. Discuss such things as the following: What would life be like with no parental authority figures and three dependent siblings? What immediate problems would you face? How would you resolve these problems or learn to cope with them?
4. Discuss relevant themes as the story unfolds: e.g., loneliness, death and the stages of grief, creative

problem-solving, inner strength, sibling rivalry, poverty, responsibility, guilt, and promises. Must promises always be kept? The students should generate both discussion and additional themes, as they must be the ones to provide the integration into personal experiences.

Writing Personal Histories

5. Discuss oral history and the importance of recording cultural heritage for future generations. Invite the students to participate in a cultural journalism project that will involve their own heritage or the traditions of an older friend or community member. Carefully model each aspect of the process. Plan for guest speakers who have special strengths in these areas.

6. Introduce students to the art of interviewing. Practice interviewing in the classroom. Brainstorm possible interview topics and model notetaking on the overhead. Make sure that each student has a personal comfort zone for the process.

7. Once interviews have been collected, write them up in class using a process approach to writing (Atwell, 1987). Note that strict attention must be given to preserving the cultural voice of the participant. Encourage students to include illustrations, family trees, favorite recipes, photographs that will copy, and any other items that relate to the theme of their section. When complete and edited, print and bind copies.

8. Host an Author's Tea! This makes a marvelous celebration for the conclusion of the unit, and it is further enhanced if those interviewed are invited for the reading of the completed personal histories. Allow the students the freedom to plan the entire morning through personally designed invitations and programs, decorations, and refreshments.

What a teaching rush this is! This study quickly blurs discipline lines and becomes, instead, a gigantic buzz of activity, discussion, and family chatter. The emphasis is on personal meaning and the acceptance of diversities that together make us all what we are.

Summary

"In a real sense, student development during early adolescence is hard to capture in generalities; these students often are described as having little in common but the fact of changing development itself" (George, 1991, p. 4). Facing significant turning points and an overlay of heavy societal demands, both young adolescents and their teachers often find these years to be difficult. It seems that adolescents often have little in common with each other or the adults who surround them. Their patterns of growth are diverse and complex, their mood swings are incredible, and their confusions are real. They turn to both schools and parents for guidance. However, they often find these havens void of understanding and concern, for these adults are struggling with their own changing roles and identities.

Current efforts to teach our children in traditional ways clearly have fallen short of the requirements presented by a rapidly changing and highly technological world. Instead of celebrating an adolescent who is fluent and articulate, we see one who is functionally illiterate by society's standards. Instead of the healthy rites of passage from childhood to adulthood, we see the student who approaches life from an attitude of indecision and peer group conformity.

Our challenge is a clear and difficult one. In order to nurture healthy young adolescents, we must find a core curriculum that will enhance their academic and social development while assuring them of the literacy levels required to meet the demands of our world. Classrooms that focus on life through the lenses of young adolescents hold merit in this challenge, but they must feature interdisciplinary teams of teachers who serve as facilitators rather than dictators of isolated curriculum mandates. This must include *all* teachers who specialize in that child—regardless of where their rooms are located and what their subjects include. These teams must be allowed the freedom found within flexible blocks of time, and their classrooms must be wrapped in an atmosphere of exploration, acceptance, structure, curiosity, and a passion for life—*all* of life. Only then will we graduate students who, (referring back to the opening quote) indeed, are truly "ready for the world."

REFERENCES

Anderson, R. C., Hiebert, E. H., Scott, J. A., and Wilkinson, I. A. G. (1985). *Becoming a nation of readers: The report of the Commission on Reading*. Washington, DC: The National Institute of Education.

Arnold, J. (1985). A responsive curriculum for emerging adolescents. *Middle School Journal* 16(3): 3, 14–18.

Arnold, J. (Ed.). (1990). *Visions of teaching and learning: Eighty exemplary middle level projects*. Columbus, OH: National Middle School Association.

Arnold, J. (1991). Towards a middle level curriculum rich in meaning. *Middle School Journal* 23(2): 8–12.

Atwell, N. (1987). *In the middle: Writing, reading, and learning with young adolescents*. Portsmouth, NH: Heinemann.

Beane, J. A. (1990). *A middle school curriculum: From rhetoric to reality*. Columbus, OH: National Middle School Association.

Beane, J. A. (1992). Turning the floor over: Reflections on a middle school curriculum. *Middle School Journal* 23(3): 34–40.

Capelluti, J., and Brazee, E. N. (1992). Middle level curriculum: Making sense. *Middle School Journal* 23(3): 11–15.

Carnegie Council on Adolescent Development. (1989). *Turning points: Preparing American youth for the 21st century*. New York: Carnegie Corporation.

Cleaver, V., and Cleaver, B. (1969). *Where the lilies bloom*. New York: Harper and Row.

Cleaver, V., and Cleaver, B. (1977). *Trial valley*. New York: Harper and Row.

Erb, T. O. (1991). Preparing prospective middle grades teachers to understand the curriculum. *Middle School Journal* 23(2): 24–28.

George, P. S. (1991). Student development and middle level school organization: A prolegomenon. *Midpoints: Occasional papers, 1.* Columbus, OH: National Middle School Association.

George, P. S., and Alexander, W.M. (1993). *The exemplary middle school* (2nd ed.). Fort Worth, TX: Harcourt Brace Jovanovich.

George, P. S., Stevenson, C., Thomason, J., and Beane, J. (1992). *The middle school—and beyond.* Alexandria, VA: Association for Supervision and Curriculum Development.

Glasser, W. (1992). The quality school curriculum. *Phi Delta Kappan 73:* 690–694.

Jones, J. P. (1990). Teacher to teacher: Getting people ready for the world. *Middle School Journal* 22(1): 46–48.

Jones, J. P. (1991). Books: Trapdoors to the imagination. *Middle School Journal* 23(1): 44–48.

Kozol, J. (1985). *Illiterate America.* New York: New American Library.

Lipsitz, J. (1984). *Successful schools for young adolescents.* New Brunswick: Transaction Books.

Lounsbury, J. H. (1991a). *As I see it.* Columbus, OH: National Middle School Association.

Lounsbury, J. H. (1991b). A fresh start for the middle school curriculum. *Middle School Journal* 23(2): 3–7.

McDonough, L. (1991). Middle level curriculum: The search for self and social meaning. *Middle School Journal,* 23(2): 29–35.

Merenbloom, E. Y. (1988). *Developing effective middle schools through faculty participation.* Columbus, OH: National Middle School Association.

National Center for Education Statistics. (1988). *A profile of the American eighth grader: NELS: 88 student descriptive summary.* Washington, DC: U. S. Government Printing Office.

National Middle School Association. (1991). Change needed to improve learning climate. *Middle Ground* 18(4): 8.

Rudman, M. K. (1984). *Children's literature: An issues approach.* New York: Longman.

Stevenson, C. (1991). You've gotta see the game to see the game. *Middle School Journal* 23(1): 13–17.

Stevenson, C., and Carr, J. F. (Eds). (1993). *Integrated studies in the middle grades: "Dancing through walls."* New York: Teachers College Press.

Toepfer, C. F. Jr., (1992). Curriculum for identity: A middle level educational obligation. *Middle School Journal* 23(3): 3–10.

Whitehead, A. N. (1929). *The aims of education and other essays.* New York: Macmillan Company.

Wraga, W. C. (1992). The core curriculum in the middle school: Retrospect and prospect. *Middle School Journal* 23(3): 16–23.

CHAPTER 11

Exploratory Curricula in the Middle Level

Jim Gill

Adolescent youth in our society always have possessed an instinctive desire to explore. By nature, young humans are curious beings. Opportunities for explorational discoveries frequently are presented to young adolescent students in their total milieu, as well as, for most, through their formal middle level education settings. The impact of the sum of those inquires and probing experiences during a crucial stage of an individual's development often has lifelong significance. A young person's philosophy regarding the meaning and scope of life often is influenced by those explorational activities.

Middle grades students are extremely curious about themselves and about the purpose of human beings in the world. They desire opportunities that invite them to participate in their own discoveries through personal involvement and experiences.

Therefore, middle level exploratory programs that address the developmental characteristics of middle grades students should be integral parts of educational programming at that level. Toepfer (1992a) emphasized that point when he stated, "Appropriately organized, middle level curriculum can assist the developmental need of the adolescents to discover who and what they are, and formulate who and what they may and can become" (p. 8).

Exploration in the Middle Grades

Exploration as a function of normal schooling is not a "faddish development" of the middle school movement of the past quarter century. It has roots in history. Schools in ancient Greece utilized exploration as a major component of programs for youth. During the 1700s, Benjamin Franklin's Academy included exploratory curricula as a primary part of its educational program in colonial America (Bergman, 1992). During the middle of the twentieth century exploration was considered to be one of the most successful aspects of the "junior high school movement" in American schools (Brazee, 1987).

Exploratory courses as specific curricula for young learners in middle grade schools constitute but a small segment of the concept of *exploration*. As the transformation of middle grades education proceeds during this decade, exploratory courses and exploration in general promise to have greater significance than in previous years. However, despite its longevity in formal education, exploration in middle grades education has not progressed dramatically, either through formal curricula or through overall program emphasis in schools. In some respects, it has taken a "back seat" to other aspects of education, even during the rapid emergence of the middle grades movement of recent years. Given the nature of the 11- to 14-year-old clientele and the apparent willingness of many middle grades educators to commit to change and improvement, it would appear that middle level education should be fertile ground for implementing adequately the concept of exploration. But often such is not the case.

Perhaps the relatively low status of exploration at the middle level is the result of inadequate advocacy. Lounsbury (1989) stated, "The dearth of information concerning the status of middle level education has long plagued this educational movement" (p. ix). The scarcity of research and evaluation on middle level education, including exploration, recently has been acknowledged. Beane (1990) aptly said, "Curriculum change is the weak link in the train of concepts that constitutes the middle school" (p. 19). His writings have been instrumental in the current focus on the issues related to curricula. Other researchers have pointed to the issue as one that has suffered from serious neglect for too long. Brazee (1987), in his forward to a special New England League of Middle Schools' publication titled *Exploratory Curriculum for the Middle Level*, stated that curriculum development had not kept pace with middle grades program development. In appealing for "A Fresh Start . . . ," Lounsbury (1991b, p. 3) urged middle level practitioners "to employ zero-based curriculum development" which would force them to analyze and justify present curricula. Given those developments, such questions as, "What curricula would be considered vital for all middle grades students?", should be asked. "What courses, if any, would be 'required?'" And, "Should there be exploration and enrichment experiences? If so, with what intensity might they be addressed?"

Research pertaining to the concept of exploration in general, and more specifically to the exploratory *content areas* or, as they are sometimes labeled the *specials* or the *arts areas*, has not always kept pace with the transition movement in the middle level. Bergman (1992) noted that curricula often have been based on "availability" rather than on what students have actually needed. Lounsbury (1991b) stated the curriculum dilemma poignantly when he wrote, "The reality is that American education has continued to give homage to a curriculum that was established in the last century under vastly different circumstances and for a vastly different student body" (p. 3).

A perusal of middle level professional literature confirms the notion that exploratory curriculum has not always been viewed by as educators having a high priority. Merenbloom (1986) created a master guide for middle school classroom teachers who desired to work in collaborative teams. Merenbloom's insight has provided tremendous structure for thousands of effective middle level interdisciplinary teams. However, his excellent work provided little substance for the guidance of teachers in the exploratory arts areas.

Exploration was given a somewhat cursory presentation in the Carnegie Council on Adolescent Development's monumental publication *Turning Points* when it stated, "A disciplined mind connotes a disposition toward inquiry, discovery, and reasoning across all subjects" (1989, p. 43). Although little endorsement of specific exploratory curricula was made in the report, it recommended that schools should "ensure success for all students" (Carnegie, 1989, p. 9). Stopping short of including exploratory curricula as one of its eight primary recommendations, the report did note that ". . . opportunities [for students] to exhibit excellence may lie outside the core program, in exploratory courses" (Carnegie, 1989, p. 49). Indices of reliable professional journals, such as the *Middle School Journal*, have contained surprisingly few entries under the topics of *exploration* and *exploratory curriculum*.

Another indication of the low status of middle level education in general, and exploratory curricula specifically, is the lack of recognition given to the level by the federal government. The United States Department of Education's program to recognize "schools of excellence" does not identify or recognize a distinct middle level category. Middle grades schools can make application in either the elementary or the secondary division. The program's criteria also fails to address the value of exploratory curricula in middle schools in the curriculum section of either the elementary or secondary division application. Another obvious lack of recognition of middle school exploratory areas is noted in the scarcity of presentations on *exploratory curriculum* at state, regional, and national conferences for middle level educators.

Some encouragement for expanding exploratory curricula was provided in 1988 when the National Middle School Association (NMSA) adopted a resolution that proclaimed, "Whereas . . . exploration is one middle school concept which is seriously compromised . . . be it resolved that middle level educators . . . encourage students to explore new areas of interest or knowledge" (NMSA, 1992, p. 32).

And, the concept of exploration in middle schools has begun to gain some attention in the literature of middle grades education. Melton, for instance, recently proclaimed, "I firmly believe that the curriculum of the middle level school is, and should be, exploratory in nature" (1992, p. 23). His article, along with other selections, was published in an exploratory edition of the *Minnesota Association of Middle Level Education Journal* (1992). Compton and Hawn's recent publication, *Exploration: The Total*

Curriculum (1993), provides the most comprehensive treatment of middle level exploration yet available. Their work provides an outline of the bases for exploration, the characteristics of exploration, required content courses, special content courses, special interest activities, planning and implementing exploratory curricula, success stories, and evaluation.

Indeed, there are many multifaceted issues regarding the concept of exploration in middle schools. The issues are extremely complex. They involve philosophy, funding, staffing patterns, and a number of special and local interest issues. Perhaps if these complicated issues are brought to the forefront and analyzed by researchers, the full significance of exploration for 10- to 15-year-old students will begin to emerge.

Traditional Exploratory Courses

Most middle grades schools segregate their courses into categories including the core or academic classes and the exploratory courses. English, social studies, mathematics, and science normally are considered part of the core classes. They generally are required courses taken by all students in a given grade or level. All exploratory courses may not always be required of every student in the school.

In their description of a "true middle school," Alexander and McEwin (1989) listed a "full-scale exploratory program" as one of its major characteristics. They noted that although it was introduced in junior high schools, the concept has been broadened in middle schools to offer the age group a "wide range spectrum of short-term courses and activities intended to help identify, explore, and develop worthwhile interests to be pursued later in and out of school" (p. 88). Many exploratory courses in middle schools are some of the same courses that were evident in successful junior high delivery models. Van Til, Lars, and Lounsbury (1961) appealed for ample provision for exploratory experiences, stating they should be "characteristic of curriculum organization for the junior high school years" (p. 341).

Although many early exploratory courses have been upgraded and modified with the advent of middle schools, and other less formal explorational opportunities have emerged recently, still additional opportunities should be provided for middle grades students if curriculum is to be truly developmentally appropriate. Common exploratory courses may include art, music, foreign languages, technology (formerly industrial arts), home living (formerly home economics), wellness, physical education, information sciences, keyboarding, and computer science. Some course offerings typically listed in "exploratory course" fields, for example, physical education, may in fact be required courses for students in most school districts. Other courses often included in exploratory programs are alternative languages, special reading, drama, careers, consumer education, and courses for exceptional students and others.

The length of exploratory class periods and the segment of the school term that they encompass, like the offerings themselves, vary greatly among middle grade schools. Other enrichment or interest-centered experiences may be offered in the form of minicourses, which may meet for lesser periods of time. Explorational experiences also are provided in middle schools through activities, clubs, and service-learning projects.

In a comprehensive survey, Alexander and McEwin (1989) assessed the status of exploratory classes in the United States in 1968 and 1988. Among their conclusions was this observation: "There were few consistent differences between the different grade organizations (6–8, 7–9, etc.) as to the offering of these traditional exploratory subjects" (p. 54). However, they did note a greater variety of exploration offerings such as activities and minicourses in middle grades schools.

During the 1940s, Gruhn defined the functions of the junior high school and identified exploration as one of its six primary functions. He contended exploration should lead pupils "to discover and explore their specialized interests, aptitudes, and abilities" as a basis for both educational opportunities and vocational decisions (Lounsbury, 1991a, p. 65).

Lounsbury has long been a proponent of exploration in education. He contends the "concept of exploration" is so central and universal at the middle level that the middle school could well be named *the exploratory school*. He pointed out that the exploratory component of the curriculum more nearly matches the nature of the age group than any other component. He stated that when properly viewed, exploration is "an approach and a point of view that should permeate the entire curriculum as well as being a particular component in the total program" (1991a, p. 61).

In the 1970s, Lounsbury and Vars (1978) proposed a three-part curriculum for the middle level. One part was named the *variable component*. The variable component of the curriculum they advocated did not focus on highly sequential or problem-focused learnings. They suggested the variable component could be provided through flexibly arranged courses and activities. The primary emphasis of this component was on exploration or "the discovery of one's interests and capabilities" (p. 98). Lounsbury and Vars also advocated a regular health and physical education program and required experiences in art, music, homemaking, and industrial arts. The components of the curriculum of any school are influenced by many factors, including mandated programs, grade level organization, staff and facilities, and the total population of the school.

Compton also highlighted the importance of exploration in middle grades curriculum. She proposed to clump the disciplines to help eliminate the myth of "separate but equal" status, which exists when the fine and practical arts, and other exploratory subjects, are offered separately from the core disciplines (Brazee, 1987). Compton's "unified curriculum" proposal included a humanities curriculum, a technology curriculum, and a personal studies curriculum.

Compton and Hawn (1993) offer excellent recommendations for middle schools. Included in their numerous recommendations was the suggestion that schools should create minicourses unique to the special interests of the students, teachers, and the nature of the community. One middle school in the Kansas City area, Leawood Middle School, has utilized clubs, including many of which are student sponsored. These serve as highly successful minicourses and provide a significant part of the opportunities for exploration. They also have engaged parents as sponsors of numerous community service programs to help meet the various needs of students.

Toepfer (1992b) pointed out the core of a school's "educational identity" resides in its curriculum and programs. He also remarked that (1) All students do not need to explore the same things at the same time; (2) All students do not need to explore the same things to the same extent; and (3) At any time some exploratory needs of students may be so urgent that they require immediate attention. (p. 9)

Programs that are not considered to be part of basic education have received critical reviews in national reports, such as the National Commission on Excellence in Education's *A Nation at Risk* (1983). Those reports normally have recommended a "return to the basics," including a more structured basic curriculum with more demanding school days and more rigorous school terms. One tactic that might counter the perception that exploratory curricula lacks vigor is to develop programs that "clearly reflect the relationship between the exploratory offering and general curricular skills" (Schneider, p. 23).

Exploratory courses, labeled by a few people as "frills," and the teachers who teach them sometimes become targets for elimination. Cuts in staff positions are more likely to be made in exploratory areas than in academics. Lipsitz (1984) concluded in *Successful Schools for Young Adolescents* that often "translating philosophy into curriculum is the most difficult feat for schools to accomplish" (p. 188).

The obvious strengths of exploratory course programs in many middle grade schools provide a case in point. It is difficult for public schools to satisfy all of society's demands. Middle grades educators often have heard criticisms leveled at exploratory courses, which are sometimes labeled "unnecessary" or nonessential in the education of young people. Yet, these courses sometimes are the only offerings in middle schools that maintain students' interests in formal schooling. Arnold (1991) suggested the exploratory areas are the very subjects in the middle school curriculum that are not boring to many students.

Despite some criticism, the exploratory curriculum has continued to maintain a substantial role in middle grades schools in the 1990s. Exploratory teachers generally are more willing to practice what is advocated by middle level experts than are many of the core teachers. Exploratory classes normally are alive with varied and engaging learning experiences. They tend to create what Stevenson appealed for when he stated, "Classes that involve reading, writing, listening, and speaking should be balanced at least in equal measure by ones that involve doing" (Stevenson and Carr, 1993, p. 24). Young adolescent learners are much more likely to participate in active learning experiences in the fine and practical arts and other exploratory areas than in the academic classes. In such classes, normally they are measured by individual outcomes; students are assessed on their own abilities and performances. The results of their efforts in exploratory classes also may enhance students' self-esteem.

Consumer feedback on exploratory courses almost always is positive. In many exploratory courses, students apply the basic principles of cooperative learning and teamwork in their pursuit of individual and collective goals. Such principles constitute much of the desired outcomes of general education. Although limited research has been conducted regarding exploratory courses and their long-term benefits for students, it is reasonable to assume the new wave of exploratory delivery models in middle level schools will meet with success.

The middle school movement owes a tremendous debt to the early proponents of exploration at the middle level. Although the proposals of the researchers previously noted and others may not have been fully implemented to their satisfaction, they have made an impact.

Improvements in middle school delivery models, such as "rotational wheels" or cycles for exploratory courses of shorter duration, have influenced positively the movement. Many middle schools have arranged for all or most students to experience exploratory classes during their initial year of middle school. Those courses normally are of shorter duration (i.e., six or nine weeks) than those formerly offered in junior high school models. A rotational scheduling pattern permits all students to engage in a variety of exploratory experiences. More students than ever before have been provided with hands-on learning opportunities through these courses. The Gwinnett County,

Georgia, middle schools use an entry wheel for exploring health and physical education, home economics, art, technology, and music. Within the technology portion of the exploratory wheel, the staff has developed a high-interest technology "wheel-within-the-course" approach. Within the technology course students may select activities from a variety of self-directed labs and interest centers. The Blue Valley (Overland Park), Kansas, middle schools use communications, art, industrial technology, home living, foreign language, and computer science in their sixth grade exploratory wheel. Compton and Hawn (1993) cite several unique and rather extensive exploratory programs in Winchester, Virginia; Shelburne, Vermont; Burlington, Massachusetts; and Winnetka, Illinois, which are purported to provide successful models for middle schools. Tremendous progress has been made in middle schools by utilizing technology in exploratory courses as a basis for improved learning opportunities.

Unfortunately, forces that drive decisions about exploratory courses frequently are local and state policies, guidelines, and requirements, along with community traditions and expectations. These forces may be restrictive and perpetuate old assumptions about what is "good" for kids. State requirements for wellness and physical education often are more limiting than the developmental needs of young adolescents require. Likewise, persons representing "community viewpoints" in the fine arts areas may push for music for a few students to the detriment of a music experience for all. Nonetheless, music program components are apt to have major influences in exploratory course delivery models. Indeed, music is likely to have a significant bearing not only on the exploratory curriculum but also on the total schedule of middle grades schools. The availability of qualified music teachers is crucial in many schools. Community traditions and expectations play vital roles in determining what curriculum is offered and when it is offered.

Teachers of Exploratory Curricula

Middle school teachers are very special educators. They possess unique traits and carry awesome responsibilities. Young adolescent students with whom they work are by nature very inquisitive as well as extremely demanding. To effectively teach these students requires special interests, skills, insights, and attitudes.

The professional literature pertaining to the credentialing of middle grades teachers has addressed the preparation and training of the teachers of the basic subjects. But what of exploratory course teachers?

Exploratory course teachers also are very special educators. The professional preparation of exploratory teachers in the middle grades has been given only cursory treatment. Frequently, the training they receive is geared less to the middle grades than that of their middle grades teaching counterparts who teach in the core curriculum areas. Exploratory area teachers frequently are certified K–12. In addition, they are isolated somewhat from other faculty members because of teaming arrangements and scheduling. They are less likely to obtain staff development opportunities geared to their individual needs.

Teachers long have been viewed as the keys to success of middle school programs. Lounsbury and Vars (1978) appealed for a "special breed" of teacher to work in middle schools. They suggested that middle school personnel should be "secure, open, empathic, positive, and caring individuals who genuinely like middle school students" (p. 1) . Perhaps in no other teaching field are these factors more needed than in the areas of exploratory courses.

Middle level environments espouse teaming and collaboration. However, exploratory area teachers often are isolated professional educators without the "belongingness" of a team. They are likely to be isolated in workplaces by facility locations, and they have less personal interaction with other professional colleagues. In fact, they frequently are required to compete with fellow exploratory teachers for student enrollment. An individual exploratory arts teacher may be the only such teacher in the school. In such cases, the success of the program rests heavily on that professional educator who may have little support from teammates or collaboration with colleagues. In some exploratory teaching fields, the instructional responsibility is not viewed as a team process but rather as an individual one.

Although exploratory teachers sometimes are organized as members of teams, they may not have students in common. Furthermore, they often have students from all grades. The preparation time provided for exploratory teachers generally is less than that of core team teachers in many middle schools.

Several issues related to middle level teacher preparation and credentialing serve as important influences in the development of quality middle level programming. During recent years, colleges and universities have made attempts to upgrade teacher preparation curricula for middle grades education. Erb (1991) identified several curricular ideals with which college students who are preparing to become middle school teachers should become familiar. Among the concepts cited were *exploration* or experiences focusing on exposure rather than mastery, *activities* or a part of the balanced curricula provided for all students, and *integration of learning*.

Recently, a great deal has been written about the concepts of exploration and integrated learning. Brazee and Capelluti (1992) advocated curriculum reform that would include the composition of a "new team." The new team could deliver the "experience curriculum" and would include staff other than the "core team" members in the building, including district employees, workers in the community, and parents. They suggested that integrated activities would result in more relevance for the learners.

Other researchers have heightened the awareness of and made recommendations for the greater use of community resources by middle grades schools. Greater use of communities as resources in middle grades education was one of the eight major recommendations for the middle level in *Turning Points* (Carnegie, 1989). Gill (1992) suggested that "community service should be mandated" (p. 1) for students in the middle grades. Service learning appears to be gaining status as a critical part of middle level education.

The issues of exploration and integration have become factors for the readiness of beginning teachers and for experienced exploratory area teachers as well. Middle grades teacher certification issues are complicated. They are difficult to assess as well as regulate. In some states, political power struggles have existed simply over the identification of the middle grades as a distinct and separate level of education. Many states have certification provisions that require subject matter content concentrations from either primary or secondary levels. Those requirements, especially for the teachers in exploratory course fields, rarely are geared exclusively to teachers credentialing to work in the middle grades. Often the expectations, requirements, and responsibilities of exploratory teachers in middle schools exceed what they were prepared to perform in teacher training institutions.

Conclusion

The primary impetus for the rapid development of the middle level movement during the past two decades has grown out of the recognition of and responses to the developmental needs of young adolescents. That solid foundation should ensure continued growth in the future.

Melton (1992) predicted the decade of the 1990s would be the decade of curriculum at the middle level and that much of this focus would center on exploration. What factors will be included in this focus? Unks (1992) suggested that an answer may be, "What is it we value in education?" (p. 46). Many complex issues pertaining to exploratory curricula and staffing patterns in middle level education are leading us to the realization that, "The exploratory program, so often kept on the periphery, is in reality the center of middle level education" (Drewry and Larkin, 1992, p. 33).

REFERENCES

Alexander, W., and McEwin, C. (1989). *Schools in the middle: Status and progress*. Columbus, OH: National Middle School Association.

Arnold, J. (1991). Towards a middle level curriculum rich in meaning. *Middle School Journal* 23(2): 8–12.

Beane, J. (1990). *A middle school curriculum: From rhetoric to reality*. Columbus, OH: National Middle School Association.

Bergman, S. (1992). Exploratory programs in the middle level school: A responsive idea. In J. Irvin (Ed.), *Transforming Middle Level Education: Perspectives and possibilities* (pp. 179–192). Needham Heights, MA: Allyn and Bacon.

Brazee, E. (1987). Exploration in the "regular" curriculum. In E. Brazee (Ed.), *Exploratory Curriculum for the Middle Level* (pp. 33–38). Rowley, MA: New England League of Middle Schools.

Brazee, E., and Capelluti, J. (1992). Middle level curriculum: Making sense. *Middle School Journal* 23(3): 11–15.

Carnegie Council on Adolescent Development. (1989). *Turning points: Preparing American youth for the 21st century*. Washington, DC: Author.

Compton, M., and Hawn, H. (1993). *Exploration: The total curriculum*. Columbus, OH: National Middle School Association.

Drewry, P., and Larkin, D. (1992). The exploratory program: The center of the middle school. *Minnesota Association of Middle Level Educators Journal* 6(2): 30–34.

Erb. T. (1991). Preparing prospective middle grades teachers to understand the curriculum. *Middle School Journal* 23(2): 24–28.

Erb, T. (1992). Encouraging gifted performance in middle schools. *Midpoints* 3(1): 1–24.

Gill, J. (1992). Community service: A mandate for the middle grades. *Dissemination Services on the Middle Grades*, 24(3): 1–4.

Lipsitz (1984). *Successful schools for young adolescents*. New Brunswick, NJ: Transaction Books.

Lounsbury, J. (1989). Foreward. In W. Alexander and C. McEwin, *Schools in the middle: Status and progress* (p. 11). Columbus, OH: National Middle School Association.

Lounsbury, J. (1991a). *As I see it*. Columbus, OH.: National Middle School Association.

Lounsbury, J. (1991b). A fresh start for the middle school curriculum. *Middle School Journal 23*(2): 3–7.

Lounsbury, J., and Vars, G. (1978). *A curriculum for the middle school years*. New York: Harper and Row.

Melton, G. (1992). Exploration and discovery. *Minnesota Association of Middle Level Educators Journal 6*(2): 23–24.

Merenbloom, E. (1986). *The team process in the middle school: A handbook for teachers*. Columbus, OH: National Middle School Association.

National Commission on Excellence in Education. (1983). *A nation at risk: The imperative for educational reform*. Washington DC: Government Printing Office.

National Middle School Association. (1992). *This we believe*. Columbus, OH: Author.

Schneider, G. (1986). Exploratory programs and educational reform—A second look. *Middle School Journal 17*(2) 3: 23–24.

Stevenson, C., and Carr, J. (1993). *Integrated studies in the middle years: "Dancing through walls."* New York: Teachers College Press.

Toepfer, C. F., Jr. (1992a). Curriculum for identity: A middle level educational obligation. *Middle School Journal 23*(3): 1–10.

Toepfer, C. F., Jr. (1992b). Exploring middle level exploratory education issues. *MAMLE Journal 6*(2): 9–13.

Unks, G. (1992). Three nations' curricula: What we can learn from them. *NASSP Bulletin 76*: 30–46.

Van Til, W., Vars, G., and Lounsbury, J. (1961). *Modern education for the junior high school years*. Indianapolis: Bobbs-Merrill.

CHAPTER 12

Advisor-Advisee Programs: Uniquely Designed to Meet the Affective Needs of Young Adolescents

Annette Digby, Samuel Totten, und Dennis Snider

Introduction

> One major challenge facing educators in the middle grades
> is how to provide early adolescents with the social and
> emotional support they need to succeed as students. As
> young adolescents strive for autonomy, as they grapple
> with learning how to regulate their own behavior and
> make responsible choices, their need for close, caring adult
> supervision and guidance is paramount. (Mac Iver, 1990,
> p. 458)

With the emergence of public school systems in America came
immediate discussions about the most appropriate structure for
meeting the needs of all students. During the late 1800s, those
discussions focused on the feasibility of only two divisions:
elementary schools (Grades 1–6) and secondary schools (Grades
7–12). Recognizing that students in Grades 7–9 had different
cognitive and affective needs from students in Grades 10–12,
educators advocated the establishment of an intermediate level
designed to bridge the gap between elementary and secondary
schools, thus leading to the establishment of junior high schools.

By the 1950s, however, the junior high school had reached a pinnacle of popularity (Johnson, Dupuis, Musial, and Hall, 1994). Even though educators and parents felt that the intermediate structure had served a useful purpose, they now began to question its effectiveness in meeting the needs of young adolescents (Johansen, Collins, and Johnson, 1990; Schurr, 1992). Citing *The Junior High School We Need* (Grantes, Noyce, Patterson, and Robertson, 1961), critics described the junior high school as "a hybrid institution, a school with an identity crisis as severe as the identity crisis endured by many of the young students within it" (George, Stevenson, Thomason, and Beane, 1992, p. 5). Over a decade later, the need to respond to the developmental characteristics of young adolescents in appropriate educational ways was reiterated in *The Middle School We Need* (Association for Supervision and Curriculum Development, 1975). Finally, efforts to address the unique needs, both cognitive and affective, of young adolescents seemed to be under way.

As middle level programs were developed and implemented, several individual components emerged as being essential to the effectiveness of the overall program. One such component is the advisor-advisee program. The purpose of this chapter is to provide an overview of advisor-advisee programs, to present principles and strategies for developing and implementing advisor-advisee programs, and to offer recommendations for those schools interested in strengthening or developing advisor-advisee programs.

Overview of Advisor-Advisee Programs

Because young adolescents are experiencing developmental changes, they often behave inconsistently, experience real and imagined fears, and display unexplained emotions (Wheelock and Dowman, 1988). Also known as *teacher advisory* programs, advisor-advisee programs are tailored to meet the diverse needs, feelings, desires, and problems resulting from such changes. Focusing on the affective needs of middle level students, Beane and Lipka (1987) presented the following description of advisor-advisee programs:

Advisory programs are designed to deal directly with the affective needs of transescents. Activities may range from non-formal interactions to use of systematically developed units whose organizing center are drawn from the common problems, needs, interests, or concerns of transescents, such as "getting along with peers," "living in the school," or "developing self-concept." In the best of these programs, transescents have an opportunity to get to know one school adult really well, to find a point of security in the institution, and to learn about what it means to be a healthy human being. (p. 40)

Rationale

During their first few years of elementary school, students are placed in self-contained classrooms. Accustomed to the security of having one lead teacher in a single classroom, students often experience difficulty and frustration while making the transition from elementary school to middle level settings. As the Carnegie Council on Adolescent Development (1989) noted in *Turning Points*, "Many large middle schools function as mills that contain and process endless streams of students. Within them are masses of anonymous youth" (p. 356). While all aspects of a sound middle level program should set out to ameliorate this concern, an excellent advisor-advisee program is uniquely qualified to address it. Discussed below are some key reasons for the development and implementation of advisor-advisee programs.

Advisor-advisee programs promote communities of learners. One of the key recommendations in *Turning Points* (Carnegie, 1989) is the need to create "small communities for learning where stable, close, mutually respectful relationships with adults and peers are considered fundamental for intellectual development and personal growth" of students (p. 9). Advisor-advisee programs are one of the many ways to establish such a "community of learners." Within the advisor-advisee learning community, students participate in collaborative activities and group projects that foster collegiality, mutual responsibility and concern, and active participation.

Advisor-advisee programs promote individual attention to students. Cited as one of the "key elements of [learning] communities" is "small group advisories that ensure that every student is known well by at least one adult" (Carnegie, 1989, p. 9). Students have an opportunity to develop a relationship with at least one adult who knows them personally, who cares about their happiness, who wants to see them succeed, and who is willing to listen to and assist with finding solutions to their problems (Muth and Alvermann, 1992). This individualized attention may result in improved student attitudes toward school, increased self-esteem, higher levels of academic achievement, and fewer management problems (Andrews and Stern, 1992).

> Having an advisor means that each child has an adult in the school to whom to turn. Each advisory group seems to develop its own personality, but what the groups share is the sense of being havens, safe ports in the storm of adolescence. (Maeroff, 1990, p. 507)

Advisor-advisee programs provide each student with an opportunity to "belong." Middle level students need to belong to a group that meets their needs for social interactions. Unfortunately, many young adolescents often feel lost within school communities; thus, they create their own sense of belonging through socially unacceptable associations (in many cases, gangs). Students who need the security of belonging to a small group will find the transition from safe, secure elementary settings to fluid, impersonal middle level settings especially problematic (Stevenson, 1992). Advisory programs provide opportunities for each student to experience a sense of belonging through activities that encourage familiarity with the school environment, with other people in the group, and with appropriate school behavior (Kronholm, Jespersen, and Fjell, 1987; Stevenson, 1992).

Advisor-advisee programs allow teachers and other staff members to be actively involved in the affective development of students. As mentioned above, middle level students need to feel that teachers are concerned about their development—cognitive, physical, and affective. More specifically, they need teachers who are more than just dispensers of knowledge and who exhibit a genuine concern for their socioemotional development (George, 1988; White and Greenwood, 1991). When students change classes and teachers several times a day, they may feel that no one teacher really cares about them or is available to discuss their problems. Advisor-advisee programs enable teachers to express concern and caring for individual students in ways that are both time efficient and personally satisfying (Cole, 1992). Ideally, advisors should serve as advocates for individual students who experience difficulty at home or with other teachers (Andrews and Stern, 1992; Maeroff, 1990; Midgley and Urdan, 1992; Stevenson, 1992).

Advisor-advisee programs assist students with interpersonal skills development. Advisory activities and small-group tasks provide opportunities for young adolescents to refine their interpersonal skills in a nonthreatening environment. Students can observe, assess, and modify their social skills, with important implications for long-term growth (White and Greenwood, 1991).

Characteristics of Successful Advisor-Advisee Programs

Successful advisor-advisee programs provide opportunities for students to identify and interact with at least one caring, nurturing adult concerned about their affective development (Allen, Splittgerber, and Manning, 1993; Glasser, 1990). A review of such successful advisor-advisee programs reveals several common characteristics, each of which will be fully discussed within the context of this chapter.

- Emphasis on characteristics and interests of students (Cole, 1992; George et al., 1992),
- Recognition of the importance of a closely knit school community (Carnegie, 1989),
- Accommodation of student and teacher diversity (Manning, 1993; McEwin and Thomason, 1989),
- Integrated curriculum (George et al., 1992),
- Provision for continuous adult guidance in a supportive environment (Andrews and Stern, 1992),

- Sensitivity to students' needs (Manning, 1993; Schurr, 1992),
- Development of short- and long-term goals (Phillips, 1986; Schurr, 1992),
- Orientation for all participants (Phillips, 1986),
- Active involvement and support by teachers and administrators (Schurr, 1992),
- Respect for students' right to privacy (Cole, 1992),
- Modeling trust and concern (Cole, 1992),
- Effective, open communication, especially with parents (Schurr, 1992),
- Small teacher-pupil ratios (Carnegie, 1989),
- Regularly scheduled, uninterrupted meeting times (Schurr, 1992),
- Strong professional development component for school personnel (George and Lawrence, 1982),
- Utilization of all interested school personnel (Stevenson, 1992).

Development of Advisor-Advisee Programs

To develop an effective and exciting advisor-advisee program, the entire school faculty and staff need to become thoroughly conversant with the unique characteristics and needs of young adolescents. Until this is done, there is little hope that the school will be as effective as possible in addressing and meeting the needs of its middle level students. As a means of coordinating efforts to create a heightened sense of awareness and concern among faculty and staff, a coordinator and steering committee should address key issues in the development of advisor-advisee programs, including those related to selection of appropriate initial planning strategies and activities, school climate, and valid, reliable field-testing of the overall program.

Initial Planning Strategies and Activities

As stated earlier, for an advisor-advisee program to be successful, all stakeholders must develop an awareness of the needs of young adolescents and an understanding of what an advisor-advisee program is and is not. One proven strategy for facilitating communication among stakeholders is the selection of an advisor-advisee coordinator. The coordinator will play a vital role in the success of an advisor-advisee program; therefore, selection of that person should occur only after careful consideration. James (1986) advocated that someone other than the principal assume this role, mainly because the principal has many other responsibilities and duties and may not be free to devote sufficient time and effort to the advisor-advisee program.

Based upon personal experience, we strongly suggest that school counselors serve as the "experts" on advisor-advisee programs because their expertise is in the affective domain. Likewise, because the advisor-advisee program will assist the overall guidance program, counselors are natural advocates of the program. An effective advisor-advisee program will assist the counselor(s) by directing to them students with serious problems who may not otherwise have sought or been referred for guidance.

If advisor-advisee programs are to be successful, Bushnell (1991) noted that the program coordinator must (1) serve as a cheerleader for advisement, (2) be an advisor to the advisors, (3) serve as a facilitator or presenter at faculty development sessions on advisory skills, and (4) be a supplier of resources. Underlying each of these roles is the need to foster awareness and enhance knowledge about advisor-advisee programs. Suggested activities designed to encourage active participation of parents, teachers, and students include visits to other program sites, panel discussions, and professional development opportunities.

On-site visits to schools with model advisor-advisee programs. Under the leadership of the program coordinator, the steering committee (consisting of teachers, parents, administrators, and students) should visit schools that have successfully implemented advisor-advisee programs. Such visits will provide them with an excellent opportunity to see advisor-advisee programs in action and to talk with teachers, students, and administrators who are involved in an ongoing program. Another purpose for an on-site visit is to examine advisory curricula currently in place at other schools. Examination of existing curricula will provide steering committee members an opportunity to see the different types of programs that exist, and should provide useful ideas as committee members coordinate efforts to develop the school's advisory curriculum.

We cannot emphasize too strongly that the advisory curriculum should reflect and meet the unique needs of the target community. At no time should a "canned" curriculum be purchased for *direct* and *total* implementation at one school. Even though commercially developed advisory materials and programs may contain excellent ideas, they are generic in design and do not address the needs and issues of local communities. On a related note, a school should never simply copy another school's curriculum. That, of course, does not preclude a school from using outstanding and particularly innovative ideas from the various curricula it has examined and previewed. Developing the curriculum locally will allow staff members to assume ownership of the program, thus increasing chances for program success.

Panel discussions. While planning, implementing, and "selling" an advisory program, an outstanding and highly effective way to examine and emphasize the various needs of young adolescents is to hold panel discussions in which the school seeks input from the following individuals: middle level counselors, individuals from social and juvenile services, and health personnel. Representing diverse perspectives, these individuals can provide powerful "bird's-eye views" of the unique needs, problems, and concerns of young adolescents. They also can share what it is like to address, day-in and day-out, the many and various problems of young adolescents. In doing so, they will reach the advisors and parents on both a cognitive and affective level as they, the advisors and parents, listen to the concerns, trials and tribulations, and successes and failures that young adolescents experience.

At some point, it also is valuable to host panel discussions led by parents sharing their unique insights, concerns, and wishes related to their children's education, particularly as they relate to the affective domain. Such panel discussions will provide the faculty and staff with rich insights regarding the students.

Throughout the development phase of an advisor-advisee program, steering committee members, in collaboration with other involved faculty, should elicit the insights, opinions, and feelings of their students. This can be accomplished in numerous ways. For example, panels of young adolescents can be invited to a series of faculty meetings or professional development opportunities in order to share and discuss their social and emotional concerns and their views of school, peers, teachers, and family members. The students can speak about what they perceive as being most important in life as well as their hopes, aspirations, anxieties, fears, joys, and other concerns. If committee members are uncomfortable impaneling a group of students, they can develop questionnaires designed to probe the social and emotional concerns of their students.

No matter which method is used, the faculty should analyze the data collected. Finally, they can use the findings to develop their advisory's philosophy, goals and objectives, and specific activities that assist students in raising and examining relevant issues.

Professional development opportunities. Obviously, professional development programs for faculty and staff should be led by the coordinator or by someone else who has been directly involved with an advisor-advisee program and who thoroughly understands the theory behind it. Equally important is the selection of appropriate activities that highlight the characteristics and needs of young adolescents.

One eye-opening experience, which is excellent to conduct during one of the professional development sessions, is to have all of the participants write a short sketch in which they reflect on their days in middle school or junior high (or between the ages of 10 and 15) and describe themselves: how they felt about themselves, how they looked, how they perceived themselves, who their friends were, how they perceived their teachers and friends, what they were going through, what their interests were, and how they got along with their families. After a time of individual reflection, participants should share their feelings with the rest of the group. This activity is very powerful in that it encourages advisors not only to reflect on their own experiences but also on those of their friends at a crucial time in their lives. It also provides them with opportunities to reflect upon their teachers' interest or lack of interest in their well-being and problems at that time in their lives. Participants also may recall how certain students were treated better than others and how even others were mistreated or ignored. This activity provides the future advisors with an opportunity to examine and reflect on a wide array of experiences and feelings that others in the group experienced. If nothing else, the participants have a valuable opportunity to reach beyond their current view of life to empathize with young adolescents.

Another outstanding activity for professional development sessions on advisor-advisee programs is to have each advisor write a short sketch on a "favorite or least favorite teacher" during middle level years (Grades 5–8). This often brings to the forefront, in a very powerful manner, those qualities and actions in teachers that are important to young adolescents. Because of that, this task is excellent for assisting advisors to be reflective concerning the attributes that young adolescents desire and abhor in teachers.

In addition to being provided a solid overview of the unique characteristics and needs of young adolescents and the rationale, goals, and objectives for a strong advisor-advisee program, future advisors also need to be taken through a series of advisory activities in order to get a feel as to how the activities should be conducted. Not only will this modeling enable advisors to ascertain the sort of sensitivity, depth, and debriefing that they need to bring to such activities, but it also will give them a sense of how students react when asked to be open and honest as they share something that is close to them. During these sessions, advisors need to have ample opportunities to discuss the purpose and value of the activities as well as ways of adapting them to their individual personalities and the personalities of their students. Too often such professional development sessions guide advisors through a series of activities but do not provide them with an opportunity to discuss how the activities truly address the social and emotional needs of young adolescents. As a result, the advisors often are left with the impression that while the activities are fun and interesting, they are not much more than a diversion from the academic work at hand. This, of course, often leads to a situation in which the advisor does not understand the value of either the advisory activities or the advisory program as a whole.

Likewise, those who conduct the professional development sessions need to make a concerted effort to discuss the crucial need to incorporate "debriefing" activities in their own advisory sessions, particularly those in which the lessons are rather complex or in which the activities might be particularly charged with emotion. Over and above that, the presenters need to model how to conduct the debriefing sessions so that they are effective, not perfunctory. This is particularly important because, in many cases, the debriefing session often is the most significant aspect of the entire advisory experience for the students. That is the point at which the participants have an opportunity to engage in reflection about the significance that the activity has in relation to certain beliefs, values, and other affective components.

School Climate

Quite obviously, the overall climate in a middle level program should be nurturing, safe, and pleasant. More specifically, it should be one that encourages mutual respect among everyone in the school, including students, teachers, staff, and visitors. It should reflect a setting in which curiosity is valued and nurtured, in which differing opinions are respected and given a solid hearing, and in which the self-esteem of everyone is important to everyone else. The entire school, including the classes, office, cafeteria, and playgrounds, should exude a genuine sense of caring. Such a climate will complement and strengthen the advisor-advisee program.

Likewise, a successful advisor-advisee program will increase the chances of a school developing a genuine climate that encourages students and teachers to care for one another. As a result, students will not only be learning about respect for others, the beauty of each person's uniqueness, and the need to resolve conflict in a constructive, logical, and civil fashion, but they also will see such behavior modeled on a daily basis.

Field-testing

The professional and curricular development of the program should take place at least one semester, if not a year, prior to the actual implementation. This will allow time for in-depth professional development, thorough analyses of the curriculum as it is being developed, and design of both short- and long-term evaluation plans. If there is not enough lead time for the development of the curriculum and if staff development is limited, then the advisor-advisee program is likely to start with little knowledge, training, or enthusiasm among staff members. These deficiencies will make the program inefficient at best and may lead possibly to its premature demise.

Many schools find that field-testing is a good concept in theory, but in many cases it is impractical for two main reasons. First, if a group of teachers tests the materials for a year, then formal implementation of the advisor-advisee program is delayed for the rest of the school community. However, if a school has the luxury of the additional year, then field-testing would be beneficial. Second, if the field-testing is to take place during the second semester, then scheduling the special advisor-advisee periods can be a problem, especially in the middle of a school year.

Implementation of Successful
Advisor-Advisee Programs

Having strong, effective interdisciplinary teams in place will assist greatly with the successful implementation of the advisor-advisee program. This is true for a number of reasons. First, if one of the goals of the middle school is to break the large organization into smaller units, then it is a logical conclusion that the smallest unit (advisor-advisee) cannot be put into place until larger sections of the school have been broken down and put into place. Kramer (1992) presented evidence that breaking the large middle school into teams contributes to the students' "feelings of being well known, liked, and supported" (p. 34). A successful advisor-advisee program takes this concept a step further by giving students an even smaller arena in which a secure environment is established that promotes feelings of being known and supported. George and Alexander (1993) indicated that the advisor-advisee program and interdisciplinary team organization are mutually supportive of each other. "When the interdisciplinary team block or level is missing, the advisory program is at risk. When advisory programs are absent, the team is on less sure footing in its work with individual students. Both need to be present for the full functioning of each" (p. 229).

According to Connors (1992), schools too often introduce advisor-advisee programs while still organized in a departmentalized structure. When this happens, students may be placed into a program where they will not see their advisor the rest of the day because the advisor is not one of their teachers. This denies other opportunities for the advisor and advisee to interact. This almost always leads to a dismal, if not useless, advisor-advisee program. Ironically, in situations like this, the blame often is placed on the program itself and not on the organizational structure.

Scheduling Advisory Periods

The schedule for the advisor-advisee program is, obviously, contingent on each school's more comprehensive, master schedule. As one looks into the scheduling of an advisor-advisee program, however, four areas need to be addressed: (1) advisory, *not* a homeroom, (2) advisor-advisee ratios, (3) frequency and length of advisory periods, and (4) faculty and staff release time.

Advisory, not *a homeroom.* An advisor-advisee program is distinctly and radically different from a typical homeroom. Therefore, there is legitimate concern that when the advisor-advisee program is a part of the homeroom during the first period of the day, much of the time spent during this time period may be taken up with administrative details and school announcements (Messick and Reynolds, 1992). The advisor-advisee class should *not* be a surrogate for a homeroom class. "Traditional junior high school arrangements that include brief homeroom meetings cannot begin to approximate the attentiveness to student needs that are possible through advisories" (Stevenson, 1992, p. 128). One way to avoid this potential problem (if the advisory period starts the day, which is what we recommend) is to separate the homeroom and the advisor-advisee program. This can be accomplished by spending the first 10 minutes of the day in a scheduled homeroom designed strictly for administrative details, such as making announcements and calling roll. Then, this can be followed by the designated advisory period. We know of one school that rings a bell after the first 10 minutes of the day, signifying that it is time to start the advisory period. In this particular school, all of the students spend the first 10 minutes in a core classroom; when the advisor-advisee program begins, students go to their advisory teacher. By scheduling advisor-advisee programs in this way, all individuals in the school (students, core and noncore teachers, and staff) realize that the advisory program is a valuable part of the school day.

Advisor-Advisee ratio. One of the key goals of an advisor-advisee program is to create a setting in which each student is well known by at least one adult in a school. If the advisor-advisee program is to be the primary vehicle for accomplishing this goal, then it is feasible to assume that a small advisory group will increase the chances for the development of a close student-teacher relationship. For this to be a viable proposition, an advisory class should be composed of no more than 20 students. Once the numbers start to climb above 20, opportunities for small-group activities and chances for student-teacher interaction decrease. With class sizes in most schools averaging between 25–35 students, it becomes virtually impossible to attain the small advisory class without utilizing noncore instructors (e.g., art, music, and media). George and Alexander (1993) recommended that if advisors have to work with 35 or more students, the program should be postponed until the numbers can be reduced. We fully concur and would even place the maximum number at 25.

This smaller class size is needed if advisors are to have a legitimate opportunity to establish a close relationship with the students and to provide quality opportunities for all students to participate on a regular basis. This is vitally significant if the goal to meet the needs of all students is to be realized. Along with certain extracurricular activities (including clubs), the advisory class is one of the best opportunities to meet the recommendation by *Turning Points* (Carnegie, 1989) that "every student should be known by at least one adult" (p. 357).

In the most successful advisor-advisee programs, the majority of the staff (both core and noncore teachers) serves as advisors. Some schools even have included the school nurse, custodial and cafeteria personnel, the speech therapist, and others as advisors. The latter, of course, would be contingent on each state education department's and school district's regulations. Utilizing both faculty and staff not only reduces the size of each advisory group, but it also gives the program greater legitimacy and ownership by a greater number of people. We also have observed that many of these nonteacher individuals are quite child centered and, when properly educated about the focus and purpose of the advisor-advisee program, are excellent advisors.

The best way to include noncore teachers is to schedule the advisory period so that it is the only activity going on at that time in the school. For example, no classes would be scheduled during the first 30 minutes of the day, thereby avoiding scheduling conflicts with the advisory program. This type of scheduling accomplishes two goals: (1) All staff members have an opportunity to be an advisor; and (2) The administration reaffirms its support of the programs and sends a clear message to the school community that the advisory program is important.

Frequency and length of advisory periods. A minimum of three days per week should be scheduled for the advisory period and preferably five days per week. Meeting with advisory groups only once or twice a week does not provide adequate time for the development of the important student-teacher relationship, which is one of the primary goals of the advisory program. If each student is to have at least one adult advocate at school, then sufficient opportunities for interaction between the advisor and advisee are needed to accomplish this objective.

Some schools have attempted to include the advisor-advisee class one day a week, but many have found that such an arrangement lacks any continuity. One day a week does not allow the advisor and students to really become a cohesive group in which honest, worthwhile conversations and activities can be conducted. Other schools have attempted to implement their advisor-advisee programs more than once a week, but only for 10 minutes or so. Again, such a schedule was found to lack the requisite time needed to conduct an activity or discussion of any value. In fact, the latter two situations did more to frustrate advisors and students than to assist in achieving the stated goals and objectives of the program. Along with a lack of adequate preparation and a solid advisor-advisee curriculum, nothing will kill an advisor-advisee program faster than a dearth of allocated time to conduct worthwhile classroom activities. Finally, it should be noted that the advisory class should be regularly scheduled at the same time of day, not matter how many days a week it is offered. That is, it should not be a "hit-and-miss" class that is tucked in when time is available.

The advisory period should last a minimum of 20–25 minutes and a maximum of 35 minutes. A period of fewer than 20 minutes does not allow time for any type of in-depth discussion of a topic or development of an activity. Conversely, if a more lengthy time is allotted (e.g., a regular class period of 45–50 minutes), advisors likely will have difficulty in maintaining the students' interests in a topic on a regular basis. A longer period also will require additional preparation time, something to be avoided if staff members are going to buy into the program.

In light of the fact that sufficient time is always a major factor (if not a headache) facing administrators and teachers when implementing new programs, it is worth noting how some schools have "found" or allocated the time for their advisor-advisee programs. Some have lengthened their school day by 20 minutes. Others have, with state approval, trimmed five minutes off each of the other classes offered throughout the school day (usually six or seven) and allocated those minutes for their advisor-advisee program. Still others have added minutes to both the beginning and end of the school day (e.g., five minutes for each) and have trimmed time off classes (one to two minutes), recesses, and lunch (five minutes).

Specifically, if a school is on a seven-period day, it may be possible (depending on state guidelines) to deduct three to four minutes from each scheduled period and dedicate those minutes to the advisory program. If a school already is on a flexible schedule, then interdisciplinary teams working with the administration may be able to build into their schedule the time needed for the advisory period. This could be accomplished with members giving up a few minutes of their time in the subject area for the advisory time. If such scheduling is done on a team-by-team basis, the rest of the building schedule will not be affected.

As might be expected, different teachers in the same school, let alone administrators and teachers in different schools, have varying opinions as to when the optimum time is to hold the advisor-advisee class. Some assert that the first thing in the morning is the best time because it sends a signal to teachers, students, parents, administrators, and others that the advisor-advisee class is important, highly valued, and not something that is simply tagged on to the end of the day or squeezed in at anytime possible between the "important core courses." Some also have argued that starting the day off with an advisory period provides students, especially those who are having problems in their classes, at home, on the playground, or simply in general, "to work through difficulties before beginning their academic work" (George and Lawrence, 1982, p. 177).

Some advisors have argued that they prefer having the advisory period just prior to lunch (when students have a tendency to become "antsy") or just after lunch (when students often become lethargic) when it is hard for students to concentrate on academics. Both of these preferences are understandable, but only if the advisor-advisee classes are truly engaging, hands-on, thought-provoking, and something that the students and advisors "give their all to." If these attributes are not evident, then the advisor-advisee class can easily degenerate into a "holding class" that is not as useful or valuable as it could or should be—if not outright useless.

Of course, that is true no matter when the time is allocated for the class. Possibly the best practice is to have the advisors vote on a time, test that out for several months, and then poll both the students and the advisors as to whether they would prefer the same or a different time and why. Based on the data, a school can either retain the same time or test out a new time and then conduct another survey, repeating the original cycle.

Most agree that if at all possible, the advisory program should not be scheduled at the very end of the day. When it is placed at that time, danger exists that the class can become a "goof-off" time, with the teachers grading papers while the students play trivial games such as tic-tac-toe and hang-man. This type of situation sends a message to the students that the advisory program is not important. In the final analysis, building-level administrators who truly believe in affective education will be able to find ways to assist advisors in scheduling time needed for an effective advisory program.

Faculty and staff release time. During the implementation stage, advisors need to have ample time to seek out, examine, and evaluate resources from a variety of sources as well as to redesign, revise, or develop new materials for their own program. This time should be allocated by the administration so that the advisors do not have to take time from their personal lives and schedules to accomplish these goals. Principals can accomplish this in various ways, all of which will be contingent upon their local situation. They may hire substitutes to teach classes while certain faculty members are engaged in ordering, reviewing, evaluating, and/or developing new curricula. Principals also may allocate money for work sessions held after school in the late afternoon or evening, on Saturdays, or during the summer; and they may seek grants (local, regional, state, or national) to support faculty and staff work sessions.

Throughout the course of the year, different faculty and staff also need to be released from their duties in order to visit other schools that have successful advisory programs. They can sit in on the advisor-advisee sessions, speak to the students and advisors about their experiences, examine the advisory curriculum materials, and participate in a variety of other information-gathering activities. Such visits assist in providing a sense of direction for a new program and are an outstanding way of gleaning powerful and innovative ideas to take back to their own schools.

Selecting Advisory Strategies and Activities

Middle level advisors have used a large number of rather eclectic and innovative strategies to thoroughly engage their students' interest and participation in their advisor-advisee class. What will be delineated herein is only a select number of those strategies—some that we have witnessed in advisor-advisee classes, some that we have come across in our perusal of advisor-advisee curricula, some we have seen on films about advisory classes, and some we have developed and used in our middle level methods courses.

At the outset, we wish to note that we think it is imperative to seek the input of the students with regard to what they find enjoyable, interesting, and effective in reaching them. This applies to both the type of curriculum (issues, concerns, topics, and content) that is addressed as well as the type of activities and strategies used to conduct the advisory class. Not only will this result in programs that the students find meaningful, but it also will send a loud and clear message that the advisors truly care about how the students feel and think. Such a method also underscores the middle level tenets that students should have a choice in what they study in school and should have opportunities to become increasingly responsible individuals.

There are numerous small-group discussion methods that are quite useful for advisory groups. Not only do these methods move the instructor from a frontal (lecture) approach, which is not conducive to engaging the students in exploring the various advisory themes and issues, but they also assist the teacher in moving the students from passive to active participants. Likewise, the use of such discussion methods signals to the students that the teacher really cares about what each individual has to say. Furthermore, by varying the strategies that are used, the advisor automatically is making the class more interesting for, as the cliché goes, "variety is the spice of life." Finally, the use of discussion strategies indicates to the students that the advisory is *their* class—that it is specifically designed to meet their social and emotional needs.

Over and above the traditional small-group strategies (such as a panel discussion or debate) for initiating discussion, the following methods are also useful for engaging students in stimulating discussions.

- Buzz groups—The advisor prepares one or two questions on a subject and has each student write a response. Then he/she places the students in small clusters of four to six to discuss their responses. Each group selects one student to serve as a recorder (not a leader), who not only takes part in the discussion but also writes down the most salient points discussed by the group. After 10 to 15 minutes, the advisor reassembles the entire class in order to hold a group discussion based on the points brought up in each group.

- Circular response—Students are asked to read selected material and then to come up with points, disagreements, and questions for discussion purposes. Once the students are in a circle, the advisor calls on one student to posit a question or a point around which a class discussion will evolve. When the discussion begins to slow down, the next student in line should posit a statement, question, or issue, prompting the discussion to start all over again.

- Contrived incident—Either the advisor or students develop a contrived or staged incident to be played out in front of the class. The activity should take between one and four minutes and be tied to the objective and goals of the advisory curriculum. Discussion of what took place as well as the meaning behind it should be used as a follow-up.

- Fishbowl—Several chairs are arranged at the front of the class for the students who will discuss the topic at hand with the advisor. As the discussion ensues, the rest of the group observes. The advisor should allow the discussion to continue as long as it is fruitful and then open it up for a class discussion or bring up a new group of students to be in the fishbowl.

Another outstanding method for engaging students in both hands-on and exploratory activities is to engage the students in a community service project. Increasing numbers of middle level faculty are initiating community projects in their schools in the belief that such projects encourage their students to learn about altruism, social responsibility, and social issues up close. Community service programs also assist in moving the students from the "I" to the "we" or from an egocentric to a sociocentric position. The advisor-advisee program is a perfect vehicle for initiating, carrying out, discussing, and studying in more depth the complexities and significance of the community service projects that the students are undertaking.

Cooperative learning is another strategy to incorporate in the advisor-advisee class. Not only will this strategy (approximately 13 different methods come under the rubric of "cooperative learning") provide the means for students to become actively engaged learners, but research clearly indicates that it has "positive effects on social, motivational, and attitudinal outcomes as well as achievement" (Slavin, 1990, p. 34). In fact, as Slavin noted, "Although not every study has found positive effects on every noncognitive outcome, the overall effects of cooperative learning on student self-esteem, peer support for achievement, internal locus of control, time on-task, liking of class and of classmates, cooperativeness, and other variables are positive and robust" (p. 53). This, of course, is ideal for an advisory program.

In addition to the above-mentioned strategies, many advisors have successfully used drama, role-playing, simulations, brainstorming, oral history, and pantomime to stimulate discussion and to provide new ways of looking at situations. Specifically, advisory programs provide an appropriate forum for teaching problem-solving skills and conflict resolution as students begin to discuss and attempt to solve personal, classroom, and school-wide problems. As Goodman and Kreidler (1993) pointed out, "[F]undamental communication greatly enhances the basic problem-solving that is at the heart of all conflict resolution. The actual problem-solving steps are quite simple: 1. Define the problem; 2. Generate alternatives; and 3. Choose a solution" (p. 77).

Other appropriate activities for use during advisory time include the study of adolescent literature as a springboard for discussing problems and conflicts that students in the advisory class are facing. No valid reason exists why the advisor-advisee program cannot be somewhat academically oriented as long as it is focused on the affective domain and is of great interest to the students. In light of that, the literature *should not* be selected for its message as much as for its interest level, relevance, and ability to engage students in thoughtful, meaningful discussion.

Obviously, the choice of appropriate strategies, activities, and topics for advisor-advisee programs is almost limitless. As stated previously, the key to selecting strategies and activities is to seek the input of students and to provide opportunities that they find enjoyable, interesting, and relevant to their needs.

Evaluating an Advisor-Advisee Program

Many schools use the first year of an advisor-advisee program as a time to evaluate what works and what does not. In addition to ongoing evaluations and reviews, schools should conduct a comprehensive annual evaluation of advisor-advisee programs. This evaluation should take place in the spring with a survey of advisors, students, and parents. The steering committee, chaired by the coordinator, should revise the curriculum based on the results of the survey.

Any dramatic changes in the curriculum and/or schedule should be done with the full knowledge of the building principal *and* all staff members involved in the advisory program. If possible, a yearly report that begins with the initial planning activities should be given to the school board. It is important that school boards be kept apprised of what the advisor-advisee program is and of what it consists. This knowledge allows the board not only to give the program official support, but it also assists each individual board member in answering questions about the program.

Coping with Dissension

In developing any new program, resistance to the program invariably will surface. This may come from teachers and/or parents. Usually this dissension is based more on feelings and beliefs than on facts and information. Teachers often experience a change in their roles from being dispensers of knowledge to dealing more directly with the affective nature of the student. For many that is an uncomfortable situation. Parents may see the new program as threatening their traditional role of addressing affective feelings. Williamson and Johnston (1991) state that dissent is necessary and valuable in any change process and that it will help proponents to plan new programs more effectively and efficiently. Ignoring dissent or blindly battling it will be counterproductive and may come back to haunt the program at a later time.

Three possible ways of dealing with resistance are to

1. Identify and address legitimate concerns while emphasizing to teachers and parents that the advisor-advisee program is designed to address those issues that are common to middle level students. For example, all young adolescents are concerned with being accepted by their peers and not being "different"; an effective advisor-advisee program will help all students understand and analyze peer relationships. It also needs to be stressed that advisory periods are not to be used for an in-depth psychotherapy program.

2. Include known dissenters on the advisory steering committee. If a person has been part of the development process, he/she will find it more difficult to criticize the program. He/she may even become the program's strongest advocate.

3. Show and emphasize that such programs are designed for the benefit of the students. As long as the program remains child centered and true to its original purpose, it will be difficult for dissenters to derail it.

In addition to addressing the concerns of those who are skeptical of the program, the school needs to be proactive. This should include extensive and continuous staff development for advisors as well as a public campaign to get the message about the program out to patrons of the school district. Information can be distributed through public meetings, news articles, and presentations to civic groups. The school also can reach out to those in the community who, for whatever reason, either cannot or will not attend meetings held at the school by holding neighborhood meetings, distributing information at work sites (with employer consent), and setting up a school booth in a local store.

Recommendations

Acknowledging that steering committees at each site should develop a program tailored to meet the unique needs of that site, we submit the following recommendations for consideration by schools interested in developing and implementing a middle level advisor-advisee program.

1. At times, a school board and/or faction in the community may become the bane of existence for a middle level advisor-advisee program. Quite frequently this results from a misunderstanding as to what the advisory class is about or from rumors that cause suspicion in certain sectors of the community. To circumvent such a situation, the steering committee should involve community members, the school board, and the parents in the development of the program. Initially the faculty may have to sell the community on the program. In doing so, the faculty should clearly and positively delineate the rationale and purpose of the program, implementation procedures, its place in the overall school curriculum, and other relevant information. If this is done at the outset of the entire process, it will help

significantly to offset or possibly avoid negative comments and resistance to it once the program is in place.

2. Key individuals (administrators, teachers, counselors, and parents) should visit schools that have successfully implemented advisor-advisee programs to glean unique and innovative ideas and to gain answers to development and implementation concerns (such as scheduling, types of professional development programs, ways to overcome resistance, and selection of activities).

3. Students should be surveyed, interviewed, and consulted about their needs, concerns, and interests *prior* to the development of an advisor-advisee program *as well as* throughout the course of the year.

4. As George and Lawrence (1982) suggested, "prior to implementing [an advisor-advisee program], schoolwide affective goals should be determined" (p. 177). Ideally, this determination should be made by the faculty, students, parents, and administrators.

5. The advisor-advisee program needs to have a structure, just as an academic class does, otherwise some advisors and many students may perceive it as simply "fun and games" or "blow-off" time.

6. Teachers and others (including administrators, counselors, parents, and central office staff) should develop the advisory curriculum that fits the needs of the community. Developing the curriculum locally will give the faculty and community ownership of the program, and it also will avoid problems that may result from purchasing a program that is not relevant to the needs of the students.

7. It is unwise and pedagogically unsound to purchase a curriculum from an educational publishing house or another middle school for the expressed purpose of implementing it *as is*. While such a method certainly may save time at the outset of the process, it also may result in the demise of the advisory program.

In the event that a school simply purchases and directly implements a canned advisory program, the teachers will not only lack ample time to think about the pros, cons, strengths, and weaknesses of the curriculum, but they also will not have had sufficient time to buy into it. Furthermore, they often will find that the suggested activities have little or no relationship to their own students' needs and will be hesitant to use it—if not reject it outright. If a curriculum does not meet the needs of the students, then it may result in a situation in which the students may find the activities boring, meaningless, and a waste of time.

This is not to say that a school cannot or should not purchase ready-made materials. In fact, purchasing materials from schools that have successful advisor-advisee programs is worthwhile for the simple purpose of ascertaining what young adolescents find of interest. Advisors may wish to borrow or copy certain activities as is from a purchased curriculum because they believe that the activity would be of use with their students. There is no need to totally reinvent the wheel.

8. Many advisory curricula are left intact from year to year without any revision. Any curriculum, however, should be organic, and this is particularly true of an advisor-advisee program. Because such a program is in place to meet the affective needs of specific students, it is imperative that the curriculum and instructional procedures be revised as appropriate each year in order to meet the special needs of the new students in the program.

9. Many schools that have two or more grades in their middle level program frequently offer basically the same curriculum from year to year. This is a quick way to kill the interest of young adolescents in the advisor-advisee program. The advisory curriculum should be distinctly different from grade to grade. The second year of the program should build on the first, but the activities have to be different, more challenging, and equally as interesting as the first year. No one, especially young adolescents, like to take the very same course over again. Not only is that a waste of time, but it is *boring!*

10. The development of the advisor-advisee program (including evaluation of other programs, curriculum development, and professional development sessions) should take place at least a semester prior to the implementation of the program; however, if possible, an entire year should be set aside for planning and development.

11. Ample, thorough, and quality professional development opportunities should be provided for the faculty

and staff involved in the advisor-advisee program both prior to and throughout the implementation of the advisor-advisee program. Such professional development opportunities should provide faculty and staff with a solid understanding of the unique characteristics and needs of the young adolescent, a thorough understanding and appreciation of the rationale for an advisor-advisee program, an ability to implement engaging methods of instruction, and the insights and means to develop and implement powerful, effective, and engaging curricula that focus on the affective domain.

The professional development program should be led by someone who has been involved with a strong advisor-advisee program and who also understands the theory behind such a program. In this way, the sessions will be oriented toward the practical and will answer questions by providing insights based upon hands-on experiences. Furthermore, such an individual will be able to serve as a troubleshooter, having gone through the growing pains of developing, implementing, and running a program.

12. Schools of education preparing preservice teachers for middle level settings need to provide their students with a thorough grounding in and understanding of the unique characteristics and needs of young adolescents. They need to prepare them to meet *all* the needs of young adolescents with special attention given to the affective domain, which frequently is neglected in teacher education programs.

Conclusion

As evidenced by their increasing popularity and documented success, middle level programs fulfill a definite, vital role within our educational system (Beane and Lipka, 1987; Kramer, 1992; Midgely and Urdan, 1992). The overall success of middle level programs, however, depends largely upon one component—the advisor-advisee program. Designed to address the unique academic and affective needs of young adolescents, such programs assist students in making the transition from elementary school to high school settings.

Just as young adolescents have unique characteristics, so do successful advisor-advisee programs. They provide opportunities for students to discuss, analyze, and formulate solutions to problems and issues common to them; they provide opportunities for extensive interaction between and among students and their advisors; they promote individual attention to students; they provide opportunities for each student to belong to a group; and they encourage faculty and staff to become involved actively in the affective development of their students. Very simply, *successful advisor-advisee programs become communities of learners* where young adolescents can experience academic, social, and emotional development within the context of a secure, nurturing environment.

REFERENCES

Allen, H. A., Splittgerber, F. L., and Manning, M. L. (1993). *Teaching and learning in the middle level school*. New York: Merrill.

Andrews, B. and Stern, J. (1992). An advisory program—A little can mean alot! *Middle School Journal 24*(1): 39–41.

Association for Supervision and Curriculum Development. (1975). *The middle school we need*. Washington, DC: Author.

Beane, J. A. and Lipka, R. P. (1987). *When the kids come first: Enhancing self-esteem*. Columbus, OH: National Middle School Association.

Bushnell, D. (1991). The middle school counselor's role in advisement. *Florida School Counselor's Newsletter 8*: 8–9.

Carnegie Council on Adolescent Development. (1989). *Turning points: Preparing American youth for the 21st century*. Washington, DC: Author.

Cole, C. (1988). *Guidance in middle level schools: Everyone's responsibility*. Columbus, OH: National Middle School Association.

Cole, C. (1992). *Nurturing a teacher advisory program*. Columbus, OH: National Middle School Association.

Connors, N. (1992). Teacher advisory: The fourth R. In J. Irvin (Ed.), *Transforming middle level education perspectives and possibilities* (pp. 162–177). Needham Heights, MA: Allyn and Bacon.

George, P. (1988). Education 2000: Which way the middle school? *Clearing House 62*(1): 14–17.

George, P. and Alexander, W. (1993). *The exemplary middle school* (2nd ed.). Fort Worth, TX: Harcourt Brace Jovanovich.

George, P. and Lawrence, G. (1982). *Handbook for middle school teaching.* Glenview, IL: Scott, Foresman and Company.

George, P. S., Stevenson, C., Thomason, J., and Beane, J. (1992). *The middle school—and beyond.* Alexandria, VA: Association for Supervision and Curriculum Development.

Glasser, W. (1990). *The quality school.* New York: Harper and Row.

Goodman, S. and Kreidler, W. J. (1993). You need lots of choices: Conflict resolution in the elementary grades. In S. Berman and P. LaFarge (Eds.), *Promising practices in teaching social responsibility* (pp. 72–86). Albany, NY: State University of New York Press.

Grantes, J., Noyce, C., Patterson, F., and Robertson, J. (1961). *The junior high school we need.* Washington, DC: Association for Supervision and Curriculum Development.

James, M. (1986). *Adviser/advisee programs: Why, what and how.* Columbus, OH: National Middle School Association.

Johansen, J. H., Collins, H. W., and Johnson, J. A. (1990). *American education: An introduction to teaching* (6th ed.). Dubuque, IA: William C. Brown.

Johnson, J., Dupuis, V., Musial, D., and Hall, G. (1994). *Introduction to the foundations of American education.* Needham Heights, MA: Allyn and Bacon.

Kramer, L. (1992). Young adolescents' perceptions of school. In J. Irvin (Ed.), *Transforming middle level education perspectives and possibilities* (pp. 28–43). Needham Heights, MA: Allyn and Bacon.

Kronholm, K., Jespersen, D., and Fjell, M. (1987). Homeroom/advisement program brings middle level adolescents, teachers closer. *NASSP Bulletin 71*(498): 113–116.

Mac Iver, D. J. (1990). Meeting the needs of young adolescents: Advisory groups, interdisciplinary teaching teams, and school transition programs. *Phi Delta Kappan 71*: 458–464.

Maeroff, G. (1990). Getting to know a good middle school: Shoreham-Wading River. *Phi Delta Kappan 71*: 505–511.

Manning, M. L. (1993). Cultural and gender differences in young adolescents. *Middle School Journal* 25(1): 13–17.

McEwin, C. K. and Thomason, J. (1989). *Who they are—how we teach: Early adolescents and their teachers*. Columbus, OH: National Middle School Association.

Messick, R. and Reynolds, K. (1992). *Middle level curriculum in action*. New York: Longman.

Midgley, C. and Urdan, T. (1992). The transition to middle level schools: Making it a good experience for all students. *Middle School Journal* 24 (2): 5–14.

Muth, K. D. and Alvermann, D. E. (1992). *Teaching and learning in the middle grades*. Needham Heights, MA: Allyn and Bacon.

Phillips, R. C. (1986). *Making advisory programs work*. Tampa, FL: Wiles, Bondi Associates.

Schurr, S. (1992). *How to evaluate your middle school*. Columbus, OH: National Middle School Association.

Slavin, R. E. (1990). *Cooperative learning: Theory, research, and practice*. Englewood Cliffs, NJ: Prentice Hall.

Stevenson, C. (1992). *Teaching ten to fourteen year olds*. New York: Longman.

Wheelock, A. and Dorman, G. (1988). *Before it's too late: Dropout prevention in the middle grades*. Chapel Hill, NC: Center for Early Adolescence.

White, G. P. and Greenwood, S. C. (1991). Study skills and the middle level adviser/advisee program. *NASSP Bulletin* 75(537): 88–95.

Williamson, R. and Johnston, J. H. (1991). *Planning for successful implementation of middle level reorganization*. Reston, VA: National Association of Secondary School Principals.

CHAPTER 13

Age-Appropriate Teaching Strategies

Mary Ann Davies *

Having fun/expressing concern. Thinking together/working alone. Asking questions/pursuing answers. Making choices/wanting direction. Like the ebb and flow of the ocean tides, teachers of young adolescents adapt their teaching to the ever-shifting needs of their students. A strong understanding of these needs and a broad repertoire of instructional practices guide teachers in effectively staying afloat in the crosscurrents of young adolescent classrooms.

What guidelines assist teachers in meeting this challenge? The responses to this question are depicted in Figure 1. Middle level teaching strategies need to be *age appropriate*, *personally meaningful*, and *actively involve students*. All effective strategies reflect these criteria.

Successful teaching at the middle level necessitates that teachers understand the developmental characteristics of this age group and adapt their instruction to meet these needs (National Association of Secondary School Principals [NASSP], 1985; Schurr, 1989; Superintendent's Task Force [STF], 1987). Teaching strategies should provide for the physical, intellectual, and social-emotional characteristics of young people. Adapting instruction to these needs provides students with opportunities to experience success, feel capable, and grow in their own potential—the ultimate goal of middle level schools.

"Middle school teachers frequently cite the lack of motivation as a primary cause of students' failure to learn" (Johnston and Markle 1982, p. 22). This lack of motivation often stems from students viewing school as disconnected from their lives, bearing little resemblance to the real world. They

> [L]earn many things, but they do not learn how the information and skills fit together. Their knowledge is disconnected, disorganized, and jumbled. . . . Much of the criticism of school-based learning refers to students who lack understanding and are unable to apply their knowledge to solve real-world problems. (Markle, Johnston, Geer, and Meichtry, 1990, p. 53)

Meaningful instruction relates content to students' lives and assures its utility in the real world (NASSP, 1985; National Science Foundation [NSF], 1978; Scales, 1992).

Involving students in their learning captures and maintains their attention (Partin, 1987). When students are mentally engaged, they actively process information. This active participation in learning promotes long-term retention (Woolfolk, 1993). In addition, active involvement facilitates the transition from concrete to formal reasoning in young adolescents (Cheatham, 1989). Thus, appropriate middle level instruction encourages participation (STF, 1987).

In summary, effective middle grades instruction is age appropriate, meaningful, and actively involves students. Embedded within this framework are more specific guidelines that assist teachers in reaching these three broader goals (see figure 1). In addition, appropriate instruction is *relevant*, provides a *variety* of experiences and materials to address learning differences, and *challenges* students to think (Allen and McEwin, 1983; NASSP, 1985; NSF, 1978; Partin, 1987; Schurr, 1989). Taking the embedded analogy a step further, each of these guidelines can be further subdivided.

The remainder of this chapter provides examples of teaching strategies that are relevant, varied, and challenging, while simultaneously addressing the three broader goals. The examples serve as models rather than as prescriptive approaches to teaching.

> The question is not "What is the best way to teach middle school students?" It is now quite clear, from the evidence of both research and practice, that there is no one right

Figure 1

Age-Appropriate Teaching Strategies

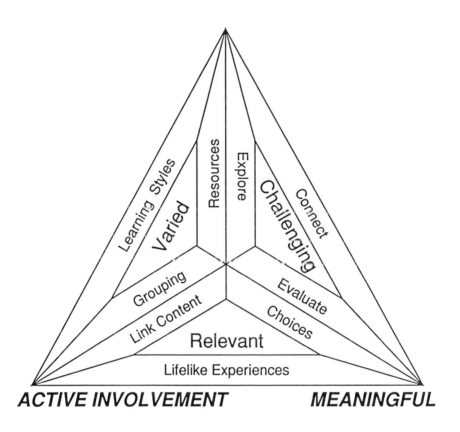

way to teach all middle school students all the time. The
method chosen depends upon the objectives of instruction,
the nature of the particular group of students being
taught, even the grade level involved. The right question
to ask about instruction in the middle school is likely to be,
"What is the right method to use for these objectives in
this area with this particular group of students?"
(Alexander and George, 1981, p. 220)

Relevant Instruction: Building Connections

Relevant instruction means connecting content to students' lives
and the world around them and providing opportunities for
making choices. Such connections and input intrinsically
motivate by making learning meaningful. When lessons are
meaningful, students seek to stay actively involved (Brophy
1987; Ericksen, 1974).

Cognitive views of learning further explain the importance
of connecting learning to students' frames of reference. They
view learning as the processes of elaborating on concepts stored
in long-term memory and actively seeking links between ideas.
Teachers activate students' prior knowledge when they connect
lessons to learners' lives. This facilitates the process of creating
mental links between prior knowledge and new information.
Building these links is the foundation for developing
understanding (Markle et al., 1990; Woolfolk, 1993). Furthermore, relating lessons to students' interests and experiences
makes abstract content more familiar and concrete, thus, more
developmentally appropriate (Brophy, 1987).

Current brain research supports the importance of relating
content to students and the real world. The brain functions as a
pattern detector. Through immersion in multiple complex and
concrete experiences, the learner finds meaning by actively
focusing on interconnections. More realistic settings provide the
natural complexity that stimulates brain growth. In addition,
lifelike experiences integrate emotion and thinking, thereby
optimizing learning. Thus, teaching that capitalizes on students'

prior knowledge and actively involves them in seeking meaning from lifelike experiences accesses the brain's potential (Caine and Caine, 1991; Healy, 1987).

Three approaches to making instruction relevant are presented: provide lifelike experiences, link content to students' lives, and include opportunities for making choices.

Lifelike Experiences

Middle level experts (Doda, George, and McEwin, 1987) suggest that effective teaching brings "students as close to the real thing as possible" (p. 5). A variety of teaching strategies create lifelike experiences for young people. These fall on a continuum of increasingly more realistic experiences. This realism motivates. "Youngsters' interests are earnest when their cultural education is firsthand, authentic, and concrete" (George, Stevenson, Thomason, and Beane, 1992, p. 76).

Artifacts. Artifacts are man-made objects and, as such, provide insight into a people's way of life. Tangible objects assist students in schema development. The variety of objects that can enhance instruction is constrained only by the teacher's imagination! A few examples follow.

- An eighth grade health teacher created realistic accident scenes with rubber and artificial blood. In sixth grade science students built a model spaceship large enough to transport the entire class (George et al., 1992).
- Artifact Dig. Students select objects representing a particular culture and/or era. These can be buried outside or in shoe box digs (Allen and McEwin, 1983). Often, archeological sites accept middle level volunteers.
- Clothing, food, music, games, art, and other objects can bring another culture alive.
- Mini-Museum. The study of any topic can be enriched through collections. For example, a fifth grade class studying the Great Depression brought in artifacts of the era from their parents and grandparents.

The mini-museum contained flour sack clothing, antiquated cameras, a clothes iron, letters from relatives,
newspaper advertisements for groceries (hamburger at 19
cents a pound), photographs, pay stubs, recipes for
inexpensive meals (tomato soup made from catsup plus
hot water), old phonograph recordings ("Happy Days Are
Here Again"), and more. (Rasinski, 1991, p. 32)

Literature. Stories make people, places, and ideas
multidimensional. Cloaked in feelings and realistic experiences,
characters mentally transport readers within the realm of the
story. Literature can help young adolescents better understand
others as well as themselves.

Young adult literature can help students "discover the
varied dimensions of adolescent experiences" (Lee and
Wiseman, 1991, p. 18). Bibliotherapy assists young people in
dealing with emotional and social issues. For example, *The
Outsiders* explores the topics of parental authority, peer
relationships, and value systems. Literature deals with life and
issues that concern young people. It creates a forum for
discussing topics that early adolescents often find difficult to talk
about—death, sex, violence, divorce, etc. (Jones, 1990).

Role plays/simulations. Role playing enables students to "try
on" the experiences of others. It assists them in understanding
actions and ideas often removed from their direct experiences.
Putting themselves in someone else's shoes aids the young
person in developing empathy and recognizing multiple points
of view, thereby moving away from an egocentric orientation.

• Pizza Hut Math.

In a unit on decimals, the teacher divided the class into
groups and gave students menus from Pizza Hut. Each
group selected a waiter or waitress who recorded orders.
Each student then ordered from the menu. Students added
decimals to figure the bill, multiplied decimals to
determine sales tax, and divided to determine each
persons' share. At the same time, they practiced the social
skills of ordering from a menu and working together. (Van
Hoose and Strahan, 1988, p. 38)

Simulations take students a step closer to the real thing. They represent an aspect of reality, modeling its complexities over time.

• Medieval Fair. Sixth grade students at Wiscasset Middle School in Maine participated in a living-history recreation of a medieval fair. They studied and researched the times and then prepared to assume the roles of medieval people at the fair, e.g., peasants, nobility, court jesters, monks, etc. On the day of the fair, students role-played their parts in costumes. Parents and guests shared in a medieval feast. "The Medieval Fair gave our students not only an experience in living history, but also a greater understanding of their place in today's world" (Collamore and Davis, 1988, p. 40).

• World War II. At Lyle Middle School in Bourne, Massachusetts, an interdisciplinary unit on World War II integrated simulated experiences with instruction.

> In the morning, students were paired in a "Headquarters" setting as either soldiers abroad (boys) or mothers on the home front (girls). . . . The students were given time (one hour every morning) to write letters to soldiers or to home. . . . During this Headquarters time newspapers reporting events that might have or indeed did take place were sold to students for five cents. Announcements were broadcast over the speaker system in the mornings giving the latest war news, an event that occurred in schools throughout America at that time. Following the first hour, students attended four flexible classes for instruction in various aspects of the war. For example, in science the developing technology of the time, radar, atomic energy development, etc., were [*sic*] examined and discussed. In history classes students read about or watched films and videotapes about the various battles and historical figures of the time. In reading, the *Diary of Anne Frank* was read and discussed. (Wibel, 1990, p. 15)

In addition, during the unit students presented ration coupons to receive lunch, lip-synched forties' hit tunes, learned the jitterbug, and participated in a culminating USO canteen.

Interdisciplinary units. Interdisciplinary units examine a central theme, topic, issue, or problem from the perspective of more than one discipline. Rather than fragmenting instruction into science, social studies, math, etc., interdisciplinary teaching focuses on the interrelationships between disciplines. This more closely resembles the real world, which is not compartmentalized into knowledge fields constrained by time limits. Thus, the very nature of interdisciplinary instruction heightens curriculum relevance (Jacobs, 1989; Vars, 1987).

> The integrative nature of interdisciplinary units encourages students to "see" the interconnectedness of the world around them. This linking renders the world more relevant by connecting content, self, and community. Understanding the links generates excitement and fuels the desire to know more. (Davies, 1992, p. 41)

Interdisciplinary units use a variety of structures and strategies to make learning more meaningful. Two examples illustrate this variety.

• City of Richmond. Students at Eastern Kentucky University's Model Laboratory School spent three weeks studying their community. The first week they attended regular classes. Each class focused on the city of Richmond from the perspective of a different discipline. For example, in social studies students explored local history by examining census data, maps, artifacts, and other primary source materials. At the end of the first week, students selected a project of interest to research individually or in small groups. Project topics were multidisciplinary, including historic homes, local fauna, environmental concerns, family trees, and local folklore. The second week students collected data and researched their projects. Hours were spent interviewing people, photographing old homes, digging through courthouse records, collecting leaves and insects, testing water, touring haunted houses, and researching at the library. Other experiences included guest speakers, a geological field trip, a walking tour of historic homes, and a community scavenger hunt of historic places. The final week students translated their research findings into a museum-style display. Peers, parents, and younger students toured the museum. Student excitement was best expressed when one said, "I can't wait until our next unit!" (Strubbe and McMahon, 1988).

• Career Linking. Koscuiszko Middle School in Milwaukee, Wisconsin, designed a series of interdisciplinary units to assist minority students in broadening their career aspirations, particularly in the fields of math and science. The unit topics covered health occupations, natural sciences, engineering, robotics, and service occupations. Each six-week unit included an introduction to the career field, a field trip to a local business, speakers from a variety of businesses, shadowing an employee for half a day in a career area of interest to the student, and participation in a variety of activities to evaluate the unit. All activities included preparation and follow-up phases (Fouad and Wiebeck, 1991).

Community projects/service. The Carnegie Council on Adolescent Development (1989), along with the National Association of Secondary School Principals (1985), recommend using community resources in the instructional program. This involves utilizing both people and places. The community is a natural setting for resolving real problems, experiencing various adult roles, and seeing the application of concepts taught in school. It provides concrete experiences for young people to explore themselves and the world around them. The following examples show a variety of ways to use the community as a resource.

• Adopt-A-Business. A team of students adopted a local business to learn how it functioned and to see the application of basic economic concepts. Students also served brief apprenticeships (George et al., 1992).

> • [A] team of 6th and 7th graders investigated their town's landfill problem, finding out how much garbage the town produced by sorting different types of refuse in their own homes, weighing it at the end of the week, and extrapolating realistic figures about the volume of types of garbage produced in their community. This was information that had not previously existed, and it helped conceptualize recycling practices that would benefit the town.

• Community Service. Community service projects address young peoples' developing sense of altruism (Beane and Lipka, 1987). "Service learning provides young adolescents with an opportunity to assume meaningful, contributing roles in their communities" (Schine, Bianco, and Seltz, 1992, p. 40). Although appropriate for all early adolescents, service learning particularly meets the needs of urban youth who often feel powerless in the face of urban problems. It shows them they can make a difference and have something worthwhile to offer (Schine et al., 1992). Service projects might include neighborhood help clubs, cleanups (Allen and McEwin, 1983), visiting nursing home residents, or working with day care centers.

Immersion programs. In an attempt to bring young people as close to the real thing as possible, a growing number of middle level schools are designing programs that immerse students in an out-of-school experience for an extended period of time. The Foxfire program and student exchanges illustrate the immersion approach.

- Foxfire Program. Eric Mortensen of North Carolina took his students to the western part of his state to experience Appalachian culture firsthand. There they got to know a community made up of Cherokee native Americans and descendants of Scotch-Irish immigrants. They heard stories of the Indian removal via the Trail of Tears. They searched for artifacts on sites of ancient Cherokee hunting grounds, learned about superstitions and the religious beliefs of fundamentalists, copied recipes for 'possum, and grew to appreciate the laconic humor and fascinating stories of these friendly mountain people. Their minds were opened to the richness of contemporary folk customs in a bicultural context that served as a microcosm of multicultural America. (George et al., 1992, p. 76)

• Exchange Program. This program paired students from a rural university community in central Kentucky with students from the bayou country in Louisiana. Schools were selected in communities exhibiting cultural and geographic differences in order to help students experience the concept of diversity. The exchange involved a trip to Louisiana by the Kentucky students, followed by a reciprocal visit to Kentucky by their Louisiana partners. Prior to the exchange, paired students wrote and called each other. During the exchange, the young people lived with the families of their partners. This gave them an opportunity to more fully experience the culture. In Louisiana, the Kentucky youth fished for crayfish, toured New Orleans, took a boat ride to an oil rig, visited a sugar factory, went to Mardi Gras parades, listened to Cajun music, and traveled the bayous. While in Kentucky, students hiked in the mountains, visited a horse park and racetrack, toured historic sites, learned how to clog, went to the state capital, and dined on the Kentucky River. Students' firsthand experiences and emotional involvement led them to a greater understanding of the underlying universality of cultures. Although they noted differences in climate, topography, food, and regional accents, they concluded that people are basically the same—young people have similar interests and feelings and share common problems (Strubbe and McMahon, 1986).

Link Content to Students' Lives

Meaningfulness is heightened by linking the content to students' interests, concerns, and prior knowledge. Adapting teaching to students' interests stimulates intrinsic motivation (Brophy, 1987). Once motivated, students become active learners. The processes of active involvement and relating content to prior experiences promote understanding (Markle et al., 1990) and enhance brain development (Caine and Caine, 1991; Healy, 1987).

Relating instruction to students' lives requires understanding the developmental needs and concerns of young adolescents. Two key developmental needs, identified by the Center for Early Adolescence, are "meaningful participation in their families, schools, and communities" and "self-definition" (Scales, 1992, p. 8). Both of these suggest that teachers of young people should provide opportunities for them to explore actively personal interests.

Four general approaches are presented for linking content to students' lives. The first three provide suggestions for making subject matter more relevant to young adolescents. The fourth approach uses student concerns and problems as the focal point of instruction.

Activate prior knowledge. Activating prior knowledge helps assure that students have the prerequisite knowledge and skills to successfully engage in an academic task. Strategies for eliciting prior knowledge follow.

- Elicit background knowledge through questions and/or administering pretests. Relate new content to previously taught units.

- Use the K-W-L strategy. Students brainstorm "What I *know*" on a topic, categorize it, and discuss sources of this information. Next, they identify "What do I *want* to know?" Upon completion of the lesson/unit, students list "What I *learned*." Relate these understandings back to the prior knowledge listed under K (Ogle, 1986).

- Incorporate the cooperative learning Think-Pair-Share strategy into lessons. In this strategy, pose a question/ problem. Everyone thinks or writes a response. Students then share their answers with a partner and together create a single new response.

- Have students map their knowledge prior to and after instruction (see figure 2).

- Guide students in thinking analogically. Start by using analogies in your teaching and then encourage students to generate their own. For example, after a brief introduction to the concept of democracy, ask students to compare aspects of democracy to the human body. What component of democracy might be compared to the cells in the body? The brain? The muscles? Heart? Then, direct students to create their own analogies for democracy (Gordon, 1970; Silkebakken and Camp, 1993).

- Use visualization or guided imagery exercises (Wood, 1991).

- Find out more about your students. What kind of music do they listen to? How do they spend their free time? Familiarize yourself with the social and environmental forces shaping their lives. Watch their favorite television shows. Listen to the music they like. This "homework" supplies you with concrete ideas on how to assist students in connection-making.

Figure 2. Concept Map

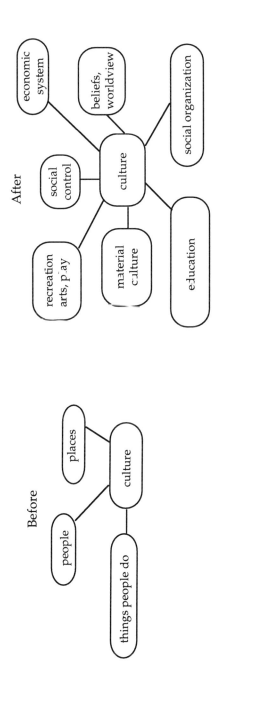

Before

people

places

culture

things people do

After

social
control

economic
system

beliefs,
worldview

culture

social organization

recreation
arts, play

material
culture

education

Realistic applications. Aid students in understanding the content by using examples and practice opportunities that derive from the learner's reality. Examples using "real" mathematics problems illustrate this approach.

- Situations taken from pupils' real lives often provide the best applications. What is the most efficient way to get to school? How early do you have to leave home to be reasonably sure you'll get to school on time? Which grocery store offers the best buys? Should quality, convenience, and other matters influence your decision? How much money will I need in order to buy a bicycle? How can I manage to get that much money? (Willoughby 1990, p. 15)

- When discussing percent problems, we started simply by asking for examples of high test scores or low test scores. "Is it possible to get 110 percent? 200 percent?" Asking the question, "If you missed two questions on a test, what do you think your score might be as a percent?", challenged the brightest as well as the slowest students, and provided an opportunity for discussion. (Harrison, 1993, p. 14)

- Have a class try to figure out how to park more cars conveniently and safely, in the school parking lot, reduce the waiting time in the school lunch line without extending the lunch period too much, synchronize traffic lights on a local two-way street for a reasonable speed in both directions. (Willoughby, 1990, p. 47)

• Give students in small groups a page from the newspaper and instruct them to write at least three word problems not using ads (Willoughby, 1990).

Affective involvement. Touching students' emotions pulls them into the learning context. It heightens their mental engagement, thereby optimizing learning (Healy, 1987). One middle level expert suggests that affective involvement is at least as important as academic instruction.

Regular experiences with the affective domain are a must for this age group as the searches for "Who Am I?" and "Who Are You?" become personal crusades for middle grade students. Their struggles for self-identity and understanding of erratic feelings or inconsistent attitudes make them very vulnerable to outside influences. It could be argued here that time spent on teaching students how to cope with their beliefs, values, perceptions, and interests is just as important, if not more so, than time spent on teaching academic content. (Schurr, 1989, p. 26)

In teaching content, look for ways to relate it to students' values or feelings. For example, when studying the Revolutionary War, start by examining conflicts between young adolescents and their parents. Explore students' feelings and sense of powerlessness. How do they react to these personal conflicts? Follow up with a discussion of the concept of revolution and examine the American Revolution. Students can compare the reactions and feelings of the patriots to their previously discussed responses (Beane and Lipka, 1987).

Another example further illustrates this strategy. While studying the Civil War, have students put themselves in the shoes of a 13-year-old boy living in Gettysburg. They can describe how they think the boy felt and compare his feelings to their own emotions in a situation of perceived threat (White and Greenwood, 1992).

Problem-centered approach. This approach derives content from the real interests and needs of young adolescents. Issues and developmental concerns of young people, along with related social concerns, become the focal points of instruction. Students investigate topics such as "getting along with others, living in school, how transescents fit in the community, understanding the messages in commercial media" (Beane and Lipka, 1987, p. 29) and themes that address both personal and social concerns. Beane (1990) suggests several ripe themes: transitions, identities, interdependence, wellness, conflict resolution, caring, justice, independence, institutions, commercialism, and social structures. Students explore these topics applying a variety of skills. By making content personally relevant, we increase the likelihood of it being used and enhance young adolescents' self-esteem (Beane and Lipka, 1987).

An example illustrates how the problem-centered approach uses concepts derived from the disciplines to examine personal concerns. The unit "Living In Our School" dealt with "why young people must go to school for such a long period of their life" (Beane and Lipka, 1987, p. 46). One unit activity and an analysis of its disciplinary content follow.

> Students developed a list of the reasons why they think they have to come to school. They interviewed family members and adults in the school setting for additional reasons. Using the one-three-six technique the students rank ordered the reasons from most important to least important with a series of why statements to support their rankings of the reasons. The students then discussed the similarities and differences in the three sets of rankings.

CONTENT	ACTIVITY
Language Arts	*Listening*—interviews, group discussions
	Speaking—interviews
	Reading—interpreting interviews, list of reasons
	Writing—interview protocols, lists of reasons
Social Studies	*Social Psychology*—general differences and similarities in the importance of school
	Sociology—importance of institutions (school) within our society; cooperation dynamics of group work
Mathematics	*Numeration*—use of ordinal numbers for ranking
	Computation—calculation of differences in rank
Aesthetic Arts	*Visual Arts*—selection of media to display findings (Beane and Lipka, 1987, p. 46)

Opportunities for Making Choices

Responsibility for Learning

Offering students a say in their learning and actions increases intrinsic motivation (Brophy, 1987; Ericksen, 1974; Wlodkowski, 1977). It gives them a greater sense of control over their learning. This sense of learning and problem ownership is critical to developing self-responsibility (Martin, 1980). Becoming a responsible young person requires exposure to many opportunities to make choices. These opportunities increase the early adolescent's *response-ability*.

Assignments/projects. Offer choices in assignments and projects. Provide a variety of options that appeal to different learning styles and interests. Examples of incorporating choice-making into assignments include the following: ask students to select 10 of the 15 problems to complete; post a chart of challenging enrichment activities for students who finish tasks early; and place several pictures on a bulletin board and instruct students to select one as a story starter.

Liala Strotman (Fusco and Associates, 1987) integrated choice-making into research projects. While studying inventors, students conducted a research project on a selected inventor. The methods of research blended requirements with options. Students were required to "complete a data collection sheet" and "read at least one biographical chapter." In addition, they selected two other sources of information. They were given several options for sharing their findings: "choice of speech, skit, radio show, puppet show, or an ingenious idea" (p. 11).

Learning contracts. The contract should include a variety of activities designed to enhance a student's understanding of a particular topic. It can include negotiable and nonnegotiable activities. Learning centers/stations, cooperative activities, films, field trips, and guest speakers provide varied formats for contract activities. Incorporate a variety of ways for students to demonstrate what they learned, e.g., exhibits, demonstrations, skits, papers, or presentations. Allow students to select their preferred format.

The activities associated with learning contracts provide a vehicle to permit the connection between previously isolated content areas and the personal interests and needs of the student. The contract allows the students to have a say in what and how they will learn. Most important, however, the use of the learning contract helps to establish a climate which clearly signals that students are valued, respected, and capable of assuming responsibility for a large portion of their learning. (White and Greenwood, 1992, p. 20)

Curriculum input. Give students a say in the content to be studied. For example, at the beginning of a unit ask students to generate questions regarding what they would like to learn. Incorporate their questions in the course of study. Solicit student suggestions for interdisciplinary unit topics. Upon completing units of study, ask students for evaluative feedback and suggestions for improving instruction (Davies, 1992).

Responsibility for One's Actions

Relationship between behavior and consequences. Assist students in seeing the relationship between their behaviors and the consequences of those behaviors. Verbalize choices the young person faces, e.g., "You can complete your assignment now or after school. The choice is yours." Connect inappropriate behaviors with logical consequences. "If you write on the desk, you will clean the desks." Arth and Freeman (1981) suggest using four questions to help young adolescents assume responsibility for their actions. "Do you know what you did wrong?" "Do you know why it was wrong?" "Do you know what to do next time?" "Do you want to go back?"

Input on rule-making. When students create classroom rules, it increases their motivation to follow them (Wlodkowski, 1977). Using criteria for evaluating the rules helps assure their reasonableness and develops critical-thinking skills. Is the rule simply and clearly stated? Is it observable? Enforceable? Necessary and fair?

Decision-making skills. Some students do not sense choices. They respond the same way to any situation. "If a child is not aware of a choice, she has no choice" (Moorman and Dishon, 1983, p. 101). Teaching problem-solving and decision-making models assists students in recognizing alternative solutions and evaluating their relative merits.

Goal-setting. Having students establish their own learning and behavioral goals increases their locus of control and heightens motivation (Brophy, 1987; Wlodkowski, 1977). Teach students to create goals that are (1) reachable in the near future; (2) specific; (3) neither too easy nor too hard (Brophy, 1987); (4) student selected; (5) written; and (6) monitored (Martino, 1993). Instructing at-risk students in these procedures helps them develop responsibility and achieve success (Martino, 1993).

Variety: Addressing Differences

Joan Lipsitz's (1984) study of exemplary schools found that they all addressed the varied developmental needs of early adolescents. "The most striking feature of the four schools is their willingness and ability to adapt all school practices to the individual differences in intellectual, biological, and social maturation of their students" (p. 167). The diversity of this age group requires utilizing a variety of instructional practices to meet their needs.

According to the Carnegie Council on Adolescent Development (1989), 25 percent of all middle level students have at-risk characteristics while another 25 percent are moderately at risk. Yet, the very nature of early adolescence places all young adolescents potentially at risk (Strubbe, 1989a; Vatterott and Yard, 1993; White and Greenwood, 1992). Strategies that most help disadvantaged learners are appropriate for all young adolescents (Ruff, 1993). "The more schools and any other institution provide success with caring, the more capable our young people will be" (Scales, 1992, p. 5).

Addressing the varied interests, learning styles, and developmental characteristics of young people creates a supportive learning environment. Such an environment provides opportunities to experience success, thereby enhancing self-esteem. Thus, effective middle level teaching mandates a variety

of experiences and resources in order to meet the diverse needs
of this age group (NASSP, 1985).

Grouping Practices

This section examines meeting varied needs through
grouping practices, addressing differences in learning styles, and
using a variety of resources. Varying group structures both
meets different learning styles and provides opportunities for
students to develop a range of skills. Class instruction, small-
group work, and individual activities should all be part of the
middle level classroom. "Decisions about apportioning time for
instruction, for individual and small-group work, and for other
activities should accommodate as fully as possible the wide
variety of learning styles and behaviors characteristic of this
developmental period" (George et al., 1992, p. 72). Using a
variety of grouping procedures addresses this diversity and
motivates students (Harrison, 1993).

Class instruction. Three national studies sponsored by the
National Science Foundation found that "[t]he dominant mode
of instruction continues to be large group, teacher-controlled
recitation and lecture, based primarily on the textbook" (Allen
and McEwin, 1983, p. 43).

Whole class instruction is a viable form of teaching *when* it
actively involves the learners in meaningful and age-appropriate
tasks. It can serve as a forum for developing a variety of skills,
such as active listening and questioning. Furthermore, lectures
efficiently transmit information, discussions clarify concepts, and
demonstrations and other forms of modeling make abstract ideas
more concrete (NASSP, 1985). These total class presentations are
appropriate when they acknowledge the interactive nature of
learning.

How can teachers make whole-class instruction more
interactive? Ask questions. Students learn more from a question-
and-answer discussion than from a straight lecture. The
Ebbinhous study found that retention drops after a lecture from
60 percent immediate recall to about 20 percent after eight weeks
(Costa, 1985). Include questions that reflect different levels of
thinking, particularly more higher-order questions (Harrison,

1993). Teachers who ask more divergent questions produce more divergent thinking in students (Costa, 1985). Adapt questions to the varied interests and levels of cognitive development of students. Be cautious, though, to challenge at-risk students with higher-level questions. One study found (Taylor and Reeves, 1993) that teachers tend to ask these students mainly recall and comprehension questions. Yet, when given higher expectations the at-risk students increased their productivity and felt better about themselves.

Incorporate strategies that actively involve all in the questioning process. For example, ask a question and direct everyone to mentally come up with an answer, pause, and then randomly sample several student responses. Also, students can signal their responses. "Signal thumbs up if you agree or thumbs down if you disagree." Or, pose a question/problem and have students think of an answer, share it with a neighbor, and then together come up with a joint response.

Active mental engagement is further stimulated by encouraging students to ask their own questions. Teach students to go beyond just asking factual and comprehension questions. Bloom's Cognitive Taxonomy provides one framework for guiding students in asking higher-order questions (Hunkins, 1976).

Group work. "The self-enhancing middle school encourages transescents to learn how to work well with others" (Beane and Lipka, 1987, p. 37). The Center for Early Adolescence identified "[p]ositive social interaction with adults and peers" as a primary developmental need of young adolescents (Scales, 1992, p. 8). Small-group instructional strategies are a natural forum for enhancing students' social and emotional development and assisting them in developing positive social interaction skills (Alexander and George, 1981).

Cooperative learning capitalizes on students' need for peer interactions. Although there are many cooperative learning strategies, ranging from highly structured to very informal, they share several common elements. The groups provide a support system, shared leadership and responsibility, heterogeneous membership, and social skill development (Jones, 1990).

Cooperative learning addresses young adolescents' developmental needs. It helps young people move away from an egocentric orientation towards a better understanding of others. In addition, it uses peer interactions as a motivational tool. Active participation, which is inherent in cooperative learning activities, matches with how young people learn. Group work meets young adolescents' need for movement. Furthermore, the heterogeneous structure assumes that all students can successfully contribute to a group, thereby providing low-achieving students with an opportunity to experience success. Finally, groups promote cognitive development through verbalization of ideas, elaboration, peer modeling of multiple perspectives, and problem-solving (Jones, 1990; NASSP, 1985).

Several other benefits are attributed to cooperative learning. One school's assessment of the benefits of cooperative learning found that students experienced "an increase in self-knowledge, in social skills, and in time management" (Gartin and Digby, 1993, p. 14). Another teacher found that heterogeneous math grouping resulted in fewer discipline problems, more engaged learning time, new friendships, and higher achievement test scores (Harrison, 1993). Group work is particularly effective with girls (Johnston and Markle, 1982) and some minorities. For example, group collaboration matches with many Native American traditional values (Jones, 1990). In addition, effective dropout programs "promote cooperative learning and group socialization skills" (Ruff, 1993, p. 11).

Peer teaching and peer helping are additional examples of group work. Both place students in leadership positions. This responsibility enhances self-esteem and teaches problem-solving (Alexander and George, 1981; Konet, 1991).

Individual activities. Individual student work addresses several learning goals. It reinforces content through practice opportunities (Woolfolk, 1993). Working alone also enables students to further develop reading, writing, and study skills. Independent work can nurture lifelong learning by focusing on the development of learning strategies, including self-monitoring skills (Jones, Palinscar, Ogle, and Carr, 1987).

Several teaching strategies incorporate individual work. The previously mentioned learning contracts allow students to select activities of interest that match with their learning styles. Learning centers present collections of materials to aid students in understanding concepts. They usually include tasks accompanied by clear directions, objectives, a feedback system, and multisensory resources. Learning centers motivate students, meet young adolescents' need for movement, provide for differences in learning styles, and often integrate the disciplines (Schurr, 1989).

> Investigation cards also enable students to work independently. These cards require a student to use a common object or topic as a springboard for observing, exploring, discovering, and investigating characteristics and concepts associated with that given object or topic. Each card outlines only one basic activity to be completed by the student, although each single activity could have several parts to it. (Schurr, 1989, p. 134)

A sample investigation card on calendars follows.

Determine all of the reasons why you think people buy calendars. Rank order them from the most popular to the least popular. Now, interview several people. Find out their reasons for purchasing a calendar. Record your findings on a graph (Schurr, 1989, p. 139). Each of these instructional approaches allows students to work at their own pace.

The most commonly encountered form of individual work consists of students independently completing a task, e.g., reading, computing problems, working on a project, or answering questions. Such tasks can be structured to set students up for success and further develop independent learning skills. Research supports the following guidelines:

1. Give clear directions. Teacher clarity aids students in successfully completing tasks (Levin and Long, 1981).
2. Provide high- and low-structure activities. Some students prefer activities that are very structured, while others want more input on *what* and *how* they learn (Dunn and Dunn, 1978). For example, when students read textual material provide those needing structure with a reading guide. An excerpt from a point-of-view reading guide follows (Wood, 1991a, p. 54).

Chapter 11—The War of 1812. You are about to be interviewed as if you were a person living in the United States in the early 1800's. Describe your reactions to each of the events discussed next.

Planting the Seeds of War:

1. As a merchant in a coastal town, tell why your business is doing poorly.

The War Debate:

2. Explain why you decided to become a war hawk. Who was your leader?
3. Tell why many of your fellow townspeople lowered their flags at half mast.

For students preferring little structure, you might assign them to read the chapter and then design their own approach to demonstrate understanding.

3. Provide self-monitoring tools. Give students a checklist specifying the evaluation criteria (rubric). Checklists help students monitor their own progress. By providing clear goals, students are more likely to meet them. In addition, rubrics encourage students to become active participants in their own assessment (Zessoules and Gardner, 1991). A sample checklist for monitoring writing mechanics follows (Wood, 1993, p. 72).

Name _____   Assignment _____

Date _____   Teacher _____

A. Content
_____ Does it make sense?
_____ Did I use new words relating to the topic?
_____ Did I use interesting words to help the reader "picture" what I wrote?
_____ Did I keep to the topic?

B. Sentence and Paragraph Structure
_____ Did I use capital letters at the beginning of each sentence and for proper nouns?

_____ Did I end each sentence with the correct punctuation?
_____ Did I write complete sentences?
_____ Did I use commas, apostrophes, quotation marks, and other punctuation correctly?
_____ Did I have any run-on sentences?
_____ Did I spell each word correctly?
_____ Did I indent the first word of each paragraph?

C. Handwriting

_____ Did I write this in my best handwriting?

Addressing Differences in Learning Styles

The National Association of Secondary School Principals (1985) recommends that middle level teachers "[p]lan instruction that accommodates individual learning styles and the different ways students think about and process information" (p. 9). Learning-styles research enumerates many benefits derived from matching instruction to students' learning styles. "Well-designed and carefully conducted research now documents that teaching students through their individual learning styles results in: (1) increased academic achievement; (2) improved attitudes toward school; and (3) reduced discipline problems" (Dunn, 1982, p. 142). Furthermore, teaching to students' learning styles addresses the needs of at-risk students who often feel that schools fail to meet their unique learning needs (Bergman, 1989). The Center for Early Adolescence (1988, p. 64) suggests that "[d]ropout prevention programs should focus on broadening and diversifying opportunities in the educational mainstream so that students with a variety of learning styles, paces, and needs can experience success." Thus, matching students with their preferred learning styles increases motivation and provides them with opportunities to experience success.

This research suggests that middle level instruction address the varied learning needs of these youngsters. Although there are many factors influencing learning, this section focuses on addressing differences in perceptual strengths. A few strategies that match with auditory, visual, and kinesthetic strengths are presented. Teaching with *variety* is the key to maintaining interest and meeting student diversity.

Auditory strategies. Neurological auditory pathways are slow to develop and are not complete until around the ages of 7 to 10 (Healy, 1987). As a result, auditory perception usually is not the strongest sense for early adolescents. Several approaches can nurture the development of this perceptual mode. Lectures, guest speakers, discussions, and cooperative learning all rely heavily on auditory perception. Accentuating key ideas through voice variation assists students in comprehending oral material. Storytelling is particularly helpful in developing communication skills (Ralston and Williams, 1983). Increasing wait-time to three to five seconds both after you ask a question and after a student responds promotes longer responses and greater involvement in discussions (Rowe, 1974). Varying your questioning procedures, including randomly calling on students, helps develop active listening skills (Levin and Long, 1981). Play games, such as "20 Questions," that rely heavily on auditory perception.

Visual strategies. Presenting information in a visual format assists concrete learners in developing their own mental images. Approaches that rely on visual perception include demonstrations, the blackboard, posters, charts, bulletin boards, pictures, and videos. Two visual teaching strategies that particularly aid academically at-risk students are visualization activities and graphic organizers (Thompson, 1988).

Research suggests that middle level students using graphic organizers achieve higher than those who do not use them (Hawk and McLeod, 1983). Graphic organizers visually represent content and highlight interrelationships. They translate abstract information into a more concrete form, aid in organizing and retrieving information, and relate new content to prior knowledge (Jones, Pierce, and Hunter, 1989).

Graphic outlines reflect the structures of the texts they represent. With training, students can construct their own graphic organizers. For example, "spider maps" describe a central idea and show the relationship of supporting details or attributes of the main idea. A model of this graphic form follows (Jones et al., 1989, p. 24).

Figure 3. Spider Map: An Example

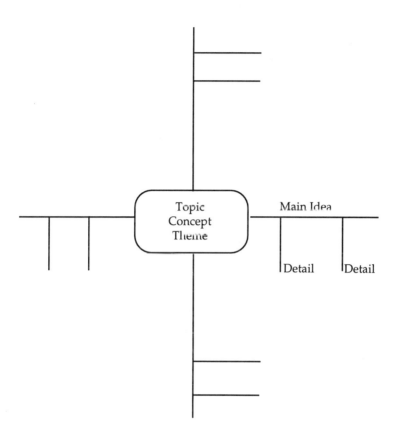

Kinesthetic strategies. Young adolescents ride a developmental roller coaster of energy highs and lows. Blended with these energy bursts are bodies experiencing periods of rapid physical growth, often accompanied by bone growth that precedes supporting muscular development. Developmental patterns may be exhibited in the classroom by bodies slouching in their seats, moving frequently to find that elusive state of being comfortable; a continuous flow of traffic to the pencil sharpener, the bathroom, the drinking fountain—any excuse to move; and feeling too tired to do anything followed by enough energy to run a five-mile race. Teachers address these developmental needs by integrating opportunities for movement into the classroom. "Activities which permit and encourage physical movement, active interactions, and psychomotor skills all cater to these erratic bursts of energy and glandular secretions" (Schurr, 1989, p. 25).

Using movement in learning accommodates the kinesthetic learner (Dunn and Dunn, 1978), focuses attention, promotes active involvement (Schurr, 1989), stimulates hemispheric integration (Houston, 1982; Williams, 1983), lays a foundation for abstract thought (Schurr, 1989), enhances creativity (Williams, 1983), serves as a memory trigger (Woolfolk, 1993), and helps young adolescents develop a more positive body image. The National Association of Secondary School Principals (1985) recommends that middle level teachers reap these benefits by capitalizing "on students' natural activity levels and integrate physical activity and hands-on instruction into the classroom procedures" (p. 10).

There are many ways to integrate movement into instruction. The following suggestions serve as idea starters.

- Use signaling as a way to monitor students' understanding. Signals should represent as close as possible the responses given. For example, "Show me on a scale from one to five with your fingers how much you learned today. What can you do to get your understanding to a five?"

- Draw pictures showing the meaning of new words and concepts. Accompany a picture with a written explanation of how the picture depicts the concept.

- Explore the differences between capitalism, socialism, communism, and anarchy. Divide students into four groups with each representing one of these systems. Each group plans a lunch for the class that would be consistent with their system's principles and manner of functioning (Williams, 1983).

- Assist students in understanding molecular bonding by assigning each one to be an atom of hydrogen, oxygen, carbon, or nitrogen. The hydrogen atoms would form one bond so these students could use one arm. Oxygen students use two arms and carbon atoms use both arms and legs. Students then find others they can bond with to form molecules or organic compounds (Williams, 1983).

- Play charades to develop vocabulary comprehension.

- Create interactive bulletin boards. For example, display a tree with three main branches. In a pocket on the bulletin board are the "leaves" describing functions of the three branches of government. Students place the leaves on the appropriate branches and self-check their accuracy.

- Use instructional approaches that naturally incorporate movement, e.g., cooperative learning, simulations, role plays, field trips, learning centers, and many games.

In addition to using strategies that address students' perceptual learning preferences, incorporate a wide variety of instructional approaches in your classroom. Arth and Freeman (1981) suggest using the "quarter system" to help you meet this goal. Divide each class into four equal time segments and use a different instructional activity for each segment (Van Hoose and Strahan, 1988). As previously mentioned, variety stimulates interest and assists in meeting differences in learning styles.

Accompany variety with fun. Lipsitz's (1984) study of effective middle level schools found that successful schools were "more elementary in tone and structure, in emphasizing fun and fantasy, and in personalizing every aspect of the school environment, these schools still appeal to the children within pseudomature adolescents" (p. 184). Activities that are perceived as fun meet young peoples' intrinsic need for fun (Glasser, 1986) and build their self-esteem by making them feel better about learning (Beane and Lipka, 1987).

Games and gimmicks are two ways to make learning fun. Creative middle level teachers develop a repertoire of gimmicks to pull young adolescents into the learning process. One teacher has students select their math homework by throwing darts at a colored dartboard. If you hit the red circle, you do the problems listed under the red column on the board, etc. (Arth and Freeman, 1981). Another teacher gives students a "Geography MasterCard" when they pass geography tests. The card enables them to earn credits redeemable at the school canteen (George et al., 1992). Fun motivates! Select varied teaching strategies that meet the diverse needs of students and that are fun.

Using a Variety of Resources

Incorporate a variety of resources with your varied instructional strategies. This variety of resources, like diverse teaching approaches, motivates and enables the teacher of young adolescents to better address students' interests and needs. Supplementing textbooks with trade books, primary source documents, media, technology, manipulatives, and other print and nonprint resources helps make abstractions more concrete (Markle et al., 1990; Wood, 1991a). The National Association of Secondary School Principals (1985) recommends using "people and places" in the community as instructional resources (p. 19). As mentioned earlier in this chapter, community resources bring students closer to the real thing. "The classroom at this level ought to be perceived by both teacher and student as a laboratory of life where units of instruction are not bound to a textbook, a lecture, or a teacher-dominated activity" (Schurr, 1989, p. 24).

In addition to the community and resources previously mentioned, technology holds the potential to motivate, remediate, challenge, and bridge the gap between schooling and the outside world. New technologies offer opportunities for active involvement in learning (Swaim, Needham, and Associates, 1984). C. W. Ruckel Middle School in Niceville, Florida, serves as an example of how technology enhances learning. For several years the school has integrated model technology, including software developed by Educational Systems Corporation, a computer resource center, and several major projects. A brief description of a few of these projects illustrates the varied applications of technology (Kean and Kean, 1992).

• AT&T Long Distance Learning Network Mindworks— Students around the globe assist each other in editing their creative writing pieces via electronic mail and telecommunication.

• National Geographic Kids Network Hello! Students around the country design and conduct science research. They collect, compile, graph, and map results using microcomputers and telecommunication systems.

• Ruckel Achievement in Mathematics—This project compares math standards in Florida schools with the standards in other countries. During the first year the school exchanged textbooks, worksheets, lessons, and tests with six other countries. In addition, students periodically chose to complete translated mathematics worksheets from other countries.

The Education Development Center (EDC) and the Technical Education Research Centers (TERC) examined how technology is integrated successfully into the curriculum. They found the keys were ongoing communication with and between teachers, along with collaboration. Teachers facilitate the use of technology by sharing materials and ideas, linking with someone more familiar with computers, revising their instruction, and sharing the responsibility for teaching with colleagues (Zorfass and Remz, 1992). Technology is another available tool for making middle level education more developmentally appropriate.

Challenging: Stimulating Thinking

As we approach the 21st century, the need for citizens adept at thinking becomes evident. We live in a time of accelerating change. The shift from an industrial to an information society exemplifies the rapidity of this change. It took 100 years to move from an agricultural to an industrial base and only 20 years to shift from an industrial to an information society (Naisbitt, 1982). This explosion of information challenges educators to assist students in understanding the complexity of the world around them and to become lifelong learners. Today and tomorrow's worlds require students capable of complex thinking.

The Carnegie Council report (1989) on young adolescent schooling highlights schools' failure to address adequately this need. "Many middle grade schools in this country fail to support and challenge youth. Nowhere is this failure more evident than in the development of American adolescents' critical reasoning and higher order thinking" (p. 42). The Goodlad (1984) study of schooling noted this failure when it found that less than 1 percent of the talk of observed teachers invited students to engage in more than recall reasoning. The National Association of Secondary School Principals (1985) confirms the need to "equip students with skills for continued learning" and self-evaluation skills (p. 5).

Activities that challenge without over-challenging spark an interest in learning (Vidler, 1977). Frequent exposure to these intellectual challenges nurtures the capacity to further engage in higher-level thinking (Costa, 1985). In other words, thinking begets thinking.

This section examines strategies to promote thinking. The strategies are divided into those that encourage students to *explore, connect,* and *evaluate.* It concludes with a problem-solving paradigm that integrates these three processes.

Explore

The exploration of ideas is driven by curiosity. The curious individual remains open to many possibilities while seeking answers to questions. The curious person tolerates ambiguity, thinks divergently, asks more and better questions, persists longer at problem-solving, and tends to achieve higher than the incurious person (Vidler, 1977). Nurturing this curiosity in young people addresses their developmental needs for "creative expression" and "self-definition" (Scales, 1992).

This intrinsic motivation to learn can be nurtured in the classroom. A number of factors stimulate curiosity, including novelty, incongruity, and complexity.

> [T]he 10–14 year old is intensely curious and imaginative and so it is an ideal time to explore the world of fantasy, creativity, and the unusual or bizarre. Mini-units on monsters, magic, mystery, or science fiction can capitalize on this passion for the make-believe. Encouraging and rewarding students for "thinking outside the box" and "marching to a different drummer" can reap dividends in motivating otherwise reluctant learners. (Schurr, 1989, p. 24)

This exploration of novel ideas develops mental flexibility—the ability to "see" varied perspectives. Such flexibility is an imperative cognitive skill for coping and adapting to times of rapid change.

The freedom to explore ideas requires a supportive classroom environment. Thinking is fostered with an inquiry approach to teaching, in which education is viewed as the exploration of the unknown, and there is an emphasis on problem-finding (Glatthorn and Bacon, 1985). Asking heuristic questions and posing problems promote a spirit of inquiry. A few guidelines will assist teachers in this process: encourage student-generated questions and problems, for these are inherently more meaningful (Willoughby, 1990); stress that there are a variety of answers and/or approaches and that there is no single best way (Johnston and Markle, 1986); challenge, yet be sensitive to each students' cognitive development (Fusco and Associates, 1987); direct students in finding the answers

themselves; structure the classroom to encourage exploration
and manipulation (Vidler, 1977); and use cooperative learning to
promote divergent thinking (Wlodkowski, 1977).

A few examples illustrate the varied approaches to
stimulating exploration.

- Use problem-solving projects. "For example, which
  grocery store in the neighborhood gives the best buys?"
  (Willoughby, 1990, p. 46). As students explore the
  question, they soon discover that the answer is neither
  simple nor straightforward.

  That's the way the world really is. Many questions that
  can be asked don't have simple answers; but we can often
  use mathematics to help us answer some of those
  questions, or at least to get a better understanding of the
  situation. (p. 47)

- Examine personal values in a variety of contexts. Davis
  (1993) provides several strategies for aiding young
  people in this exploration process. Use brainstorming.
  For example, "Why is it important to be honest? List all
  of the ideas you can think of" (p. 32).
- Reverse brainstorming generates a different perspective.
  "What can we do to lose friends or make people not like
  us?" (p. 32) The "what would happen if . . . " strategy
  guides students in beginning to develop hypothetical
  reasoning. "What would happen if everyone were a
  thief?" (p. 32)

- Present problem-solving projects that encourage original
  solutions. Bruce La Valle's middle level students
  "design, scale, and construct an energy-efficient solar
  home" (Fusco and Associates, 1987, p. 15). He provides
  opportunities to explore concepts by using a variety of
  concrete materials, including informational packets with
  illustrations, solar experiments, slide presentations, and
  examples of energy-efficient homes. After delving into
  this information, students design their original homes
  and defend their constructions.

- Create a mini-book on a selected topic. One teacher has students create a mini-history-book on a current event. The book includes required components, e.g., cover, preface, bibliography, article summaries, charts, concept maps, etc. In addition, it promotes divergent thinking through varied activities such as designing and administering a survey, drawing a political cartoon, designing a campaign slogan or button, etc. (Larkins, 1992).

Connect

The brain naturally seeks patterns and looks for relationships between ideas (Caine and Caine, 1991). Teaching strategies that aid students in pattern-seeking use the brain's natural strengths. Looking for the links between concepts develops analytical thinking and assists students in understanding the connections between new information and prior knowledge. In addition, it renders content more meaningful by having it more closely represent the complexity of the outside world.

Bringing students as close to the real thing as possible and interdisciplinary instruction both offer opportunities for examining connections. Other strategies that also encourage connection-making follow.

Futures Wheel. The futures wheel forecasts the potential effects of any decision, event, or change. It addresses the following questions: "What consequences might this decision have?" And, "How are these effects linked?" It visually displays both the more obvious consequences and the ripple effect those consequences can have on other variables (Durbin, 1982).

In the center circle, place the decision, event, or change. In the second-order circles, state consequences that might follow directly from the event. In the third-order circles, name the possible effects of the second-level consequences, and so on. As students complete a futures wheel, they begin to see that the process of examining consequences of a decision or event can continue endlessly. Looking beyond the obvious effects reveals a web of many interactive elements. This is an effective tool for

examining content-related issues ("What effects might a decision
to raise taxes produce?") and personal decisions ("If I decide to
experiment with drugs, what effects might that decision have?").
Figure 4 (Strubbe, 1989b) illustrates using the futures
wheel to postulate effects of technology that increases the
average life span to 125 years.
  Micro/macro matrix. The effects of a decision or action often
are examined only from the perspective of the individual.
Creating a micro/macro matrix encourages looking at the
consequences from broader perspectives. This framework asks,
"What choices do I have in making this decision?" "How might
each alternative affect both me and others?" The same model is
used to compare effects on a nation, the world, or any other
perspective (Fitch and Svengalis, 1979). The earlier discussion on
linking content to students' lives includes numerous strategies
for guiding youth in seeking connections in the learning process.
See figure 5.

Evaluate

  Evaluation is the process of making and defending a
judgment. It involves critical reflection that can focus on oneself
or on external variables. Examining the desirability or
effectiveness of one's own actions and those of others develops
metacognitive self-monitoring skills along with integrating
cognition and affect (Beyer, 1987; Costa, 1985). Evaluative
thinking guides students in making decisions that best serve
themselves and others. Strategies that promote self-evaluation in
the learning process follow.
  Journals/incomplete sentences. Both journals and incomplete
sentences are designed to guide students in reflective thinking.
For example, upon completing an assignment, students might
respond to an incomplete sentence that encourages self-
reflection. For example, "The most important thing I learned was
_____ because _____." People who
think about their thinking become better thinkers (Beyer, 1987;
Costa, 1985; Willoughby, 1990).

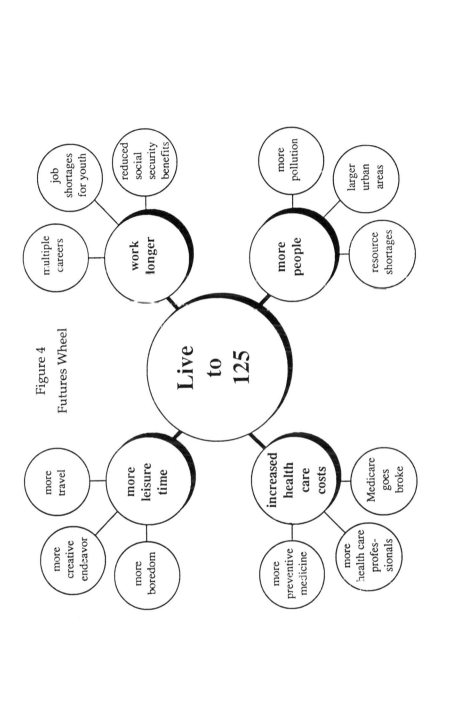

Figure 4
Futures Wheel

Live to 125

work longer
- multiple careers
- job shortages for youth
- reduced social security benefits

more people
- more pollution
- larger urban areas
- resource shortages

more leisure time
- more travel
- more creative endeavor
- more boredom

increased health care costs
- more preventive medicine
- more health care professionals
- Medicare goes broke

Figure 5. Example of Making Connections

	Effect on Individual	Effect on Others
Choice A		
Choice B		
Choice C etc.		

Self-evaluation devices. "Perhaps the most powerful way to connect evaluation devices to self-perceptions is through the use of self-evaluation by learners" (Beane and Lipka, 1987, p. 37). Evaluating one's learning and using this feedback to establish learning goals increases students' locus of control. This, in turn, aids students in viewing themselves as lifelong learners. Checklists, questions, and rubrics listing evaluation criteria all facilitate self-evaluation. An excerpt from a research evaluation sheet illustrates how self-evaluation can nurture metacognitive thinking (Fusco and Associates, 1987, p. 13).

> The easiest part of this project . . .
> The hardest part of this project . . .
> What still confuses me is . . .

Something I would like to know more about . . .
A strategy that I discovered was . . .
What fascinated me about my topic was . . .
I learned that I work this . . .
A person that I helped was . . .
Something I will do differently on the next project . . .

Value judgments. In addition to evaluating thinking processes, evaluation can focus on making value judgments. These judgments may pertain to a personal decision/action, or they may apply to the actions of others. They indicate preferences or judgments of "best/worst." Incomplete sentences are effective ways to elicit judgments. "The best candidate is _____ because _____." Having students rank order choices from "most desirable" to "least desirable" engages them in evaluative thinking. Furthermore, problem-solving models include an evaluative phase for examining alternatives generated. Opportunities for self-reflection and evaluative thinking assist young adolescents in their developmental task of self-identity (Schurr, 1989).

Problem-solving models integrate the thinking processes of exploring, connecting, and evaluating. They facilitate the development of complex thinking processes (Presseisen, 1985). The Future Problem Solving (FPS) model designed by E. Paul Torrance illustrates the integration of higher-level thinking skills. The model develops logic along with imagination. The steps in the model are (Crabbe, 1985; Kurtzberg and Kurtzberg, 1993):

1. Problem Situation. Students are given a "fuzzy situation" that summarizes the issues. They research the general topic using a variety of strategies, e.g., interviews, surveys, field trips, speakers, and readings.

2. Problem Identification. Students brainstorm possible subproblems related to the situation. They identify problems by categories such as moral/ethical, political, economic, social, etc.

3. Underlying Problem. Students synthesize the sub-problems into one general problem statement that incorporates the subproblems.

4. Alternative Solutions. Using the previously identified categories, students brainstorm possible solutions within each category.

5. Criteria Formation. At this phase, students develop five criteria for evaluating the solutions. Next, they rank order their solutions based on the identified criteria.

6. Best Solution. Based on the above criteria, students identify the best solution and defend their selection.

This process can be used with any problem. It actively involves students, and it develops a repertoire of higher-ievel thinking skills.

Summary

Effective middle level teaching strategies are developmentally appropriate, personally meaningful, and actively involve students. Adapting instruction to young adolescents' needs enables them to experience success and grow in their potential. Variety in grouping practices, instructional approaches, and resources assist in meeting the diverse needs of young adolescents. Relating content to students' lives and providing them with challenging experiences heighten motivation and promote active involvement. As a result, young people grow to view learning as a lifelong interactive and enjoyable process.

NOTES

*Additional works by the author of this chaper may be found in the bibliography under both the names Davies and Strubbe.

REFERENCES

Alexander, W. M., and George, P. S. (1981). *The exemplary middle school.* New York: Holt, Rinehart, and Winston.

Allen, M. G., and McEwin, C. K. (1983). *Middle level social studies: From theory to practice.* Columbus, OH: National Middle School Association.

Arth, A., and Freeman, L. M. (1981). The gimmick as an instructional tool. *Middle School Journal* 12(4): 4–7.

Beane, J. A. (1990). *A middle school curriculum, from rhetoric to reality.* Columbus, OH: National Middle School Association.

Beane, J. A., and Lipka, R. P. (1987). *When the kids come first: Enhancing self-esteem.* Columbus, OH: National Middle School Association.

Bergman, S. (1989). *Discipline and guidance: A thin line at the middle level school.* Reston, VA: National Association of Secondary School Principals. ERIC Document Reproduction Service No. 284-922.

Beyer, B. K. (1987). *Practical strategies for the teaching of thinking.* Needham Heights, MA: Allyn and Bacon.

Brophy, J. (1987). Synthesis of research on strategies for motivating students to learn. *Educational Leadership* 45: 40–48.

Caine, R. N., and Caine, G. (1991). *Making connections: Teaching and the human brain.* Alexandria, VA: Association for Supervision and Curriculum Development.

Carnegie Council on Adolescent Development. (1989). *Turning points: Preparing American youth for the 21st century.* Washington, DC: Carnegie Corporation.

Center for Early Adolescence and the Massachusetts Advocacy Center. (1988). *Before it's too late: Dropout prevention in the middle grades.* Carrboro, NC: Author.

Cheatham, J. (1989). Piaget, writing instruction and the middle school. *Middle School Journal* 20(4): 14–17.

Collamore, J. A. P., and Davis, L. (1988). A medieval fair brought history alive. *Middle School Journal* 20(1): 39–40.

Costa, A. (1985). Teacher behaviors that enable student thinking. In *Developing minds, a resource book for teaching thinking.* Alexandria, VA: Association for Supervision and Curriculum Development.

Crabbe, A. B. (1985). Future problem solving. In A. Costa (Ed.), *Developing minds, a resource book for teaching thinking*. Alexandria, VA: Association for Supervision and Curriculum Development.

Davies, M. A. (1992). Are interdisciplinary units worthwhile? Ask students. In J. H. Lounsbury (Ed.), *Connecting the curriculum through interdisciplinary instruction*. (pp. 37–41). Columbus, OH: National Middle School Association.

Davis, G. A. (1993). Creative teaching of moral thinking. *Middle School Journal* 24(4): 32–33.

Doda, N., George, P., and McEwin, K. (1987). Ten current truths about effective schools. *Middle School Journal* 18(3): 3–5.

Dunn, R. (1982). Teaching students through their individual learning styles: A research report. In *Student learning styles and brain behavior* (pp. 142–151). Reston, VA: National Association of Secondary School Principals.

Dunn, R., and Dunn, K. (1978). *Teaching students through their individual learning styles: A practical approach*. Reston, VA: Reston Publishing Company.

Durbin, P. (1982). New techniques and old values. *J. C. Penney Forum*, January, 10–11.

Ericksen, S. C. (1974). *Motivation for learning*. Ann Arbor, MI: University of Michigan Press.

Fitch, R. M., and Svengalis, C. M. (1979). *Futures unlimited: Teaching about worlds to come*. Washington, DC: National Council for the Social Studies.

Fouad, N. A., and Wiebeck, V. (1991). Career linking. *Middle School Journal* 23(1): 36–38.

Fusco, E. and Associates. (1987). *Cognitive matched instruction in action*. Columbus, OH: National Middle School Association.

Gartin, B. C., and Digby, A. (1993). Staff development on cooperative learning strategies: Concerns and solutions. *Middle School Journal* 24(3): 8–14.

George, P. S., Stevenson, C., Thomason, J., and Beane, J. (1992). *The middle school and beyond*. Alexandria, VA: Association for Supervision and Curriculum Development.

Glasser, W. (1986). *Control theory in the classroom*. New York: Harper and Row.

Glatthorn, A. A., and Bacon, J. (1985). The good thinker. In A. Costa (Ed.), *Developing minds, a resource book for teaching thinking*.

Alexandria, VA: Association for Supervision and Curriculum Development.

Goodlad, J. (1984). *A place called school*. New York: McGraw-Hill.

Gordon, W. J. J. (1970). *The metaphorical way of learning and knowing.* Cambridge, MA: Synectics Education Press.

Harrison, J. S. (1993). Strategies for the heterogeneous math class. *Middle School Journal* 24(4): 10–16.

Hawk, P. P., and McLeod, N. P. (1983). Graphic organizer: An effective teaching method. *Middle School Journal* 14(3): 20–22.

Healy, J. M. (1987). *Your child's growing mind: A guide to learning and brain development from birth to adolescence.* New York: Doubleday.

Houston, J. (1982). *The possible human*. Los Angeles: J. P. Tarcher.

Hunkins, F. (1976). *Involving students in questioning*. Needham Heights: Allyn and Bacon.

Jacobs, H. H. (1989). The growing need for interdisciplinary curriculum content. In H. Jacobs, *Interdisciplinary curriculum: Design and implementation* (pp. 1–11). Alexandria, VA: Association for Supervision and Curriculum Development.

Johnston, J. H., and Markle, G. C. (1982). What research says to the practitioner—about motivating students. *Middle School Journal* 13(4): 22–24.

Johnston, J. H., and Markle, G. C. (1986). *What research says to the middle level practitioner.* Columbus, OH: National Middle School Association.

Jones, J. P. (1990). Bibliotherapy: Bringing adolescents home to themselves. *Middle School Journal* 22(2): 44–46.

Jones, B. F., Palinscar, A. S., Ogle, D. S., and Carr, E. G. (Eds.). (1987). *Strategic teaching and learning: Cognitive instruction in the content areas.* Alexandria, VA: Association for Supervision and Curriculum Development.

Jones, B. F., Pierce, J., and Hunter, B. (1989). Teaching students to construct graphic representations. *Educational Leadership* 46(4): 20–25.

Kean, D. M. and Kean, D. K. (1992). Using model technology. *Middle School Journal* 23(5): 44–45.

Konet, R. J. (1991). Peer helpers in the middle school. *Middle School Journal* 23(1): 13–15.

Kurtzberg, R. L. and Kurtzberg, K. E. (1993). Future problem solving: Connecting middle school students to the real world. *Middle School Journal* 24(4): 37–40.

Larkins, B. (1992). The election in your classroom: Election connections for critical thinking skills. *New England League of Middle Schools Journal* 5(3): 24–28.

Lee, S., and Wiseman, D. (1991). Touching the lives of young adolescents with award winning books. *Middle School Journal* 22(5): 18–20.

Levin, T., and Long, R. (1981). *Effective instruction.* Alexandria, VA: Association for Supervision and Curriculum Development.

Lipsitz, J. (1984). *Successful schools for young adolescents.* New Brunswick: Transaction Books.

Markle, G., Johnston, J. H., Geer, C., and Meichtry, Y. (1990). Teaching for understanding. *Middle School Journal* 22(2): 53–57.

Martin, R. J. (1980). *Teaching through encouragement.* Englewood Cliffs, NJ: Prentice-Hall.

Martino, L. R. (1993). A goal-setting model for young adolescent at risk students. *Middle School Journal* 24(5): 19–22.

Moorman, C., and Dishon, D. (1983). *Our classroom: We can learn together.* Englewood Cliffs, NJ: Prentice-Hall.

Naisbitt, J. (1982). *Megatrends, ten new directions transforming our lives.* New York: Warner Books.

National Association of Secondary School Principals. (1985). *An agenda for excellence at the middle level.* Reston, VA: Author.

National Science Foundation. (1978). *Early adolescence: Perspectives and recommendations.* Washington, DC: U.S. Government Printing Office.

Ogle, D. M. (1986). K-W-L: A teaching model that develops active reading of expository text. *The Reading Teacher* 39: 564–570.

Partin, R. L. (1987). Fifteen guidelines for developing attention-holding lessons. *Middle School Journal* 18(2): 12–13.

Presseisen, B. J. (1985). Thinking skills: Meanings, models, materials. In A. Costa (Ed.), *Developing minds, a resource book for teaching thinking* (pp. 43–48). Alexandria, VA: Association for Supervision and Curriculum Development.

Ralston, Z. T., and Williams, W. R. (1983). Storytelling: An old art form with real instructional potential. *Middle School Journal* 14(2): 26–27, 29.

Rasinski, T. V. (1991). Inertia and reading: Stimulating interest in books and reading. *Middle School Journal, 22*(5): 30–33.

Rowe, M. (1974). Wait-time and rewards as instructional variables, their influence on language logic and fate control: Part 1: Wait-time. *Journal of Research in Science Teaching* 11: 81–94.

Ruff, T. P. (1993). Middle school students at risk: What do we do with the most vulnerable children in American education? *Middle School Journal* 24(5): 10–12.

Scales, P. C. (1992). From risks to resources: Disadvantaged learners and middle grades teaching. *Middle School Journal 23*(5): 3–9.

Schine, J. G., Bianco, D., and Seltz. J. (1992). Service learning for urban youth: Joining classroom and community. *Middle School Journal* 23(4): 40–43.

Schurr, S. L. (1989). *DYNAMITE in the classroom: A how-to handbook for teachers.* Columbus, Oh· National Middle School Association.

Silkebakken, G. P. and Camp, D. J. (1993). A five-step strategy for teaching analogous reasoning to middle school students. *Middle School Journal* 24(4): 47–50.

Strubbe, M. A. (1989a). An assessment of early adolescent stress factors. In D. B. Strahan (Ed.), *Middle school research: Selected studies, 1989* (pp. 47–59). Columbus, OH: National Middle School Association.

Strubbe, M. A. (1989b). Thinking skills. *Focus 17*: 1–6.

Strubbe, M. A. and McMahon, S. (1986). They're not a small town, they're one big family. *National Association of Laboratory Schools Journal 10*(2): 55–64.

Strubbe, M. A. and McMahon, S. (1988). Scavenging for the past. *Southern Social Studies Quarterly 14* (2): 57–62.

Superintendent's Task Force. (1987). *Caught in the middle: Educational reform for young adolescents in California schools.* Sacramento, CA: California State Department of Education.

Swaim, J., Needham, R., and Associates. (1984). *In search of excellence: The national reports—implications for middle schools.* Columbus, OH: National Middle School Association.

Taylor, R. and Reeves, J. (1993). More is better: Raising expectations for students at risk. *Middle School Journal* 24(5): 13–18.

Thompson, M. (1988). Specific teaching and learning strategies for academically at–risk students: What works. Paper presented at the meeting of the National Middle School Association, Denver, CO.

Van Hoose, J., and Strahan, D. (1988). *Young adolescent development and school practices: Promoting harmony.* Columbus, OH: National Middle School Association.

Vars, G. F. (1987). *Interdisciplinary teaching in the middle grades.* Columbus, OH: National Middle School Association.

Vatterott, C., and Yard, G. J. (1993). Accommodating individual differences through instructional adaptations. *Middle School Journal* 24(5): 23–28.

Vidler, D. (1977). Curiosity. In S. Ball (Ed.), *Motivation in education* (pp. 17–43). New York: Academic Press.

White, G. P., and Greenwood, S. C. (1992). Empowering middle level students through the use of learning contracts. *Middle School Journal* 23(5): 15–20.

Wibel, W. H. (1990). How do you teach about war? *Middle School Journal* 22(2): 14–15.

Williams, L. V. (1983). *Teaching for the two-sided mind.* New York: Simon and Schuster.

Willoughby, S. S. (1990). *Mathematics education for a changing world.* Alexandria, VA: Association for Supervision and Curriculum Development.

Wlodkowski, R. J. (1977). *Motivation.* Washington, DC: National Education Association.

Wood, K. (1991a). Changing perspective to improve understanding. *Middle School Journal* 22(1): 52–56.

Wood, K. (1991b). Customary practice and indicated directions: Instruction in the middle grades. *Middle School Journal* 23(1): 52–56.

Wood, K. (1993). Assessing writing performance across the curriculum. *Middle School Journal* 24(3): 67–72.

Woolfolk, A. (1993). *Educational psychology.* Needham Heights, MA: Allyn and Bacon.

Zessoules, R. and Gardner, H. (1991). Authentic assessment: Beyond the buzzword and into the classroom. In V. Perrone (Ed.), *Expanding student assessment* (pp. 47–71). Alexandria, VA: Association for Supervision and Curriculum Development.

Zorfass, J. and Remz, A. R. (1992). Successful technology integration: the role of communication and collaboration. *Middle School Journal* 23(5): 39–43.

CHAPTER 14

Transcending Classroom Management: Assisting the Development of Caring, Responsibility, and Community in the Middle School Classroom

Bruce Smith

> By declaring that man is responsible and must actualize the potential meaning of life, I wish to stress that the true meaning of life is to be discovered in the world rather than within man or his own psyche, as though it were a closed system . . . being human always points, and is directed, to something, or someone, other than oneself—by giving himself to a cause to serve or another person to love—the more human he is and the more he actualizes himself. What is called self-actualization is not an attainable aim at all, for the simple reason that the more one would strive for it, the more he would miss it. In other words, self-actualization is possible only as a side-effect of self-transcendence. (Frankl, 1992, p. 115)

This is not your typical "how-to" chapter on classroom management, which is the traditional way of looking at the teaching of the social curriculum of the classroom (see Doyle, 1986). Instead, I offer a different approach to teaching the social curriculum of middle schools—a way that I believe is more consistent with the theories, conceptions, and goals of the middle school movement.

First, I examine some core conceptions of classroom management to expose the notion of control, coercion, accountability, and competition. Then, focusing on the social and cultural nature of classrooms, I offer a different way of looking at the teaching of the social curriculum with the notions of caring, persuasion, assistance, responsibility, and community. I describe and explain the sociocultural contexts of schools by introducing an ecocultural perspective and model of teaching, learning, and schooling, which focuses on classroom activities and the social interactions and transactions between teachers and students. Using this model as a framework, I suggest four important goals for assisting the development of caring, responsibility, and community in the classroom. Finally, I describe five types of activities that can assist the attainment of these goals: opportunistic planning, inquiring, social problem-solving, helping, and transcending activities. I present an approach to teaching the social curriculum of the middle school that can assist in the development of not only good learners but, more importantly, good people.

> Education worthy of the name is essentially education of character," the philosopher Martin Buber told a gathering of teachers in 1939. In saying this, he presented a challenge more radical and unsettling than his audience may have realized. He did not mean schools should develop a unit on values or moral reasoning and glue it onto the existing curriculum. He did not mean that problem children should be taught how to behave. He meant that the very profession of teaching calls on us to try to produce not merely good learners but good people. (Kohn, 1991, p. 497)

Unfortunately, it is difficult to find a term for this different perspective. Stevenson (1992) titled a chapter in his book "Organizing for Responsibility and Harmony." Kohn (1990, 1991) uses terms such as *altruism* and *caring*. Others have used the terms *community* (see Etzioni, 1993; Lickona, 1991; Sergiovanni, 1993), *service* (see Coles, 1993), and *solidarity* (see Bowers and Flinders, 1990; McLaughlin, 1992). Considering these many terms, it seems there are essentially three components that need to be covered. First is a verb that connotes the action of teachers and students and constitutes the task of teaching the social curriculum. In terms of classroom management such verbs include *managing, establishing, organizing, maintaining, repairing, disciplining,* etc. The key is to convey a sense of teaching that is social, interactive, and nonauthoritative. Thus, I use the terms *assisting, constructing, nourishing, awakening,* and *caring*.

Second, I use the term *community* to convey the essence of a group of students, teachers, and/or staff who are working cooperatively and harmoniously for some common good. Finally, I use the term *responsible* to convey the essence of the individual in such a community—an individual who freely chooses to transcend selfishness to become a productive member of the community. Therefore, the phrase for the teaching of the social curriculum is *assisting the development of caring, responsibility, and community.*

It is my belief that solutions to management problems must be constructed by teachers and students by using a process of inquiry that leads teachers and students to inquire into themselves, others, and their unique school and classroom contexts. Thus, this chapter is written to stimulate your thinking and feeling about certain ways of looking at middle school classrooms, students, and the teaching of the social curriculum. It is an attempt to persuade you to begin a process of inquiry that could lead you to see middle school classrooms, teachers, and students differently.

An Analysis of Some Core Conceptions of Classroom Management

This section provides an analysis of some of the core conceptions of the field of classroom management: (1) the conceptions of the effective teacher, (2) control, (3) accountability, and (4) the relationship between the academic and social curriculum. It describes alternative conceptions that form the base of the different approach offered.

The first disagreement with the traditional perspective of classroom management is with the conception of the effective teacher and the type of "inquiry" effective teachers are supposed to use to solve their problems. The concept of the effective teacher has led teachers to rely on how-to methods and expert advice in solving their problems. Instead, I borrow Bruno Bettelheim's (1987) term a *good enough* teacher (rather than an effective teacher) which he discussed in his book *A Good Enough Parent: A Book on Child-Rearing* (1987). Every teacher should read this book because it is applicable directly to teaching. While every teacher strives to become the perfect teacher, this is an unreachable goal. Becoming an effective teacher also is an unreachable goal. Largely because of the way the specific teacher effectiveness research was done, there has never been a teacher who exhibited all or most of the effective behaviors described in the massive teacher effectiveness literature (see Shulman, 1986). Therefore, I suggest that a teacher should strive to become a *good enough* teacher.

The concept of a good enough teacher is not a lowering of expectations. Bettelheim (1987) said a good enough teacher is one who reflects upon his or her own life experiences, values, beliefs, goals, conceptions, and personal knowledge of a situation to get a feeling for what things mean to students. By doing so this teacher acquires new understandings and meanings of his or her life experiences, her or his students, and the situation; and these new understandings and experiences guide the teacher's thinking, feeling, and behaving in daily activities and problem situations.

Many times teachers have asked me to tell them how to solve a behavior problem in their classrooms with only a handful of descriptors of the student or the situation. They usually are surprised when I tell them they are the experts of the situation, and that I need much more information to make suggestions. They have good intentions and the student's best interest at heart, but they are after the "right" way of handling the situation, and the key to finding that answer is to find some expert to tell them what to do. Fortunately, they are adding my suggestions to a great deal of personal knowledge and opinion that they already have considered. They are weighing options and searching for clues as they creatively work through the problem. As a result of this search, they may develop a deeper understanding of themselves, the student(s), and the situation. This type of inquiry describes what is meant by a good enough teacher, and the rest of this chapter is written with this type of inquiry in mind.

A second disagreement with the traditional perspective of classroom management is the view that the teaching and learning of the social curriculum supports the teaching and learning of the academic curriculum. The goal of classroom management from this traditional perspective is the development of *responsible* or *accountable* learners. Taylor and Johnsen (1986) view these two concepts as dramatically different.

> Responsibility presumes that humans have the potential to act as free moral agents guided by deliberation and internal sanctions, in choosing their acts in the light of the consequences. Responsible action can be intense but it is never mindless. Accountability, on the other hand, means being subject to giving an account to an external agent who has prespecified a minimum standard to be achieved. Accordingly, accountable action can be intense but is often mindless. Responsibility requires freedom to make choices; accountability requires constant surveillance. The two are opposing concepts. (p. 16)

Responsibility is not some sort of "accountability to self." Responsibility is a social concept (see Taylor and Johnsen, 1986). Just as accountable people give an account to an external agent, responsible people are directed by something external as well—a cause that is greater than oneself. The key difference between accountability and responsibility is in the idea that responsible people act as free moral agents. This idea of giving students the status of free moral agents changes the concept of teaching and managing from one of controlling and coercing students into thinking, feeling, and behaving certain ways into a notion of persuading students to consider thinking, feeling, and behaving in these certain desired ways (see Strike and Soltis, 1992) and assisting them in their efforts.

The idea of allowing students to choose to act rightly or wrongly probably scares most teachers. One reason may be that these teachers may have a negative view of human nature (Kohn, 1991). That is, they may think that given the opportunity to choose, most students would choose to act wrongly, especially in terms of "toeing the line" and doing school work.

Kohn (1990, 1991) provides strong arguments for considering the "brighter side of human nature," citing numerous research findings that suggest that teachers do not need to be frightened by giving students the status to make their own choices. Nor, it appears, do teachers have to coerce, bribe, threaten, or punish students into acting appropriately. In terms of middle school students, Stevenson (1992) has written an entire text from the standpoint of looking at the brighter side of students' natures. Of course, it would be absurd to suggest that we do not have a darker side; we see and hear evidence of this daily. The assumption is, however, that given the choice, all of us would tend to choose to act in what we believe is a good and just way.

However, schools are not particularly set up to allow for such choices to be made; middle schools are no exception. Being able to control students is probably a major goal of most teachers. The literature is full of suggestions and methods that will help middle school teachers control their students' behavior (e.g., see Canter, 1989; Reed, 1991; Schockley and Sevier, 1991). From the beginning of the school year, a major task of teachers is to establish authority in the classroom. The very term *management* connotes a position of authority and control over a number of important decisions. Managers hold their workers accountable to them; this is just as true in classrooms as it is in business. However, the suggestion from many notable educators is that the very controlling nature of classroom management may be responsible for the seeming lack of responsible behavior and much of the inappropriate behavior in classrooms (e.g., see Comer, 1990; Glasser, 1990; Goodlad, 1990; McCaslin and Good, 1992).

Stevenson (1992) summarizes this argument nicely:

> The authority issue tends to be much clearer and more predictable in schools than in homes. The traditional message at school is simply "Obey!" Whatever the rule may be, whoever is giving the orders, the dictum remains. Youngsters are left with the choice only to obey or not obey, to pay attention and learn or to pretend. And what is even more disturbing is a syndrome in which apparent mindless submission to obedience on the surface is often countered with devious actions of the child's own

choosing. There is something about totalitarian rule that provokes rebellious or deceitful behaviors among people needing to assert their individuality, whether it is a pretense of doing one's work or petty larceny or the malevolent drug and alcohol abuse. Middle-level educators must be awake to the actuality that, given opportunity and examples, early adolescent youth is capable of creditable reasoning and responsible decision-making. (p. 215)

A major disagreement with a caring approach is voiced something like this: "I generally agree with what you are saying, but my kids have to learn the curriculum by the end of the year. We have to control them somehow or they won't do their work." The general feeling is that kindness and caring, while crucial, are somehow independent of or even in opposition to the types of learning and behavior needed in an effective classroom.

The types of strict external control procedures used in schools to ensure academic achievement (such as compelling, powerful, and seductive rewards; real or implied threats; strong punishments; intense public evaluation and normative comparisons; and/or forced, individual competition) do not appear to work, especially in the long run (Comer, 1990; Glasser, 1990; Goodlad, 1990; Kohn, 1986, 1990). Taking control of a classroom and school through the typical means of motivating students to learn not only does not work, it actually produces the opposite effects from what is intended in all children, even those who are high achievers (Deci and Ryan, 1991; Ford, 1992; Ryan, Connell, and Deci, 1985; Ryan and Stiller, 1991). Such external control orientations decrease self-regulation and self-management and facilitate compliance and defiance (Ryan et al., 1985).

On the other hand, a great deal of research has shown that a social curriculum characterized by cooperation and community typically leads to increased academic learning and development, increased motivation to learn, and increased self-esteem (Comer, 1990; Ford, 1992; Glasser, 1990; Goodlad, 1990; Kohn, 1986, 1991). The development of perspective-taking and empathy, for example, is an important cognitive skill that promotes general problem-solving (Kohn, 1990, 1991). Furthermore, as Kohn (1991) points out, caring for others does not mean that one also will not care for oneself, develop oneself through learning, or enjoy oneself in learning activities.

Kohn (1986, 1991) suggests we mistakenly have linked the concepts of competitiveness and excellence. A notion of excellence based on competitiveness leads us in attempts to triumph over others and to focus on winning instead of doing well in the activity, enjoying the activity, or helping others do well or enjoy the activity (Deci, Betley, Kahle, Abrams, and Porac, 1981; Kohn, 1986). The argument is for a notion of quality learning and excellence based on cooperation, caring, and community. There is a growing body of research to support this notion; in fact, many of our leading educational reformers, such as Comer (1990), Glasser (1990), Goodlad (1990), Sarason (1990), and Tharp and Gallimore (1988), believe that the solution to our educational problems lies with the development of a social curriculum similar to the kind described in this chapter.

The social and academic curricula should be consistent and interrelated, with both focusing on matters of caring, responsibility, and community. Matters of values, morality, and spirituality must be infused into the curricula of schools (see Brandt, 1993; Etzioni, 1993; Lickona, 1991). This line of reasoning and research has led several educators to offer alternative approaches that are built upon notions of caring, cooperation, responsibility, and community (e.g., see Bowers and Flinders, 1990; Glasser, 1990; Kohn, 1990, 1991; McLaughlin, 1992).

Placing the Teaching and Learning of the Social Curriculum of Schooling in a Sociocultural Context

One of the more pervasive findings from the classroom management research is that the behaviors of teachers and students are best understood by viewing them within the specific classroom activity in the specific classroom in the specific school in which they take place (Brophy and Good, 1986; Doyle, 1986; Evertson, 1989; Good and Brophy, 1986). Unfortunately, even from the massive classroom management literature, the best answer to the question, "What should I do about this misbehavior?" is, "It depends on the situation." What is required is that teachers must begin to situate their behaviors and their students' behaviors in the sociocultural contexts of their classrooms.

Stevenson (1992) suggests that middle grade teachers should become like anthropologists inquiring into the culture(s) of their students. This is a good metaphor for teachers, and it fits nicely with the general findings from the classroom management literature and the concept of a good enough teacher.

This section describes an ecocultural perspective, which differs from other versions by placing the notion of caring, responsibility, and community at its core. This can be used by a teacher to begin to understand and interpret the culture of his or her classroom. Developed originally in the field of anthropology (see Weisner, 1984), this perspective and model of socialization has since been applied to education (see Keogh and Weisner, 1993; Smith 1992; Tharp and Gallimore, 1988).

The ecocultural model of teaching, learning, and schooling deals with the complex nature of the relationships between the sociocultural, interactional, and individual contexts of the school and classroom. It offers one explanation for the mutual influences of each of these contexts for the development of teachers and students. The major focus of this perspective is on the interactional settings in which culture is both enacted and created by the participants in various activities in the classroom and school. Although culture is powerful, administrators, teachers, and students can exert some influence on their own and others' development by the ways they plan and prepare for activities and interact with others. By *accommodating* the opportunities and the constraints of the culture, a teacher can assist her or his development, the development of her or his students, and begin to change the culture through the ways she or he plans classroom activities and interacts with students.

The key to understanding this ecocultural perspective is to focus on the transactions between people in context. Virtually all of the major psychological and educational theories used to explain teaching and learning focus on individuals as if they could be isolated from the people with whom they interact and the activities they are undertaking (see Bruner, 1990; Kohn,

1990). To understand individuals, we need to focus on the social nature of development and the social relationships and activities through which the individual is formed and helps to form others.

This sociocultural notion of the self is especially important because of the middle grade students' "hunger for self-definition . . . and affirming their existence" (Stevenson, 1992, p. 332). This crucial developmental domain of middle grade students, noted by several important psychologists and educators (see, especially, Elkind, 1984; Erikson, 1968; Spence, 1984; Stevenson, 1992), is viewed differently from an ecocultural perspective, which places this notion of the self in a sociocultural context. Bruner (1990) provides a lucid description of such a notion of self in his important work, *Acts of Meaning*.

> Self . . . must be treated as a construction that, so to speak, proceeds from the outside in as well as from the inside out, from culture to mind as well as from mind to culture. . . . Kenneth Gergen was one of the earliest among the social psychologists to sense how social psychology might be changed by the adoption of an interpretivist, constructivist, and "distributive" view of . . . the construction of Self. In this work two decades ago, he set out to show how people's self-esteem and their self-concept changed in sheer reaction to the kinds of people they found themselves among, and changed even more in response to the positive or negative remarks that people made to them. Even if they were asked merely to play a particular public role in a group, their self-image often changed in a fashion to be congruent with that role. Indeed, in the presence of others who were older or seen to be more powerful than they were, people would report on "Self" in a quite different and diminished way from their manner of seeing themselves when in the presence of younger or less-esteemed people. And interacting with egoists led them to see themselves one way, with the self-effacing another. . . . In the distributive sense, then, the Self can be seen as a product of the situations in which it operates, the "swarms of its participations," as Perkins puts it. (pp. 108–109)

Ecocultural theory provides one conceptual framework for understanding the situations in which one operates and participates. To understand the development of the self from an ecocultural perspective, one must first grasp the situations in which children form relationships and learn the valued and appropriate ways to think, feel, and behave. These situations of participation are activity settings—patterned and repetitive settings of interactions and transactions that comprise culturally valued, goal-oriented activity. Schools, then, may be best viewed as part of a complex ecocultural system within which children and youth are being socialized by their interactions and transactions with adults and their peers as they participate in typical school and classroom activities. The situated-in-school self of the student, then, can be viewed as a product of these activities in which he or she has participated and currently is participating. The same, of course, can be said for the situated-in-school selves of teachers.

From an ecocultural perspective, one cannot separate or isolate the teacher or students from the school and classroom contexts in which they are interacting (see Rogoff, 1990; Tharp and Gallimore, 1988). One can only make sense of their actions by understanding the culture in which these actions take place. And, one can only solve problems in context by understanding the culture in which these problems take place. Through the choice of certain activities and the ways in which the teacher and students plan and participate, they have some control over their introspection and how they perceive themselves and others and over *what they are becoming*. The extent to which people have some influence over what they are becoming is dependent upon their ability to accommodate the opportunities and constraints of the school and classroom context (Baker-Sennett, Matusov, and Rogoff, 1993; Tharp and Gallimore, 1988). Responsible teachers and students do so freely—as free agents who actively (and interactively) accommodate and mediate the constraints and opportunities of the context and create their own opportunities in ways that are consistent with their own personal goals, values, and beliefs (Baker-Sennett et al., 1993; Tharp and Gallimore, 1988).

By focusing on interactions and viewing them within a developmental framework, the role of the teacher is defined as a mentor or guide who assists students to higher levels of skill in thinking, feeling, and behaving independently (see Tharp and Gallimore, 1988). This Vygotskian perspective of activity and process (see Rogoff, 1990; Tharp and Gallimore, 1988; Wertsch, 1985) suggests an interesting twist to the idea of how students become independent and responsible—they do so through interdependence and interaction with responsible people *while acting responsibly*. By doing so, students learn how to think, feel, and behave freely as responsible people.

Middle School Teachers' Goals for Teaching the Social Curriculum

Goals for teaching the social curriculum in middle schools can be reached when one realizes that *all* middle school students already have within them the ability and desire to achieve these goals (see Stevenson, 1992). For example, all middle school students have participated in numerous activities in which they both were cared for and cared for others. Our major problem as teachers is that we have been socialized to believe that we must bribe, entice, punish, and in other ways "get" selfish students to act responsibly rather than realizing that we can, instead, merely assist these students to awaken and develop the social and prosocial skills and dispositions that are already within them (see Kohn, 1990, 1991; Stevenson, 1992).

These goals are as applicable to teachers as they are to students. In fact, from the social-interactional perspective of teaching as assisting and guiding, it is essential that teachers already have awakened and developed some mastery of the following goals within themselves to be able to assist the development of these skills and dispositions in students (see Rogoff, 1990; Tharp and Gallimore, 1988).

Prosocial Orientation

The first general goal for teaching the social curriculum of middle schools is taken from Kohn (1990), and it involves enhancing a prosocial orientation in students and assisting the development of perspective-taking and empathy skills. A prosocial orientation refers to the tendency to act "voluntarily and intentionally to benefit someone else" (Kohn, 1990, p. 63). However, as Kohn (1990) points out, the term *prosocial* does not deal with the underlying motivation of why the person has acted to benefit another. Nor does taking the perspective of another guarantee that the prosocial action was undertaken for altruistic reasons. In fact, a great deal of research on perspective-taking has investigated competitive situations in which taking the perspective of an opponent gives one an upper hand in the competition (Kohn, 1990).

Empathic understanding is necessary but not sufficient for altruistic, helping, and caring actions (Kohn, 1990). Trying to understand the feelings of another by recreating how one feels in a similar situation does not guarantee that the other feels the same. And it limits our empathy to similar situations with which we have some direct experience. According to Kohn (1990), we need a view of perspective-taking and empathy that maximizes our understanding of and identification with others.

> Feelings are particular to the person who feels them, and empathy, properly understood, is a way of taking account of that fact. But it also is a way for one person to acknowledge that the feeling of the other is saturated in his otherness. . . . The topic here is not pain but *her* pain, and from my perspective the fact that it cannot be reduced to my pain is highly significant. (pp. 134–135)

Contextual Awareness

A second goal for teaching the social curriculum in middle schools is to become contextually aware. Middle school teachers and students must begin to investigate, interpret, and understand the sociocultural and historical contexts of schools—

they must become aware of the influences of these contexts and contextual levels on their own development and the development of others. According to Brookfield (1987), this is a crucial component of adult critical thinking.

> When we are aware of how hidden and uncritically assimilated assumptions are important to shaping our habitual perceptions, understandings, and interpretations of the world, and to influencing the behaviors that result from these interpretations, we become aware of how context influences thoughts and actions. Critical thinkers are aware that practices, structures, and actions are never context-free. (p. 8)

This is a crucial goal from an ecocultural perspective because it is through understanding and accommodating the opportunities and constraints of the particular school and classroom contexts that teachers and students can begin to guide their own development in desirable ways. But more important, by becoming contextually aware, teachers and students can begin to realize that they are first and foremost social beings in a social world. This social world is about human interactions and human relationships. Teachers and students are connected with each other because of this social context, and they need to begin to focus on their interactions and relationships with each other.

Moral Imagination

A third goal for the teaching of the social curriculum is to awaken and nourish the moral imagination of teachers and students—to assist and engage in moral reflection (Coles, 1986, 1989). In education, we must begin to realize that our lives in and out of classrooms have "moral sides" to them (Coles, 1986). Teachers and students' lives are full of moral dilemmas. So are most of the texts, novels, and (auto)biographies we teach and learn about in schools. We can unite teachers and students' moral lives with these moral lessons through reflection. The meanings that are made can assist moral and social development.

Thus, teachers and students must not only focus on their interactions and relationships with each other; they also must begin to understand that they are not only responsible for themselves but for others as well. Further, they must begin to understand that they also are connected with others outside of school and that together they form a community. Teachers and students must become more community responsible as well— they must develop a social-ethical consciousness (Stevenson and Carr, 1993a).

Self-Introspection and Meaning-Making

A final goal for the teaching of the social curriculum involves assisting self-introspection and meaning-making for the development of individual teacher's and student's social selves. It is an equally important developmental dimension for middle school students and adults (Bruner, 1990; Elkind, 1984; Erickson, 1968; Frankl, 1992; Linde, 1993; Spence, 1984). We all constantly must create and recreate a coherent sense of self that expresses: (1) who we are and why and how we got that way; (2) who we are becoming and why and how we are becoming this; and (3) who we want to be and why and how we can get there.

We must not forget, however, that this sense of self is socially constructed and embedded (Bruner, 1990; Kohn, 1990; Linde, 1993). Through our interactions *with* others we communicate, negotiate, exchange, create, and revise our life stories (see Bruner, 1990; Linde, 1993). This is a crucial point. Self-introspection involves social interaction in which people tell each other, in so many ways, their and others' life stories. Together, teachers and students create and continuously re-create their and others' sense of selves.

However, this social process of introspection needs some direction. It is the teacher's duty to persuade and assist students in realizing that they are socially responsible and caring persons. A goal of teachers, then, should be to develop responsibility and caring in their students. To do so, responsibility, caring, helping, and community must become part of all teachers and students' life stories.

These four goals are aimed at assisting the development of good people. They focus on the development of values, commitment, duty, and a "sense of the desirable" (see Nissan, 1992). Teaching values in schools may make many educators nervous. But this unease is based on the idea that schools, as they exist now, are value free. They clearly are not (see Kohn, 1986, 1990; Lickona, 1993). The issue is not whether we should teach values in the schools, it is whether we should be teaching the values that we already are teaching.

> We must concede that a prosocial agenda is indeed value-laden, but we should immediately add that the very same is true of the status quo. The teacher's presence and behavior, her choice of text, the order in which she presents ideas, and her tone of voice are as much a part of the lesson as the curriculum itself. So, too, is a teacher's method of discipline or classroom management saturated in values, regardless of whether those values are transparent to the teacher. In short, to arrange our schools so that caring, sharing, helping, and empathizing are actively encouraged is not to introduce values into a neutral environment. It is to examine the values already in place and to consider trading them in for a new set. (Kohn, 1991, p. 499)

The Ecocultural Context of Middle Schools: Constraints and Opportunities

Focusing on individual students or teachers does not capture the social and cultural nature of schooling. Teaching and learning are social acts embedded in a cultural context and can only be interpreted and changed by understanding this cultural context—by understanding the opportunities and constraints that middle school teachers and students face. Despite the middle school movement, teaching, learning, and schooling in the typical middle school remain remarkably similar to that in junior high schools throughout the country (Cuban, 1992; Stevenson, 1992).

Many of the goals and visions of the middle school movement were offered in the early 1900s as part of the reform movement of the junior high school. The very institution that the middle school movement seeks to reform was built upon many of the very same principles! Cuban (1992) offers a fascinating historical case study of the American junior high school reform movement of the 1900s, which has direct implications for the present middle school movement.

Just like the middle school movement, the junior high school movement sought to create a school that was aimed specifically at meeting the unique developmental needs of early adolescents at that time. Originally, junior high schools were envisioned as vastly different from high schools. Slowly, however, the powerful cultural, economic, political, and social forces of the time squelched the movement and created a mini-version of the high school. This same powerful influence of the American culture is responsible for the failure of most present-day middle schools to realize the middle school vision and create a truly different type of school.

The ecocultural model describes and explains how and why the organization of the high school powerfully influences the activities that administrators, teachers, and students undertake in middle schools. Strong ecocultural forces influence who does what in middle schools; what and how they teach and learn; why they teach and learn this way; and where, when, and how long they teach and learn. Cuban mentions such strong ecocultural forces as an economic structure tied to academic achievement, test scores, and parent and community approval. Strong public and professional beliefs and values and a rich history give high schools and what they do a higher status than the "lower level" feeder elementary, middle, and junior high schools. A political structure dictates such things as certification requirements, curriculum, and management policies based, ultimately, on a high school model of individual achievement, competition, individual learning, and obedience (see also Kohn, 1986, 1990; McCaslin and Good, 1992). One can begin to sense the power of these forces and understand the reasons why well-meaning middle school reforms, in all probability, will eventually turn back to the traditional ways without broad systemic reforms.

Such a broad view of reform allows us to place the blame of the seeming failure of educational reform on various levels of the educational system and culture, instead of just on teachers (McCaslin and Good, 1992). Clearly, broad and sweeping changes in the ecocultural niche of middle schools are necessary for the middle school movement to be realized in most schools.

Fortunately, there are documented accounts of middle schools and isolated middle school classrooms that have achieved many of the lofty goals of the middle school movement (Atwell, 1987; Cuban, 1992; Herndon, 1985; Marshall, 1973; Phillips, 1978; Stevenson, 1992; Stevenson and Carr, 1993a; Wiggington, 1985). The suggestion from the ecocultural model is that these schools and teachers are able to accommodate the pressures of the broad socioeconomic and cultural forces and the idiosyncratic pressures of the specific situation. Culture is powerful, but so too can be individuals in that culture who adapt, adjust, and manipulate external constraints and find and take advantage of the opportunities provided to teach students in ways that they see fit. For school districts or schools to have achieved these goals is exemplary, but for isolated teachers to have achieved them is courageous (Beane, 1993; Freire, as cited in Brookfield, 1987).

Stevenson and Carr (1993b) identify several factors that would inhibit and constrain middle school teachers from attempting such innovations in their classrooms. Many of these factors are largely due to external forces, such as a lack of administrative, parental, and collegial support; insufficient planning time; a lack of resources; inflexible scheduling; curriculum and evaluation expectations; and a general ennui of mindless conformity to the traditional ways of teaching and managing middle grade students.

However, there are more personal reasons Stevenson and Carr (1993b) describe that appear to constrain innovation in the middle school classroom. The first is fear.

> Many teachers are afraid to let go of professional habits that have brought them comfort in the midst of an onslaught of changing students and changing school

policies. . . . Teachers who give in to their fear are inclined
to stick to their routines and preoccupation with order and
control. (p. 193)

A second personal factor is the level of difficulty of
innovation. Personal change and innovation in the classroom
require a great deal of time and effort. Third, such innovation
involves students taking on more responsibility and teachers
giving up authority and control. It is difficult for most teachers to
give up control of their classroom to anyone, especially students.
Doing so introduces a great deal of risk. With students assuming
more responsibility, there is more likelihood of management
problems (Doyle, 1986). Further, with more flexibility in the
curriculum and classroom activities, there is more uncertainty.
And, finally, choosing alternative ways of teaching and learning
can be viewed as choosing against colleagues, superiors, and
experts. Thus, more of the burden of blame for failure rests on
the teacher who chooses to be innovative.

Of course, these personal reasons also are strongly
influenced by the external forces described above. Yet, there are
too many accounts of teachers who have successfully challenged
the system for middle school teachers to just give up and give in
to the power of the middle school culture. Furthermore, there is
a growing body of research that suggests that teachers can exert
much more choice over what they teach and how they teach it
than most teachers believe. For example, Goodlad's (1984)
massive study suggests that teachers often assume a great deal of
responsibility in planning and teaching. A major finding of the
planning literature is that teachers can assume much more
responsibility in planning instruction and management. Studies
of enthusiastic, committed, and exemplary teachers suggest that
these teachers became so by "fighting" against conformity and
by manipulating the system (Feiman-Nemser and Floden, 1986;
LeCompte and Dworkin, 1991). The suggestion, from an
ecocultural perspective, is that culture also provides many
opportunities for teachers to be innovative and to make
significant changes in their classrooms. Taking advantage of
these opportunities requires teachers to be contextually aware—
to actively seek out these opportunities. This requires critical
thinking, the investment of time and energy, courage, and a

commitment to make change on the behalf of students (Kohn, 1990; Stevenson and Carr, 1993b).

Planning Activities That Can Awaken and Assist the Development of Caring, Responsibility, and Community

This section describes the importance of planning in the development and "success" of classroom activities and introduces children's planning, suggesting that if the teacher were to plan *with* students, it not only would assist students to assume more responsibility, but it also would assist in the development of student planning skills. This section fuses the teacher- and children-planning literatures to describe planning as a social activity. In everyday events, such as children planning their play or teachers planning tomorrow's lessons, planning processes take place within a sociocultural context and often involve interaction with others (see Baker-Sennett et al., 1993).

From a sociocultural perspective, Baker-Sennett et al. (1993) define planning as an everyday problem-solving approach, as a "process involved in developing approaches to handling problems" (p. 255). This process can take place prior to the activity being planned and during the activity as it unfolds. By viewing planning as a process, Baker-Sennett et al. (1993) focus on its dynamic and sociocultural nature.

> We argue for the importance of viewing planning as a process of transformation of opportunities for upcoming events, with development involving learning to plan opportunistically—planning in advance of action or during action according to the circumstances, flexibly anticipating constraints and opportunities, and adapting to circumstances. (p. 254)

This view of planning contrasts sharply with the traditional views that say the key to effective classroom management is effective advanced planning (see Doyle, 1986; Emmer, Evertson, Clements, and Worsham, 1994; Evertson, 1989; Evertson and Harris, 1992). Success in planning, from an effectiveness view, involves the acquisition of effective planning behaviors and mental plans or blueprints *and* an increase in *advanced* planning. The very same can be said for the traditional view of children's planning (Baker-Sennett et al., 1993). Effective planning from both traditional perspectives is viewed as an acquired skill that develops relatively independently of particular circumstances and involves a capacity and a set of mental plans to formulate effective plans of action in advance.

A sociocultural perspective of planning does not discount advanced planning (Baker-Sennett et al., 1993). Advanced planning allows for a careful consideration of possible constraints and opportunities and provides an assurance that all parts of the plan are organized and in place. Planning in advance can avoid costly errors, eliminate wasted time, and guide an individual's actions so that he or she may pay attention to more important and immediate aspects of the particular situation. Most importantly, advanced planning in collaboration with others (such as students) can increase the coordination of efforts in the planned activity as well as assist in the development of advanced planning skills (Baker-Sennett et al., 1993).

In the middle school classroom, a close relationship between the teacher and students should develop. By neglecting to investigate students' interests and goals before and during action, this relationship suffers. Furthermore, a great deal of research now suggests that an overreliance on advanced planning stifles flexibility, improvisation, and creativity (Baker-Sennett et al., 1993; Clark and Peterson, 1986). Yet, flexibility, improvisation, and creativity appear to be especially important in complex social activities, such as those in classrooms, in which unpredictability and changing circumstances are common (Baker-Sennett et al., 1993). Improvisation allows the individual to take advantage of unfolding circumstances and adjust to new information. This opportunistic advanced planning involves the formulation of flexible, tentative, skeletal plans, which are manipulated, fine-tuned, altered, and elaborated on during the activity.

This conception of planning explains the types of planning described in the book *Integrated Studies in the Middle Grades: "Dancing through Walls"* (Stevenson and Carr, 1993a). In the second chapter of this book, Stevenson and Carr explain the planning framework that was used by the teachers to plan their integrated studies. This skeletal framework allowed for a great deal of flexibility in the planning of the studies and ensured that the teachers would allow for flexibility and improvisation in their classroom activities. At the heart of this planning was a focus on the developmental characteristics and goals of students. Much of the planning in these studies, both before and during the action, was done with the students. Tentative plans and goals were devised, and these were altered and/or elaborated with the students.

Going into a year, unit, or activity with skeletal plans that allow for flexibility and improvisation is not being unprepared. It is, actually, being better prepared for the complex and often unpredictable classroom context. (See Doyle, 1986, and Gump, 1987, for excellent descriptions of this complex context.) It does, however, demand a different type of teaching that was described several decades ago by Dewey (1916, 1938) and G. H. Mead (1934) and more recently by several others, such as Schön (1989), Shulman (1989), and Sirotnik (1989), as *reflective teaching*—continuously learning about teaching and developing oneself as a democratic, moral teacher by reflecting upon one's experiences. As Schön (1989) says:

> People sometimes think about what they are doing. Phrases like "thinking on your feet," "keeping your wits about you," and "learning by doing" suggest not only that people can think about doing but also they can think about doing something while doing it." (p. 199)

Schön terms this type of reflection *reflection-in-action*, and it is virtually synonymous with Baker-Sennett et al.'s (1993) conception of planning in action.

Teachers are not the only ones who need to be reflective; students do too. And by reflecting-in-action *with* students, teachers will be assisting in developing in students the skills and desires to be reflective in their practices.

Such reflective teaching and learning demands continuous debate, dialogue, deliberation, and reasoning (Shulman, 1989). Sirotnik (1989) refers to this type of teaching and learning as critical inquiry, which includes being "playful with one's ideas, being inventive and creative, being reflective with respect to one's practice" (p. 108). But the conception of reflection is not just a cognitive process; it carries with it an emotional and moral base. The major goal of reflection in schools for Dewey (1916, 1938) was to create a microcosm of the broader democratic society in which American schools were embedded. In a collaborative search for knowledge through reflection, dialogue, and deliberation, personal moral theories of both teachers and students would be exposed and be open for consideration and development. Reflection for Dewey was moral reflection.

Planning to meet these goals will not necessarily guarantee that teachers and students will engage in activities that will help them be more caring, responsible, or help build a community. Teachers and students must begin to focus on and change the processes by which they plan. Langer (1989) argues that a preoccupation with outcomes can make us mindless as we automatically use the same processes to meet new goals. The types of goals set forth above require different processes of planning and teaching, and these require a "mindful," deliberate focus. In addition to being flexible and creative, planning and teaching also must be critical, which involves an inquiry into the cultural origins of everyday problems and the inherent cultural values that flavor typical problems and solutions. Only then can we begin to see that the mindless reliance on control runs counter to the values and goals of democracy. And only then can teachers and students begin to mediate these cultural forces of control and begin to create a responsible and caring community in the classroom.

Activities That Awaken and Assist Caring, Responsibility, and Community

By losing oneself in the cause of helping others and building a community in the classroom, the student will not only find and develop in herself or himself responsibility, caring, and a sense of community, but she or he also will be learning about and developing a social self through introspection. The power of narratives or stories can evoke introspection and meaning-making (Bruner, 1990; Coles, 1989). The focus of both the academic and social curricula of schools should be on stories, whether it is students casually talking about their lives with others as they complete a project together, listening to others as they try to solve a classroom behavior problem, cooperatively learning about World War II, watching and discussing the popular movie *The Mighty Ducks* on a rainy day, or reading and discussing the book *Of Mice and Men*. Done with moral reflection, these stories can awaken and nourish the moral imagination of teachers and students to assist their social, moral, and intellectual development and provide models and guidance for living a good, just, and moral life (Coles, 1989).

Because students should learn cooperatively for both academic and social reasons, most learning in middle school classrooms should take place in groups. Although grouping students for learning is an important planning task, the typical grouping practice based on academic ability (tracking, streaming, or leveling) is not substantiated by research for academic, social, or moral reasons (George, 1988; Kulik and Kulik, 1984; Slavin, 1987; Stevenson, 1992). Not only does this practice produce, at best, negligible effects on learning, it is discriminatory and runs counter to the vision and goals of the middle school movement (George, 1988; Stevenson, 1992). Student groups should be formed to allow the students to help each other and to learn from others' various abilities and talents.

Four types of classroom activities are (1) inquiring activities, (2) social problem-solving activities, (3) helping activities, and (4) transcendence activities. They are not necessarily separate activities, but I will discuss them separately here.

Inquiring Activities

Inquiring activities are activities in which the teacher and students are trying to understand more fully some aspect of other people's lives and their own lives. Stevenson (1992) devoted a whole chapter to understanding through inquiry activities. Inquiry can be directed at others or the self, through such tasks as keeping a reflective journal. Even when the inquiry is not directed at the self, the inquirer can learn more about herself or himself by learning about other ways of looking at the world and, thus, looking at and questioning the ways that she or he looks at the world. Inquiry should focus, for the most part, on critically learning about people in the classroom. It also should be directed at other fictional or nonfictional people through book research, interviewing, etc.

Stevenson (1992) suggested that teachers and students in middle schools should be like anthropologists, inquiring into and learning about the culture of the classroom and school. Teachers can learn a valuable lesson from anthropology by realizing that a minimum requirement for learning about a person is patiently observing and listening to the person *while sharing typical activities with the person*. By doing so, teachers and students can get to know what others' lives are like—they can learn about each other. A massive restructuring of classroom activities is not required.

Learning about each other may be more than just a social aspect of classroom learning groups (Gallimore and Goldenberg, 1992; Tharp and Gallimore, 1988). Conversation in learning activities can have academic as well as social benefits. This instructional conversation can be an important aspect of teacher-led instruction as well (whole-group, small-group, or one-on-one activities). Through conversations in the classroom, teachers can not only assist their students to higher levels of cognitive, emotional, and behavioral performance, but teachers and students can get to know each other intellectually, personally, socially, and morally. Certainly, social conversations are crucial but also are academic and moral ones. The typical one-way teacher-led question-and-answer activities in classrooms are not conversations (see Gallimore and Goldenberg, 1992; Tharp and Gallimore, 1988). In these activities, which are really more like interrogations, the teacher usually knows the answer to the question asked. This type of interchange is typically not a part of meaningful conversations in which, instead, questions are asked to obtain information that is not known by the person asking the question.

In more Socratic and assistive types of instructional conversation, the "teacher" (who can be the teacher or a student in the classroom) asks questions or poses a problem to students where both do not know the answer or solution. There often is not a right answer to the question, or there are multiple good solutions to the problem. The instruction comes when the teacher, who is more skilled in solving such problems, assists the performance of the student in solving such problems while they seek a solution together. This type of instruction involves dialogue, deliberation, and conversation, and it is important for both academic and social learning—for solving the problem and for learning about each other.

Social Problem-Solving Activities

Social problem-solving activities include conflict resolution and mediation of interpersonal conflict activities. Many of the most difficult questions and problems that middle school students have are social. It is inevitable that there will be interpersonal conflicts in the classroom. Together, middle school teachers and students can help resolve such real social conflicts. By doing so, teacher and student mediators will not only be helping students resolve a real conflict, but they also will be assisting these students to be more able to help themselves and others resolve future conflicts. Such activities have the potential for fostering other types of cognitive, moral, and social growth and development as well. Furthermore, relationships can mature and deepen from successful conflict resolution (Peterson, 1989).

Steinberg (1989) suggests that, "Young people are much more likely to resolve their differences when they—with the help of trained peers—sit down together, name what has been going on without focusing on blame, and work out a solution" (p. 5). But it is important to point out that such reflection and deliberation may need to be assisted in middle school students, who may still have trouble understanding another's perceptions and points of view. The research on social problem-solving, conflict resolution, and student mediation suggests that such processes need to be learned and practiced before solutions to real problems can be sought (Glasser, 1975, 1977, 1986, 1990; Stevenson, 1992). Teachers must have the skills necessary to maturely resolve conflicts in order to assist students in developing these skills (Stevenson, 1992).

There exists a number of readings on social problem-solving, conflict resolution, and student mediation. (Please see Stevenson, 1992, page 239, for an excellent list of readings.) Stevenson's (1992) description of conflict resolution and student mediation is a good start. In the field of classroom management, a major part of Glasser's (1990) educational adaptations of reality therapy and the development of responsibility in students is built upon the activity of mature social problem-solving in the classroom. The use of Glasser's (1975, 1977, 1986) reality therapy in the classroom for individual and group problems has been described adequately elsewhere (see Emmer et al., 1994; Jones and Jones, 1990). Lickona (1991) describes how to use conflict resolution in class meetings and provides references and information on several conflict resolution programs.

It is useful to think of interpersonal conflict as interpersonal *goal* conflict (Ford, 1992; Peterson, 1989). Many times a specific conflict between two or more people who are in continuous close contact, such as students and teachers, are often the result of a conflict of deeper feelings, beliefs, and basic goals that goes beyond the particular incident. This perspective of goal conflict is especially useful for looking at those conflicts between the teacher and students. While it is important to consider the goals of the teacher and students when planning and enacting activities, there are numerous contextual and personal constraints in middle schools and classrooms that work against the alignment of multiple interpersonal goals (Ford, 1992). Thus, some type of conflict resolution process that can bring teacher and student goals out into the discussion will probably be necessary.

Helping Activities

Helping activities are activities in which teachers and students perform classroom, school, and/or community services. They are helping something or someone other than themselves. A recent entire edition of *Educational Leadership* (Brandt, 1993) was dedicated to character education. Much of this literature focuses on worthwhile service outside the classroom and school. However, we must not neglect helping activities in the classroom. It would probably be impossible to build both caring relationships and a community in the classroom without them (see Etzioni, 1993; Lickona, 1991, 1993; Noddings, 1984, 1988). Helping activities do not exclude academics. A growing body of evidence suggests that students may be better able than teachers to assist the cognitive development of other students in many academic activities because their cognitive developmental levels are closer to those of the students who need assistance (Rogoff, 1990).

All students can and should be helping others in the class, school, and community. Stevenson (1992) argues that all students in the middle classroom are both willing and capable of helping others. As Curwin (1993) suggests, when "we help at-risk students, we inadvertently give them the message that they are in an inferior position. Reversing this role builds pride. Students feel good when they see themselves as genuinely useful. Helping others is therapeutic" (p. 36). Of course, at-risk students do need help. But, when it is given in an atmosphere in which they also are helping and feeling useful, the negative effects of such help will be diminished.

Transcendence Activities

Transcendence activities refer to activities in which the teacher and/or students transcend themselves and "lose" themselves in social activity. This can occur "individually" as one transcends her or himself and feels connected and as one with the activity and physical surroundings. Teachers and/or students can lose themselves in harmonious interactive effort. Such feelings of unity and transcendence have been described in the literature by Baumeister (1991), Csikszentmihalyi (1990), Ford (1992), and Maslow (1971) from a more individual view in terms of what the individual gets out of these "peak" or "optimal" experiences. I am unaware of any such educational social-interactional perspectives that have focused on the growth of a group through the sharing of such experiences. However, in my life I have felt such group harmony and unity as my team, class, or family became connected—indeed were created and constructed—through joint activity towards shared goals.

There appears to be a great need to lose oneself at times, especially for adolescents and, especially, in times of personal turmoil or trouble (Baumeister, 1991). Baumeister has given a persuasive argument that much alcohol and drug abuse, suicide, sexual masochism, bulimia, and other self-destructive behaviors are attempts to escape the self. Herein lies a dilemma with the emphasis on introspection and the development of the self. Just as it appears that there is a great need for middle school students (and teachers) to find themselves (Stevenson, 1992), there also is a great need for them to lose themselves (Baumeister, 1991). Unfortunately, middle school students often choose destructive ways to forget themselves. There is a great need for middle schools to provide constructive activities so that students can lose themselves in appropriate ways. Transcendence activities can provide such a constructive way.

Yet, if Frankl (1992) was right, transcending oneself in a relationship or in helping someone or giving oneself up to a cause can have a profound influence on what one becomes. Herein lies an answer to the dilemma posed above. By losing themselves in proactive activities, middle school students will, as a by-product of these activities, also "find" themselves, when they want to, as responsible, caring individuals in the social community of the classroom and school.

Conclusions and Implications

So, as you begin a journey of inquiry and renewal—a journey that could ultimately lead you to see middle schools and teaching and learning in different ways, remember the words of the poet T. S. Eliot:

> And the end of all our exploring
> Will be to arrive where we started
> And know the place for the first time.

We are a people in trouble. And, although schools are filled with well-meaning and hardworking people, they are, for the most part, very nasty places. We reward, bribe, threaten, punish, and otherwise control, put-down, and discriminate against all sorts of students. Administrators do this to teachers, as do teacher educators to preservice teachers. No wonder students can be so nasty, too. But there are some glimmers of hope—islands of caring and community in a sea of traditional competition and control.

Middle school students need these moral models to guide them in becoming good people, in living a kind and caring life, in transcending selfishness, and in becoming responsible members of their communities, this country, and the world. Next to their parents and family, who could be better models and guides than the people who are teaching them. Although such a change sounds radical, it is really just about a change in the ways we see and make sense of what happens in middle schools and classrooms. Yes, this does require a great deal of effort, inquiry, humility, and courage. But, most of the tools, materials, skills, and dispositions are already in middle school classrooms within teachers and students, as Kohn (1990) so eloquently reminds us at the end of his book.

> No imported solution will dissolve our problems of dehumanization, egocentricity, coldness, and cruelty. No magical redemption from outside of human life will let us break through. The work that has to be done is our work, but we are better equipped for it than we have been led to believe. To move ourselves beyond selfishness, we already have what is required. We already *are* what is required. We are human and we have each other. (pp. 267–268)

REFERENCES

Atwell, N. (1987). *In the middle: Writing, reading and learning with adolescents.* Portsmouth, NH: Heinemann.

Baker-Sennett, J., Matusov, E., and Rogoff, B. (1993). Planning as a developmental process. In H. W. Reese (Ed.), *Advances in child development and behavior* (Vol. 24) (pp. 253–281). Orlando, FL: Academic Press.

Baumeister, R. F. (1991). *Escaping the self: Alcoholism, spirituality, masochism, and other flights from the burden of selfhood.* New York: Basic Books.

Beane, J. A. (1993). Forward: Teachers of uncommon courage. In C. Stevenson and J. F. Carr (Eds.), *Integrated studies in the middle grades: "Dancing through walls"* (pp. vii–x). New York: Teachers College Press.

Bettelheim, B. (1987). *A good enough parent: A book on child-rearing.* New York: Vintage Books.

Bowers, C. A., and Flinders, D. J. (1990). *Responsive teaching.* New York: Teachers College Press.

Brandt, R. S. (Ed.). (1993). Character education [Special issue]. *Educational Leadership 53*(3): 5–97.

Brophy, J., and Good, T. L. (1986). Teacher behavior and student achievement. In M. C. Wittrock (Ed.), *Handbook of research on teaching* (3rd ed.) (pp. 328–375). New York: Macmillan.

Brookfield, S. D. (1987). *Developing critical thinkers: Challenging adults to explore alternative ways of thinking and acting.* San Francisco: Jossey-Bass.

Bruner, J. (1990). *Acts of meaning.* Cambridge, MA: Harvard University Press.

Canter, L. (1989). *Assertive discipline for secondary educators.* Santa Monica, CA: Canter and Associates.

Clark, C. M., and Peterson, P. L. (1986). Teachers' thought processes. In M. C. Wittrock (Ed.), *Handbook of research on teaching* (3rd ed.) (pp. 255–296). New York: Macmillan.

Coles, R. (1986). *The moral life of children.* Boston: Houghton-Mifflin.

Coles, R. (1989). The call of stories: Teaching and the moral imagination. Boston: Houghton-Mifflin.

Coles, R. (1993). *The call of service: A witness to idealism.* Boston: Houghton-Mifflin.

Comer, J. P. (1990). Home, school, and academic learning. In J. I. Goodlad and P. Keating (Eds.), *Access to knowledge: An agenda for our nation's schools* (pp. 23–42). New York: College Entrance Examination Board.

Csikszentmihalyi, M. (1990). *Flow: The psychology of optimal experience.* New York: Harper and Row.

Cuban, L. (1992). What happens to reforms that last? The case of the junior high school. *American Educational Research Journal 29*(2): 227–251.

Curwin, R. L. (1993). The healing power of altruism. *Educational Leadership 51*(3): 36–39.

Deci, E. L., Betley, G., Kahle, J., Abrams, L., and Porac, J. (1981). When trying to win: Competition and intrinsic motivation. *Personality and Social Psychology Bulletin 7*: 79–83.

Deci, E. L., and Ryan, R. M. (1991). A motivational approach to self: Integration in personality. In R. Dienstbier (Ed.), *Nebraska symposium on motivation, Vol. 38: Perspectives on motivation* (pp. 237–288). Lincoln: University of Nebraska Press.

Dewey, J. (1916). *Democracy and education*. New York: Macmillan.

Dewey, J. (1938). *Experience and education*. New York: Macmillan.

Doyle, W. (1986). Classroom organization and management. In M. C. Wittrock (Ed.), *Handbook of research on teaching* (3rd ed.) (pp. 392–431). New York: Macmillan.

Eliot, T. S. (1971). The complete poems and plays, 1909–1950. New York: Harcourt, Brace, and World.

Elkind, D. (1984). *All grown up and no place to go: Teenagers in crisis*. Reading, MA: Addison-Wesley.

Emmer, E. T., Evertson, C. M., Clements, B. S., and Worsham, M. E. (1994). *Classroom management for secondary teachers* (3rd ed.). Needham Heights, MA: Allyn and Bacon.

Erickson, E. (1968). *Identity, youth, and crisis*. New York: Norton.

Etzioni, A. (1993). *The spirit of community*. New York: Crown.

Evertson, C. M. (1989). Classroom organization and management. In M. Reynolds (Ed.), *Knowledge base for the beginning teacher* (pp. 59–70). Elmsford, NY: Pergamon Press.

Evertson, C. M., and Harris, A. H. (1992). What we know about managing classrooms. *Educational Leadership 49*(7): 74–78.

Feiman-Nemser, S., and Floden, R. L. (1986). The cultures of teaching. In M. C. Wittrock (Ed.), *Handbook of research on teaching* (3rd ed.) (pp. 505–526). New York: Macmillan.

Ford, M. E. (1992). *Motivating humans: Goals, emotions, and personal agency beliefs*. Newbury Park, CA: Sage Publications.

Frankl, V. E. (1992). Man's search for meaning: An introduction to logotherapy. Boston: Beacon Press.

Gallimore, R., and Goldenberg, C. N. (1992). Tracking the developmental path of teachers and learners: A Vygotskian perspective. In F. K. Oser, A. Dick, and J. Patry (Eds.), *Effective and responsible teaching: A new synthesis* (pp. 203–221). San Francisco: Jossey-Bass.

George, P. S. (1988). Tracking and ability grouping: Which way for the middle school? *Middle School Journal* 20(1): 21–28.

Glasser, W. (1975). *Reality therapy: A new approach to psychiatry*. New York: Harper and Row.

Glasser, W. (1977). 10 steps to good discipline. *Today's Education* 66: 60–63.

Glasser, W. (1986). *Control theory in the classroom*. New York: Harper and Row.

Glasser, W. (1990). The quality school: Managing students without coercion. New York: Harper and Row.

Good, T. L., and Brophy, J. (1986). School effects. In M. C. Wittrock (Ed.), *Handbook of research on teaching* (3rd ed.) (pp. 570–604). New York: Macmillan.

Goodlad, J. I. (1984). A place called school: Prospects for the future. New York: McGraw Hill.

Goodlad, J. I. (1990). Common schools for the common weal: Reconciling self-interest with the common good. In J. I. Goodlad and P. Keating (Eds.), *Access to knowledge: An agenda for our nation's schools* (pp. 1–22). New York: College Entrance Examination Board.

Goodnow, J. J. (1987). Social aspects of planning. In S. L. Friedman, E. K. Scholnick, and R. R. Cocking (Eds.), *Blueprints for thinking: The role of planning in cognitive development* (pp. 179–201). Cambridge, MA: Cambridge University Press.

Gump, P. V. (1987). School and classroom environments. In D. Stokols and I. Altman (Eds.), *Handbook of environmental psychology* (Vol. 1) (pp. 691–732). New York: John Wiley and Sons.

Herndon, J. (1985). *Notes from a schoolteacher*. New York: Simon and Schuster.

Jones, V. F., and Jones, L. S. (1990). *Comprehensive classroom management: Motivating and managing students* (3rd ed.). Needham Heights, MA: Allyn and Bacon.

Keogh, B. K., and Weisner, T. (1993). An ecocultural perspective on risk and protective factors in children's development: Implications for learning disabilities. *Learning Disabilities Research and Practice* 8(1): 3–10.

Kohn, A. (1986). *No contest: The case against competition: Why we lose in our race to win.* Boston: Houghton Mifflin.

Kohn, A. (1990). *The brighter side of human nature: Altruism and empathy in everyday life.* New York: Basic Books.

Kohn, A. (1991). Caring kids: The role of the schools. *Phi Delta Kappan* 72(7): 496–506.

Kulik, J. A., and Kulik, C. L. (1984). Effects of ability grouping on secondary school students: A meta-analysis of evaluation findings. *American Educational Research Journal 19*: 415–428.

Langer, E. (1989). *Mindfulness.* Reading, PA: Addison-Wesley.

LeCompte, M. D., and Dworkin, A. G. (1991). *Giving up on school: Student dropouts and teacher burnouts.* Newbury Park, CA: Corwin Press.

Lickona, T. (1991). *Educating for character: How our schools can teach respect and responsibility.* New York: Bantam Books.

Lickona, T. (1993). The return of character education. *Educational Leadership 51*(3): 6–11.

Linde, C. (1993). *Life stories: The creation of coherence*. New York: Oxford University Press.

Marshall, K. (1973). *Law and order in grade 6-E*. Boston: Little, Brown.

Maslow, A. H. (1971). *The farther reaches of human nature.* New York: Viking.

McCaslin, M., and Good, T. L. (1992). Compliant cognition: The misalliance of management and instructional goals in current school reform. *Educational Researcher 21*(3): 4–17.

McLaughlin, H. J. (1992, April). *Seeking solidarity and responsibility: The classroom contexts of control and negotiation.* Paper presented at the meeting of the American Educational Research Association, San Francisco.

Mead, G. H. (1934). *Mind, self, and society*. Chicago: University of Chicago Press.

Nissan, M. (1992). Beyond intrinsic motivation: Cultivating a "sense of the desirable." In F. K. Oser, A. Dick, and J. Patry (Eds.), *Effective and responsible teaching: A new synthesis* (pp. 126–138). San Francisco: Jossey-Bass.

Noddings, N. (1984). *Caring: A feminine approach to ethics and moral education.* Berkeley, CA: University of California Press.

Noddings, N. (1988). Schools face "crisis in caring." *Education Week 8*(14): 32.

Peterson, D. R. (1989). Interpersonal goal conflict. In L. A. Pervin (Ed.), *Goal concepts in personality and social psychology* (pp. 327–361). Hillsdale, NJ: Lawrence Erlbaum Associates.

Phillips, J. (1978). "A cave, a dam, a river." *Phi Delta Kappan 59*: 703–704.

Reed, D. F. (1991). Effective classroom managers in the middle school. *Middle School Journal 23* (1): 16–21.

Rogoff, B. (1990). *Apprenticeship in thinking: Cognitive development in social context*. New York: Oxford University Press.

Ryan, R. M., Connell, J. P., and Deci, E. L. (1985). A motivational analysis of self-determination and self-regulation in education. In C. Ames and R. Ames (Eds.), *Research on motivation in education, Vol. 2: The classroom milieu* (pp. 13–51). Orlando, FL: Academic Press.

Ryan, R. M., and Stiller, J. (1991). The social contexts of internalization: Parent and teacher influences on autonomy, motivation, and learning. In M. L. Machr and P. R. Pintrich (Eds.), *Advances in motivation and achievement, Vol. 7: Goals and self-regulatory processes* (pp. 115–149). Greenwich, CT: JAI.

Sarason, S. B. (1990) *The predictable failure of educational reform: Can we change course before it's too late?* San Francisco: Jossey-Bass.

Schockley, R., and Sevier, L. (1991). Behavior management in the classroom: Guidelines for maintaining control. *Schools in the Middle 1* (2): 6–9, 11–12.

Schön, D. A. (1989). Professional knowledge and reflective practice. In T. J. Sergiovanni and J. H. Moore (Eds.), *Schooling for tomorrow: Directing reforms and issues that count* (pp. 188–206). Needham Heights, MA: Heights: Allyn and Bacon.

Sergiovanni, T. (1993). *Building community in schools*. Alexandria, VA: Association for Supervision and Curriculum Development.

Shulman, L. S. (1986). Paradigms and research programs in the study of teaching: A contemporary perspective. In M. C. Wittrock (Ed.), *Handbook of research on teaching* (3rd ed.) (pp. 3–36). New York: Macmillan.

Shulman, L. S. (1989). Teaching alone, learning together: Needed agendas for the new reforms. In T. J. Sergiovanni and J. H. Moore (Eds.), *Schooling for tomorrow: Directing reforms and issues that count* (pp. 166–187). Needham Heights, MA: Allyn and Bacon.

Sirotnik, K. A. (1989). The school as the center of change. In T. J. Sergiovanni and J. H. Moore (Eds.), *Schooling for tomorrow:*

Directing reforms and issues that count (pp. 89–113). Needham Heights, MA: Heights: Allyn and Bacon.

Slavin, R. E. (1987). Ability grouping and student achievement in elementary schools: A best evidence synthesis. *Review of Educational Research 57*: 293–336.

Smith, B. (1992, April). Teachers' implicit constructions of key elements necessary to consider when planning a lesson: A qualitative criticism. Paper presented at the meeting of the American Educational Research Association, San Francisco.

Spence, D. (1984). *Narrative truth and historical truth: Meaning and interpretation in psychoanalysis.* New York: Norton.

Steinberg, A. (Ed.). (1989). Talking it out: Students mediate disputes. *Harvard Education Letter 5*: 4.

Stevenson, C. (1992). *Teaching ten to fourteen year olds.* New York: Longman.

Stevenson, C., and Carr, J. F. (Eds.) (1993a). *Integrated studies in the middle grades: "Dancing through walls."* New York: Teachers College Press.

Stevenson, C., and Carr, J. F. (1993b). Epilogue: Daring to dance . . . or not. In C. Stevenson and J. F. Carr (Eds.), *Integrated studies in the middle grades: "Dancing through walls"* (pp. 183–201). New York: Teachers College Press.

Strike, K. A., and Soltis, J. F. (1992). *The ethics of teaching.* New York: Teachers College Press.

Taylor, W. D., and Johnsen, J. B. (1986). *Resisting technological momentum.* 85th Yearbook, Pt. 1: National Society for the Study of Education. Chicago: University of Chicago Press.

Tharp, R. G., and Gallimore, R. G. (1988). *Rousing minds to life: Teaching, learning, and schooling in social context.* New York: Cambridge University Press.

Weisner, T. S. (1984). Ecocultural niches of middle childhood: A cross-cultural perspective. In W. A. Collins (Ed.), *Development during middle childhood: The years from six to twelve* (pp. 335–369). Washington, DC: National Academy Press.

Wertsch, J. V. (1985). *Vygotsky and the social formation of mind.* Cambridge, MA: Harvard University Press.

Wiggington, E. (1985). *Sometimes a shining moment.* New York: Doubleday.

CHAPTER 15

Physical Education and Athletics within the Middle School Philosophy

Cathy D. Lirgg

Although a few examples can be found in the 1950s and earlier, the middle school is a relatively recent phenomenon, having emerged primarily in the 1960s (Lounsbury, 1992). Kohut (1988) called it "possibly the most exciting educational enterprise in decades" (p. 17). Almost any book or article written about the middle school reminds the reader that the middle school was developed to "meet the needs of young adolescents." A similarly frequent charge of the middle school is to "bridge the gap between elementary school and high school."

As a discipline within the middle school, physical education can play a large role in meeting the needs of young adolescents. This chapter will address that role by showing how physical education can fit under the umbrella of the middle school philosophy. To do this, however, it is important to establish an understanding of what the middle school is and where its roots originated. Through the years physical education has been a part of young adolescents' education, although the content emphasis has changed during the last century. As the middle school movement takes hold throughout the United States, physical education must contribute in a manner consistent with the philosophy and practices of the middle school in general.

What is the middle school? Where did its roots originate? Who are the students it educates? Most importantly for this chapter, where and how does physical education fit into this structure?

Although some of these questions are addressed elsewhere in this book, the first section of this chapter will examine briefly the history and philosophy of the middle school in order to establish a background from which to build. Throughout this section, implications for physical educators will be noted where appropriate. Because one purpose of the middle school is to meet the needs of young adolescents, the second section will focus on the diverse physical, intellectual, emotional, and social characteristics of middle schoolers, with special emphasis on the physical. A discussion of the needs and motivations of the emerging adolescent and the implications of those motivations on physical educators also is included. The last section will discuss the unique role of physical education in a middle school setting, including curriculum and instruction and the intramural versus interscholastic sports debate.

From Junior High to Middle School

Schools designed specifically for emerging adolescents are not new. Junior high schools, comprised predominantly of students in Grades 7–9, appeared as early as 1909. By 1970, there were close to 8,000 junior high schools in the United States (Lounsbury, 1992). Originally, junior high schools promised fundamental changes in school organization, curriculum, instruction, and student outcomes. However, as often happens with institutionalized social reform, goals were scaled down and the junior high school eventually came to be viewed as nothing more than a junior version of the high school (Cuban, 1992).

Initially, the junior high school was itself an innovative reform. Breaking the traditional 1–8, 9–12 organizational structure, its goals were similar to the present middle school concept: to meet the needs of young adolescents and to bridge the gap between elementary school and high school. According to the 1918 *Report of the Commission on the Reorganization of Secondary Education* (Cuban, 1992), junior high schools were to be places where students could explore their own aptitudes, and where they had some choice as to the kinds of interests they wished to pursue. However, junior high school reformers often had multiple agendas, and this led to the charge that the junior high school was ambiguous or uncertain about its mission (Cuban, 1992). Hence, it was not surprising that it became essentially a miniature high school, incorporating such high school practices as departmentalization, subject-centered curriculum, teacher-controlled lessons, and tracking.

Physical education in the junior high school virtually patterned itself after its high school counterpart. Students were scheduled into classes a specified number of times during the week. These were inflexible as to time of day. Occasionally, students could choose from varied course offerings, but most likely instruction revolved around team and individual sports and fitness activities. As at the high school, interscholastic sporting events were the rule rather than the exception. Schools would field one (or in some cases two) teams at each grade level. Intramurals were relegated a backseat to interschool competition.

Some educators saw the "problem" of the junior high school not so much in its intentions as in its implementation (Holyoak and Weinberg, 1988; Lounsbury, 1992). In fact, Lounsbury (1992) called the middle school movement "the renaissance of the real junior high school" (p. 12). Nevertheless, the junior high school, while paradoxically firmly rooting itself as an educational institution, received an abundance of criticism (Cuban, 1992). A new reform, the middle school, began to emerge for basically two reasons: a dissatisfaction over the junior high school's ability to meet the needs of the emerging adolescent, and the earlier maturational trend of students today than at the beginning of the century, when the junior high concept was first introduced (Hannan, 1974).

The Middle School Concept

The most obvious difference between the junior high school and the middle school is grade structure. To accommodate the earlier maturation of students, middle schools typically are comprised of students beginning with either Grade 5 or 6 and continuing through Grade 8. Although most middle schools house the sixth, seventh, and eighth grades, there has been no research to indicate that any one combination of middle school grade levels is superior to another (Kohut, 1988). Ninth graders are deemed more like tenth graders than eighth graders and are incorporated into the high school. Although this grade structure difference between middle school and junior high school carries important implications, the middle school concept involves much more than simply exchanging a ninth grade for a fifth or sixth grade (McDonald and Tierno, 1979).

The middle school should bridge the gap between elementary schools and high schools by a unique implementation of its curriculum. Some of the techniques that successful middle schools have been using are individual (developmentally appropriate) instruction, interdisciplinary teaming, flexible scheduling, innovative programs, advisor-advisee programs, and cooperative learning.

Although it would be difficult to pinpoint a universal middle school curriculum, Toepfer (1992) has suggested a framework for organizing curriculum activities at the middle school level that incorporates six curricular functions. The six curricular functions are integration, exploration, guidance, differentiation, socialization, and articulation. These functions will be defined briefly below, with implications for physical education given where appropriate.

Integration deals with the process of helping students learn how to learn. In the middle school, students should be given a broad knowledge base and the skills necessary for subsequent learning. Learning experiences should be at the student's developmental level and provide opportunities for success, as well as for remediation. In physical education, students should be provided an opportunity to refine basic skills, as well as be exposed to a wide range of activities. Most important is the teacher's responsibility to design activities at each individual's skill level so that success can be attained. This responsibility includes helping young adolescents who are behind in skill "catch-up" to their classmates through developmentally appropriate activities.

Exploration is concerned with examining the usefulness of a subject to real life and having students apply that knowledge to current issues in their lives. An appreciation for movement, sport, and fitness for lifelong health must be developed early. To accomplish this goal, activities that are presented must be shown to be worthwhile or useful, as well as fun, to the middle school student. Links between life as it is now for the middle schooler and how it will be 10 years or more from now must be established. The establishment of these links, however, will not be made exclusively through lectures; students must discover for themselves and reach their own conclusions. Physical educators must provide these opportunities and constantly challenge their students to think about their future, as well as to evaluate their present.

Guidance activities assist students in making immediate and future choices. Although middle schools should employ counselors to assist students, teachers should play an important role. Adviser-advisee programs allow teachers and students to interact in small groups in noninstructional settings. If this program is available in a middle school, all teachers, including physical educators, should participate.

Differentiation speaks to the varying developmental levels in the middle school. Several alternative learning arrangements, such as those mentioned earlier, are vital to the curriculum. In physical education, skill level will vary widely among individuals. This fact necessitates planning that provides adequate success for students at all skill levels. In addition, various teaching styles need to be explored. For example, some students within a certain activity might profit from a command approach, while others may thrive when guided discovery is used. The bottom line is that physical educators should teach to the individual.

Socialization incorporates the recognition of the importance of successful social interaction in a young adolescent's life; that is, social maturity comes from successful social interaction. Young adolescents need to be taught social skills to communicate and interact effectively. The physical education class is well equipped to undertake this curricular function. Preparing objectives that specifically speak to effective social interaction is important at the middle school level. Understanding concepts such as sportsmanship, teamwork, or respect for diversity of ability simply will not just happen. They must be planned for and discussed, not only within *teachable moments* (i.e., although not planned, discussing issues as they come up during situations in class), but also within the context of the scheduled lesson. For example, although grouping by ability allows opportunities for optimizing success, if used exclusively this practice may lead to *motor elitism* (the "I'm skilled, but you're not" syndrome). Some of these practices also may lead to imposed stereotypes (e.g., boys are good at sports, girls are bad at sports). If boys and girls are placed together in a physical education class, this type of narrow thinking needs to be addressed specifically by the teacher and not ignored.

Articulation, the last curricular function, deals directly with the concept of bridging the gap between elementary and high school by minimizing gaps and providing overlap from school unit to school unit. To this end, middle school curricula should be planned in cooperation with both elementary and high schools in the area. The implications for physical education in this area are often ignored. Physical education programs need to be designed so that students are not, for example, learning to dribble a basketball at each grade level. Basic locomotor and manipulative skills should be taught in the elementary grades, while exploration of how these skills can be incorporated into sports, games, and activities occurs at the middle level. This articulation pattern should lead to a refinement of chosen skills at the high school level. Building on skills learned at the elementary level will only be as successful, however, as the elementary instruction. While this is true for any subject, far too often children enter middle school with poor fundamental motor skills. Students who do not possess the fundamentals of movement will be limited in their ability to master both sport and fitness skills. The middle school teacher must be flexible enough to address those skills in students who are deficient, while at the same time providing growth and exploration in skills for those students who already have mastered the fundamentals.

While the middle school does not have a universal curriculum in the sense of having a clearly identified purpose or theme (Beane, 1990), the organization and methodology of the middle school should reflect a clear focus. This focus should be on the needs of the young adolescent. The effectiveness of a middle school can be found in the answer to this question: "To what extent does the school's program meet the developmental characteristics and learning needs of the students in that school?" (Toepfer, 1992, p. 213) These characteristics and needs are the focus of the next section, with a special emphasis given to the physical dimension.

The Middle School Student

Physical Characteristics

The age range of 10–14 years, which encompasses middle school, is a period of intense change. Although students are developing more mature intellectual and social capacities than they previously possessed, change occurs most noticeably in the physical domain. Changes in height, weight, muscle mass, and secondary sexual characteristics are rapid and sometimes frightening to the young adolescent. While this change is inevitable, its onset is not similar for boys and girls. Furthermore, among each gender, rates of maturation vary considerably.

Boys and girls are very similar in biological characteristics before puberty; after puberty, however, they are quite different (Keogh and Sugden, 1985). Girls tend to reach the onset of puberty, on average, around age 10 or 11. Boys reach puberty about two years later. The rapid growth spurt characterized by puberty lasts approximately two and a half to three years, with peak height velocity, the period of most rapid growth in height, occurring on the average between ages 11 and 12 for girls and between ages 13 and 14 for boys. Girls generally grow an average of three inches a year during puberty, while boys average about four inches. The growing period for boys also lasts slightly longer than for girls. For both genders, peak weight velocity occurs after peak height velocity. Puberty also results in an increase in adipose tissue, with girls acquiring more than boys, sometimes at a rate of 50 percent greater (Payne and Isaacs, 1991).

In addition to the growth in height and weight, hormonal changes influence genitals and secondary sexual characteristics as well as muscle mass. Some of the changes may be dramatic and confusing to many young people, and physical education classes often magnify these changes. Locker rooms provide avenues for comparisons—comparisons that dramatize the individual variations in rate of growth and development. For this reason, facilities such as individual shower stalls and dressing areas should be available to students who may wish to use them. In addition, coeducational classes can be especially embarrassing at this age. A typical middle school physical education class may contain what appears to be predominantly physically mature young women, a few physically mature young men, a few prepubertal girls, and several prepubescent boys. In physical education, unlike most other subjects, teachers must deal with these individual physical differences and plan activities, as well as structure groups, to take into consideration strength and overall physical maturity differences.

Because of the many physiological changes taking place in a young adolescent's body, sugar is pumped into the body at a high level. It is used for energy and then depleted. The result can be periods of intense activity followed by lethargic behavior (Holyoak and Weinberg, 1988). The physical educator must recognize and understand these occurrences and incorporate both high intensity and low activity into the lessons.

Several cautions should be made to the physical educator regarding students entering puberty. First, because peak height velocity occurs before peak weight velocity, students, especially boys, may not be as strong as they seem based on their height (Payne and Isaacs, 1991). Activities that are considered collision or contact sports, such as football, wrestling, and basketball, should be supervised carefully and structured to prevent injury or damage to still growing bones. In addition, the growth spurt in adolescence occurs at a different speed for different body parts. This fact contributes to the adolescent awkwardness that occurs frequently during puberty. Not all students will go through this awkward stage, but the physical educator certainly must understand this phenomenon.

Second, boys who are early maturers will have a definite advantage over late maturers and girls because of hormonal changes that provide an increase in muscle mass. However, late maturers will catch up and often be taller than early maturers because they have had longer to grow. Cutting athletes from teams at the middle school level is discouraged strongly because it is highly unfair to the late maturers (Payne and Isaacs, 1991).

Third, girls who are early maturers will probably display greater proportions of body fat compared to their less-mature counterparts. Because of this increase in body fat, many adolescent girls tend to be weight conscious. Comparisons to their prepubescent weight may cause some girls of this age to acquire habits that may lead to anorexia or bulimia. In fact, the high-risk population for the onset of anorexia is between ages 12 and 18 (Romeo, 1984). Physical educators, especially coaches, should be careful when suggesting or, in the case of sports such as gymnastics, swimming, and dance, ordering girls to lose weight because the young adolescent may be psychologically vulnerable to a coach's orders. Teachers and coaches should be particularly attuned to the warning signs of eating disorders.

Fourth, all students should be educated regarding the implications of their body changes and be given the opportunity to discuss their concerns with an adult. As mentioned earlier in this chapter, guidance should be an integral part of any middle school program. This guidance process should deal not only with academic subject choice but also with items of personal concern, such as maturation issues. The guidance process must be integrated to include not only guidance counselors but also school health personnel and physical educators.

Finally, the physical changes occurring during the middle school years also bring about a sense of restlessness. Middle schoolers need to be physically active. They also want freedom, but they are afraid to lose certain securities (Williamson and Johnston, 1991). Physical education programs need to be structured in such a way that students are given plenty of on-task time and are guided in their learning instead of always being told what to do.

Social, Emotional, and Intellectual Characteristics

Probably the most important need of young adolescents lies in the social area: the need for friends. Friends represent an important act of choice for young adolescents because they have little control over most other areas of their lives (Milgram, 1992). The peer group for most young adolescents consists of same-sex friends, although there are some exceptions (Stafford, 1982). Therefore, while coeducational activities, if conducted correctly, might help to eliminate gender stereotypes, young adolescents need activities in which they can participate exclusively with those of their own gender. The physical education program should provide both types of opportunities.

Furthermore, group membership becomes extremely important. Peer pressure can be quite prominent as young adolescents struggle to fit in somewhere. Schools must recognize these needs and plan activities both formally and informally that address them (Campbell, 1991). The physical education staff becomes important in structuring intramural activities in which everyone can participate and be a member of a team. Discussions in physical education classes about individual differences in such areas as personality, gender, race, and ability will allow students the opportunity to understand some of their feelings and can work to eliminate some societal evils, such as racism, sexism, and motor-elitism.

Emotionally, middle schoolers are quite fragile. Because they lack the experience to put things into perspective, events often are blown out of proportion (Campbell, 1991). A seemingly small issue, such as that dealing with hair or clothes, can make a huge impact on a middle schooler's daily life. Teachers need to understand this urgency and help the student cope with events without devaluing the student's very real feelings.

Middle school students also struggle with self-concept and self-esteem issues. Again, open communication between peers and between students and adults is crucial as social validation is important in order to build and maintain a positive self-concept. Because students of this age are easily discouraged and lose self-confidence easily, they need adults who are interested and genuinely care about them (Irvin, 1992; Milgram, 1992).

Although self-esteem is an important topic for all young adolescents, young girls are especially vulnerable to a decrease in self-esteem as they enter the middle school years (Brutsaert, 1990). Eccles and Midgley (1989), however, suggest that it is not the age of the student that contributes to the decrease in self-esteem. They argue that the environment contributes to changes in student motivations and beliefs. For example, schools that emphasize competition, social comparison, and ability at this heightened period of self-focus particularly are harmful at this age. However, the school environment may not be the only source of competition among middle school students. The media, with its emphasis on socially correct apparel, such as Nike Air Jordan's and Polo shirts, invites competition in a domain within a middle schooler's life that to him or her is seen as vitally important—personal appearance. Knowing these things, physical educators must make special efforts to provide opportunities for success while downplaying competition in any sense.

Research on the self-esteem of young adolescents often has been undertaken in junior high schools, at the transition from sixth to seventh grade. As Eccles and Midgley (1989) point out, the transition to the middle school occurs earlier than to the junior high school, making comparisons of students' belief systems in these two schools difficult. Invariably, age is a confounding factor in this type of research. If, however, the environment does contribute or is related to shifts in students' belief systems (e.g., self-esteem), instructional patterns more than likely are the key. At this stage, more research employing middle schools needs to be conducted to identify instructional patterns that may contribute specifically to positive self-esteem of young adolescents. Even so, this type of research may prove difficult because of the individual nature of the students themselves. However, research consistently makes clear that experiencing success can contribute greatly to enhancing self-esteem.

Intellectually, students are beginning to think in the abstract. *Beginning* is the important word here. For example, while some students may be capable of recognizing complex defensive or offensive strategies in a sport such as basketball, many students will be confused trying to learn one defensive formation. Physical educators must not only recognize physical differences, but they also must understand the cognitive differences in their students and plan accordingly in their lessons. For example, choices of strategies in games need to be gradually increased so that the blossoming abstract abilities of students can be developed without appearing overwhelming.

Students also are acquiring the ability to respond to such abstract thoughts as putting themselves in another's shoes, empathizing, and seeing another's point of view (Steinberg, 1985). These characteristics can be discussed in physical education classes with much more response and understanding than before. The opportunities afforded by teachable moments relating to the above characteristics need to be incorporated into classes so that these issues can be made relevant to the immediate environment of the middle schooler. Middle schoolers learn best when they are able to apply knowledge to current situations. This application is true not only as it relates to facts, but also as it relates to feelings and emotions.

Middle school children are unique individuals, even within their own peer groups. However, they have many things in common. They have an abundance of energy but tire quickly. They are undergoing a sometimes frightening period in their lives when, at times, the body seems to control their lives. They are learning important personal and social skills while increasing their ability to think abstractly. They live in the present, a present that dictates their subsequent emotions and actions. They are experiencing threats to their self-confidence and self-esteem and combat those threats by tying closely into a peer group for support.

The middle school must provide an avenue to explore the many feelings young adolescents are experiencing. Each subject's curriculum and instructional process should have the student at the heart of this process. The next section examines the philosophy underlying the curriculum in physical education and the guidelines established specifically for the middle school student.

The Physical Education Program

Physical education at the middle school level has taken on greater importance since the publishing of *Turning Points* in 1989, a highly regarded report of a task force on the education of young adolescents by the Carnegie Council on Adolescent Development. The Carnegie Council determined that young adolescents need to be healthy in order to learn. It acknowledged that the physical and mental health dimensions of educating youth virtually have been overshadowed by the emphasis on academics. The whole student has not been educated. The council suggested two areas in which health and fitness can be greatly improved.

The first area falls under the auspices of health care at the middle school level. Every student should be ensured access to health services. While physical educators are not directly responsible for this service, they often are the ones who are in a position to screen potential problems and bring those problems to the attention of the proper authorities. The school nurse and the physical educator might work together through physical education classes to screen such conditions as scoliosis.

The second area directly impacts middle school physical education. The Carnegie Council (1989) advocated regular physical education and involvement in sport and fitness activities. They believed that physical education should not be a "sorting program" that focuses on the most talented. Every student should be able to achieve at least moderate success at some type of physical activity. That means that schools must, by necessity, offer a wide range of activities, and it is suggested that schools join with parks and recreation departments to make this possible. For example, outdoor recreation sponsored jointly by the school system and the recreation department can provide opportunities, such as risk management and challenge activities, not usually found in the normal curriculum of middle school physical education (Chandler, Hamilton, and Ralph, 1991).

Finally, the report notes that fitness is the key ingredient to good physical and mental health and must be a goal of the instructional program of all students.

Placek (1992) has raised the issue of the location of physical education in the middle school curriculum. Physical education often is thought to have a separate, activity-centered curriculum. Placek suggests that we begin to integrate physical education into the core interdisciplinary curriculum of the middle school. The middle school, with its emphasis on flexible scheduling, team teaching, and cooperative learning strategies, offers a unique opportunity for integration to occur. As she notes, integration will not be an easy task; however, physical educators must be proactive in showing administrators that physical education is of vital importance to young adolescents and that it indeed has an important place in the core curriculum.

Given that physical education should play an important role in the education of the middle school student, each school district is left to decide what type of program to implement and how to incorporate the goals of middle school within its own physical education and middle school curriculum. Although some suggestions have been offered previously in this chapter, this section will explore several guidelines from various professionals in the field concerning how to accomplish this very important task.

Philosophy

The fact that there is no national curriculum in physical education at any level can be both a hurdle and a blessing. On the one hand, physical educators constantly must plan lessons without the benefit of a book that describes units in a specified order. Arguably, not having a national curriculum has contributed to the repetitive teaching of skills at different grade levels. However, school districts or communities often disagree as to what is important to their children in the physical domain. A middle school in urban Miami may teach many different skills and have different values than a small school in rural Montana, and rightly so. Some school districts may believe that lifetime sports are the most important for their students to learn, while another school may stress physical fitness.

The underlying basis of any curriculum in physical education should be a well-developed philosophy. Siedentop, Mand, and Taggart (1986) have developed several beliefs that are relevant to middle school physical education. Together they represent a physical education philosophy for today's secondary schools and include, among others, the following statements:

> Health-related fitness is of major importance to the well-being of our society and a necessary element in physical education programs. . . .
>
> Physical education is valuable in its own right and does not need to be justified by reference to academics. . . .
>
> The major values to be gained through participation in physical education are skill, the joy of physical exertion, the realization of clear-cut objectives, appropriate relationships to authority, the acceptance of responsibility, cooperative relationships, security in the rituals of rules and customs that define sport, the adventure of risk, the ability to defer goals, and measuring oneself against clearly defined and widely accepted measures of quality. . . .
>
> The values to be derived from participation in physical education are appropriate to females and males, rich and poor, to normal and exceptional students. . . .
>
> The values available through participation in sound physical education programs are particularly relevant to the major developmental tasks of adolescents and to ignore this aspect is to deny what has been known for centuries. . . .
>
> The many activities that comprise physical education have no particular hierarchical value in terms of their importance to the participant even though they may have more or less value relative to specific goals for the educator. . . .
>
> If physical education is to survive and thrive as a school subject, it must demonstrate tangible outcomes and students must show recognizable achievement gains. . . .
>
> Equal educational opportunity is fundamental to the maintenance of our democratic society, and physical education should be in all school curricula and equally accessible to all students. . . .

> Physical education can be central to the education of
> youth if it is characterized by commitment, intimacy, and
> achievement. . . .
> To be successful, physical education needs to extend
> beyond the school and the school day. . . .
> The role of the teacher is critical to the success of the
> physical education program. (excerpted from pp. 22–28)

These beliefs provide an example of a well-designed philosophy of physical education. Whether a school district adopts these statements or develops a philosophy of its own should be left up to that individual school district. The point, however, is that without a philosophy, curriculum development becomes a hit-or-miss endeavor. Siedentop et al. (1986) note that if physical education, at any level, wishes to shape its own future, it cannot do so without arriving at some clear formulation of basic beliefs. Physical educators *must* be able to articulate what quality physical education at the middle school level is all about. No one else is in a better position to do so.

Guidelines for Programming

The Middle and Secondary School Physical Education Council of the National Association for Sport and Physical Education [NASPE] (1992a)[1] recently revised a position paper developed a few years earlier concerning guidelines for middle school physical education. Included in these guidelines are program characteristics; characteristics of the middle school student; goals of the instructional program (developed by the Physical Education Outcomes Committee of NASPE, 1992b)[1]; curriculum; teachers; student health and safety; scheduling, time allotment, and class size; facilities, equipment, and supplies; and measurement and evaluation. While it is not the intention of this chapter to reiterate everything in this position paper, some of the key concepts from *Guidelines for Middle School Physical Education* (NASPE, 1992a) relevant to this chapter will be reviewed.

Program characteristics. Program characteristics suggested by the council fall in line with the overall philosophy of the middle school concept discussed earlier in this chapter. The council believes that every student should have a home base and teacher who provides continuing guidance and assistance with daily decision-making. Learning opportunities should be balanced to address the three major goals of the middle school: a) personal development of the middle schooler, b) continuing learning skills, and c) effective use of appropriate knowledge. The instructional design should be characterized by a focus on individual progress that utilizes many curricular options and individualized instruction where appropriate. Interdisciplinary teaming also should be utilized for cooperative planning, instruction, and evaluating. Finally, the council believes that a wide range of exploratory activities that promote socialization, develop interest, and enrich leisure time is necessary.

Curriculum. The middle school curriculum in physical education should be comprehensive and well balanced in order to enhance the psychomotor, cognitive, and affective domains through movement. It should contain offerings in conditioning and physical fitness, individual and dual sports, team sports, gymnastics, rhythms and dance, track and field, aquatics, and outdoor activities. In addition, the council lists several beliefs specifically about physical activity programs. Council members feel that middle school programs should

- Allow students to participate in physical activity on a regular basis equivalent to five times per week.
- Have philosophy and program goals that are consistent with the educational goals of the school and that reflect the needs of middle school students.
- Represent a transition from the elementary program to the high school program accomplished by giving the students opportunities to participate in short exploratory units as well as longer ones.
- Utilize specific instructional objectives for each unit.
- Provide activities developed on a continuum so that each student can progress on an individual basis.
- Offer a variety of activities regardless of students' levels of physical development.
- Allow students to assess and evaluate both their physical and social selves.

- Provide opportunities for remediation of motor and fitness skills.
- Provide experiences that promote motor skill and fitness development.
- Provide opportunities for students to select and perform activities.
- Reflect a multimedia approach.
- Provide for interaction and coordination with other school disciplines.
- Provide skills and concepts for the pursuit of lifelong personal wellness.
- Develop skills that enable students to apply technology to the development of personal wellness.
- Develop an appreciation of physical activity and its effect on total well-being.

Student health and safety. The council also provides several guidelines regarding student health and safety. Students should wear clothing appropriate to the activity, with showering and change of clothing encouraged after vigorous activity. Scheduling should take into account physical maturation and skill development levels. It is especially important that teachers take size and strength considerations into account for competitive situations. Teachers need to receive, as well as report, pertinent student medical information. A written policy for providing first aid and reporting accidents should be available at each school. Facilities and equipment should be maintained daily. Locker rooms and activity areas should be continuously supervised.

Time allotment and class size. The Middle and Secondary School Physical Education Council recommends daily directed physical education instruction of sufficient length for meaningful learning to occur. The actual program should be planned so that students are provided maximum involvement and opportunities for optimal achievement. Finally, class size should be similar to academic class sizes.

The council believes that implementation of these guidelines, plus others that were not highlighted here, should result in sound and tenable physical education programs in the middle schools. Of course, quality of teaching is a determining factor in whether the program will be successful. One standard of the quality of teaching is how well student outcomes are met. The next section takes a look at some outcomes for middle school students in physical education.

Outcomes

Although a national curriculum does not exist, for the first time physical educators and curriculum planners have a guide that gives direction to the development of standards for student achievement. In 1986, the NASPE formed a committee to reflect the focus of the current national education reform movement. The committee, comprised of physical educators, completed what became known as the Physical Education Outcomes Project (NASPE, 1992b, p. 7). This committee developed two sets of guidelines.

The first defined what it means to be *a physically educated student*. To accomplish this task, the committee identified several statements using the verbs *has, is, does, knows,* and *values*. For example, the physically educated student demonstrates proficiency in a few forms of physical activity" (HAS); "assesses, achieves, and maintains physical fitness" (IS); "selects and regularly participates in lifetime physical activities" (DOES); "understands that wellness involves more than being physically fit" (KNOWS); and "cherishes the feelings that results from regular participation in physical activity" (VALUES).

The second set of guidelines dealt with specific and measurable outcomes (or *benchmarks*) for students in Grades 2, 4, 6, 8, 10, and 12. At each of these grade levels, outcomes were identified and tied with a verb from the definition of a physically educated student. Each benchmark begins with a stem: "As a result of participating in a quality physical education program, it is reasonable to expect that the students will be able to. . . . " and goes on to list several benchmarks for various activities. Benchmarks for sixth and eighth grades are relevant to middle school physical education. The following two sections provide examples of benchmarks for these grades.

Sixth grade. As a result of participating in a quality physical education program, it is reasonable to expect that the students will be able to

- Consistently throw and catch a ball while guarded by opponents (HAS).
- Monitor heart rate before, during, and after activity (IS).
- Participate in games, sports, dance, and outdoor pursuits, both in and outside of school, based on individual interests and capabilities (DOES).
- Identify benefits resulting from participation in different forms of physical activities (KNOWS).
- Seek out, participate with, and show respect for persons of like and different skill levels (VALUES).

Eighth grade. As a result of participating in a quality physical education program, it is reasonable to expect that the students will be able to

- Combine skills competently to participate in modified versions of team and individual sports (HAS).
- Participate in an individualized fitness program (IS).
- Identify and follow rules while playing sports and games (DOES).
- List long-term physiological, psychological, and cultural benefits that may result from regular participation in physical activity (KNOWS).
- Respect physical and performance limitations of self and others (VALUES).

These benchmarks are not substitutes for curriculum planning. Teachers should add and delete benchmarks as deemed appropriate by the school and the community. They will, however, help teachers document what students are learning in physical education and represent reasonable levels of achievement.

Physical education in the middle school should be more than a seasonal representation of team sports, more than mere physical activity. It should combine rules, strategies, history, background, safety procedures, benefits, and lifestyle applications. It should help students become aware of their personal wants and needs in order to make choices about activities that are available to them (Tenoschok, 1984). The middle school is the ideal time to make physical activity a regular and important dimension of one's lifestyle (Batesky, 1991).

The physical education curriculum also transcends the school day instructional period. It plays a large role in helping students prepare to use their newly learned skills in such areas as intramurals or interscholastic sports. The final section of this chapter will explore the intramural versus interscholastic sport debate in the middle school.

Interscholastic Competition or Intramurals?

The question of athletic competition at the middle school level is a volatile one, spurred on by our society's desire to produce winners. Proponents of interscholastic competition for middle schoolers point to the community pride that interscholastics develops and the importance of middle school interscholastics as a *feeder* system for the high school program, which in turn serves as an even greater source of community pride (Huggins and Hunt, 1987; Redfearn, 1981). Further, some feel the athletically gifted student should have available the opportunity to expand his or her talents by competing in an arena of similar-ability athletes. Although these arguments are popular with selected parents and community members, many educators and physicians who deal directly with middle school youth are more cautious in their appraisal of the benefits of interscholastic sports for this age group.

There are three basic types of athletic competition frequently found at the middle school level. The first type is *intramurals,* where students compete within their own school. Frequently, students are organized into teams, such as by homeroom. Often, this type of competition takes place during the lunch hour or directly after school. Intramurals are structured and are highly supervised, usually by physical education and classroom teachers throughout the building. Benefits of this type of competition are that it allows maximum participation for everyone and is housed within the school, during or immediately following the school day. Also, it can be closely tied to physical education instruction. Unfortunately, coaching in this setting is minimal.

Extramurals refers to structured competition involving only teams within a school district. For example, a school district with three middle schools may structure events between schools. Schools often will sponsor more than one team in a sport to allow for greater participation. These teams are given coaching similar to an interscholastic team. Three benefits of this type of competition are reduced traveling time to games and traveling costs, greater participation by students than would be offered in a true interscholastic program, and the availability of coaching. Frequently, under this type of arrangement, the emphasis is on playing and not on winning. All players must play a designated amount of time.

Interscholastic competition usually is reserved for the elite athlete. Tryouts are held and teams are cut to a certain size. Some sports, such as football, can allow greater team size but, frequently, not everyone will play in a game. Winning is generally emphasized, although this need not be the case in all situations, especially in school districts where the philosophy is to play everyone. Competition is between school districts, which often necessitates greater travel time. A benefit of this type of program is that it usually caters to the advanced athletes and offers them an opportunity to increase their skills, similar to advanced level academic programs that many school districts provide. In addition, interscholastic coaches generally are more knowledgeable about the sport they coach.

As noted earlier in this chapter, physical characteristics of middle schoolers vary widely. Some boys and girls are well into their pubertal years, while others have not even begun puberty. As a result, a particular age group of youth may have some children who are far superior in strength and skill than are others. Because interscholastic competition most frequently is set up by grade level, this structure virtually guarantees dominance by the early maturing youth (Redfearn, 1981). Often, however, the outstanding middle school athlete may have difficulty making the high school team because he or she is surpassed in size by later maturing athletes (Payne and Isaacs, 1991). In addition, because rate of growth during puberty is accelerated, some youth who may appear strong on the basis of their taller and heavier appearance may suffer from epiphyseal injuries (injuries to the growth plates in the bones) because they possess insufficient strength for certain contact sports such as football and wrestling (Cherry, 1974).

There appear to be two primary questions in this debate. The first question concerns competition in general. "Is competition healthy for middle school youth? Can they handle the pressure of winning and the pain of losing? Are they equipped to learn skills in a competitive situation?"

The second question deals specifically with the desirability of interscholastic competition in middle school. "If competition is desirable, who will the opponent be? How much extra time will be given these special teams during the day? How will teams be chosen and who will coach? What sports should be offered?"

Intramurals?

Let us consider the first primary question: "Should middle school students compete in sport?" Some would have us believe that competition at any age level is unhealthy and should be avoided (Kohn, 1986). However, this suggestion is somewhat unrealistic. Left alone with a bat and ball, most children automatically will form their own games with their own rules that are amazingly fair for all the children who are playing. These bat-and-ball games resemble baseball or softball, although they most likely will not be played exactly as such. The point here is that children will organize themselves into games for the sake of competition (rarely do children get together to hit ground balls to one another).

Competition is an important part of life, largely because a part of competition involves cooperation. If two groups of children are playing touch football and one group decides that the endline is the oak tree, and the other group wants the endline to be the edge of the garage, there will be no game and no competition. When a group of youngsters saves their collective allowances for three weeks to buy a net for the playground basket, you have cooperation in preparation for competition.

If we assume that competition is not good, we need go no further. Even intramurals (especially team sports) should be eliminated. However, if we believe that competition can be worthwhile, is competition automatically beneficial to middle school youth?

The opinion of many sport psychologists is that competition can be good or bad—depending on the social context in which it is taking place. If winning is emphasized and players are treated as miniature adults by coaches who yell at them, who give them "win one for the Gipper" halftime talks, who keep game statistics and award most valuable players trophies, then competition can certainly be harmful. If competition is organized around fair play, equal opportunity, and skill development, and if coaches know the physical, mental, and emotional capacity of their young charges, the benefits of competition readily should outweigh the anxiety of losing. Indeed, research suggests that most children do not find athletic competition highly stressful (Scanlan and Passer, 1978, 1979) and that competitive athletics have been found to produce no more anxiety than physical education classes, band competitions, or academic tests (Simon and Martens, 1979; Skubic, 1955).

One important key to *good* competition is that everyone (students, coaches, administrators, and parents) understands the middle school philosophy and how that impacts competition at the middle school level. Individuality must be respected and, therefore, youngsters of all abilities should have the opportunity to participate. Games should be organized so that every member of the team plays at least a minimum amount of time (Gentry and Hayes, 1991; Riemcke, 1988). In addition, several different sports, both team and individual, should be offered so that everyone has a greater opportunity to be successful.

Another important key is hiring coaches who have a fundamental understanding of the middle school youngster. Often coaches who are hired from outside the school or from other levels, such as the high school, may lack this vital understanding. In these cases, training programs must be made available. While excellent coaching education programs such as the Program for Athletic Coaches' Education and the American Coaching Effectiveness Program[2] exist, a middle school district may want to supplement the material to deal specifically with characteristics of middle school youth and the middle school and district philosophy.

Can individuals learn during a competitive situation? Research has shown that learning new skills in a competitive situation is less than ideal. Martens (1969) found that the presence of an audience impaired learning of a complex motor skill in a laboratory. The nature of competition suggests that there probably will be an audience present to watch. For youngsters who are less skilled, this situation most likely will produce a lesser performance than would have occurred without the presence of an audience. For this reason, a school district might allow competition but not allow spectators. Or the competition may be in the form of intramurals held during the school day or during lunch hour.

However, research also has shown that competition can improve performance if a task is well learned. In general, Wankel (1972) found that the performance of high-ability individuals was improved with competition, but low-ability individuals performed better in a noncompetitive situation. One obvious solution to this dilemma (other than eliminating competition for the lesser skilled) is to increase the skill level of participants. This can be achieved through well-directed practices; however, during intramurals, little practice time and coaching may be available. The burden of improving skills so that competition can be enjoyed falls squarely on the shoulders of the physical educators.

The physical education curriculum plays a vital role in improving ability. Activities that are offered competitively, initially should be taught in physical education classes. Here, students can learn a wide range of skills and become familiar with strategies and rules in a noncompetitive environment. Through physical education, all students should achieve at least moderate success in some type of physical activity (Carnegie, 1989). They should, at minimum, attain the competence necessary to participate confidently in intramurals. Quality daily physical education can assist students in acquiring that confidence. The goal of physical education should not be to become a sorting program that focuses only on the most talented (Carnegie, 1989). Being physically educated should involve knowing the joy and exhilaration of moving well and experiencing the freedom and fun of any movement, even if it is not performed at a high level (Mueller, 1990).

Interscholastic Sports?

The second primary question, and the main debate question: "Should there be interscholastic sports at the middle school level?" First, it must be remembered that middle school encompasses Grades 5–8. What may be beneficial for eighth graders may be detrimental to fifth graders. For example, a recent survey of physicians and athletic directors in the state of Arkansas found that the majority of respondents were against interscholastic sports before the eighth grade (Gentry and Hayes, 1991). On the contrary, some educators believe that there are no conclusive reasons why any middle school child should be subjected to competition in the form of interscholastics (Redfearn, 1981).

Community pressure often plays a role in whether or not schools have interscholastic athletics. It is vitally important that the philosophy of the school be reflected in all school functions. If a philosophy of "all must play" is advanced, which seems to best reflect the general middle school philosophy, the school must convey that philosophy to the public and structure programs to reflect it.

This does not necessarily eliminate the more elite interscholastic program. In fact, the Carnegie Council report (1989) acknowledges that interscholastic sports may be desirable as a way to recognize young people for excellence. However, the report is quick to note that opportunities for athletic competition under no circumstances should be limited to interscholastic sport. If a school has a fine intramural program or extramural program in which everyone who wishes can belong to a team and participate, then interscholastic sports for a select group of individuals may fit into the philosophy. Too often, however, most of the budget and an abundance of energy are used to create interscholastic sports while only lip service is paid to intramurals. The priorities in this situation are backwards.

Which of these choices is best for middle school children? If one looks to the philosophy of the middle school in general to answer this question, the answer should be that programs that allow participation for anyone who wishes to play are the most desirable. Because of the need to cater to the wide range of individuals at the middle school level, a wide variety of activities should be available. Often, this is not financially possible for interscholastic sports. It may, however, be possible at the extramural level and certainly is possible at the intramural level. Individual differences in maturation must be addressed when setting up any program so that competition is fair, and all are provided an opportunity to improve skill. Although inter-scholastics might allow fair, competition by choosing homo-geneous (more mature, better-skilled) individuals, it eliminates many students from the process.

This debate can only be resolved by each school district examining what it believes to be important in the life of a middle school child. The saying "form follows function" can be used here to show how a program (the form) should follow the philosophy (the function). By staying in tune with a sound philosophy that is based on research and knowledge of the needs of young adolescents, an athletic program can be developed that greatly enhances the well-being of the adolescent.

In conclusion, because physical education and athletics cut across many different disciplines and allow for learning in several domains, a sound middle school physical education class and/or athletic team can be a place of growth for both student and teacher. If teachers understand the needs of students and if the vision of the school can focus on those needs, the program, as well as the students, should flourish. However important a good philosophy and a well-rounded curriculum may be, the key is the teachers who implement the program. A commitment to the philosophy of the middle school and to understanding the middle school student are the first steps in presenting a sound middle school physical education program. The next step requires energy. Let us hope that the energy of middle school physical education teachers parallels the energy of their charges. What an exciting place those classes would be!

NOTES

1. Copies of full reports can be obtained by contacting the American Alliance for Health, Physical Education, Recreation, and Dance, 1900 Association Drive, Reston, VA 22091-1599.

2. The Program for Athletic Coaches' Education was developed by the Youth Sport Institute at Michigan State University, East Lansing, MI, and is administered by Vern Seefeldt. Rainer Martens at Human Kinetics Publishers, Champaign, IL, heads the American Coaching Effectiveness Program.

REFERENCES

Batesky, J. (1991). Middle school physical education curriculum: Exposure or in-depth instruction? *Middle School Journal* 22(3): 7–11.

Beane, J. A. (1990). Rethinking the middle school curriculum. *Middle School Journal* 21(5): 1–5.

Brutsaert, H. (1990). Changing sources of self-esteem among girls and boys in secondary school. *Urban Education* 24: 432–439.

Campbell, S. H. (1991). Are middle school students normal? Early adolescents and their needs. *Schools in the Middle* 1(2): 19–22.

Carnegie Council on Adolescent Development. (1989). *Turning points: Preparing American youth for the 21st century.* Washington, DC: Author.

Chandler, G. L., Hamilton, M., and Ralph, B. (1991). The place of outdoor challenge. *Middle School Journal* 22(3): 12–16.

Cherry, P. (1974). Interscholastic athletics for the middle school: Yes or no? *Middle School Journal* 5(1): 13–15.

Cuban, L. (1992). What happens to reforms that last? The case of the junior high school. *American Educational Research Journal* 29: 227–251.

Eccles, J. S. and Midgley, C. (1989). Stage-environment fit: Developmentally appropriate classrooms for young adolescents. In C. Ames and R. Ames (Eds.), *Research on Motivation in Education* (vol. 3), (pp. 139–186). Orlando, FL: Academic Press.

Gentry, D. L. and Hayes, R. L. (1991). Guidelines for athletic programs in the middle school. *Middle School Journal* 22(3): 4–6.

Hannan, T. P. (1974). Middle school—the need to establish a unique identity. *Middle School Journal* 5(1): 9–10.

Holyoak, C. and Weinberg, H. (1988). *Meeting needs and pleasing kids: A middle school physical education curriculum*. Dubuque, IA: Kendall/Hunt.

Huggins, E. B. and Hunt, S. B. (1987). Intramural programs or interscholastic sports in the junior high schools: An assessment of attitudes of principals in Kentucky. *Journal of the National Intramural-Recreational Sports Association* 11(2): 38–43.

Irvin, J. L. (1992). Developmentally appropriate instruction: The heart of the middle school. In J. L. Irvin (Ed.), *Transforming middle level education* (pp. 295–313). Needham Heights, MA: Allyn and Bacon.

Keogh, J. and Sugden, D. (1985). *Movement skill development*. New York: Macmillan.

Kohn, A. (1986). *No contest: The case against competition*. Boston: Houghton Mifflin.

Kohut, S. (1988). *The middle school: A bridge between elementary and high schools*. Washington, DC: National Education Association.

Lounsbury, J. H. (1992). Perspectives on the middle school movement. In J. L. Irvin (Ed.), *Transforming middle level education* (pp. 3–15). Needham Heights, MA: Allyn and Bacon.

Martens, R. (1969). Effects of an audience on learning and performance of a complex motor skill. *Journal of Personality and Social Psychology* 12: 252–260.

McDonald, W. E. and Tierno, M. J. (1979). From junior high school to middle school: the story of one conversion. *Middle School Journal* 10(1): 20–23.

Milgram, J. (1992). A portrait of diversity: The middle level student. In J. L. Irvin (Ed.), *Transforming middle level education* (pp. 16–27). Needham Heights, MA: Allyn and Bacon.

Mueller, L. (1990). What it means to be physically educated. *Journal of Physical Education, Recreation, and Dance 61*(3): 100–102.

National Association for Sport and Physical Education. (1992a). *Guidelines for middle school physical education.* Reston, VA: American Alliance for Health, Physical Education, Recreation, and Dance.

National Association for Sport and Physical Education. (1992b). *Outcomes of quality physical education programs.* Reston, VA: American Alliance for Health, Physical Education, Recreation, and Dance.

Payne, V. G. and Isaacs, L. D. (1991). *Human motor development: A lifespan approach.* Mountain View, CA: Mayfield.

Placek, J. H. (1992). Rethinking middle school physical education curriculum: An integrated, thematic approach. *Quest 44:* 330–341.

Redfearn, R. W. (1981). Junior high school/middle school inter-scholastics: Too much, too soon. *Middle School Journal 13*(1): 10–14.

Riemcke, C. (1988). All must play—the only way for middle school athletics. *Journal of Physical Education, Recreation, and Dance 59*(9): 82–84.

Romeo, F. F. (1984). Anorexia nervosa in the middle school. *Middle School Journal 15*(4): 16–18.

Scanlan, T. K., and Passer, M. W. (1978). Factors related to competitive stress among male youth sport participants. *Medicine and Science in Sports 10:* 103–108.

Scanlan, T. K. and Passer, M. W. (1979). Sources of competitive stress in young female athletes. *Journal of Sport Psychology 1:* 151–159.

Siedentop, D., Mand, C., and Taggart, A. (1986). *Physical education: Teaching and curriculum strategies for grades 5–12.* Mountain View, CA: Mayfield Publishing Company.

Simon, J. A. and Martens, R. (1979). Children's anxiety in sport and nonsport evaluative activities. *Journal of Sport Psychology 1:* 160–159.

Skubic, E. (1955). Emotional responses of boys to little league and middle league competitive baseball. *Research Quarterly 26:* 342–352.

Stafford, E. (1982). The unique middle school student: An unknown ingredient. *The Physical Educator* 39(1): 38–42.

Steinberg, J. (1985). *Adolescence*. New York: Knopf.

Tenoschok, M. (1984). Physical education: A middle school basic. *Middle School Journal* 16(1): 26–27.

Toepfer, C. F., Jr. (1992). Middle school level curriculum: Defining the elusive. In J. L. Irvin (Ed.), *Transforming middle level education* (pp. 205–243). Needham Heights, MA: Allyn and Bacon.

Wankel, L. M. (1972). Competition in motor performance: An experimental analysis of motivational components. *Journal of Experimental Psychology* 8: 427–437.

Williamson, R. and Johnston, J. H. (1991). *Planning for success: Successful implementation of middle level reorganization*. Reston, VA: National Association of Secondary School Principals.

Concluding Remarks

Michael J. Wavering

> America's challenge in preparing its youth is truly a
> formidable task. But many proven and promising
> solutions exist. We do not lack the knowledge to transform
> the education of young adolescents. What we need is the
> leadership and the will. (Carnegie Council on Adolescent
> Development, 1989, p. 85)

The issues, descriptions, needs, solutions, and prospects outlined
in *Educating Young Adolescents: Life in the Middle* provides the
knowledge to transform the education of our youth. If we were
able to provide inspiration and guidance with this effort, we will
have been successful.

Ten- to fifteen-year-old youths arguably are the most
complex and difficult students to educate in our system of
schooling. Time and again these youngsters make fateful choices
that affect them for the rest of their lives. Hopefully, they are
making these choices based on accurate information; too often
they are not. The schools that serve these youth need to be
concerned as much or more with the life-affecting decisions that
young adolescents are making as with the content of courses.

Schools for young adolescents need to be places that
respect developmental changes and employ teachers who are
specially equipped to teach at the middle level and who also
genuinely like youth of this age. Administrative structures
should reflect and support effective teaching and learning, and
curricula and teaching strategies must be young adolescent
compatible. Schools need to be warm, friendly places—places

that may represent for some young adolescents the only safe haven currently in their lives.

Middle level schools should be places where it is safe to make mistakes, because we can learn from our mistakes, and where *all* individuals are respected as persons of worth and intelligence. Schools should encourage students to develop through their experiences lifelong attitudes toward learning, because learning is life.

Young adolescents know far more than schools and society credit them. Some of this knowledge is incorrect or partially correct, but this knowledge must be challenged by potent teaching—teaching that is more than telling; teaching that is interactive and cooperative. These challenges can only be executed in an environment of trust and fun. Trust is gained through respect for each individual—a respect that seeks to understand each individual. Fun is not antithetical to a learning environment, but rather is a necessary part of growth in and out of school (Glasser, 1986).

Thus, the successful middle level school should be a place where the components of a clear and driving philosophy, appropriately prepared teachers, adults who understand the developmental needs of young adolescents, supportive administrative structures, and curricula tailored to youth all interact to provide the synergy of complex, successful human and humane enterprises. When this comes together, education for young adolescents is not for youth caught in the middle, but for youth in the middle of it all.

REFERENCES

Carnegie Council on Adolescent Development. (1989). *Turning points: Preparing American youth for the 21st century.* Washington, DC: Author.

Glasser, W. (1986). *Control theory in the classroom.* New York: Perennial Library.

Contributors

Rebecca S. Bowers is an assistant professor at Old Dominion University in Norfolk, Virginia. Her teaching and research interests are in the areas of preservice teacher preparation and development, curriculum and instructional integration, multicultural education, mathematics education, and science education. Dr. Bowers received an Ed. D. degree from the University of North Carolina at Greensboro.

Judith A. Brough is chair and associate professor in the Education Department at Gettysburg College in Pennsylvania. She received her Ed.D. degree from the State University of New York at Buffalo, where she concentrated on curriculum planning and development with a specialization in middle level education. Dr. Brough is active nationally in the National Middle School Association and the Middle Level Council for the National Association of Secondary School Principals.

Mary Ann Davies is an associate professor at Southern Utah University in Cedar City, Utah. She has had nine years experience teaching middle level students. Dr. Davies is a regular contributor to National Middle School Association publications and has made numerous presentations at local, state, and national meetings. She received her Ed. D. degree from Virginia Polytechnic Institute and State University.

Annette Digby is an assistant professor and Assistant Dean at the University of Arkansas, Fayetteville. She has published in the areas of middle level education, public school/university partnerships, and cooperative learning. Dr. Digby received an Ed. D. degree from the University of Alabama.

Jim Gill is the principal of Leawood Middle School in Leawood, Kansas. He is active in the National Middle School Association and currently serves on the Board of Trustees. Dr. Gill has been a middle level teacher, counselor, and administrator since 1964. He has an Ed. D. degree from the University of Kansas.

Michael James is an associate professor in the Department of Curriculum and Instruction at Wichita State University. Among other publications, Dr. James wrote the 1986 monograph *Advisor/Advisee Programs: Why, What and How* for the National Middle School Association. He received his Ed. D. degree from the University of Arizona.

Jeanneine P. Jones is an assistant professor at the University of North Carolina at Charlotte. She has taught eighth grade in an exemplary middle school for 15 years and was the author of the "Teacher to Teacher" column in the *Middle School Journal*. Dr. Jones has made numerous presentations at state and national meetings. She received an Ed. D. degree from the University of North Carolina at Greeensboro.

Cathy D. Lirgg is an assistant professor at the University of Arkansas, Fayetteville. She has four years experience in teaching and coaching in the public schools and nine additional years of experience teaching at a small college. Dr. Lirgg received a Ph. D. degree in physical education and exercise science from Michigan State University.

DeWayne A. Mason is an assistant professor at the University of California, Riverside. He is a former middle level teacher and principal, and he received a Ph. D. degree from the University of Missouri, Columbia. Dr. Mason's areas of professional interest are school effects, school and classroom organization, curriculum design, and instruction.

Rebecca Farris Mills is an associate professor at the University of Nevada, Las Vegas. She is involved actively in the American Educational Research Association special interest group on middle level education, and she is a member of the National Middle School Association Research Committee. Dr. Mills has published in the *Middle School Journal*, *Research in Middle Level Education*, and *Schools in the Middle*. She earned her Ed. D. degree at the University of Arkansas, Fayetteville.

Beverly Woods Reed is the director of the Arkansas Leadership Academy for Leadership Training and School-Based Management and an assistant professor at the University of Arkansas, Fayetteville. Dr. Reed was a secondary mathematics teacher, a counselor, an assistant superintendent and superintendent, and the assistant superintendent of education for the state of Arkansas. She earned her Ed. D. degree at the University of Arkansas.

Charles Russell is an adjunct professor at the University of Arkansas, Fayetteville, and the director of secondary curriculum for Rogers Public Schools, Rogers, Arkansas. Dr. Russell has served as a secondary school teacher, an assistant superintendent, and a visiting professor of educational administration. He earned an Ed. D. degree from the University of Arkansas, Fayetteville.

Bruce Smith is an assistant professor of special education at Henderson State University in Arkadelphia, Arkansas. His research interests include inquiring into his own teaching at the college level and the prevention of mild disabilities through responsible teaching of the social curriculum of elementary and middle schools. He earned a Ph. D. degree from the University of California at Los Angeles. Dr. Smith taught elementary and middle grades students with learning disabilities and emotional disturbances for 10 years in Los Angeles.

Dennis Snider is the director of the Center for Middle Level Education, Research, and Development at the University of Arkansas, Fayetteville. He was principal for nine years at Old

High Middle School in Bentonville, Arkansas. Mr. Snider is the past president of the Arkansas Association of Middle Level Education and currently serves as its executive director. He is a member of the Board of Trustees of the National Middle School Association and a Ph. D. candidate in curriculum and instruction at the University of Arkansas.

Samuel Totten is an associate professor of curriculum and instruction and was the codirector of the Center for Middle Level Education, Research, and Development at the University of Arkansas, Fayetteville. Dr. Totten has coedited *Social Issues in the English Classroom*, *Social Issues and Community Service at the Middle Level*, and *Middle Level Education: An Annotated Bibliography*. He received an Ed. D. degree from Columbia Teachers College.

Dionne M. Walker is a Ph. D. candidate at the University of Arkansas, Fayetteville, majoring in kinesiology. She has taught physical education and health to middle school students and has coached at all levels, middle school through college. Ms. Walker earned a masters degree in kinesiology from the University of Arkansas.

Michael J. Wavering is an associate professor at the University of Arkansas, Fayetteville. He taught six years at the middle level, and part of his current assignment entails supervising student teachers in middle level settings. An active area of research is the development of logical reasoning in young adolescents. Dr. Wavering received a Ph. D. degree from the University of Iowa.

Index

SOURCE BOOKS ON EDUCATION

BILINGUAL EDUCATION
A Source Book for Educators
by Alba N. Ambert and Sarah Melendez

TEACHING SCIENCE TO YOUNG CHILDREN
A Resource Book
by Mary D. Iatridis

SPECIAL EDUCATION
A Source Book
by Manny Sternlicht

COMPUTERS IN THE CLASSROOM ... WHAT SHALL I DO?
A Guide
by Walter Burke

SCHOOL PLAY
A Source Book
by James H. Block and Nancy R. King

COMPUTER SIMULATIONS
A Source Book to Learning in a Electronic Environment
by Jerry Willis, Larry Hovey, and Kathleen Hovey

PROJECT HEAD START
Past, Present, and Future Trends in the Context of Family Needs
by Valora Washington and Ura Jean Oyemade

ADULT LITERACY
A Source Book and Guide
by Joyce French

MATHEMATICS EDUCATION IN SECONDARY SCHOOLS AND TWO-YEAR COLLEGES
A Source Book
by Louise S. Grinstein and Paul J. Campbell

BLACK CHILDREN AND AMERICAN INSTITUTIONS
An Ecological Review and Resource Guide
by Valora Washington and Velma LaPoint

SEXUALITY EDUCATION
A Resource Book
by Carol Cassell and Pamela M. Wilson

REFORMING TEACHER EDUCATION
Issues and New Directions
edited by Joseph A. Braun, Jr.

EDUCATIONAL TECHNOLOGY
Planning and Resource Guide Supporting Curriculum
by James E. Eisele and Mary Ellin Eisele

CRITICAL ISSUES IN FOREIGN LANGUAGE INSTRUCTION
edited by Ellen S. Silber

THE EDUCATION OF WOMEN IN THE UNITED STATES
A Guide to Theory, Teaching, and Research
by Averil Evans McClelland

MATERIALS AND STRATEGIES FOR THE EDUCATION OF TRAINABLE MENTALLY RETARDED LEARNERS
by James P. White

RURAL EDUCATION
Issues and Practice
by Alan J. DeYoung

EDUCATIONAL TESTING
Issues and Applications
by Kathy E. Green

THE WRITING CENTER
New Directions
edited by Ray Wallace and Jeanne Simpson

TEACHING THINKING SKILLS
Theory and Practice
by Joyce N. French and Carol Rhoder

TEACHING SOCIAL STUDIES TO THE YOUNG CHILD
A Research and Resource Guide
by Blythe S. Farb Hinitz

TELECOMMUNICATIONS
A Handbook for Educators
by Reza Azarmsa

CATHOLIC SCHOOL EDUCATION IN THE UNITED STATES
Development and Current Concerns
by Mary A. Grant and Thomas C. Hunt

DAY CARE
A Source Book
Second Edition, by Kathleen Pullan Watki and Lucius Durant, Jr.

SCHOOL PRINCIPALS AND CHANGE
by Michael D. Richardson, Paula M. Short, and Robert L. Prickett

PLAY IN PRACTICE
A Systems Approach to Making Good Play Happen
edited by Karen VanderVen,
Paul Niemiec, and Roberta Schomburg

TEACHING SCIENCE TO CHILDREN
Second Edition
by Mary D. Iatridis with a contribution by
Miriam Maracek

**KITS, GAMES AND MANIPULATIVES
FOR THE ELEMENTARY SCHOOL
CLASSROOM**
A Source Book
by Andrea Hoffman and Ann Glannon

PARENTS AND SCHOOLS
A Source Book
by Angela Carrasquillo
and Clement B. G. London

PROJECT HEAD START
*Models and Strategies for the
Twenty-First Century*
by Valora Washington
and Ura Jean Oyemade Bailey

**INSTRUMENTATION
IN EDUCATION**
An Anthology
by Lloyd Bishop and Paula E. Lester

**TEACHING ENGLISH
AS A SECOND LANGUAGE**
A Resource Guide
by Angela L. Carrasquillo

**SECONDARY SCHOOLS
AND COOPERATIVE LEARNING**
Theories, Models, and Strategies
by Angela L. Carrasquillo

**THE FOREIGN LANGUAGE
CLASSROOM**
Bridging Theory and Practice
edited by Margaret A. Haggstrom,
Leslie Z. Morgan, and Joseph A. Wieczorek

EDUCATING YOUNG ADOLESCENTS
Life in the Middle
edited by Michael J. Wavering